C000061101

Churchill's Greatest Fear

By the same author

Wall of Steel: The History of 9th (Londonderry) HAA Regiment, RA (SR); North-West Books, Limavady, 1988

The Sons of Ulster: Ulstermen at War from the Somme to Korea: Appletree Press, Belfast, 1992

Clear the Way! A History of the 38th (Irish) Brigade, 1941–1947; Irish Academic Press, Dublin, 1993

Irish Generals: Irish Generals in the British Army in the Second World War; Appletree Press, Dublin, 1993

Only the Enemy in Front: The Recce Corps at War, 1940–1946; Tom Donovan Books, London, 1994

Key to Victory: The Maiden City in the Second World War; Greystone Books, Antrim, 1995

The Williamite War in Ireland, 1689–1691; Four Courts Press, Dublin, 1998

A Noble Crusade: The History of Eighth Army, 1941–1945; Spellmount, Staplehurst, 1999

Irish Men and Women in the Second World War; Four Courts Press, Dublin, 1999

Irish Winners of the Victoria Cross (with David Truesdale); Four Courts Press, Dublin, 2000

Irish Volunteers in the Second World War; Four Courts Press, Dublin, 2001

The Sound of History: El Alamein 1942; Spellmount, Staplehurst, 2002

The North Irish Horse: A Hundred Years of Service; Spellmount, Staplehurst, 2002

Normandy 1944: The Road to Victory; Spellmount, Staplehurst, 2004

Ireland's Generals in the Second World War; Four Courts Press, Dublin, 2004

The Thin Green Line: A History of the Royal Ulster Constabulary GC, 1922–2001; Pen & Sword, Barnsley, 2004

None Bolder: A History of 51st (Highland) Division, 1939–1945: Spellmount, Staplehurst, 2006

The British Reconnaissance Corps in World War II; Osprey Publishing, Oxford, 2007

Eighth Army in Italy: The Long Hard Slog; Pen & Sword, Barnsley, 2007

The Siege of Derry 1689: The Military History; Spellmount, Stroud, 2008

Only the Enemy in Front: The Recce Corps at War, 1940–46 (revised p/bk edn); Spellmount, Stroud, 2008

Ubique: The Royal Artillery in the Second World; Spellmount, Stroud, 2008

Helmand Mission: With the Royal Irish Battlegroup in Afghanistan, 2008; Pen & Sword, Barnsley, 2009

In the Ranks of Death: The Irish in the Second World War; Pen & Sword, Barnsley, 2010

The Humber Light Reconnaissance Car 1941–45; Osprey Publishing, Oxford, 2011

Hobart's 79th Armoured Division at War: Invention, Innovation and Inspiration; Pen & Sword, Barnsley, 2011

British Armoured Divisions and Their Commanders 1939–1945: Pen & Sword, Barnsley, 2013

Victory in Italy: 15th Army Group's Final Campaign; Pen & Sword, Barnsley, 2014

Churchill's Greatest Fear

The Battle of the Atlantic
3 September 1939 to 7 May 1945

Richard Doherty

Pen & Sword
MILITARY

First published in Great Britain in 2015 by
Pen & Sword Military
an imprint of
Pen & Sword Books Ltd
47 Chur ﹕ Street
Barnsley
South Yorkshire
S70 2AS

Copyright © Richard Doherty 2015

ISBN 978 1 47383 400 2

The right of Richard Doherty to be identified as the Author of this
Work has been asserted by him in accordance with the Copyright,
Designs and Patents Act 1988.

A CIP catalogue record for this book is available from the British
Library

Typeset in Ehrhardt by
Mac Style Ltd, Bridlington, East Yorkshire
Printed and bound in the UK by CPI Group (UK) Ltd,
Croydon, CRO 4YY

Pen & Sword Books Ltd incorporates the imprints of Pen & Sword
Archaeology, Atlas, Aviation, Battleground, Discovery, Family
History, History, Maritime, Military, Naval, Politics, Railways, Select,
Transport, True Crime, and Fiction, Frontline Books, Leo Cooper,
Praetorian Press, Seaforth Publishing and Wharncliffe.

For a complete list of Pen & Sword titles please contact
PEN & SWORD BOOKS LIMITED
47 Church Street, Barnsley, South Yorkshire, S70 2AS, England
E-mail: enquiries@pen-and-sword.co.uk
Website: www.pen-and-sword.co.uk

Dedication

For all who served in the Battle of the Atlantic,
especially those who lost their lives.

Twilight and evening bell
And after that the dark!
And may there be no sadness of farewell
When I embark.

Contents

Maps

Illustrations

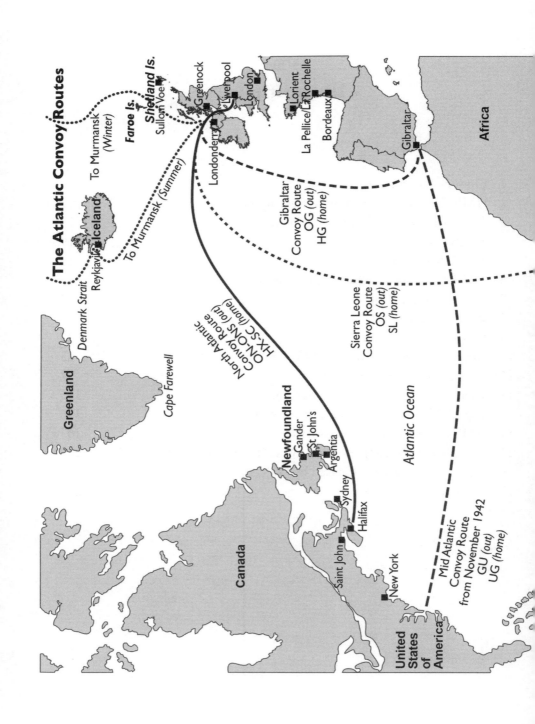

The Atlantic Convoy Routes

Shetland Is.
Sullom Voe
Faroe Is.
To Murmansk (Winter)
Greenock
Liverpool
London
Lorient
La Pellice/La Rochelle
Bordeaux
Londonderry
Gibraltar
Africa
To Murmansk (Summer)
Reykjavik Iceland
Denmark Strait
Greenland
Cape Farewell
Gibraltar Convoy Route
OG (out)
HG (home)
Sierra Leone Convoy Route
OS (out)
SL (home)
North Atlantic Convoy Route
ON, ONS (out)
HX-SC (home)
Newfoundland
Gander
St John's
Argentia
Sydney
Halifax
Saint John
New York
Canada
United States of America
Atlantic Ocean
Mid Atlantic Convoy Route from November 1942
GU (out)
UG (home)

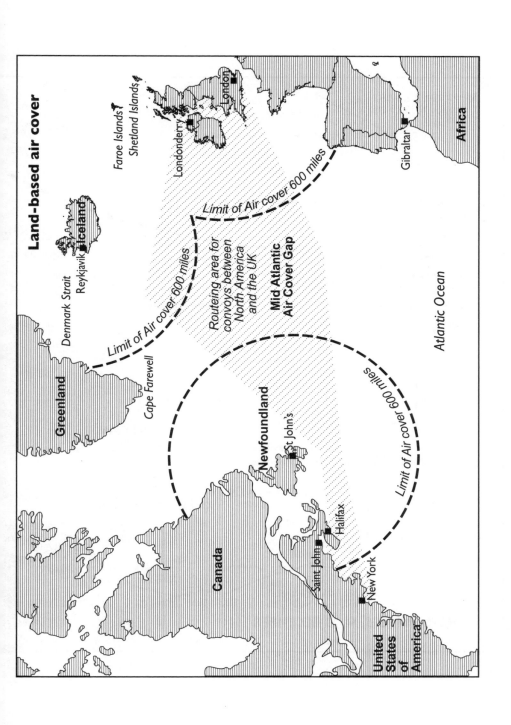

Land-based air cover

Faroe Islands

Shetland Islands

London

Londonderry

Iceland

Reykjavik

Denmark Strait

Limit of Air cover 600 miles

Cape Farewell

Greenland

Limit of Air cover 600 miles

Routeing area for convoys between North America and the UK

Mid Atlantic Air Cover Gap

Gibraltar

Africa

Newfoundland

St John's

Atlantic Ocean

Canada

Halifax

Limit of Air cover 600 miles

Saint John

New York

United States of America

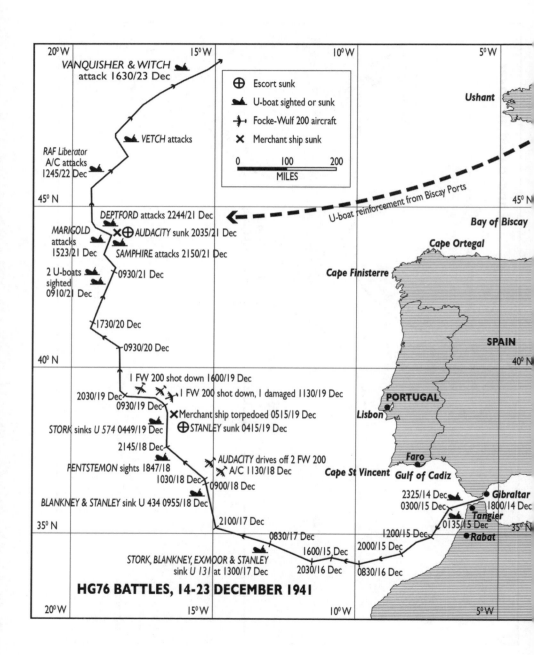

Legend:
⊕ Escort sunk
🛥 U-boat sighted or sunk
✈ Focke-Wulf 200 aircraft
✕ Merchant ship sunk

0   100   200
MILES

20° W   15° W   10° W   5° W

VANQUISHER & WITCH
attack 1630/23 Dec

Ushant

VETCH attacks

RAF Liberator
A/C attacks
1245/22 Dec

45° N   U-boat reinforcement from Biscay Ports   45° N

DEPTFORD attacks 2244/21 Dec

Bay of Biscay

MARIGOLD
attacks
1523/21 Dec

AUDACITY sunk 2035/21 Dec

Cape Ortegal

SAMPHIRE attacks 2150/21 Dec

2 U-boats
sighted
0910/21 Dec

0930/21 Dec

Cape Finisterre

1730/20 Dec

40° N

0930/20 Dec

SPAIN

40° N

1 FW 200 shot down 1600/19 Dec

2030/19 Dec

1 FW 200 shot down, 1 damaged 1130/19 Dec

0930/19 Dec

PORTUGAL

STORK sinks U 574 0449/19 Dec

Merchant ship torpedoed 0515/19 Dec

Lisbon

2145/18 Dec

STANLEY sunk 0415/19 Dec

PENTSTEMON sights 1847/18

AUDACITY drives off 2 FW 200
A/C 1130/18 Dec

Faro

1030/18 Dec

0900/18 Dec

Cape St Vincent   Gulf of Cadiz

BLANKNEY & STANLEY sink U 434 0955/18 Dec

2325/14 Dec

Gibraltar

0300/15 Dec

1800/14 Dec

35° N

2100/17 Dec

Tangier

0135/15 Dec

35° N

0830/17 Dec

1200/15 Dec

1600/15 Dec

2000/15 Dec

Rabat

STORK, BLANKNEY, EXMOOR & STANLEY
sink U 131 at 1300/17 Dec

2030/16 Dec

0830/16 Dec

HG76 BATTLES, 14-23 DECEMBER 1941

20° W   15° W   10° W   5° W

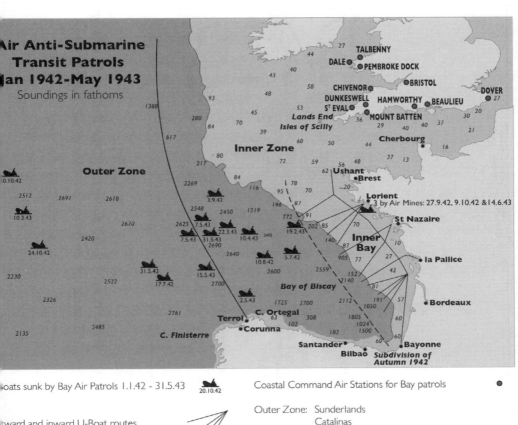

oats sunk by Bay Air Patrols 1.1.42 - 31.5.43

tward and inward U-Boat routes
00 fathom line under escort

fathom line

Coastal Command Air Stations for Bay patrols

Outer Zone: Sunderlands
Catalinas
Liberators
Inner Zone: Whitleys
Wellingtons
Hudsons
Inner Bay: Night-flying aircraft and day fighters only

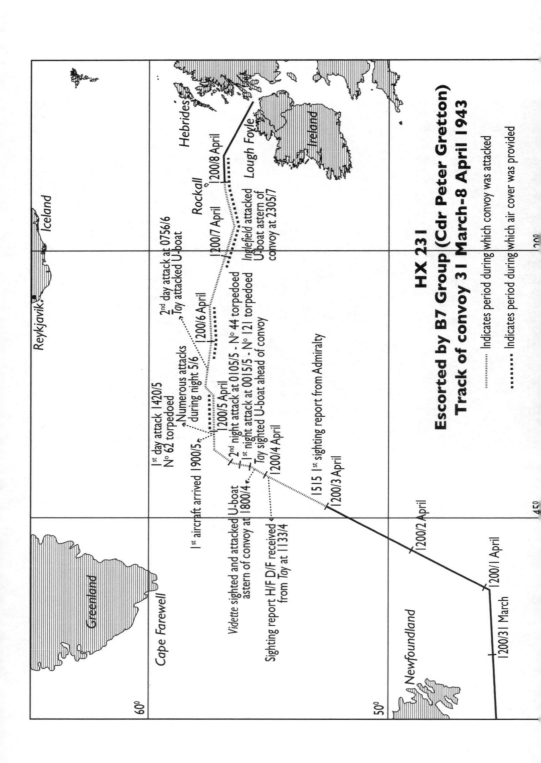

Reykjavík

Iceland

Greenland

Cape Farewell

60°

Newfoundland

50°

Hebrides

Rockall

Lough Foyle

Ireland

1st day attack 1420/5
N° 62 torpedoed

2nd day attack at 0756/6
Tay attacked U-boat

Numerous attacks
during night 5/6

1200/6 April

1st aircraft arrived 1800/4

Vidette sighted and attacked U-boat
astern of convoy at 1800/4

1200/5 April

2nd night attack at 0105/5 - N° 44 torpedoed
1st night attack at 0015/5 - N° 121 torpedoed

Tay sighted U-boat ahead of convoy

1200/4 April

Sighting report H/F D/F received
from Tay at 1133/4

1515 1st sighting report from Admiralty

1200/3 April

1200/8 April

1200/7 April

Inglefield attacked
U-boat astern of
convoy at 2305/7

1200/2 April

1200/1 April

1200/31 March

45°

30°

HX 231
Escorted by B7 Group (Cdr Peter Gretton)
Track of convoy 31 March-8 April 1943

·········· Indicates period during which convoy was attacked

••••••••• Indicates period during which air cover was provided

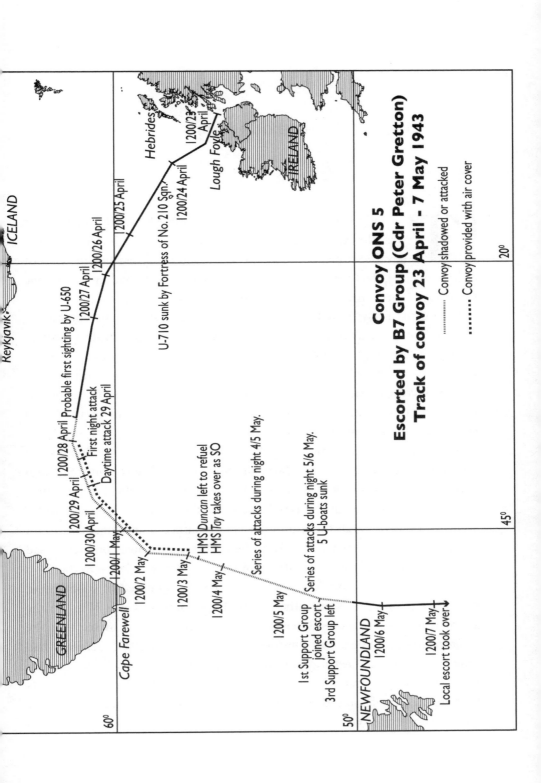

Convoy ONS 5
Escorted by B7 Group (Cdr Peter Gretton)
Track of convoy 23 April - 7 May 1943

.... Convoy shadowed or attacked
········· Convoy provided with air cover

ICELAND

Keykjavik

GREENLAND

Hebrides

IRELAND

Lough Foyle

1200/23 April

1200/24 April

1200/25 April

U-710 sunk by Fortress of No. 210 Sqn.

1200/26 April

1200/27 April

1200/28 April Probable first sighting by U-650

First night attack

Daytime attack 29 April

1200/29 April

1200/30 April

1200/1 May

Cape Farewell

1200/2 May

1200/3 May HMS Duncan left to refuel
            HMS Tay takes over as SO

1200/4 May

Series of attacks during night 4/5 May.

Series of attacks during night 5/6 May.
5 U-boats sunk

1200/5 May

1st Support Group
joined escort
3rd Support Group left

NEWFOUNDLAND
1200/6 May

1200/7 May
Local escort took over

60°

45°

50°

20°

Introduction

'The only thing that ever really frightened me during the war was the U-boat peril.' So wrote Winston Churchill of the naval campaign in which Germany's submarine, or U-boat (*Unterseeboote*), fleet threatened to destroy the United Kingdom's maritime lifelines to North America, the Commonwealth and Empire.

Britain has always relied on merchant ships to sustain life and commerce. During the First World War, Germany came close to defeating Britain through a campaign of submarine warfare in the first Battle of the Atlantic. Lessons were learned: the importance of aircraft – flying boats and airships played a critical part in defeating the U-boats: the importance of the merchant marine was emphasized; without it Britain could neither pursue a land war in Europe nor be assured of survival.

The Admiralty re-introduced the convoy system as war loomed in 1939 and took control of the Merchant Navy on 26 August, but the Royal Navy was otherwise not well prepared. The large numbers of escort ships necessary to protect convoys were lacking and few aircraft were available for escort duties. Although the Admiralty later assumed operational control of Coastal Command, the Cinderella of the RAF's operational commands had to make do with stop-gap aircraft unsuited to the tasks assigned to them.

Hitler's Germany should have appreciated the potential of submarines, but other than a few naval officers, the high command was blind to the strategic possibilities of submarine warfare. Hitler failed to see that the *U-bootwaffe* could be a war-winning weapon. Thus, in 1939, Germany had only a small U-boat fleet and a maritime policy that placed more importance on surface ships, a shortsightedness that deprived the Third Reich of its best chance of defeating Britain since most of what Britain needed for basic survival was imported.

Germany entered the war with fewer than fifty U-boats, including short-range coastal boats unable to operate in the Atlantic. Germany's maritime threat rested on surface raiders, aircraft and U-boats. In spite of the German reputation for thorough planning, those elements were unco-ordinated. Even the *Kriegsmarine*'s small U-boat fleet inflicted severe damage on Britain's merchant shipping – and on the Royal Navy – and held the advantage until May 1943, when the balance swung against them through the conflation of several factors – tactics, escort ships, air cover, weaponry, detection systems, operational research, plus the courage and dedication of merchant seamen and the crews of the Allied navies. May 1943 was not the end. The Battle of the Atlantic raged until the last days of war. The *U-bootwaffe*'s final victim, *Avondale Park*, was sunk by *U-2336* on 7 May 1945, the day before VE Day.

This book is an outline of the Battle of the Atlantic, examining how it was fought and how strategy, tactics, leadership and weaponry, with developing electronics, intelligence and operational research, played their part. The term 'Battle of the Atlantic' was coined by Winston Churchill for what became the longest campaign of the Second World War, and for which he established a special government committee, such was his level of concern about the battle, especially the U-boat threat, his greatest fear.

Acknowledgements

My interest in the Battle of the Atlantic goes back many years. I still have an original but battered 1957 paperback edition of Captain Donald Macintyre's *U-boat Killer* that I bought while at primary school. A few years later I remember buying and reading Jost Metzler's *The Laughing Cow: A U-boat Captain's Story* but by then I had moved on to grammar school (and found *U-69*'s symbol and its origin intriguing since it presented me with a French construction that I had yet to learn in class). Sadly, the original copy of Metzler's book has long since disappeared although I do have a replacement. My buying both books so many years ago suggests a long-time fascination with the Battle of the Atlantic and with both sides of the campaign.

I had the advantage of growing up in the Londonderry of the 1950s and 1960s when the city's port was often busy with visiting warships from many nations taking part in NATO exercises. The nearby HMS *Gannet*, the Royal Naval Air Station at Eglinton, was the training facility for the Fleet Air Arm's shipboard anti-submarine airmen – and where the re-formed German navy's air arm, the *Marineflieger*, trained and worked up on the Fairey Gannet, less than a dozen years after the war ended. Eglinton also hosted an annual open day with spellbinding air displays and, of course, an emphasis on naval and maritime reconnaissance aircraft. A few miles farther down the road, RAF Ballykelly, a Coastal Command station, from which flew Avro Shackletons, also hosted NATO guests for exercises, including RCAF Argus ASW aircraft and Lockheed Neptunes from several nations. The growl of piston engines frequently filled the air above us as Coastal Command maintained its Constant Endeavour.

The city was still a Royal Navy base, housing HMS *Sea Eagle*, the Joint Anti-Submarine School (JASS) in which the skills of both Royal Navy and Royal Air Force personnel were honed, often by men with hard-earned experience of anti-submarine warfare in the Battle of the Atlantic.

Taking that trip back in time reminds me that my very first expression of thanks in this book has to be to my late father, a soldier who had served in the Second World War and who taught his two sons much about ships and aircraft. Since he never talked about the horrors of war it was many years after his death that I realized that J. J. Doherty had undertaken several wartime voyages during which the U–boat threat was very real.

Commander Peter Campbell has been a great source of advice on anti-submarine warfare on which he is an authority, having served at HMS *Sea Eagle*. Ever courteous, Peter is also the epitome of the professional naval officer. When I told him of my intention to write this book he made me a gift of Captain Mike O'Kelly's short account of the Battle of the Atlantic. Although brief, Captain O'Kelly's book provides an excellent summary of the battle to May 1943. Since it comes from an expert on the subject – he also served at HMS *Sea Eagle* and was a specialist in anti-submarine warfare – I found it invaluable. My sincere thanks go to Peter for his advice and support.

Over the years the Naval Historical Branch at Portsmouth has been a great help in my research and I extend my gratitude to its knowledgeable staff who are steeped in the proud traditions of the Senior Service and respond enthusiastically to requests for assistance.

In London the Imperial War Museum is a priceless asset for the historian and researcher and its library, archive of personal recollections, including many recorded interviews, and photographic collection are all world class.

The National Archives at Kew hold many documents relating to the Battle of the Atlantic and the staff there are always helpful, knowledgeable and professional. I am grateful to the staff of the search and the reading rooms for all their help on my many visits.

Whenever I visit the National Archives it is a pleasure to meet my good friend Bob O'Hara, who served in the Royal Navy, and our discussions range over many and varied topics. Bob and his research team can be relied upon to provide documents that I need when I don't have time to travel to Kew. Their efforts have also helped this book and I am very grateful to them.

Ernie Cromie of the Ulster Aviation Society is an authority on all matters related to aviation in Northern Ireland, especially the role of the Royal Air Force's Northern Irish bases in the Battle of the Atlantic. As a friend of Squadron Leader Terence Malcolm Bulloch, Ernie was able to provide information on Terry Bulloch's wartime service from his logbooks as well as answering many questions about operations from Northern Ireland, the deployment of the Consolidated B-24 Liberator in Coastal Command and the complicated question of just how many very-long-range (VLR) Liberators really served. Ernie's exhaustive research, and evidence from Terry Bulloch, convince me that only those Mark Is issued originally to No.120 Squadron were truly VLR machines.

Squadron Leader Allan Thomas was the captain of a Nimrod MR2 before retiring from the Royal Air Force a decade ago. An oceanographer and authority on airborne anti-submarine warfare, I am grateful to Allan for his assistance and advice with elements of this book, especially with the development of ASV radar, and for clarifying what I believed to have been an urban myth.

George Jackson is a retired US Navy officer who specialized in anti-submarine warfare and to whom I am grateful for the information he provided on MAD – magnetic anomaly detection.

A special word of thanks is due to Platon Alexiades for his advice on German cyphers and their codenames that ensured that at least one error did not make it into the text.

Charles Messenger, one of the UK's best-known military historians, lent me his unpublished manuscript of a book on convoy ONS5. This convoy, which was at sea from 22 April to 12 May 1943, was the centre of one of the pivotal battles in the campaign and Charles's diligently researched account was invaluable in covering that crucial period of the Battle of the Atlantic. Not only am I grateful for the loan of the manuscript but I look forward to seeing it in print before too long.

Arguably the leading authority on the Battle of the Atlantic today is Professor Marc Milner of the University of New Brunswick, Fredericton, where he is Director of the Brigadier Milton Fowler Gregg VC Centre for the Study of War and Society. I thank Marc for his advice and support and, as the bibliography shows, his books, which have been invaluable.

The Linen Hall Library, Belfast, and the Central Library, Londonderry, helped my research and were able to obtain books that were otherwise difficult to track down. My thanks go to both institutions for their unfailing courtesy and help.

I first met John P. Cosgrove and his late wife, Patricia, from Washington DC, almost a quarter of a century ago when I was asked to host them and tell them something of the role of the River Foyle and Londonderry Port in the Battle of the Atlantic. We became good friends and have maintained contact ever since. During the Second World War John served on the destroyer escort USS *Gendreau* in the Pacific and had no direct involvement with the Atlantic war. However, he has long been involved with the Destroyer Escort Sailors Association and served on its national executive as well as chairing the editorial board. John was able to introduce me to many aspects of the history of the DEs in the Atlantic and very kindly provided me with the three volumes of *Trim But Deadly*, the history of the DEs. In addition he enabled me to make contact with many former DE sailors, US Navy, Coast Guard and even Royal Navy, who have shared their memories.

Dr Paul Clark MBE is a household name in Northern Ireland where he has long been the face of UTV News. Paul has a real passion for the military history of the island of Ireland in the twentieth century, as evidenced by the many programmes he has made on the subject. One programme was a study of the role of Londonderry in the Battle of the Atlantic, made for UTV in 2000 by Chris Orr's TV Derry, in which I was privileged to be involved. During the research for that programme Joan McClean of Chris Orr's team 'discovered' former Lieutenant Commander John Scott DSC* who had been living quietly in the city since the war. John earned his first DSC for destroying a U-boat that was targeting the SS *Rimutaka*, which was carrying the Duke and Duchess of Gloucester to Australia. John Scott's story is told on page 257 and Paul's programme when broadcast was dedicated to Lieutenant Commander Scott who had died in the meantime. I thank Paul, Chris and Joan for their work.

Ian Henderson also has a deep-rooted interest in military history and, over many years, has done much to promote the story of the Battle of the Atlantic, including writing a detailed account of Operation DEADLIGHT, the Allied destruction of the U-boats after VE Day, in *After The Battle*, No.36. My thanks are also due to Ian for his assistance, advice and contacts.

The maps and line drawings in this book are the work of Tim Webster who has helped me on many previous occasions and was especially valuable on this volume due to his extensive knowledge and love of ships. I am most grateful to Tim for all his hard work.

Working with the Pen and Sword team has always been a pleasure and this was no exception. For his support and encouragement, I am grateful to Brigadier Henry Wilson while Matt Jones is a professional and very patient production manager and Jon Wilkinson's jacket design skills are second to none. My thanks also go to Mat Blurton and Katie Noble of Mac Style for their work on the book.

As always, special thanks go to my wife Carol, my children Joanne, James and Catríona, son-in-law Steven and grandchildren Cíaran, Katrina, Joshua and Sophie for their patience, understanding and support.

Richard Doherty
Co. Londonderry
August 2015

Chapter One

The importance of Britain's maritime commerce is demonstrated by the merchant service which, in 1939, had about half the world's merchant shipping tonnage.[1] The title Merchant Navy had been granted by King George V to honour the sacrifice of the merchant marine in the Great War when 14,879 seamen and over 11,000,000 tons of shipping were lost to U-boats.[2] An even higher price was to be exacted in the Second World War with over 30,000 lives and more than 14,000,000 tons lost.[3]

Most of the deaths and ship losses were attributable to submarines in both wars. The idea of the submarine had been about for centuries but it did not become a viable weapon until the late-nineteenth century when its ability to hide beneath the waves added a new dimension to warfare. The first successful submarine action occurred in February 1864, during the American Civil War, when the Confederate submersible *Hunley* sank the USS *Housatonic.*

Subsequently the United States became the birthplace of the modern submarine through the work of the Irish engineer John Phillip Holland. Funded by the Fenian Brotherhood, Holland designed and built the *Fenian Ram*, now in a New Jersey museum, fell out with his backers and turned to the US Navy which had earlier rejected his ideas. A new design, combining electric power for underwater travel and a conventional fuel engine for surface travel, was bought by the US Navy and commissioned as the USS *Holland* in October 1900.

The Royal Navy bought Holland-class submarines – *Holland 1* survives in the Submarine Museum in Gosport – while Germany was also developing submarines. The Imperial Navy's first, *U-1*, commissioned in 1906, was double-hulled (a French innovation), with a kerosene (paraffin) engine, and a torpedo tube. It was followed by a boat half as big again with two torpedo tubes (*U-2*), but it was 1912–13 before a German diesel submarine emerged. In August 1914 Germany had forty-eight submarines in service or being built with twenty-nine operational. Germany had also supplied Russia with submarines, the Imperial Navy deploying the first operational submarine fleet during the Russo–Japanese War. Although Japan had purchased five Holland boats these saw no action. Other nations – including France, Italy and Greece – had small submarine fleets, but the largest in August 1914 was the Royal Navy's: seventy-seven boats in service with fifteen building.[4]

Submarines demonstrated their effectiveness when *U-9* sank three Royal Navy cruisers in under an hour on 22 September. However, it was attacks on merchant ships that showed their full strategic potential and raised a moral dilemma. By attacking merchantmen bound for British ports German submarines could strangle Britain's trade but there were agreed conventions for attacking merchant shipping. Under these 'Prize Rules', the crew of the merchantman had to be allowed to leave their vessel before it was sunk but conforming to such rules negated the submarine's main advantage by forcing it to engage its target while surfaced and remaining so as the crew abandoned ship.

The Germans declared an exclusion zone around the British Isles in which British vessels would be sunk without warning; neutral ships were also liable to attack. Germany was moving towards unrestricted submarine warfare, which Admiral Alfred von Tirpitz believed would knock Britain out of the war.

When, in May 1915, the Cunard liner *Lusitania* was torpedoed off Ireland with the loss of 1,198 lives there was international outrage. All but eleven of 139 American passengers were killed, prompting an American protest, following which Germany's chancellor, Theobald von Bethmann-Hollweg, supported by Kaiser Wilhelm, ordered Tirpitz to restrict attacks to identifiably British vessels. Neutrals were to be treated according to the Prize Rules and passenger ships were not to be attacked. This persisted until 1917 when Germany resumed unrestricted submarine warfare, a decision that led to the United States' declaration of war on 6 April 1917.

Submarines had continued attacking British ships. December 1916's losses prompted one commentator to write that 'it was … a question whether our armies could win the war before our navies lost it'. By February 1917 Germany had over 100 U-boats, a scale that had its own effect since numbers are always important in battle. Although the Royal Navy had the world's largest submarine fleet in 1914, these were seen as defensive patrol vessels and no serious attention was given to anti-submarine warfare. Germany's offensive deployment of submarines forced the Admiralty to study countermeasures. The first effective depth charges were not produced until June 1916 and anti-submarine vessels did not have enough for effective action until early-1918, in spite of the concept of a 'dropping mine' having been mooted in 1911; Admiral Sir George Callaghan, Commander-in-Chief Home Fleet, had asked for some in July 1914. By then the depth charge was recognized as the best anti-submarine weapon.

Rapid development in depth-charge technology followed with depth-charge throwers supplementing stern rails for dropping charges. Another development, the 'howitzer', fired a charge to between 1,200 to 2,600 yards although fewer than 400 were delivered by the end of 1917. The concept would appear again in the Second World War.

Effective use of depth charges required knowing where the submerged target was. In 1915 the hydrophone was introduced, able to detect the sound of a moving submarine underwater at up to two miles. It was limited by being able only to indicate the target's proximity and the vessel using it had to be stationary since its own engines, and passage through the water, drowned out external sounds. A stationary ship could become a sitting target.

In late-1916 the Anti-Submarine Division was created. Its work led to significant advances in hydrophone technology. In 1917 Captain C. P. Ryan, of the Hawkcraig Experimental Station, devised a directional hydrophone while the Board of Invention and Research produced another. Both were soon being used to train hydrophone operators as hydrophones were fitted to many naval vessels. A further refinement, from George Howard Nash, a civilian inventor, was the 'fish' hydrophone, a torpedo-shaped device towed by the sub-hunter; almost 200 were delivered by November 1918, although production only began in October 1917.

Hydrophone equipment was also used in submarines, allowing commanders to detect targets. Another Great War scientific development was a shipboard transmitter emitting a fan-shaped beam ahead of a ship travelling at up to 15 knots. Although this 'Electrical Detector' did not see operational service it demonstrated its potential before the war ended, when it equipped seven ships.

The Electrical Detector provided good indication of the bearing of a submerged target, although its depth-finding capabilities were less reliable. It could not detect a surfaced submarine, nor maintain contact with a submerged target at less than 100 yards and could give false returns from underwater phenomena, although experienced operators would learn to distinguish these from submarines. Nonetheless, the Electrical Detector was recognized as the future of submarine-detection equipment and given the codename by which it was known for decades: ASDIC, allegedly an acronym for *A*llied *S*ubmarine *D*etection *I*nvestigation *C*ommittee. No such committee existed.

The work that produced ASDIC was carried out for the Anti-Submarine *Division* by the Board of Invention and Research, using quartz piezoelectric crystals to create an underwater active sound detector. For security, neither quartz nor sound experimenting were mentioned; early work was dubbed 'supersonics', which became ASD'ics, ASD indicating Anti-Submarine Division. Quartz piezoelectric crystals became asdivites. The acronym ASDIC owed its birth to ASD'ics. In 1939 Oxford University Press asked the Admiralty for the origin of ASDIC, or asdic, and the resultant shuffling of files between departments and individuals produced the answer that it was an acronym of the committee referred to above. The passage of years and changing personalities in a bureaucracy probably prompted this conclusion, rather than any deliberate attempt to deceive; by then there was no need for such secrecy.[5] (The modern *OED* gives the origin of asdic as 'from *ASD*, prob. repr. Anti-Submarine Division, + ic'.)

The Admiralty, by conscripting civilian craft, mainly trawlers and drifters, as anti-submarine vessels, created an auxiliary patrol that eventually numbered over 3,000 vessels. However, two warship classes became major anti-submarine vessels. Although the Germans had begun submarine action early in the war, a reduction in intensity after the *Lusitania* sinking gave the Royal Navy time to react. With small craft needed for anti-submarine warfare, this led to the rebirth of the sloop; no fewer than 112 were built between 1915 and 1918 and designated Flower-class. Capable of speeds between 16.5 and 17.5 knots, they proved sufficiently versatile for the anti-submarine role, although intended initially as patrol or minesweeping vessels. The other small warship, the P-Boat, or P-sloop, displaced only

612 tons, with a speed of 20 knots, two guns and two 14-inch torpedo tubes, and had hardened steel bows for ramming.

By 1917 there was another anti-submarine weapon: air power. The RNAS (Royal Naval Air Service), formed on 1 July 1914, had discharged missions including bombing, torpedo-dropping, air defence and reconnaissance. It also encompassed maritime reconnaissance and anti-submarine warfare. Co-ordination between surface warships and airships or flying boats became another critical element in the battle.

The newly-developed medium of wireless also entered the equation. Although the Germans enjoyed an advantage in this field, this worked against them. Transmitting on the 800-metre wavelength, the German navy's principal wireless station was near Berlin, at Nauen. Its transmissions could be picked up in the Mediterranean and Balkans, as far afield as the USA to the west, China to the east, and southern Africa to the south. With Zeppelin airships and U-boats contacting distant bases, the German command embraced radio enthusiastically. That enthusiasm, and the extent to which U-boats employed radio, provided considerable assistance to the Admiralty's Naval Intelligence Division, whose Room 40 OB ('Old Block' of the Admiralty building) monitored transmissions to good effect. Room 40, under Admiral Sir Reginald 'Blinker' Hall, Director of Naval Intelligence, was the precursor of the Operational Intelligence Centre (OIC). Thanks to the Russians presenting the Royal Navy with a German naval signal book, recovered from the cruiser *Magdeburg*, sunk in the Baltic after running aground, Room 40 could decrypt German naval signals throughout most of the war.

The elements necessary to prosecute anti-submarine warfare successfully were available to the Royal Navy which refused to accept the most important, convoy, which had been in its gift all along. Why? Its effectiveness was proven: Henry V's army sailed to France in 1415 in a 1,200-ship convoy, following the examples of King John, two centuries earlier, and Edward III in 1346. Convoys protected Spanish ships sailing from the New World, were important in the mid-seventeenth century Dutch wars, and throughout the Napoleonic period. The 1798 Compulsory Convoy Act was used to ensure the safe arrival of merchantmen carrying vital supplies to Britain, thus sustaining the ability to continue the war against Napoleon.

In spite of this record the system was not implemented by the Admiralty when the threat arose. Admiralty thinking had changed in the nineteenth century. After the Compulsory Convoy Act was repealed in 1872, Their Lordships reviewed their war plans which had:

> a mesmerizing influence on attitudes to trade protection until well into the twentieth century. The Admiralty saw the empire as a single entity bound together by the sea lanes ... If these routes were severed, then Britain would be ruined. In May 1885 the Foreign Intelligence Committee considered ... trade protection but convoy was not included as an option ... Blockade of the enemy's bases was to be left to the battle fleet while cruisers patrolled the sea lanes ... the Admiralty had missed the wood for the trees: it was not the sea lanes that needed protection but the ships ... which sailed along them.[6]

Alfred Thayer Mahan suggested that a 'properly systematized and applied' convoy system would have more success 'than hunting for individual marauders – a process which, even when thoroughly planned, still resembles looking for a needle in a haystack'.[7] Mahan identified warships protecting convoys as defensive, seen as *wrong* by naval officers imbued with the Nelson spirit of engaging the enemy more closely. On the other hand, cruising sea lanes was seen as *right*: acting offensively. The Royal Navy considered its task the offensive one of hunting down and destroying enemy submarines but, in spite of the technological resources and weaponry, submarines were as dangerous as ever in spring 1917. By then only forty-six U-boats had been lost, including six to the actions of British destroyers.

Some naval officers supported the concept of escorted convoys and had a very real contemporary example: merchant ships between Harwich and Holland were escorted after July 1916 with obvious results. Convoys were introduced, under French pressure, on cross-channel sailings, described as 'controlled sailings' by the Admiralty, to deliver coal to France.[8] Escorted convoys to Scandinavia followed. Beatty 'was given grudging permission' for this measure, which reduced 'a 25 per cent loss rate' to 0.24 per cent.[9]

Still the Admiralty resisted escorted convoys for ocean trade routes, believing that a convoy offered a bigger target and that merchant officers lacked the skills to maintain station. This view was held by the First Sea Lord, Admiral Sir John Jellicoe, ignoring the evidence of the Harwich–Holland convoys and those to Scandinavia.

Although Lloyd George claimed credit for the adoption of the system for ocean trade, this was not entirely true. When Germany renewed unrestricted submarine warfare in 1917, he asked Sir Maurice Hankey, Secretary to the War Cabinet, to report on the system. Hankey pointed out that the Grand Fleet used the convoy principle by deploying destroyer screens, while convoys were used for troopship movements. He concluded that convoy offered 'great opportunities for mutual support by the merchant vessels themselves, apart from the defence provided by their escorts' as weapons on merchantmen could be used.

Pressure was growing to introduce convoys. Admiral Beatty, commanding the Grand Fleet, argued that forces being deployed to hunt U-boats should be used to protect merchant ships. The successful transporting of British and Imperial troops to the Western Front supported his argument: all had sailed in protected convoys almost within sight of the German High Seas Fleet and enemy naval forces based in Belgium with no losses.

The Admiralty changed its stance in late-April 1917. Such were that month's losses that Lloyd George announced his intention to visit the Admiralty on the 30th. He claimed this visit as the critical spur in introducing ocean convoys but others had probably played greater roles. Admiral Duff, of the Anti-Submarine Division, argued strongly for convoys in a remarkable *volte face* from someone who, hitherto, had raised 'Every possible objection to [a convoy system], many ... based on false figures and false assumptions'.[10] 'Duff's case was so well researched and so cogently argued that the paper must have been weeks if not months in preparation'.[11]

On 27 April Jellicoe wrote to the First Lord saying that Royal Navy command of the surface of the oceans would be useless if German submarines were paralyzing the lines of communication. Once accepted, the principle was implemented quickly. The United States Navy, which had entertained reservations similar to the Royal Navy's, was also soon converted.

In April 1917, the last full month before convoys were introduced for transatlantic shipping, U-boats had sunk 881,027 tons. June also showed high losses – 696,720 tons – but losses reduced in August and thereafter as convoy protection became more effective. In the last three months of 1917 only 702,799 tons of shipping were lost. Losses reduced throughout 1918.

The Germans countered with new tactics, including surface attacks by night and using groups of U-boats to intercept convoys. Although unsuccessful, these would form part of the *U-bootwaffe*'s operational tactics in the Second World War.

It had been a close-run thing. In May 1917 the government's shipping adviser, Sir Chiozza Money, advised that the absolute minimum shipping necessary to keep the country supplied with essential foodstuffs was 4,812,000 tons. Over the following nine months 2,909,155 tons were lost; less than half that tonnage was launched while almost 1,000,000 tons of damaged shipping was under repair. The safety margin was below 700,000 tons. Germany's U-boats had come very close to knocking the United Kingdom out of the war, a lesson the Admiralty took to heart, as did German submariners.

At the core of the problem had been the novelty of the threat, the Naval Staff's lack of experience, and the consequent absence of rigorous analysis. Indeed there had been no Naval Staff until 1912, a point Churchill emphasized:

> At least fifteen years of consistent policy were required to give the Royal Navy that widely extended outlook upon war problems and of war situations without which seamanship, gunnery, instrumentalism of every kind, devotion of the highest order, could not achieve their due reward.
>
> Fifteen years! And we were to have only thirty months!

The Anti-Submarine Division was even less experienced, with about a month to get into its stride.

The lessons of the first U-boat campaign were hard learned and would not be forgotten by the Royal Navy, but politicians reduced the Navy's effectiveness in the inter-war years and the service itself placed too much faith in asdic. Only in the years immediately preceding the Second World War were measures to counter the shortage of suitable escort vessels taken, but the vital air element of anti-submarine warfare was relegated to a Cinderella role. Fortunately, Hitler's Germany made even more serious errors.

Chapter Two

Exhausted, and their treasuries much diminished, by war, the victors welcomed peace and the opportunity to reduce expenditure on armed forces. In the United Kingdom, not only were wartime conscripts demobilized but the regular forces were reduced. The most expensive service, the Royal Navy, provided an obvious target; as Terraine comments 'the only cheap item in the Navy's locker was an Able Seaman'.[1]

In May 1919 the Naval Staff proposed a fleet of thirty-three battleships, eight battle-cruisers, sixty light cruisers and 352 destroyers,[2] an optimistic aim swept aside by what became known as the 'Ten Year Rule'. This assumed that Britain and its empire would not be involved 'in any great war' for ten years; Churchill, as Chancellor of the Exchequer in 1928, decreed that this should be a rolling ten years. Estimates for the Royal Navy, already reduced from £171,000,000 to £90,000,000 in 1919, dropped to £58,000,000 by 1923 and an average £64,300,000 between 1920 and 1938, by which date re-armament had begun. However, the Navy had suffered such deep cuts that it had much catching up to do.

The inter-war years also saw several international agreements to reduce fleets with the Washington conferences of 1921–22 setting limits on ship numbers and sizes. Britain wanted submarines banned, but the French opposed this and, eventually, no limitations were set. Of course, the vanquished were banned completely from having submarines. The Five-Power naval treaty between Britain, the United States, Japan, France and Italy curtailed battleship construction by these nations with many battleships under construction finished as aircraft carriers.

The emphasis on surface ships may have helped ensure that anti-submarine warfare became a backwater. Since Germany was not allowed submarines, there was no urgency to develop operational doctrine, weaponry, tactics or detection equipment. Thus this element of the Navy's role suffered from neglect, exacerbated by reducing the number of small ships suitable for escort duties. Whereas, in November 1918, there had been

466 destroyers and flotilla leaders, by September 1939 the number had fallen to 201 destroyers and sloops. A hundred of the destroyers of 1939 were Fleet destroyers, neither available nor suited for escort work. However, some Great War anti-submarine veterans remained in the service, thus ensuring the intellectual legacy of the victors of the first Battle of the Atlantic. So, too, did a number of submariners, among whom Max Horton would play a leading role in the second Battle of the Atlantic. Others with vital experience returned from the reserve or were called back.

In spite of the Great War experience, an emphasis on surface vessels persisted. Moreover, Jellicoe, visiting Australia, New Zealand and India shortly after the war, pointed out the possibility of conflict with Japan, bringing a reprimand from the Admiralty but prompting the Naval Staff to consider this very possibility. Should such a war break out, a major naval base at Singapore would be necessary.[3] This became a reality, and money that might have been spent on ships was invested in Singapore. In the Admiralty it was believed that the major battles of the next war would be fought east of Singapore by surface fleets; the emphasis remained on surface vessels. Although Japan had been allied to the UK since 1902 the alliance was not renewed after 1922.

The UK was not the only state where surface ships dominated thinking. Japan was building the biggest battleships yet seen, the United States continued with its capital ship programme, albeit abiding to international agreements, and Italy and France did likewise. Neither Italy nor France signed the 1930 London Naval Treaty, in which Britain, Japan and the USA agreed overall tonnage and tonnage limits for cruisers, destroyers and submarines. As well as armament limitations for each class, the London Treaty agreed that no new capital ships would be laid down before 1937. When, in 1934, the Geneva disarmament conference, convened in 1932, broke down, Japan announced its withdrawal from the Washington and London treaties when these expired in 1936. By then the political situation in Germany had changed dramatically with the rise of Adolf Hitler and the Nazi Party.

Having prosecuted a submarine campaign in the Great War, and been first to recognize the submarine's offensive potential, the German navy might have been expected to give more importance to U-boats than surface vessels in a re-armament programme. That did not happen. The *Marineleitung* (Naval Command), which became *Oberkommando der Marine* (OKM), or Naval High Command, in January 1936, proved as capital-ship minded as its contemporaries. The commander-in-chief of the *Kriegsmarine*, as the *Reichsmarine* had become, Eric Raeder, was a big-ship man; naval supremo since 1928, he would remain in post until 30 January 1943.

Raeder was determined to build a strong navy, defying and circumventing the restrictions of Versailles. Clandestine arrangements were made to build ships and equipment, including submarines. Recognition of the strategic importance of Britain's maritime communications pointed towards making war on British merchant shipping and Raeder appointed a committee under Vizeadmiral Günther Guse, his deputy chief of staff, to outline the strategic basis on which to build the navy. His chief staff officer, Kapitän zur See Hellmuth Heye, argued that Germany should not engage the Royal Navy in surface actions but should attack British trade routes with fast, lighter ships. However, Admiral Carl Witzell, of the ordnance department, disagreed, arguing that only the heaviest ships could see the Atlantic striking force break through to attack the trade routes. Witzell carried the day, suggesting that the naval staff, or at least the strategy committee, remained wedded to the idea of the capital ship in particular, and surface ships in general. The U-boat fleet commander (the *Führer der U-boote*, or *FdU*; also *Befehlshaber der U-boote* (*BdU*), chief of the U-boat service) was not consulted. Heye believed that British sound detection was so advanced that U-boat attacks on British naval forces could not be guaranteed to achieve success. Nor did he believe that U-boats could be used successfully in 'cruiser war' on the ocean but would have to operate in 'a more or less stationary role'.

This view was not accepted by all. Admiral Hermann Böhm, who would command the fleet, saw the strategic possibilities in a war against Britain as being, firstly, deployment of U-boats and mines; secondly, raids against the ships of the Royal Navy's strategic blockade; and, finally, mercantile warfare. Even Böhm's considered submission did not divert Raeder from his big-ship navy project. By January 1939 the committee had recommended a 'balanced fleet'. This became the Z Plan (Z stood for *Ziel*, or target), due for completion in 1948. On 18 January 1939 Hitler approved the plan and the allocation of materials but the target was to be achieved in six years rather than ten.[4]

The Z Plan called for six Class-H battleships, displacing over 56,000 tons (with main armaments of eight 16-inch guns, to be increased to 17-, 19- and even 20-inch guns, the last in the final design which would displace over 130,000 tons). Of the other vessels planned, the Bismarck-class included both *Bismarck* and *Tirpitz*, while the Gneisenau-class was also of two ships, the other being *Scharnhorst*, plus twelve 30,000-ton battle-cruisers and five heavy cruisers. There were also three *Panzerschiffe* (armoured ships), dubbed 'pocket battleships' by the British press, mounting 11-inch guns on a cruiser hull. Sixty-five cruisers, including five heavy, twenty-four light and thirty-six scout, were to be built, plus seventy destroyers, seventy-eight torpedo boats and 249 submarines. Of the submarines, 162 were to be Atlantic types, the others being coastal (sixty) and special purpose. Eight aircraft carriers were planned.[4]

Raeder and his committee described this as a 'balanced fleet' but the only sense in which it was balanced was in including something for everyone. As a practical fleet it made little sense, although the aircraft carriers indicated some semblance of modernity. Terraine describes the plan as 'worse than rubbish; it was fantasy of a kind that men in positions of power entertain at their peril'[5] while Padfield questions Raeder's intelligence and moral courage since he must have known that the plan was beyond the ability of German shipbuilding to achieve, not only due to lack of capacity but, more importantly, because there was insufficient steel for the ships *and* army and Luftwaffe demands.[6] Fantasy maritime planning had met fantasy economics. Even more fantastic was that responsibility for overseeing Germany's economy had been given to Hitler's right-hand man, Hermann Göring, a morphine addict with dubious credentials in economics. Although a fighter ace in the Great War, Göring had no staff experience and thus no skills in high-level organization. As head of the Luftwaffe he was unlikely to accord any priority to naval plans. Such was the way in which the Nazis ran Germany that the various elements of governance operated as if in discrete silos. This also applied to the armed services with intense rivalry between navy and air force.

One name seems to have been omitted from this account of German naval preparations for war: Karl Dönitz. Since he was, successively, head of the *U-bootwaffe*, commander-in-chief of the Kriegsmarine and Hitler's successor as Führer, it can be difficult to realize that, in the inter-war years, Dönitz was not highly placed in the command structure. That explains why his voice was not listened to in the discussions of the navy's special committee, why his arguments were not heard and appreciated, and why the U-boat service entered the war with an operational fleet far short of what Dönitz wanted. However, in spite of this, it was Dönitz who endowed the small submarine service with effectiveness, even though it had to struggle not only with a shortage of boats but also with defective weapons.

Dönitz had entered the Kaiser's navy as a cadet in 1910, joining the cruiser *Breslau* two years later. In September 1913 he was gazetted *leutnant zur see* (sub-lieutenant) and was still with *Breslau* eleven months later when, with the battle-cruiser *Goeben*, following a bombardment of French ports in Algeria, she raced across the Mediterranean, pursued by Royal Navy vessels, to the Dardanelles and thence to Constantinople, where both hoisted the Turkish flag, that country entering the war on Germany's side. Dönitz remained in the Black Sea until 1916 when he went home to join the submarine service.

On 3 January 1917 Dönitz passed out of U-boat school to join *U-39* at Pola. Under the command of Walter Forstmann, Dönitz proved ideally suited to the submarine service. Such was his ability that he was appointed to command *UC-25*, a minelayer, also based at Pola in the Adriatic. In two cruises as *UC-25*'s captain, Dönitz earned the Knight's Cross of the Hohenzollern Order. His next command was *UB-68*, in which, due to an inherent structural fault, he and his crew were captured in the Mediterranean in September 1918, although his chief engineer died when he opened the seacocks to scuttle the boat.

Dönitz thus ended the war as a prisoner. Repatriated in July 1919 he was one of 1,500 naval officers allowed to resume naval careers. As with most Imperial Navy officers, Dönitz was imbued with an anti-British spirit, seeing the Royal Navy as Germany's main enemy. Captivity probably increased that feeling which never diminished.

Since the rump of the navy in which Dönitz served had no submarines there was no immediate opportunity to resume his submariner's career. However, there was a determination to circumvent the provisions of the Versailles treaty and the torpedo-boat flotilla permitted to Germany was exercised as a submarine flotilla, it being recognized that surfaced submarines were torpedo boats. The surface-attack tactic developed by submariners in the later stages of the war was refined by torpedo–boats acting as submarines in inter-war exercises.

Dönitz's career path in the 1920s and 1930s took him to the Torpedo, Mine and Intelligence Inspectorate at Kiel where he served as a *Referent*, or adviser, and the *Marineleitung* in Berlin. Attending a staff course, he came to the attention of Raeder, then a rear admiral (*konteradmiral*) and, having served as navigator on the flagship of the Commander-in-Chief Baltic, he returned to torpedo boats as a *korvettenkapitan* commanding a half-flotilla of these vessels which were being used as U–boat substitutes on exercises. Dönitz's command 'found and destroyed' an 'enemy convoy' during one night exercise in 1929.[7] As he moved on to the naval base at Wilhelmshaven and then back to sea, commanding the light cruiser *Emden*, his path crossed those of some of the men re-shaping Germany. The impression he made on them was a key factor in his rise, as was his enthusiastic embrace of Nazism.

Dönitz was not among those who viewed Hitler only as an upstart Austrian corporal. Instead he saw him as a man to be admired, one who could restore Germany to its proper station in the world. Hitler appealed to naval officers such as Dönitz because his

racial and world views were nothing more than the propaganda of Imperial Germany rendered more brutally simple in his crude mind, and therefore keyed in with the naval officers' basic prejudices … [and] most naval officers who met Hitler personally were impressed. He had the Kaiser's extraordinary memory for technical detail and interest in ship design and weaponry; he appeared to have the future of the Navy at heart; above all he spoke of the future of Germany in terms they approved.[8]

Taking Padfield's argument a step further, Terraine notes that:

The misreading of the frame of mind of men brought up in the Imperial Navy is really only an extension of a still widespread misreading of Wilhelmine Germany itself, based on sentimentality and a nostalgia for a German version of the '*Grande Époque*' which is largely a figment of imagination; as a German writer [C. H. Müller-Graaft] has said, it is only a part-truth that Hitler was the destroyer of Germany.[9]

Dönitz must have felt justified in his trust of Hitler when, in February 1935, the latter ordered the open resumption of submarine building and the official rebirth of the submarine service. The immediate effect on Dönitz was to have him appointed to command the new service. Due to take *Emden* on a Far East cruise he was disappointed at not being able to do so. Moreover, he believed that the new submarine force would be only 'a small and comparatively unimportant part' of the planned new fleet.

The German decision to begin building submarines again had the First Sea Lord, Admiral of the Fleet Lord Chatfield, decrying the 'insidious submarine and aircraft' while opining that 'our methods are now so efficient that we will need fewer destroyers in the North Sea and the Mediterranean'. Padfield notes a 1935 Admiralty affirmation that asdic had 'virtually extinguished the submarine menace'.[10] This confidence was widespread and even persuaded the Naval Staff, in 1937, to declare that the submarine-induced problems of 1917 would never be repeated, while Sir Samuel Hoare, First Sea Lord, averred to the House of Commons that 'the submarine is no longer a danger to the security of the British Empire'.[11] So taken in by this was Winston Churchill that he wrote to Prime Minister Neville Chamberlain in March 1939 telling him that 'The submarine has been mastered'.

How good was this equipment in which so many reposed so much faith? Asdic had developed little, largely thanks to financial parsimony, and was limited in three critical respects. Its range was no better than 2,500 yards (2,286m or about 1.25 nautical miles) and then only in good conditions. On average, range was about 1,300 yards. Operationally, this meant that a submarine could fire its torpedoes without coming within detection range. Asdic's second limiting factor was the loss of contact with the target at about 200 yards, allowing a submarine's commander to take evasive action as his attacker closed, so that the pattern of depth charges, launched from the hunter's stern, would miss. However, asdic's greatest drawback was the third limiting factor: it could only detect a submerged target; it could not pick up a surfaced submarine. And the German submarine service had developed the night-time surface-attack tactic, which was being refined in training, using torpedo boats as submarine substitutes.

In contrast to what appears to be unwarranted confidence, some critical decisions had been taken in Britain since Hitler's rise to power. A belated increase in Royal Navy strength was underway, but building warships is a time-consuming business, as is recruiting and training crews to bring ships to war readiness. The building programme suffered from the attentions of bureaucrats more interested in saving money than in ensuring that the country could defend itself. Thus, while the 1933 Naval Estimates included *one* 'convoy sloop', it was 1936 before the Admiralty had approved a detailed specification for such a vessel.

As late as February 1939 Treasury civil servants had the naval estimates reduced to £149.5 million (almost twice the 1937 figures, but much ink and as much frustration were expended on achieving the increase) and it was those estimates that finally laid significant 'emphasis on convoy escorts'. That emphasis was to be found in plans for forty Hunt-class destroyers and fifty-six Flower-class corvettes, a design based on a whale-catcher but quick and easy to build and suitable for construction in small shipyards. Although intended for coastal convoy escort duties, the Flowers became the mainstay of the ocean escort groups. The first Hunts were launched in December 1939 and, eventually, over eighty were built in four sub-classes[13] while the first Flowers followed down the slipways. In all, 225 Flower-class and sixty modified-Flower-class corvettes were built, serving with the Royal and

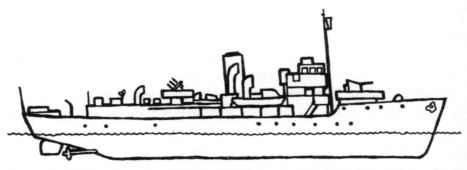

Figure 1: A Flower-class corvette. These little ships provided the backbone of the oceanic escort groups although they had been intended for coastal escort duties.

Figure 2: HMS *Londonderry*, one of the pre-war Grimsby–class sloops that proved to be excellent escort vessels.

Royal Canadian Navies, the US Navy and other Allied navies. An improved corvette, the Castle–class, followed, of which fifty-three were built.

There would be other escorts, including sloops, designed specifically to protect convoys, with frigates following later. These types took more time to build, were more expensive and demanded much larger shipyards than the corvettes. The decisions to build all these vessels were taken just in time. They were almost too little too late.

Before the building programme, a major decision was reached. Although the House of Commons learned in 1935 that the convoy system would not be introduced at once on the outbreak of war, a Shipping Defence Advisory Committee was established in 1937. On the advice of Admiral Sir William James, Deputy Chief of the Naval Staff (DCNS), it was agreed that the system would be implemented in possible war areas. James was among the serving senior officers who remembered the lessons of the Great War; he had been in charge of Room 40, another organization that had been allowed to diminish in the post-war years. Terraine notes that the decision did not receive with unanimous approval.

At last a 1917 lesson had sunk in – but not universally, and not without difficulty, whatever history might say: shipowners and merchant masters were not all best pleased … the Red Duster and the White Ensign did not readily seek each other's company.[14]

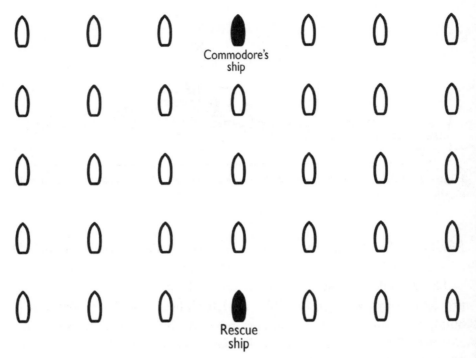

Figure 3: The organisation of a typical convoy with 35 merchantmen and an escort of six warships. Later in the war larger convoys were introduced as they were proved to be safer and were less of a strain on escorts.

Meanwhile the Kriegsmarine was producing its new fleet. Dönitz lobbied for a stronger submarine force than in the Z Plan and the number was increased from 249 to 300 boats. As head of the U-boat force, he was also refining operational tactics. He argued that only the *U-bootwaffe* could engage British shipping while German armies fought their way to the French Atlantic seaboard. Such thinking was reflected in a speech made by Hitler to his commanders on 23 May 1939:

If Holland and Belgium are successfully occupied and if France is also defeated, the fundamental conditions for a successful war against England (sic) will have been secured. England can then be blockaded from Western France at close quarters by the air force, while the Navy with its U-boats can extend the range of the blockade. When that is

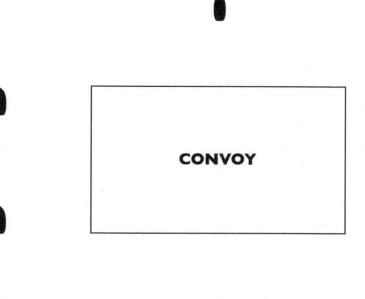

Figure 4: Typical positioning of escorts.

done, England will not be able to fight on the Continent and daily attacks by the Air Force and Navy will cut her life-lines. The moment England's supply routes are severed, she will be forced to capitulate.[15]

Dönitz's book *Die U-Bootwaffe* was published in early 1939. Had Naval Intelligence Division read it then, the Royal Navy might have been better prepared. However, NID did not obtain a copy until 1942, by which time the working out of its thesis was all too familiar. In the book, Dönitz stressed that the U-boat was to be the Kriegsmarine's principal offensive weapon with merchant ships the prime targets. He did not discuss group tactics but expressed his belief in night attacks, for which he believed the U-boat, with its low silhouette, was suited ideally. This targeting of merchantmen, and the enemy's maritime communications, was, explained Dönitz, the true purpose of warfare at sea.[16]

This thinking had been opposed in German naval circles. Admiral Heye, who believed in the effectiveness of asdic almost as strongly as the Admiralty, thought that U-boats could have only limited success. His October 1939 paper on sea warfare against Britain led to the concept of a 'cruiser U-boat', a large vessel capable of 25 knots surfaced, armed with four 5-inch (127mm) guns. This proposal did not become reality, although the Types IXD-1 and -2 retained elements of the concept.

Meanwhile Dönitz continued training his submariners and planning for operational deployment. War-gaming operations in the Atlantic with a varied force of U-boats, including fifteen Type VIIs and Type IXs, plus surface ships, against a strong enemy force protecting five convoys indicated that spreading boats too thinly meant that three convoys were not even spotted in the great expanse of ocean. However, Dönitz identified a solution to the problem, one that would play a critical part in defeating the U-boats. He intended using radio to direct boats towards targets from a shore-based headquarters, thus concentrating groups, or packs, of U-boats against convoys.

Submarines were cheaper than Raeder's big ships, much easier to build, with less of a drain on scarce raw materials, and required much less manpower to operate, but 300 could not be built and in service before war began. Hitler had accelerated the move to war and, instead of having time to build up to the 300-strong fleet, Dönitz would have to make do with what was available in September 1939. Although his full strength at that time was fifty-seven boats in commission, not all were available for operations; eight were training and trials' boats and his Type IIs were not suitable for use in the Atlantic. By 1 September only thirty-eight Type VIIs and IXs had been completed.

One staff appreciation produced in the *Marineleitung* drew attention to the dangers posed by aircraft from aircraft carriers, pointing out that carrier-borne aeroplanes would force U-boats to remain submerged, unable to maintain contact with their targets. The writer of that appreciation arguably demonstrated more prescience than most of his contemporaries in identifying the way aircraft might affect U-boat operations. However, it would be some time before carrier-borne aircraft could play a major role. Although land-based aircraft and flying boats already had an anti-submarine role, as late as April 1940 this was still defined as 'anti-submarine co-operation [with ships] generally'.[17]

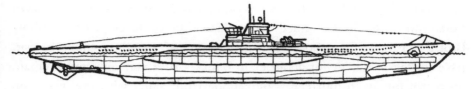

Figure 5: Type VII U-boat. The VIIC was the backbone of the U-boat fleet from 1941, with 568 commissioned, and serving in most theatres.

In 1936 the Royal Air Force created three operational commands: Fighter, Bomber and Coastal (there was also a Training Command). This reorganization was a preparation for the expansion schemes to increase RAF strength as more and newer aircraft left the factories. However, the threat of war meant that Fighter and Bomber Commands received priority over Coastal Command in the expansion programme. When Coastal Command came into being on 14 July 1936, under Air Marshal Sir Arthur Longmore, it included two front-line groups. That autumn, when Air Marshal Philip Joubert de la Ferté succeeded Longmore, the command still had only eight squadrons equipped with six different aircraft types. Most were obsolescent: four squadrons flew biplane flying boats such as the London, Scapa, Singapore and Rangoon, while two were torpedo-bomber squadrons with the equally dated Vickers Vildebeest. Two were re-equipping with a new design, the twin-engined Avro Anson general reconnaissance (GR) aircraft. However, the Anson, with limited range and payload, was no real threat to U-boats. Price makes an interesting comparison of the Anson, introduced to Coastal Command in 1936, and the Blackburn Kangaroo, introduced into the newly-formed RAF in 1918 for similar duties. The Kangaroo's bomb load was four 230lb anti-submarine bombs while the Anson could carry only four 100lb bombs; the Kangaroo also had greater endurance than the Anson. Perhaps the only point on which the Anson scored better was in crew comfort. Price also compares the Lockheed Hudson, introduced in 1939, with the Kangaroo: against the Kangaroo's four 230lb bombs the Hudson carried four 250lb bombs; both had six-hour endurance.[18]

As Coastal Command expanded, new squadrons formed. No.228 Squadron re-formed in December 1936, but with biplane flying boats before re-equipping to yet another of the same, the Supermarine Stranraer.

However, during 1938, the first Short Sunderland flying boats joined No.210 Squadron.[19] This four-engined, monoplane aircraft, developed from Short Brothers' Empire flying boat was to give sterling service throughout the war. Able to stay in the air for about eight hours – later versions could remain on patrol for up to fourteen – the Sunderland, along with the American Consolidated Catalina, proved formidable. Although ordered by the RAF before the war, the first Catalinas did not enter service until 1941; the prototype flew in 1935 and Catalinas entered service with the US Navy in 1936. Twin-engined, and not as large as the Sunderland, the 'Cat' had longer range and would prove a valuable addition to Coastal Command.[20] (The US Navy recognized the RAF name Catalina for the aircraft in 1941.)

Irrespective of their other capabilities, no Coastal Command aircraft was equipped with effective anti-submarine weapons when war began. Standard RAF bombs, known as general-purpose (GP) bombs, were available but had little effect on most vessels, least of all submerged U-boats. Scant attention appears to have been paid to developing air-dropped anti-submarine munitions in the inter-war period, largely due to cost restraints. It would be some time before aircraft became a fully-fledged threat to submerged U-boats. Peacetime parsimony also ensured that there was no airborne detection system for Coastal Command aircraft but this, too, would come in time. Once such a system became available to aircraft carrying effective anti-submarine weapons, the lives of enemy submariners would become even more perilous.

On 1 December 1937 an Air Ministry directive outlined the wartime role of Coastal Command as:

> trade protection, reconnaissance and co-operation with the Royal Navy. It guaranteed that the aircraft ... would only be employed on other duties when the threat to our sea communications was insignificant, and thus not only met the Admiralty's views regarding the function of aircraft allocated to naval co-operation but eliminated its apprehensions regarding the diversion of Coastal Command aircraft.[21]

By the outbreak of war Coastal Command had almost 450 aircraft, mostly Ansons, with about half available for front-line duties, and close to 10,000 personnel. Only twenty-seven Sunderlands were in service; thirty Vildebeests and twenty-six Londons and Stranraers remained with squadrons. There were also fifty-three Lockheed Hudson light bombers, improvised from the Lockheed 14 airliner, which the British Purchasing Commission had ordered off the drawing board in 1938; the first entered squadron service in May 1939.[22]

Joubert de la Ferté had been succeeded as Air Officer Commanding-in-Chief (AOC-in-C) by Air Marshal Sir Frederick Bowhill but left a lasting legacy in the form of one of his first innovations – an Area Combined Naval/Air Headquarters in which

> RAF and RN officers sat side by side controlling their respective formations in all air/sea operations and exercises – the real beginning of a vitally necessary mutual co-operation in defence of Britain's sea lifelines. If certain members of the higher 'brass' remained strictly partisan, at least at this rather lower level mutual respect, understanding and enthusiasm found a comfortable billet, to the benefit of all. Indeed, at relatively junior command level a degree of willing co-operation had always existed, if only on an individual basis. Differences in custom, language and attitudes had usually been matters of good-hearted banter between the two shades of blue uniform; so different from the entrenched and often bitter 'wars' waged along the Whitehall corridors of power.[23]

As a former sailor – Bowhill's career began as a midshipman in 1898 – the new AOC-in-C was able to build on the work of his predecessors, whose careers had begun in the Army, and prepare the command for its wartime years, when it would come under Admiralty operational control. He also moved his headquarters from Lee-on-Solent to Eastbury Park, Northwood, and with it the pattern for the future Command Operations Room. This was simplicity itself: the control centre included a wall covered by a map showing movements of all ships and aircraft and other relevant information and, facing this, three small rooms, one for each service, although the Army Room was taken over by the Air/Sea Rescue operations' controller. Northwood was close enough to London to allow contact with the chiefs of both the Naval and Air Staffs throughout the war.[24]

Coastal Command was placed on operational status on 2 September 1939, the day before the UK declared war on Germany. It would remain operational until June 1945, played an increasingly important role in the protection of Britain's maritime trade and, in co-operation with the Royal Navy, helped bring about the defeat of the *U-bootwaffe*. As we shall see, that co-operation was in stark contrast to the manner in which German forces operated. Although there was some co-operation between the Kriegsmarine and Luftwaffe, with the latter's Focke-Wulf Fw200 Condor four-engined bombers deploying in support of the former, German joint-service planning and operations were but a shadow of that achieved by their British opponents. Nor was the Fw200 the most reliable of aircraft; based on an airliner, it was fragile with a tendency to break up, and only 276 were built.[25] The Germans had other problems, not least the unreliable nature of their torpedoes early in the war.

When war was declared on Sunday 3 September 1939 neither side was prepared fully or adequately. The early months would be a learning experience for both British and Germans although they would give a very strong impression that the German navy and, in particular, its *U-bootwaffe* was in the ascendancy.

Chapter Three

The opening months of war were described as the 'Phoney War', due to the lack of action on land in Europe. However, there was no 'Phoney War' at sea: the war was only hours old when the *U-bootwaffe* claimed its first victim: the Donaldson Line's SS *Athenia*.

Athenia sailed from Glasgow for Montreal on 1 September but was to call at Belfast and Liverpool to collect passengers, leaving Liverpool in the afternoon of the 2nd, by which time there were over 1,100 passengers, including many Jewish refugees; crew members numbered 315. With a blackout in force, navigation lights were dimmed sailing through the Irish Sea and the North Channel into the Atlantic. News of the declaration of war was received before noon on Sunday with a notice posted for the attention of passengers. Otherwise, life continued as normal with many passengers enjoying the afternoon sunshine on deck.

As his ship steamed into the Atlantic, Captain James Cook had no idea that a U-boat lay ahead. *U-30*, a Type VIIA, was one of fourteen Type VIIs and IXs to leave Kiel and Wilhelmshaven on 19 August – another two followed soon after – to deploy around the British Isles ready for war. Fourteen Type II boats had also deployed to the North Sea on 25 August while two 'pocket battleships', *Graf Spee* and *Deutschland*, had slipped into the Atlantic undetected. What was worse, the Royal Navy (and the RAF) was entirely oblivious of this; as one officer, holding what would soon become a key position, remarked, 'Our Intelligence was not so much inefficient as totally inadequate'.[1]

U-30 had already passed through the Irish Sea, at one stage hearing Royal Navy vessels pass over. On the 3rd the submarine was surfaced about 250 miles north-west of Ireland and some sixty south of Rockall. Leutnant zur See Fritz Julius Lemp, the commander, was in the conning tower. At about 4.30pm German time (it was three hours later by GMT) he spotted *Athenia* travelling at speed – her maximum was about 15 knots – and zig-zagging. From this, and the fact that she appeared to be outside normal shipping routes, Lemp deduced he was looking at an armed merchant cruiser, a conclusion reinforced by her being blacked out. Lemp ordered his crew to prepare for a submerged attack, cleared the conning tower and dived.

The ensuing tragedy held a hint of farce. Lemp ordered two torpedoes to be fired, but the second did not launch. Since it was 'live' in its tube, several nervous moments passed before it was cleared. Not long after leaving the tube, the torpedo exploded. The first struck *Athenia*, which was soon dead in the water. Meanwhile, radio operator Georg Hügel had picked up distress signals from the liner, indicating that she was a merchant ship. When Hügel reported this Lemp surfaced to check and consulted the boat's register of ships. He ordered *U-30* to leave the scene and did not report the sinking to U-boat HQ.[2]

Athenia's sinking in contravention of Hitler's orders began a propaganda war. The German propaganda ministry claimed that she had been sunk deliberately by the British, on orders from Churchill, First Lord of the Admiralty. Hitler was concerned that the incident would have the same effect on American public opinion as the *Lusitania* sinking in 1915 and lead to United States' involvement in the war, especially as twenty-eight of the 127 dead were Americans. However, American opinion was mixed, former-President Hoover even opining that the Germans could not be so clumsy as to commit such an act; North Carolina's Senator Robert Rice Reynolds, an anti-Semitic and Anglophobic isolationist, claimed that Germany had no reason to sink a liner, but added that Britain had – to inflame the American people.[3]

Raeder, believing that the closest boat to the incident was over seventy miles away, assured the Americans that the Kriegsmarine had had no part in it. When *U-30* returned to Wilhelmshaven on 27 September Lemp told Dönitz what had happened. Dönitz sent him to Berlin to tell Raeder who, in turn, informed Hitler. Lemp was not court-martialled as he appeared to have made a genuine mistake, but *U-30*'s log was altered to suit the official line. Not until the Nuremberg trials was an official German admission of responsibility forthcoming.[4]

Athenia may have been sunk in direct contravention of Hitler's orders, but those orders changed greatly before long. By increments between 23 September and 17 November, restrictions on U-boats were eased so that any darkened ship, including liners 'clearly identifiable as hostile', in a zone out to 20 degrees West (20W), could be attacked. Unrestricted submarine warfare had begun.

It is impossible to avoid the conclusion that Admirals Raeder and Dönitz and the German Naval Staff had always wished and intended to introduce unrestricted warfare as rapidly as the political leaders could be persuaded to accept the possible consequences.[5]

By the end of November 1939 U-boats had taken a heavy toll of Allied shipping; eighty-nine ships (340,275 tons) had been sunk. A further twenty-five were lost in December, bringing the toll since the outbreak of war to 114 ships and 421,156 tons.[6]

Of those ships lost, only twelve had been in convoy while five had straggled. In return, the *U-bootwaffe* had lost nine boats, roughly a sixth of the fleet, including three to mines. German mines had caused more Allied shipping losses than had submarines in November and December, but the Admiralty knew that increased production in German shipyards would see more submarines at sea, increasing the risk to Allied merchantmen. Dönitz saw a gloomier picture, noting on 23 October that his losses – then seven boats – 'must lead to paralysis of U-boat warfare if no means can be devised of keeping them down'.[7]

Both sides had learned lessons. The Royal Navy had lost two major ships to submarines, the aircraft carrier *Courageous* and the battleship *Royal Oak*. *Courageous* was torpedoed by *U-29* on 17 September, going down with 518 of her crew of 1,260. Having already sunk three ships, Leutnant zur See Otto Schuhart was nearing the end of his patrol and was searching for a convoy in the Western Approaches when he spotted *Courageous*, which was part of a Royal Navy group hunting for submarines. Two of her four escorting destroyers had gone to assist a merchantman, making the carrier more vulnerable. *U-29* was not well positioned to attack until *Courageous* turned into the wind to allow her aircraft to land on. Presented with an ideal target, Schuhart took full advantage and, from under 3,000 yards, fired three torpedoes. Two struck the carrier which sank in fifteen minutes, the first major Royal Navy warship to be lost in the Second World War and the *U-bootwaffe*'s first major success.

Schuhart and his crew were decorated, but an even more spectacular success occurred less than a month later when Kapitänleutnant Günther Prien took *U-47* into the Scapa Flow anchorage and sank the elderly battleship HMS *Royal Oak*, which lay at anchor in perceived safety. In a remarkable display of seamanship, Prien steered into the confines of the anchorage and, with his second salvo, sent *Royal Oak* to the bottom; the ship sank in thirteen minutes. Of Prien's first salvo, only one hit *Royal Oak* but the explosion was judged to be internal or an air attack. Under twenty minutes later, the second salvo struck and 833 men perished as the battleship sank. Not surprisingly, Prien became the idol of the Kriegsmarine and was decorated by Hitler with the Knight's Cross, the first submariner, and only the second member of the Kriegsmarine, to be so decorated; each crew member also received the Iron Cross. Prien became known as the 'Bull of Scapa Flow' (*Der Stier von Scapa Flow*) and adopted a snorting bull emblem for *U-47*, a device also used by his 7th U-boat Flotilla.

The sinkings of *Athenia*, *Courageous* and *Royal Oak* had significant psychological consequences. *Athenia*'s loss had initiated the beginning of a major change in the German rules of engagement, providing an augury of the struggle to come in the Atlantic. *Courageous* had been engaged in hunting submarines and her loss indicated the flaws in the tactical deployment of hunting groups that included such valuable capital ships. *Royal Oak*'s demise, Dönitz considered, would prompt the Admiralty to move the Home Fleet from Scapa to improve its defences. Believing the fleet would be dispersed to Loch Ewe, the Firth of Forth and Firth of Clyde, he 'initiated appropriate U-boat operations in all these localities'. Largely minelaying, those operations resulted in damage to the battleship *Nelson* and the crippling of the cruiser *Belfast*,* although *U-33* was lost.[8]

However, as well as the nine submarines lost in 1939, the *U-bootwaffe* faced other problems. The campaign was not as effective as Dönitz and his commanders had hoped. Under operational conditions, many boats had developed faults that had not been evident in peacetime training, when,

---

* *Belfast* spent over two years in the dockyard undergoing repairs and having improvements made to her armour, armaments and radar. She returned to service in November 1942, three years after being mined.

against Dönitz's recommendations, they were restricted to diving no more than 150 feet.[9] During operational cruises, boats had suffered faults due to poor design or bad workmanship, including valves and seals that did not work properly, as well as defective engine mountings. Many had to be docked for lengthy repairs, reducing the fleet's strength and its operations. Dönitz believed that some of 1939's losses might have been due to such defects. The severe winter of 1939–40 also saw boats confined to port by thick ice.

Perhaps the worst problem was that of defective torpedoes, a problem so severe that Dönitz includes much of a chapter on it in his *Memoirs*.[10] There had been suspicions from the early days of war – the torpedo that failed to launch from *U-30* during the attack on *Athenia* was an early example – and would grow worse in 1940. While *U-29* had claimed *Courageous* on 17 September, *U-39* had come close to sinking the Royal Navy's most modern aircraft carrier, *Ark Royal*, on the 14th. The *Ark* was saved by faulty German workmanship. Off the Orkney Islands, Kapitänleutnant Gerhard Glattes had spotted the carrier and manoeuvred into a firing position. About a half mile from his target, Glattes fired two torpedoes. Both failed to reach *Ark Royal*, exploding less than 100 yards from the carrier and signalling the presence of a U-boat. HM Ships *Faulknor*, *Firedrake* and *Foxhound* started a search and *Foxhound*'s captain was able to see *U-39* below him as he unleashed his depth charges. Glattes's boat was blown to the surface and its crew abandoned her before she sank; the crewmen were rescued by the destroyers. *U-39* had become the first U-boat sunk in the war. Less than a week later *U-27* was captured; from his prison camp her captain smuggled a message to Dönitz telling him that three torpedoes had been fired but had exploded prematurely. Further misfire reports were received as boats returned to base, including *U-56* which, finding herself among the Home Fleet on 30 October, had fired three torpedoes at HMS *Nelson*. None exploded, although two struck the battleship; the third missed, exploding at the end of its run. On 31 October Dönitz noted in his HQ war diary:

> At least 30 per cent of torpedoes are duds. They do not detonate or they detonate in the wrong place … Commanders must be losing confidence in their torpedoes. In the end their fighting spirit must suffer.[11]

During the Norwegian campaign the problem worsened. Dönitz received reports of attacks failing because of defective torpedoes. He records that U-boats made thirty-six attacks and that a 'most meticulous examination' indicated that, but for torpedo failures, a number of Allied warships and transports would have been damaged or sunk.[12]

Investigations into the cause of so many misfires, begun in late 1939, were hampered by the freezing over of the Baltic that winter, preventing the use of the practice ranges and committing U-boats to the Norwegian campaign without an effective weapon. Raeder established a Torpedo Commission to identify and resolve the causes of the problems. Eventually, it was appreciated that the torpedoes' magnetic and percussion pistols were at fault. The magnetic, or MZ, pistols and the percussion, or AZ, pistols were developments of First World War pistols, but 'a good deal more complex (and more liable to go wrong)'. This was an example of German engineering hubris that was also evident in over-complex tanks such as the Panther and Tiger and in the standard infantry machine guns, the MG34 and MG42.

U-boats used two types of torpedo, the G7a and the G7e, the latter designed for submarine launch. The G7a's compressed-air motor left a trail of bubbles, whereas the electrically-driven G7e made no track, but travelled at a maximum 30 knots, slower than a destroyer; therefore it was intended principally for use against merchantmen. G7e torpedoes had an inherent fault making them run deeper than intended, causing many to pass under their targets without exploding. This fault was known but its cause was not discovered until January 1942 when U-94, on an Atlantic patrol, radioed HQ to report that an inspection of a torpedo had revealed 'a marked excess of pressure ... in the balance chambers', the compartment containing the hydrostatic valve controlling the horizontal rudders and running depth. While U-94's crew should not have been performing an on-board inspection, it was fortuitous that they did: they had identified the G7e's problem. It was then up to the engineers to produce a solution. [13]

For such a scandal, scapegoats were necessary. Vizedmiral Götting and Konteradmiral Wehr filled that role and were dismissed. Wehr and some officials were court-martialled, with Wehr and two others found guilty. Yet warnings seem to have been ignored, not least by Dönitz who makes no mention of them in his *Memoirs*.

In a 1946 official publication,[14] the first phase of the Battle of the Atlantic is defined as the period from 3 September 1939 to June 1940.[15] Dissecting the battle into eight phases was the result of work for the Admiralty in the late 1940s by a former U-boat captain, staff officer at U-boat Headquarters and Dönitz's son-in-law, Günter Hessler. Hessler worked with another former captain and staff officer, Alfred Hoschatt; their definition is accepted by most British historians. In his *Memoirs*, Dönitz uses a starting date of July 1940, considering what had gone before as outside that struggle. Marc Milner defines the September 1939 to March 1940 period as 'opening skirmishes'.[16] Irrespective of Dönitz's assertion, that U-boats were in the Atlantic, sinking merchantmen, from the first day of war argues strongly for dating the start of the Battle of the Atlantic as 3 September 1939. Milner's 'opening skirmishes' were part of the overall battle, marking a phase when opposing forces realized some of their weakness, whether in weaponry and equipment or in tactics.

The first six months of the long struggle which was to last for six years can be described as the opening skirmishes before battle was fully joined. During these skirmishes each side probed the other's defences and learnt what it was up against.[17]

Convinced of the effectiveness of the wolfpack tactic, Dönitz was keen to put it into operation but lacked sufficient boats to do so. A plan to deploy nine against convoys from Gibraltar in October 1939 failed for several reasons, including dockyard delays. Only three boats were available which, on the 17th, attacked a convoy, sinking three or four ships. Torpedo failures meant that other targets were spared. One boat ran out of torpedoes and the others lost contact with the convoy, which had air cover.[18]

This indicated the shape of things to come. More boats would allow Dönitz to adopt the wolfpack as a standard tactic against convoys. Another indicator of future operations was the presence of air cover. Although ineffective for attacking U-boats at this stage, due to inadequate weaponry and lack of airborne detection equipment, the presence of one aircraft over a convoy was a deterrent, preventing boats operating on the surface in daylight. An Anson or Hudson might be incapable of inflicting any real damage, but could summon a warship.

Macintyre makes an interesting observation on air escorts to convoys in the First World War. Ninety-six ships were sunk from the 16,000 in ocean convoys and 161 from the 68,000 in coastal and short sea convoys; only five fell victim when both air and sea escorts were operating, in spite of the aircraft lacking effective weapons to attack submerged submarines.

Sadly, these operations, carried out by the RNAS, had not been recorded in the *Naval* histories of the war but in those of the new Royal Air Force which absorbed the RNAS in 1918. As a result, the air escorts' success had been lost in the detail of air battles and bombing raids.[19] Small wonder that Coastal Command was the Cinderella of the RAF. In autumn 1939, as each side, in Macintyre's words, probed the other's defences, Coastal Command was fighting to catch up, through expansion, new aircraft, new weapons (radar had been fitted to a few aircraft by January 1940) and new bases.

In the winter of 1939–40 the maritime conflict continued. *Graf Spee*, damaged in battle with Royal Navy ships, was harried into Montevideo where, unable to stay in the neutral port long enough to make the necessary repairs to his ship, Captain Hans Langsdorff chose to scuttle her and commit suicide. The Battle of the River Plate gave the Royal Navy a much-needed morale boost and removed a major German surface ship from the Atlantic. *Graf Spee*'s sister ships, *Scheer* and *Deutschland* (subsequently renamed *Lützow*), had also been to sea. *Deutschland* had been relatively unsuccessful compared to *Graf Spee*; the latter sank nine merchantmen, the former only three. *Scheer* went on to become the most successful surface raider. Not surprisingly, the Admiralty saw the German surface fleet as the greater threat at this time, since the Kriegsmarine also deployed nine converted merchant ships as auxiliary cruisers. The cruiser *Admiral Hipper*, first of a planned class of five, was also in commission as were the battleships (battle-cruisers by Royal Navy definition) *Scharnhorst* and *Gneisenau*, which had slipped into the Atlantic in November 1939, while two Bismarck-class battleships were nearing completion. For all the attention being paid to the German surface fleet the *U-bootwaffe* would prove the greater threat.

At the end of December 1939 only thirty-nine U-boats were in service with fewer than ten at sea at any time. The larger Atlantic boats were deployed around the British Isles, off the coasts of Ireland, in the south-western approaches to the Channel, and off the Scottish coasts. Off the east coast of Britain, the smaller U-boats preyed on shipping and laid magnetic mines. Minelaying was concentrated initially in coastal channels and off the Thames and Tyne before being extended to Liverpool Bay and the Clyde.

As 1940 dawned there was a lull in U-boat attacks, partially due to weather conditions but also because of German preparations for operations in Norway and north-western Europe. Nonetheless, the leading U-boat commanders, well trained and with operational experience, were evolving the surface night attack that would for a time frustrate the escorts and cause so many losses in the convoys.[20]

Chapter Four

Spring 1940 brought a lull in the Atlantic. Surface raiders were operating but the ocean was free of submarines, which had been recalled to protect German shipping in the invasion of Norway. During the Norwegian campaign the *U-bootwaffe* suffered four boats sunk and two damaged. One, sunk by a Swordfish from HMS *Warspite*'s catapult, was the first despatched by a naval aircraft. Other German losses were attributed to lack of familiarity with asdic's capability, especially true of training-boat commanders deployed operationally.

Atlantic operations did not resume until May when boats re-entered the south-western approaches, by which time German armies had invaded France and the Low Countries and the British Expeditionary Force was retreating. Ships and aircraft that would otherwise have been protecting convoys were redeployed to support the evacuation from France, as were Coastal Command squadrons, a very different role from that for which they had trained. Operation DYNAMO, the evacuation of the BEF, resulted in losses of escort ships and crewmen, increasing the time it would take to build up escort forces to meet the demands that would be made of them.

The fall of France was a boon to the *U-bootwaffe* with major naval bases on the Atlantic coast available to the U-boats, increasing their effectiveness, acting, in modern parlance, as a 'force multiplier'. No longer would boats have to journey around the north of Scotland to enter the Atlantic. From Brest, Lorient, St Nazaire, la Rochelle/la Pallice and Bordeaux, they could cross the Bay of Biscay and interdict the convoy routes, cutting 450 miles off the previous outward journey from Germany, thereby increasing patrol time; even the 250-ton coastal U-boats could deploy into the Atlantic. Fritz Julius Lemp's *U-30* was the first boat to put into any of these bases, docking at Lorient on 7 July 1940.[1] In addition to the French bases, the Kriegsmarine also had Norwegian ports.

Alongside strategically-sited naval bases the Germans had gained new airfields for the Luftwaffe for use in attacks on Britain and in the Battle of the Atlantic. Long-range aircraft, principally Fw200 Condors, operating from airfields in western France could search for and attack convoys far out at sea and direct U-boats to them. French airfields also increased the risk of bombing for Britain's ports and cities, bringing the entire United Kingdom within range of Luftwaffe bombers. New Luftwaffe airfields in Norway would also play a part in the campaign against the convoys.

The Germans had seized many French ships, including some equipped with asdic. The Admiralty feared that this would allow the *U-bootwaffe* to develop tactics to frustrate asdic, but this fear was probably overrated. Nonetheless, with German surface raiders at large in both North and South Atlantic – and soon to round the Cape into the Indian Ocean – the overall situation for the United Kingdom was as bleak as could be imagined. With France defeated, most of Europe overrun, Italy entering the war on Germany's side on 10 June, a non-aggression pact between Germany and the USSR, and the United States' policy of neutrality, it seemed as if Britain stood alone against Germany. Only the Commonwealth and Empire stood with the United Kingdom in what Churchill called 'Britain's darkest hour'.

Britain relied more than ever for survival on the Atlantic commerce routes and the Merchant Navy, but merchant ships sailing the Atlantic became the prime target for a renewed U-boat campaign. In the first four months of 1940, in spite of the lull in U-boat operations in the Atlantic, merchant shipping losses had totalled 239 vessels, or 706,653 tons (Table 1), of which 110 ships (376,077 tons) had been lost to submarines.

In May the Luftwaffe accounted for forty-eight ships. Air attacks, plus interdiction by Kriegsmarine *S-boote* (*Schnell-boote*, fast boats, known as E-[for enemy] boats to the Allies), forced the re-routeing of inbound convoys through the north-west approaches. Western Approaches Command Headquarters was in Plymouth but the change of emphasis to routes around the north of Ireland meant Plymouth was no longer suitable. The HQ was to be transferred to Liverpool, although it was 7 February 1941 before the new headquarters opened in Derby House.[2] Ten days later, Admiral Sir Percy Noble succeeded Admiral Martin Dunbar-Nasmith as Commander-

Table 1

Mon	U-boats	Aircraft	Mines	Warships	Aux raiders	S-boats	Other causes/NK	Total
Jan	111,263 (40)	23,693 (11)	77,116 (21)	-	-	-	2,434 (1)	214,506 (73)
Feb	169,566 (45)	853 (2)	54,740 (15)	1,761 (1)	-	-	-	226,920 (63)
Mar	62,781 (23)	8.694 (7)	35.501 (14)	-	-	-	33 (1)	107,009 (45)
Apr	32,467 (7)	13,409 (7)	19,799 (11)	-	5,207 (1)	151 (1)	87,185 (31)	158,218 (58)
Totals	376,007 (110)	46,649 (27)	187,156 (61)	1,761 (10)	5, 207 (1)	151 (1)	89,652 (33)	706,653 (239)

in-Chief, Western Approaches, the latter becoming Commander-in-Chief, Plymouth. No.15 Group Coastal Command also moved from Plymouth to Liverpool and, under Air Vice-Marshal James Robb, assumed responsibility for the north-west approaches.

> In … Derby House an operations room was started, and there a plot was maintained which was a duplicate of the Trade Plot in the Admiralty, with which it was linked by direct telephone. There, under the direction of a highly skilled staff from both Services, the naval and air sides of the Atlantic battle were fully integrated, and a constant watch was maintained over the whole vast battlefield and over the hundreds of warships, merchantmen and aircraft involved in the unremitting prosecution of the campaign.[3]

Sir Percy Noble's instructions from the Admiralty were defined clearly: he

> would be directly responsible for the protection of trade, the routeing and control of the outward and homeward-bound ocean convoys and measures to combat any attacks on convoys by U-boats or hostile aircraft within his command.[4]

By summer 1940, as the Battle of Britain raged over southern England, the Admiralty was fighting another battle less obvious to the British people. The Battle of the Atlantic was becoming one of wills, of operational tactics, of intelligence, of weapons and technology on and under the surface of the ocean and in the air above. Skilled U-boat commanders continued wreaking havoc in convoys with minimal escorts: at times, the sole escort for forty merchantmen might be a single armed merchant cruiser (AMC) or an obsolescent battleship. Such was the shortage of anti-submarine escort vessels that convoys might only have two small ships as protection.

At the end of May it was possible only to escort outbound convoys about 200 miles to the west of Ireland, between longitude 12 and 15 West (W), where the outward-bound convoy's escort left to rendezvous with a homeward-bound convoy. Meantime, the outbound convoy sailed in formation for about another twenty-four hours before the ships broke away to make their way to their destination ports. By July the outbound close-escort range had been extended to 17W and in October was further extended to 19W. Even this was not enough as the U-boats continued to move beyond the escorts' range, sinking many unescorted vessels at little risk. On 17 August Hitler declared a complete blockade of the British Isles and warned that neutral ships would be sunk on sight.[5] The French Atlantic ports allowed U-boats to range as far as 25W, well beyond the range of escorts, while air cover from UK bases was effective only to about 15W, except for the few Sunderlands available. A similar pattern prevailed for eastbound convoys. Escorted by ships of the Royal Canadian Navy for about 400 miles, after which the mid-ocean escort, often a solitary AMC, took over, these convoys, too, provided rich targets. Such was the tonnage being sunk that U-boat crews dubbed this period 'the happy time'.

U-boat commanders employed a tactic initiated in the Great War and refined by Dönitz between the wars: the surface attack. Using the submarine as a torpedo boat, this removed the threat of detection by asdic, which could not detect a surfaced target. Remaining at extreme range in daylight the boats closed on the convoys at dusk. With little more than conning towers showing, they were difficult to spot, especially as they stayed on the convoy's dark side; if spotted they could always dive. They usually shadowed an escort, to hide the boat's wake, before firing at selected targets and turning to escape. If not counter-attacked, a boat might reload its tubes and attack again before dawn.[6]

During September U-boats began stalking unescorted ships, attacking them with gunfire. Fifty-nine merchant ships (295,335 tons) were sunk by U-boats that month, forty in convoy. Among those in convoy was the SS *City of Benares*, a loss that caused outrage. The Ellerman Lines' vessel, the commodore's ship of OB213, carried 191 passengers, of whom ninety were children being evacuated to Canada by the Children's Overseas Reception Board (CORB), in spite of Churchill's instruction that no British children be taken overseas. On the night of 17 September OB213's escort of a destroyer and two sloops reached the limit of their endurance and turned for home, unaware of a U-boat stalking the convoy.[7]

Kapitänleutnant Heinrich Bleichrodt, commanding *U-48*, had just sunk HMS *Dundee*, the sole escort to SC3, and was moving farther west when he found OB213. He attacked on the surface, from behind, in the early hours of the morning. Weather conditions favoured him; the high seas of a rising north-westerly gale hid *U-48*. Bleichrodt's first salvo of two torpedoes failed to hit, but a single torpedo sixteen minutes later struck the stern and exploded. *City of Benares* immediately began to settle. Fifteen minutes later the ship was abandoned. Of the 407 aboard, more than half – 260 – perished, including seventy-seven child passengers, the youngest only two years old.[8]

There was outrage in Britain and the United States and the Germans were accused of a war crime. In response, they, describing the liner as a legitimate target, accused the British government of ignoring German warnings about such targets by allowing children to be transported in a war zone. Bleichrodt could not have known there were children on the ship.

U-boats continued their heavy toll of merchant ships, whether in convoy or alone, in autumn 1940. In that third week of September, eleven ships of a homebound convoy were sunk by two U-boats while, during the October full-moon period, thirty-one were lost from two convoys that were 'cut to pieces'.[9] Terraine notes that the 'first effective pack action against a convoy' began on 6 September and lasted until the 10th; the target was SC2, fifty-four ships which had sailed from Sydney, Cape Breton Island. The attack was initiated when the German naval radio-intercept service, *B-Dienst*, picked up the Admiralty signal detailing the convoy's rendezvous with its escort. Dönitz ordered four boats to intercept. The first to make contact, *U-65* (von Stockhausen), was driven off. However, *U-65* followed SC2 and reported its position, thus allowing the others to plot interception courses. In spite of a Force 8 gale, Gunther Prien in *U-47* found the convoy before dawn on the 7th and sank three ships. As dawn broke, Sunderlands forced the boats under. On the night of 8/9 September the attack was resumed by *U-47*, *U-99* (Kapitänleutnant Otto Kretschmer) and *U-28* (Kapitänleutnant Günter Kuhnke), with the latter sinking another ship, as did Prien. However, the arrival of seven escort ships, although not in a formal, trained group, and the attentions of aircraft, brought the battle to an end. Nonetheless, SC2 had lost almost 10 per cent of its ships. The pack tactic was effective and would be used again in October, with devastating consequences.[10]

Dönitz describes a ravaging attack in October, beginning on the night of the 16th/17th when Bleichrodt in *U-48*, operating north-west of Rockall, made contact with the homebound SC7. Another five boats, *U-46* (Endrass), *U-99* (Kretschmer), *U-100* (Schepke), *U-101* (Frauenheim) and *U-123* (Moehle), already east and north of Rockall Bank, were directed towards the convoy. When *U-48* lost touch, having been attacked, the other boats formed into line abreast at right angles to the convoy's presumed route to regain contact, a lengthy operation that had to be undertaken well to the east of the convoy's last known position so that boats had time to take up their new dispositions, make sure that they were well in advance of the convoy and placed so that it would be daylight by the time it appeared. They were in place by the morning of the 18th and the convoy ran into the line that afternoon. In a series of night surface attacks, seventeen ships were sunk.[11]

With torpedoes expended, three boats turned for France. Meanwhile, Prien had found another eastbound convoy, HX79, west of Rockall Bank. *U-46*, *U-48* and *U-100* were still available to attack while *U-38* (Kapitänleutnant Heinrich Liebe) and *U-28* (Kuhnke) were advised of the opportunity. *U-28* was too far from HX79 to join an attack, so the operation fell to the other five, which, during the night of the 19th/20th, sank fourteen ships. Thus SC7 and HX79 were the two that the Admiralty described as having been 'cut to pieces'. The writer could have modified his text to note that three convoys had been shattered with the loss of thirty-eight ships since, on the night of the attack on HX79, U-boats also attacked HX79A, sinking another seven ships. No U-boats were lost in these attacks.[12] Macintyre notes the loss rates in HX79 and SC7: 24.5 per cent and 58.8 per cent respectively.[13]

By the end of October, during which sixty-three ships were lost, the toll of merchant ships, British, Allied and neutral, since September 1939 had risen to 1,026 (almost 4 million tons). More than half, 568 ships and over 2 million tons, were British. Thus far, U-boats had destroyed 471 ships (over 2 million tons), 250 of which (1.25 million tons) were British.[14] Attacks by aircraft and surface ships had also taken a huge toll. An example of the threat from surface ships came when HX84, which sailed from Halifax, Nova Scotia, on 28 October, was about midway across the Atlantic.

HX84 had left Canada with a Royal Canadian Navy local escort, which handed over to the mid-ocean escort, a single ship, the AMC HMS *Jervis Bay*, commanded by Captain Edward Stephen Fogarty Fegen. A Great War veteran recalled to service when war broke out, Fegen – described by Alistair MacLean as 'a big tough 47-year-old bachelor Irishman, son of an admiral, grandson of a captain, already twice decorated for his gallantry'[15] – had the task of ensuring 'the safe and timely arrival' of HX84 in the United Kingdom. While the convoy would reach Britain, Fegen would never see his homeland again. *Admiral Scheer* had sailed from Gdynia on 23 October, slipped into the Atlantic undetected in bad weather, through the Denmark Strait, and was searching for targets, guided by German naval intelligence. *Jervis Bay* was no match. Against *Scheer*'s main armament of six 11-inch guns and secondary battery of eight 5.9-inch guns, the converted liner possessed only seven 6-inch guns that had to be fired over open sights and lacked the range of the other's weapons. Not for nothing were AMCs dubbed 'Admiralty Made Coffins'. Kapitän Theodor Krancke had a fast, well-armoured warship with excellent fire-control equipment and two spotter float-planes that confirmed the position of the convoy – *B-Dienst* had already provided details of the convoy's course and speed.

When the German was spotted and identified, Fegen signalled the Admiralty, providing their first indication that *Scheer* was at sea. Fegen ordered the convoy to scatter and make smoke. To protect it, he chose to engage *Scheer*, which had altered course to attack and opened fire from 17,000 yards. *Scheer*'s first salvo fell around *Cornish City*, the commodore's ship, without causing damage. Before the second salvo was in the air, *Jervis Bay* was steaming towards the foe. With no doubt of the outcome, Fegen placed his ship in harm's way to force the German to concentrate on him. Every minute that the cruiser did so was another minute for the merchantmen to escape.

Before long *Jervis Bay* had suffered such severe damage that she could steam only in a straight line. Her commander was wounded mortally.[16] Still the puny British ship held the attention of Krancke, who kept out of range of Fegen's 6-inch guns. Captain John O'Neill, of the *Cornish City*, told an Irish newspaper in 1945:

Within 15 minutes of the epic encounter beginning, *Jervis Bay* was a raging inferno from stem to stern. Billows of smoke soared skywards from the slowly sinking cruiser, from which now and then a solitary salvo was returned in answer to the fire of the raider. As dusk was falling and the smoke ... exceedingly dense, it was difficult for the attacker to see the prey.[17]

With German shells still crashing into her, *Jervis Bay* sank below the waves with Fegen standing on what remained of his bridge, his shattered arms hanging limply. His last moments were witnessed by Captain Sven Olander, of the Swedish ship *Stureholm*, which recovered sixty-five of Fegen's crew from the ocean. Roskill tells how the convoy had scattered immediately

and made good use of its smoke-making apparatus, while the escorting warship unhesitatingly challenged her redoubtable adversary to a most unequal duel. The result was a foregone conclusion, but Captain Fegen's action gained enough time to save all the convoy save five ships. He was awarded a posthumous Victoria Cross for his gallantry and self-sacrifice.[18]

Krancke had failed to make best use of his overwhelming superiority. In a five-month raiding operation, however, he sank thirteen merchantmen and captured three, as well as sinking *Jervis Bay*. His tally totalled over 115,000 tons. Milner describes the winter of 1940–41 as 'the last gasp of the German surface threat in the Atlantic', a point underlined by the cruise of *Scharnhorst* and *Gneisenau*, which began in late-January. Both cleared the Denmark Strait to enter the Atlantic on 4 February.[19]

A major target awaited them: HX106. Forty-one ships had sailed from Halifax on 30 January and the local escort had handed over to the elderly battleship HMS *Ramillies*, with her maximum speed of 21.5 knots (but a practical speed of 15 knots) and armament of four 15-inch and fourteen 6-inch guns. Among *Ramillies'* officers was Harry Barton, who recalled that the lookout, Lieutenant John Dreyer, identified as *Scharnhorst* a large ship with its superstructure just above the horizon. *Ramillies* went to action stations, but *Scharnhorst* was seen to steam away. What was not known at the time, but was revealed by Kriegsmarine records after the war, was that *Gneisenau* had been out of sight below the horizon.[20] In this case, the presence of the obsolescent battleship had deterred an attack. *Scharnhorst*'s captain had suggested that he draw off *Ramillies* while *Gneisenau* destroyed the convoy, but Admiral Günther Lutjens, in overall command, had demurred. Hitler had instructed his senior naval officers not to engage British capital ships and Lutjens was not prepared to disobey. Had he turned a blind eye, *Scharnhorst*, with her modern 11-inch guns, outranged *Ramillies*'s main guns and was about ten knots faster. However, Lutjens may also have been thinking that *Ramillies* would put up a fight similar to that waged by *Jervis Bay*.

HX106 did not make Liverpool unscathed as *U-96* sank two stragglers that fell behind on 10 February and were sunk three days later.[21]

The attacks on SC7 and HX79 proved the pack tactic's value. Destroying thirty-one ships and savaging two convoys demonstrated the validity of the tactic, which would be a major element in operations in the Atlantic as more U-boats became available. The underlying principle was that the concentration represented by a convoy had to be met by a similar concentration of U-boats, something that was possible through advances in communications.[22] Dönitz had also been quick to redeploy boats following the change of convoy routeing to the north-west approaches.

It may seem that the advantages all lay with the *U-bootwaffe* but there were already some chinks of light in the battle against Dönitz and his boats. Although small, these were chinks nonetheless. One was the establishment of additional escort bases. Dönitz refers to the British occupation of Iceland on 8 May 1940 'with the object of obtaining naval and air bases for their escort forces'.[23] He omits to mention that the occupation of Iceland by Britain and Canada was intended not only to provide escort bases, but to pre-empt a German invasion: Iceland was then part of a joint kingdom with Denmark, which the Germans had already overrun. Little over a month after this, the Royal Navy also established an escort base at Londonderry on the river Foyle in Northern Ireland.[24] Subsequently named HMS *Ferret*, Londonderry would become the most important escort base in the Battle of the Atlantic and the most westerly available in the British Isles. The Admiralty had hoped to use the Treaty Ports in Ireland, which had been handed over to the Irish government in October 1938, but the Irish prime minister, Éamon de Valera, could not be prevailed upon to allow British forces to operate from Irish soil. (The RAF had thought that a Coastal Command flying-boat squadron, either No.210 or No.228, might move to Bantry Bay 'if [a] base [became] available'.) [25]

The Londonderry escort base, and air bases in Northern Ireland, played a crucial role in the developing battle. Dönitz also mentions Churchill obtaining fifty American destroyers in return for the United States being granted the use of naval and air bases in Newfoundland, Bermuda and the West Indies.[26] However, the bases in Newfoundland (not then part of Canada) and Bermuda were 'granted as a gift'; the use of 'similar bases in British Guiana and five of our West Indian colonies' was the subject of the agreement that brought fifty ex-USN destroyers to the Royal Navy.[27] Perhaps the most important aspect of this agreement was that Britain could reduce her commitments to defending those bases as United States' forces moved in. While an additional fifty destroyers for escort work seemed a good deal on paper, those who sailed in them were not convinced.

the ex-US ships ... required significant modification and working up before they would be ready to enter service with the Royal Navy. On the face of it, they were manna from heaven for the hard-pressed North Atlantic escort force, but on closer examination this much-lauded aid from America seemed less than generous.[28]

The destroyers, dubbed Town-class in British service, were old, built during the Great War, and mothballed thereafter. Under 1,000 tons, they were narrow, with high superstructure and four funnels, making them top-heavy. They could make 30 to 35 knots, but were difficult to handle and rolled excessively in heavy seas. Uncomfortable ships in which to live and fight, the Royal Navy made the best use it could of them. In 1940 they were very welcome additions to an embattled fleet; no one looks a gift horse in the mouth.[30]

Other developments of which the Germans were unaware included the beginning of a programme to fit radar to escort vessels and ASV radar to Coastal Command aircraft. Over time, both innovations would make the tactic of operating on the surface increasingly dangerous. Meanwhile, however, that practice, which rendered asdic 'blind', robbed escort commanders of a detection system on which they had relied. As Terraine comments, this tactic had taken the Royal Navy by surprise.[31]

Royal Navy officers were also studying German operating procedures to identify effective countermeasures. The greatest problem at the end of 1940 remained the shortage of escort ships, a problem exacerbated by the increasing number of convoys. We have noted the SC convoys, slow convoys from Sydney, Cape Breton Island, Nova Scotia, to the UK, which had begun in August, as a summer-only addition to the HX convoys. These continued into the winter, 'even though an ocean escort could not always be provided, and the fierce North Atlantic gales sometimes scattered the labouring merchantmen far and wide on the waters'.[32]

New escort vessels had been ordered before the war; Flower-class corvettes were entering service in increasing numbers, the first, *Arabis* and *Gladiolus*, commissioning in April 1940. Originally, these small ships (925 tons and 205 feet long) had been intended to escort coastal convoys but their endurance proved suitable for oceanic work, even though the little vessels were

> extremely uncomfortable and exhausting to their crews in the stormy Atlantic. Yet they crossed and recrossed that ocean escorting the slow convoys in all weathers and it is hard to see how Britain could have survived without them.[33]

Several classes of sloop were in service when war broke out, with newer classes under construction. The first of the latter, HMS *Black Swan*, had been commissioned in January 1940 but would not join Western Approaches Command until May 1941, following repairs after bomb damage off Norway in April 1940. Sloops already in service were modified for the escort role; further modifications followed in the course of the war. The almost thirty sloops in commission in 1940 were worked hard, with one often providing the ocean escort for a convoy. While acting as lone escorts to SC1 and SC3, the Hastings-class HMS *Penzance* was sunk on 24 August and the Shoreham-class *Dundee* on 15 September. (*Bittern*, name-ship of her class, had been sunk by air attack in April.)

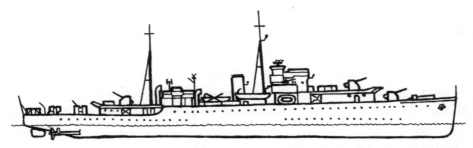

Figure 6: HMS *Black Swan*, name ship of her class, gave excellent service during the war. One of her sister ships, HMS *Flamingo*, was transferred to the re-formed German navy in 1959 and renamed *Graf Spee*.

Frigates designed specifically as ocean-going anti-submarine escort ships had been ordered but took longer to build; the first were not laid down until 1941. The first frigates ordered were of the River class, lightly-built warships for which orders were placed with several British and Canadian yards. The first eight built in Canada were intended for the United States Navy but, on completion, were handed over to the Royal Navy under Lend-Lease. With a crew of 140, they were armed with two 4–inch quick-firing (QF) guns in single-gun turrets and 126 depth charges, later increased to 150; from entry into service they were also fitted with the forward-firing Hedgehog multiple-launch spigot mortar. The Rivers would be followed by the Loch-class frigates, improved Rivers with superior anti-submarine armament and hulls designed for prefabrication.

River- and Loch-class frigates would be supplemented by the Captain class, American destroyer escorts (DEs), supplied under Lend-Lease in 1943–44, the only full class of Royal Navy warship not built in British yards, although based on British designs. British-built Hunt-class destroyers were designed for escort work but, being unsuited to Atlantic operations, were restricted generally to the North Sea and Mediterranean.

Coastal Command's situation had improved by the end of 1940. However, the command had been balanced towards the east of the British Isles, to patrol the northern exits into the Atlantic, with most bases established with that aim in view, although there was a single station in Northern Ireland, at Aldergrove in County Antrim, home to No. 502 (Ulster) Squadron. In

November 1938 the squadron had been transferred to Coastal Command and equipped with Ansons. Although the Anson could carry only 100lb bombs, 502 patrolled off the north coast of Ireland, but, in September 1940, began re-equipping with Armstrong Whitworth Whitleys, with a greater range than the Anson and a heavier bomb load. By then, it had been decided to abandon anti-submarine bombs in favour of naval depth charges.

It would take time to establish bases farther west in the British Isles, but several were already being constructed, or planned, in Northern Ireland and the Hebrides. Flying boats could operate from Plymouth – RAF Mount Batten – and Pembroke Dock, but there were still insufficient Sunderlands to cover the Western Approaches and northern Norway. Sunderland production was slow, as its manufacturers, Short Brothers, were also building the RAF's first four-engined bomber, the Stirling, and bomber manufacture had priority. However, by the end of 1940 some Sunderlands had been fitted with ASV Mark I, improving their effectiveness in the anti-submarine role. Also fitted with the new equipment were some Hudsons, but fewer than fifty aircraft carried the radar in December 1940.

Even without ASV equipment, Coastal Command aircraft had demonstrated the contribution they could make to fighting the U-boats. On 30 January 1940 a Sunderland of No.228 Squadron had achieved the command's first success against a submarine. *U-55*, commanded by Kapitänleutnant Werner Heidel, had sunk a ship on the 21st, followed by two more in OA80G on the 30th. When *U-55* struck at OA80G, some ninety miles south-west of the Isles of Scilly, the convoy had the sloop HMS *Fowey* as escort, although two destroyers were ordered to assist. The Sunderland, from Pembroke Dock, located *Fowey* and the French destroyer *Guépard*, which was rescuing survivors from a stricken ship, as well as the reinforcing destroyers, HM Ships *Whitshed* and *Valmy*. Thirty minutes later the Sunderland spotted *U-55* on the surface. The boat appeared unable to submerge and the aircraft attacked, dropping bombs and machine-gunning it. The bombs were unlikely to cause any major damage but the machine-gunning could kill or injure crewmen. (Early Sunderlands carried only a single machine gun in the nose turret; this would later be increased to two and as many as four fixed-forward-firing guns would be fitted to some machines.)

The aircraft then guided the escorts to *U-55*, the crew of which scuttled their boat before being picked up by *Fowey*. *U-55*, on its first war patrol, had sailed on 16 January and had sunk six ships before being despatched. Although the authoritative website Uboat.net claims that the Sunderland dropped depth charges, this was not the case since such munitions were not available for aircraft at that time. Roskill describes this as 'the first joint air-sea success in the U-boat war' and notes that 'the U-boat would probably have got away but for the presence of the Sunderland'.[33]

The destruction of *U-55* was a joint success for air and sea escorts but an isolated one:

> This episode ... demonstrates how lacking we were in anti-submarine warfare at that time. There was just one success in the month for Coastal Command, although there were at least twenty-two U-boats at sea. ... Most obvious was that two ships in convoy could be sunk so close to our shores, and that only one Sunderland was sent on a strike. There was a gross lack of cover ... available from the Royal Navy and Coastal Command. The shortage of aircraft was demonstrated by only one Sunderland out of all types being sent at a critical time.[34]

Coastal Command aircraft made seventeen attacks on U-boats 'with negative results' during June 1940; clearly the anti-submarine bombs were not effective, but, at that time,

> a depth charge specifically designed for use by aircraft was not available, and initially a compromise was reached with the use of a naval 450lb depth charge modified for aircraft use. These, however, could only be carried by flying boats.
> It was to be 1941 before land-based aircraft, such as No.221 Squadron's Wellingtons, were able to take three or four of these 450lb depth charges; but then that squadron was to be lost to the Command by being posted to the Middle East.[35]

By late-August the U-boats' operational area was pushed out to 20W, initially between 45N and 57N but extended to 62N in mid-October. This meant that most U-boat operations were beyond the range of UK-based Coastal Command aircraft. However, the occupation of Iceland allowed the building of air bases there, but the first aircraft deployed were obsolescent Fairey Battles, single-engined bombers with a three-man crew, and unsuited to maritime patrolling. Fortunately, they were replaced by Hudsons of No.269 Squadron, which had become operational on the Lockheed aircraft in mid-July 1940 and moved to Iceland between mid-April and late-July 1941. Although the Hudson was still restricted to carrying bombs rather than depth charges, the squadron provided a deterrent and, since Reykjavik was another 14 degrees west of the airfields in Northern Ireland, extended Coastal Command's westward reach. However, there remained the Mid-Atlantic Gap, south of Cape Farewell, where U-boats would remain safe from air attack for another two years.

Sunderlands of No.204 Squadron also moved to Iceland in April 1941, but only until August when the squadron transferred to West Africa to protect Sierra Leone convoys. No.204 was succeeded in Iceland by No.209, which followed its predecessor's pattern by remaining there for five months before going to Africa, in this case East Africa, to work over the Indian Ocean. Individual U-boats were spotted off West Africa in July 1940 when a ship was sunk, followed by another in August but none were reported in those waters again until the winter: four ships were sunk in November, followed by five in December and three in January 1941. Although there were no losses in February, March saw renewed aggression with fifteen ships sunk; ten were lost in April and 'losses shot up' to thirty-two in May. All attacks occurred within 600 miles of an air base. Not until January 1941 did Sunderlands deploy to the region but only one arrived in January; two others, damaged at Gibraltar, did not reach Sierra Leone until March.[36]

Although the story of HX84 has already been told, it is worth adding a brief note on how it was assisted by a Sunderland while re-assembling on its approach to its destination. The convoy:

Received excellent support from Coastal Command, including help from a radar-equipped Sunderland, which used its ASV Mk I set to locate one of the U-boats trying to establish contact – the first airborne radar contact with a U-boat.[37]

With surfaced U-boats attacking at night, the Royal Navy and Coastal Command faced a major problem during 1940. ASV and ship-mounted radar were in their infancy, and there was no effective means of illuminating a target at night: flares were not practicable at the low altitudes at which air attacks were made. Moreover, there was no low-level bombsight. For surface escorts, asdic could not detect a surfaced U-boat.

The search for solutions to these problems led to increased co-operation between the Royal Navy and Coastal Command. On 7 August 1940 Sir Frederick Bowhill wrote to the VCNS and Vice Chief of the Air Staff (VCAS) about U-boat operations in the Western Approaches, prompting a discussion at the Admiralty three days later. This led to a programme for co-operation in anti-submarine warfare being initiated. Although limited, the programme, under Captain Philip Ruck-Keene,

> was to become a feature of the Allies' ASW, that is, close co-operation between Coastal Command and the navies. In 1940, however, it was not very obvious, due to the Royal Navy's lack of escort vessels and Coastal Command's lack of aircraft.[38]

There was a very clear, positive outcome from a meeting chaired by the VCNS at the Admiralty on 23 September, at which Bowhill was present. It was agreed that full use of current ASW capabilities was not being made; that depth charges were necessary against submarines; that operational control and administration of the joint effort should be made from a new command in the north-west; and that a practice of holding weekly review meetings at the Admiralty to examine existing ASW methods and possible new means of protecting convoys should be instituted.[39]

Following that meeting, No.15 Group was included as part of the new Area Combined Headquarters (ACHQ) 'which was not just the control centre for the North-Western Approaches, but also the "nerve centre" of the Battle of the Atlantic'.[40] Such initiatives were at the operational level but, at the strategic level, the British approach was also focused sharply, as Dönitz acknowledges.[41]

There was a very marked contrast between the co-operation within the UK forces and the lack of such in the German forces. Dönitz had no equivalent of Coastal Command on call and the attitude of Luftwaffe chief Hermann Göring was one of rivalry rather than support. Although I./*Kampfgeschwader* 40 (I./KG 40), equipped with Focke-Wulf FW200 Condors, was based near Bordeaux from July 1940, it was January 1941 before Dönitz was given operational control of the unit and its aircraft,[42] even though they had been carrying out anti-shipping operations.

Under command of *Fliegerführer Atlantik*, the FW200s had flown reconnaissance missions over the Atlantic, reporting convoys. They had also supported Luftwaffe operations against Britain with maritime reconnaissance and meteorological reconnaissance flights, taking off from Bordeaux–Merignac, flying out to the west of Ireland on a semi-circular route that took them to Norway, whence they would make the return trip a day or two later. By late-summer 1940 Condors were also attacking ships, sinking 90,000 tons of Allied shipping in September and October. A Condor of I./KG40 attacked and set on fire the 42,000-ton liner *Empress of Britain* on 26 October 1940 off Donegal, *U-32* sinking the damaged, under-tow ship with two torpedoes two days later; the liner sank in four minutes. In turn, *U-32* was sunk by the destroyers *Harvester* and *Highlander* on 30 October. The *Empress of Britain*, a Canadian Pacific liner, was 'the only one of our "giant liners" to fall victim to the enemy'.[43]

When Dönitz gained operational control over KG40, he gave it the role of locating convoys and guiding the U-boats to them. This was easier in the planning and theory than in practice. It was soon discovered that the airmen's navigational skills were poor compared to those of the sailors, nor could the Condors follow a convoy discreetly, while their time on station was limited by their endurance; the farther into the ocean the sighting was made, the shorter the time they could shadow ships. In practice, U-boats guided Condors to convoys, as with HG53, sighted by Kapitänleutnant Asmus Nicolai Clausen's *U-37* off southern Portugal on 8 February 1941.

Clausen attacked that night, sinking two ships; a third would follow. He also called in Condors, which arrived during the 9th. Never before had German aircraft been seen in that area and the FW200s sank another five ships. This attack was the only instance in the Atlantic of a successful

German combined operation using submarines, surface vessels and aircraft. The surface ship, the heavy cruiser *Admiral Hipper*, operating off the Azores, was ordered to join the attack. By the time *Hipper* arrived, on 11 February, only one straggler remained for her to pick off, but a *B-Dienst* intercept then led to her being diverted to a fresh target, SL(S)64, homebound, unescorted, from Sierra Leone. On the 12th *Hipper* fell upon the convoy, sending seven of the nineteen merchantmen to the bottom.

The Condors sank several ships in convoy in early-1941, including seven from OB290 on 26 February, sunk by bombs from six planes (the most successful German air operation against ships in the Atlantic).[44] Although the strategic situation was worrying to the British commanders – *Scharnhorst* and *Gneisenau* were at sea at this time, and U-boats continued their toll – it was frustrating for Dönitz, who could not obtain the number of submarines he wanted. He argued 'forcibly and unequivocally' for 'a large number of U-boats as quickly as possible', to 'achieve decisive results', but his pleas seemed to be in vain.[45] He contrasts this with what was happening on the British side. Noting that Churchill's history of the Second World War emphasized his own belief that U-boats were Britain's greatest danger, and that 'the Germans would have been wiser to have staked everything on the U-boat', he describes how Churchill 'acted in accordance with this belief' as the driving force in organizing anti-U-boat measures, taking the chair of the Battle of the Atlantic Committee, established to co-ordinate efforts to ensure victory in the struggle. With the committee including the War Cabinet, several other ministers, the First Sea Lord, the Chief of the Air Staff and scientific advisers, it seemed that all British resources were drawn together to combat the U-boats. In contrast, there was no parallel organization under Hitler in Germany, prompting Dönitz to bemoan that 'We were very far from staking our all on the U-boat', the weapon that Britain most feared.

Dönitz assessed rightly that, to the British, 'the Battle of the Atlantic was a conception which they could all easily visualize, and a fact, the supreme significance of which they all readily appreciated'. In Germany, however, the 'gaze was fixed on the continental land battles', the German view being that those battles would also end British sea power. The 'continentally-minded German Government and High Command of the German Armed Forces' were unable to realize that the U-boats could decide the outcome of the war.[46]

Chapter Five

It is both easy and arrogant for the historian sitting comfortably with the benefit of hindsight and a mass of official records to indicate turning points, great or small, in the course of events. For those involved it was rarely possible to see turning points at all. This was certainly the case with the campaign against the U-boats, but the effectiveness of the convoy system could be seen. Terraine notes that, in the first five months of war, 'out of 5,756 ships which had sailed in convoy, the U-boats had only succeeded in sinking four'.[1] Nonetheless, many ships in convoy had been lost to U-boats in 1940, especially in the later months, as German commanders attacked at night on the surface.

In September 1939 there were still some in authority who considered that the Royal Navy should take offensive action by deploying hunting groups, each of about five ships, supported by reconnaissance aircraft, to seek and destroy U-boats. Those espousing this concept included the First Sea Lord, Sir Dudley Pound, and the First Lord of the Admiralty, Winston Churchill.

> Nothing can be more important in the anti-submarine war than to try to obtain an independent flotilla which could work like a cavalry division on the approaches, without worrying about the traffic or U-boat sinkings, but could systematically search large areas over a wide front. In this way these areas would become untenable to U-boats, and many other advantages would flow from the manoeuvre.[2]

Churchill did not appreciate that tactics suited to a land battlefield do not translate to a war at sea. Nor were there enough ships to create hunting groups *and* escort convoys. Vice Admiral T. H. Binney's committee, reviewing anti-submarine warfare in the early weeks of war, concluded that 'the best position for anti-submarine vessels is *in company* with a convoy. For the present, every AS vessel with sufficiently good sea-keeping qualities should be employed with convoys rather than dispersed in hunting units'. Binney's committee also likened the task of the hunting groups to 'looking in a dark room for a black cat that isn't there'.[3]

HMS *Courageous* had been lost while conducting one such 'cavalry sweep'. Although common-sense prevailed eventually, and the emphasis switched to escorting convoys, this 'extraordinary ambivalence',[4] as Roskill describes it, was still present in early-1940 and 'no clear direction regarding the policy ... was issued by the Admiralty to the commands chiefly concerned'.[5] The VCNS not only agreed with the Binney Committee recommendations but also noted that 'this is the principle adopted'; but it was clear that many asdic-equipped ships were being misused in a fashion not only applauded but encouraged by Churchill and Pound. Yet:

> Not the least important lesson to be learnt from a study of the early months of the U-boat war is that the enemy would be most easily found in the vicinity of the quarry which he was seeking, that his purpose could best be frustrated by protecting the quarry as strongly as possible and that escorting convoys would therefore produce abundant opportunities for a vigorous tactical offensive against the enemy – once he had shown himself.[6]

The lesson would be absorbed but Terraine points out that, rather than being attributable to 'wilful blindness', the hunting group concept owed something to the fact that 'escorts did not kill many U-boats in [the First World] war' although the general lesson had been 'that individual U-boats were generally reluctant to attack convoys, and unsuccessful when they did so'.[7]

Nor was the escort fleet the only element of Britain's armoury served inadequately by its masters. Although Coastal Command was playing an increasing part in protecting shipping and deterring U-boats, and both naval and air chiefs recognized the potential of increased co-operation between escort ships and aircraft, there remained one serious blind spot: there was no effective anti-submarine weapon. The anti-submarine bomb used by the Fleet Air Arm (FAA) and the RAF was ineffective. Proposals had been made to the Admiralty, from officers commanding aircraft carriers, and the

Air Ministry, that depth charges suitable for aircraft should be developed. Although the Admiralty had received such proposals before war began, no research was undertaken. As late as 17 April 1940, when there was no doubt that the anti-submarine bomb was ineffective, the Air Ministry chose not to carry out further investigations into development of air-dropped depth charges. So how did such depth charges become available?

The man who ensured that depth charges for aircraft were developed and produced was the sailor-turned-airman Air Marshal Bowhill. Bowhill's intervention had the Air Ministry's ruling eased sufficiently to allow trials of air-dropped depth charges to continue and almost entirely through his efforts were such weapons introduced in mid-1940. Initially on a very small scale, this led to the introduction of a depth charge suitable for a greater range of aircraft by spring 1941.'This was to prove by far the most effective anti-submarine weapon placed in the hands of both naval and RAF aircrews during the entire course of the war.'[8]

The anti-submarine bombs in use in 1939 and 1940 had superseded those of the Great War, which had been 'poor in shape and bad ballistically' but their replacements, 100lb, 250lb and 500lb bombs, were little better.[9] With only about half the bomb's weight being explosives, there was little power to damage a submarine. The complicated double-action fuse caused the bomb to detonate immediately on striking a surfaced submarine, but a short delay was built in should it fall into the water.

The *Naval Staff History* notes that:

It is to be observed that in 1937 the Naval Air Staff had expressed a preference for the 100lb A/S bomb to the heavier depth charge. The arguments ... ranged round the supposed advantage in the probability of hitting with a stick of several light bombs over that with a lesser number of heavier ones. The lethal radius, however, of the 100lb bomb against a submerged submarine was eventually found to be not more than 2 feet, a discovery which largely nullified the theory of the 'stick'.[10]

Even the 500lb bomb needed to detonate within eight feet of a U-boat's hull to cause lethal damage. That bombs could also skip off the surface and detonate in the air was a major problem: it led to the downing of an Anson that, accidentally, bombed a British submarine, and of FAA dive-bombers attacking an enemy target.

Dropping the bombs was no easy matter as Coastal Command aircraft were fitted with the Mark IX bombsight, requiring a straight-and-level approach at 3,000 feet or higher. Since a surfaced U-boat was likely to dive very quickly on spotting an aircraft, leaving no opportunity for a pilot to fly 'by the book', he would be compelled to dive to an altitude where bombs would be dropped after sighting by the 'mark one eyeball'.

To use depth charges against U-boats, FAA and Coastal Command aircraft had first to find their targets. In adverse weather conditions spotting a surfaced U-boat was extremely difficult; at night it was impossible. The solution lay in equipping aircraft with a radar set that could detect a surfaced submarine. Although popular wisdom has long been that radar was a British invention, this was not so: work on developing radio direction finding (RDF in British parlance until the American 'radar' supplanted it) had been undertaken in several countries, including Germany. What made British work unique was the use of radar to create the world's first fully-integrated air defence system. With radio, telephone links to RAF fighter and Royal Artillery gun-control rooms, observers on the 'inland' side of the detector beams, and well-trained personnel, radar created a system that gave the defenders a major advantage during the Battle of Britain. Moreover, even if an element of it – say, a gun-control room – was disabled by enemy action, the overall system could continue; it was almost self-repairing. But the early long-range radars, Chain Home, used to detect enemy aircraft before they left continental airspace, were huge bulky equipments with large aerial arrays. Nothing like that could fit into an aircraft.

However, parallel work had been underway in other forms of radar. Sir Henry Tizard, Chairman of the Aeronautical Research Committee since 1933, had been most anxious to develop air defence radar and to that end Robert Watson-Watt's team in the Radio Department of the National Physical Laboratory applied their energies. Meanwhile, at the Bawdsey Research Station, Dr Edward Bowen's team was developing airborne radar to detect other aircraft – AI, or airborne interception, for night-fighters – and ASV, or air-to-surface vessel, to detect ships at sea. Bowen had begun work in 1936 with a four-man team. They faced two major problems: the airborne radar unit's wavelength had to be much shorter than that of Watson-Watt's ground sets, since a long-wavelength set would not fit into or onto an aircraft; the transmitter's size and weight were also critical in ensuring that it could be fitted in fighter aircraft.

Bowen's team proved the feasibility of their concept through experiments with a modified television receiver in a Handley-Page Heyford bomber fitted with a basic directional aerial system. Beaming transmissions at the Heyford from a ground-based radar station, the test proved 'that radio energy reflected off one aircraft could be received in another' as operators in the aircraft could observe the echo signals.[11] As research progressed, and Bowen's team doubled in size, a small radar with a high-powered transmitter and sensitive receiver, operating on 240 MHz, then a very high frequency, had been constructed and was ready to be fitted into an aircraft. There was a problem, however, as safety experts were concerned that its high power might create sparks that could ignite fuel. When the team proved that this would not happen, the set was fitted in an Anson in July 1937.[12]

The trials proved successful with clear returns received from warships at five miles. Due to poor weather conditions on the second day of trials, the equipment had a more rigorous testing than anticipated, even being used to assist the Anson's navigator make landfall through thick cloud. Ships detected included the aircraft carrier *Courageous*, the battleship *Rodney*, and the cruiser *Southampton*, all in conditions that would have made conventional reconnaissance impossible. Even aircraft taking off from *Courageous* were detected. Bowen reported that 'these results encourage the hope that it will ultimately be possible to discover and locate ships at sea ... up to about ten miles from an aircraft'.[13]

In spite of such successful trials, work on air defence radar took priority, absorbing the bulk of available funds and manpower. Bowen and his team continued their work, one aspect of which was deciding how aerials should be fitted to aircraft. This required a compromise as the ideal solution, a series of aerials radiating in a compass rose from the plane, was impracticable, not least since it would cause considerable drag and upset the machine's handling characteristics. Extensive experimentation concluded that a forward-looking aerial array transmitting in a fan-shaped beam ahead of and below the aeroplane with wing-mounted, outward-angled (at 30 degrees) receiver aerials to pick up the direction of the returning echoes was the best solution. This would allow the operator to advise the pilot on the course to steer so that signals from both receivers would be of equal strength, indicating a target directly ahead. Several months before war broke out, this system had been proved in further trials, although there remained much work to be done before a fully-operational ASV radar was available.[14]

Initially, ASV was intended to detect ships but it became clear that it might also be able to detect smaller targets, including surfaced U-boats. Following an enquiry from Admiral Somerville in late 1939, the first version, ASV Mark I, was tested in a Hudson against the submarine *L-27*. With the Hudson at 1,000 feet, *L-27* was visible on radar at three miles, broadside on; the Hudson crew could pinpoint its location. Continued testing revealed that, at 6,000 feet, detection range increased to six miles.[15]

By the end of 1939 another aerial array, a sideways-looking system with five dipoles atop the fuselage, had been tested on a Whitley. Later reduced to four, this was the transmitter element, measuring eighteen feet in length overall. Two twelve-foot-long receiving aerials, mounted on the fuselage sides, were known as Sterba arrays. Overall, this gave longer range and better resolution. Dubbed LRASV, long-range ASV, the range was two-and-a-half times that of the forward-looking system; surfaced submarines could be detected at ten to fifteen miles.

As the first ASV sets were being fitted to Coastal Command Hudsons and Sunderlands, the Royal Aircraft Establishment (RAE) at Farnborough was developing its successor. Only about 200 ASV Mark I sets were produced. Fitted in relatively few Sunderlands and Hudsons, it was very much a work in progress with many of the hallmarks of new equipment: poor reliability, high maintenance and costing much time in training operators. Nonetheless, it pointed the way to the future and gave operators valuable experience.

ASV Mark II was a marked improvement. A 1.5-metre radar (although it operated at 1.7 metres or 176MHz) it was engineered properly and proved more reliable, with a range up to thirty-six miles. Minimum range was about a mile. Thousands of sets were manufactured in forward- and sideways-looking variants and fitted in various Coastal Command aircraft. However, only the sideways-looking LRASV was effective against U-boats.[16]

The new radar was claimed to have scored its first success on 30 November 1941 when a Whitley Mk VII of No.502 Squadron equipped with ASV depth-charged *U-71* in the Bay of Biscay. Although the Whitley was credited with sinking *U-206* this boat was not present; *U-71* was the boat attacked – she escaped unscathed.[17] Since mid-1941 the use of ASV Mark II had seen a 20 per cent increase in daytime attacks on U-boats. Although nocturnal attacks were possible, these were usually ineffective because the airmen were unable to see the submarine due to the radar's one-mile minimum range; aircrew had to revert to the 'mark one eyeball'.[18] However, an ASV-equipped Swordfish made the first successful night attack on a U-boat on 21 December 1941.[19] Such attacks were the exception for many more months, but work was underway to develop a solution to the problem of the night-time blind spot.

The scientists' role was crucial. They were responsible not only for developing ASV radar but for better explosives, improvements to ships and aircraft and the means of breaking the German Enigma code. As the war progressed, they became even more important; the work of a British group led to the development of the cavity magnetron, the first of which was tested in February 1940 and, in turn, made possible centimetric radar; this became ASV Mark III and took the air war against the U-boats to a new level.[20]

Another major factor was the availability of more escort ships and aircraft. Not only was the Royal Navy short of escort ships when war began but the ships it did have lacked the fuel capacity to escort a convoy across the Atlantic, a journey involving escorts in travelling many more nautical miles than the merchantmen since the warships had to shepherd the latter, nipping around the convoy and racing to attack U-boats or investigate sightings. Giving escort ships 'longer legs' became a priority with the problem solved by the expedient of refuelling at sea from tankers in the convoys. Meanwhile, shipyards contributed as more corvettes came off the slips, as well as additional sloops and the new frigates. Some older destroyers were modified for escort duties and the strength of the escort fleet was increased. Above all, the increasing numbers of ships made the difference, proving, as Nelson said in 1805, that 'Numbers only can annihilate'. The bases in Iceland and the Londonderry base more than proved their worth as force multipliers; it was no coincidence that when the *U-bootwaffe* made its formal surrender to the Royal Navy it did so at Londonderry on 14 May 1945.

In spite of friction within the Air Ministry, and Bomber Command's antipathy, more aircraft became available for Coastal Command and increasing numbers were fitted with ASV. The problem of the blind spot in darkness in that last mile before a target was solved by fitting searchlights to aircraft to illuminate surfaced U-boats. Very long range aircraft, in the form of the American Consolidated B-24 Liberator, were supplied, but never in sufficient numbers and almost 'too little too late', as were improved versions of the Short Sunderland, capable of greater endurance, fitted with better ASV and carrying improved weaponry, while another product of the Consolidated company arrived in 1941 – the PBY-5, or Catalina, flying boat. (A single PBY-4 Catalina had been delivered to the Marine Aircraft Experimental Establishment at Felixstowe in June 1939 but there seems to have been little urgency in providing Catalinas for Coastal Command.) When Sir Arthur Harris became AOC-in-C Bomber Command in 1942 he demonstrated a jealous attitude to four-engined bombers, arguing that such aircraft belonged to his command and refusing to allow the transfer of any to Coastal. His argument will be familiar: he considered Bomber Command to be an offensive arm and Coastal to be defensive.

Worse still, Harris was actively antagonistic to Coastal Command, telling Churchill in a minute dated 17 June 1942 that it was 'merely an obstacle to victory'.[21] Terraine describes this 'as one of the more unpleasing ironies of the war' since, on the date Harris wrote that note, the facts supported a different conclusion. Between 1 January and 30 June, only twenty-one U-boats had been sunk, of which six and a half had been destroyed by aircraft, meaning that air action was involved in 30.9 per cent of U-boat losses. Going further, Terraine notes that British air action was involved in 16.6 per cent of those losses, but that Coastal Command had not made any claims for the sinking of U-boats.[22] (A Fleet Air Arm Swordfish had sunk one in the Mediterranean, two had been sunk by US Navy Hudsons off Newfoundland, one by a US Navy Mariner flying boat west of the Bermudas and one by a British Hudson in the Mediterranean; another, damaged by a Swordfish in the Mediterranean, had been torpedoed and sunk by another U-boat.)[23] It was clear that air action had a detrimental effect on U-boat operations, the simple presence of an aircraft usually being enough to force a boat to submerge.

That picture changed in July when eleven boats were lost, with aircraft sinking five and sharing one with surface vessels; two were attributable to Coastal Command planes. In August ten boats went down, five to aircraft. Another ten were lost in September, three to aircraft and one shared while October saw nine of sixteen lost U-boats sunk by aircraft, with another shared. In November thirteen boats were lost, seven to aircraft. December saw only five boats lost, one to aircraft. Almost half the U-boats sunk in those six months had been despatched by aircraft with Coastal Command responsible for just over a fifth of such sinkings.[24]

While aircrew and sailors grappled with the U-boats, and scientists worked on or refined methods of detection and weaponry, another group fought a silent war. These were the intelligence specialists whose role, not generally well known at the time and misunderstood in more recent times, was to prove of inestimable value to anti-submarine operations. Since the 1970s there has been a popular belief that Ultra was the most important factor in winning the battle against Dönitz's U-boats. Without doubt, Bletchley Park and Ultra were important, but, in operational terms, two other factors were at least as important: radar and radio intercepts.

We have already noted aspects of the radar story, and made some mention of radio intercepts, especially the German use of radio for operational command and control of U-boats. Through this practice Dönitz and U-boat Command played a major part in their own defeat. There was a certain amount of hubris in the fact that the Germans seemed not to appreciate that their enthusiastic use of radio could provide their foes with a weapon to use against them. Some of this hubris may have been due to the capture of British codebooks from the merchantman *City of Baghdad*, sunk by the raider *Atlantis* in the Indian Ocean on 11 July 1940.

The Admiralty was unaware of the loss of those codebooks. The German boarding party had been surprised to discover them in the weighted bags in which they were to be dropped into the ocean. However, the ship's Indian crew, pitched into a war they did not understand and which was none of their concern, had panicked, creating pandemonium. It seems that, in the confusion created by the shelling of *City of Baghdad* and the breakdown of discipline, the codebooks had been forgotten.

Atlantis's prize was a real boon for the Kriegsmarine and, especially, the *U-bootwaffe*. Using the British codes, the German naval intelligence service, *B-Dienst*, could decipher signals to convoy commodores. (*B-Dienst*, *Beobachtungsdienst*, was one of a number of German cryptology departments, underlining again German failure to conduct operations on a co-ordinated inter-service basis. Typical of the Nazi regime, these departments failed to share information effectively, thus wasting much time and energy.) In late 1942 *B-Dienst* was also able to break the Admiralty code for escorts and from December was reading some 80 per cent of such signals, although not always in time to take action. Even when a new code was introduced by the Admiralty in June 1943 *B-Dienst* was able eventually to read it. Had the Germans introduced a centralized signals intelligence organization, such as Bletchley Park, they might have created a much more effective weapon.

Using intelligence provided by *B-Dienst*, Dönitz was able often to deploy boats into patrol lines across the planned course of a convoy. When *B-Dienst* deciphered signals in time to allow Dönitz to take advantage of it the effects could be disastrous, as with SC2 in September 1940. Not only was information provided to U-boat Command in time but Dönitz could deploy a wolfpack against the convoy, leading to the loss of five ships. However, there was another aspect to this method of command and control. Dönitz was exercising command and control at a tactical as well as an operational level, leaving only the final attack to individual captains. The increased volume of radio traffic generated allowed the Allies to listen in and use it to locate packs and individual boats.[25]

The U-boats were not the only German vessels using radio in this fashion. When the battleship *Bismarck*, having sunk HMS *Hood*, was making for the safety of Brest, she shook off the chasing British ships, which lost radar contact. However, Admiral Günther Lütjens, commanding the German squadron (although his other ship, *Prinz Eugen*, had taken an independent course to France), sent lengthy radio messages to Naval Group West HQ in Paris which were intercepted by the Admiralty and *Bismarck*'s course was determined. There then occurred one of those errors with which the history of warfare is replete: Admiral Tovey, commanding the pursuers, 'gained the impression … that the *Bismarck* was breaking back to the north-east'. This caused Tovey to reverse his course and lose further ground. In London it had been determined that *Bismarck*'s destination was Brest and ships of the Home Fleet and of Force H, away to the south-east, were ordered to proceed on that assumption. Thus radio intercepts had played a role in the hunt for the *Bismarck* but not with the results that might have been hoped for.[26]

At this stage, some of Coastal Command's new Consolidated PBY-5 Catalina flying boats enter the story. Although ordered before the war, No.209 Squadron, based at Lough Erne in County Fermanagh, had only begun converting to the Catalina in April and was operational with some of the long-range machines, the first RAF squadron so equipped. On 26 May, three days after the loss of *Hood*, Catalina Z, piloted by Flying Officer Dennis Briggs, spotted *Bismarck*.[27] Briggs' aircraft came under heavy accurate fire from the battleship but he radioed a report before losing contact. He placed *Bismarck* '690 miles slightly north of west from Brest'.[28] Since the Catalina was very much a new arrival in Coastal Command, some US Navy aircrew had been attached to familiarize their RAF counterparts with it. One American, Ensign Leonard B. 'Tuck' Smith, was in 209/Z that day, acting as co-pilot, and it was he who spotted *Bismarck*. Since the United States was still neutral, no mention was made of Smith's role at the time.

Following confirmation of the German ship's position, Admiral Somerville's Force H was able to engage the foe on the 27th and Swordfish from HMS *Ark Royal* attacked *Bismarck*, damaging her steering gear. With *Bismarck* now unable to do other than steam in a circle, Tovey's ships were able to catch their quarry and pound her with their heavy guns. Captain Phillip Vian's 4th Destroyer Flotilla also joined in the final action, Vian having diverted his five destroyers on picking up the Catalina's report. Although some survivors from *Bismarck* were rescued by British ships, the recovery operation had to be curtailed due to the threat of U-boat attack. Ironically, Lütjens had asked for U-boat support and Dönitz had withdrawn boats from anti-convoy operations to protect *Bismarck*. Only one boat seems to have been in a position to do any damage to Force H, but had already expended its torpedoes.[29]

Bismarck, with her sister ship *Tirpitz*, and other German surface vessels had been considered the main threat to commerce in September 1939. That threat had now been reduced and overtaken by that from the U–boats but the Kriegsmarine's major surface units still worried the Admiralty. The operation to sink *Bismarck* had emphasized the importance of Coastal Command with the Catalina proving its value. However, only small numbers had been received and production of the Sunderland was proving a headache, caused by the manufacturers, Short & Harland, who seemed none too interested in improving production rates. In mid-1941 Shorts' factory at Rochester in Kent was delivering four Sunderlands each month, a rate scheduled to increase to five in 1942. A new Sunderland factory at Windermere in the Lake District was to supply only two per month, with the first not expected until March 1942, while at Dumbarton 'a peak production of three boats per month' was all that was called for. That left the Short & Harland factory in Belfast where production might have been increased but a Ministry of Aircraft Production (MAP) letter to the Admiralty on 13 October 1941 indicated that the company was not 'even attempting to put their backs into Sunderland production ... some 2,000 operatives [on Stirling production] are temporarily redundant'. MAP was trying to have those men transferred to Sunderland production until work on Stirlings resumed some two to three months later.[30]

Air Chief Marshal Sir Charles Portal, Chief of the Air Staff (CAS), wrote to Joubert on 6 November 1941 (Joubert had returned to Coastal Command as AOC–in–C on 14 June, succeeding Bowhill):

The production of Sunderlands in recent months has been most disappointing and has only just met the wastage of the existing five squadrons. The programme provides for a peak of fifteen per month by March 1942. Reviewing Sunderland production generally, I feel that this aircraft is suffering, and has been long suffering from complete lack of interest on the part of all concerned and is badly in need of publicity and drive. If the Service really needs Sunderlands this need should be emphasized.[31]

The shortage of Sunderlands was exacerbated by another flying boat, the Saunders-Roe Lerwick, proving so problematical that it had to be withdrawn in May after several had been lost. Following a spell operating the ill-fated

Lerwick, No.209 Squadron became the RAF's first operator of the PBY-5 Catalina. Fortunately, the first Catalinas were arriving at this time, although their introduction to service was not straightforward. The Battle of the Atlantic Committee, at its second meeting on 26 March, heard that:

> Two Catalinas ... had been operational during the week, but one had been lost on its first operational flight. In addition, two further Catalinas had been delivered, one of which would be operationally fit the following day.[32]

Churchill ordered a weekly report on the status of the Catalina and so the next meeting of the committee, on 2 April, was told that seven had been delivered, of which one had been lost, two were serviceable, two were under repair and two were with training units.[33] Reports on Catalina deliveries were presented to the weekly meetings for months thereafter.

This chapter illustrates the many difficulties facing Britain in the early phase of the Battle of the Atlantic. While there were many causes for concern, there were also signs that matters would improve, although those signs could often be identified as such only in retrospect. Occasionally there were what appeared to be positive signs – such as that supposed sinking of a U-boat by an ASV-equipped Whitley on 30 November 1941 – that turned out to be false indicators, but proved good for morale.

Also good for morale was the news that six U-boats were sunk in March 1941, including three commanded by some of Germany's leading U-boat 'aces'. (The true total was five boats.)[34] On 8 March, Günther Prien, the 'Bull of Scapa Flow', was lost when HMS *Wolverine* depth-charged *U-47* south of Iceland. Macintyre describes the incident in which Prien perished, noting that Prien was overbold and ventured too close to OB293. Commander James Rowland's HMS *Wolverine* came suddenly on Prien as a squall of rain cleared, forcing *U-47* to crash dive. Depth charges damaged her propeller shafts. Prien surfaced after dark, hoping to escape the destroyer, but Rowland had remained in intermittent asdic contact and *U-47*'s shafts produced an obvious rattle on *Wolverine*'s asdic, leading the destroyer to her target. Another depth-charge assault smashed *U-47*'s hull. Following a 'vivid flash' and explosion from the depths, wooden debris floated to the surface to tell of her end.[35]

Eleven days later, Joachim Schepke's *U-100* was hunted down and depth-charged by HM Ships *Walker* and *Vanoc*, escorting HX112; Macintyre was commanding 5th Escort Group from *Walker*. *U-100* was forced to the surface, rammed and sunk by *Vanoc*. Schepke was killed, crushed between his periscope and the crumpled bridge of his boat by *Vanoc*'s bows; only six crewmen survived. *Walker* sank another boat only thirty minutes later, Kretschmer's *U-99*, which had been operating with Schepke's boat. Three men died but the majority, including Kretschmer, survived.[36]

Schepke had been a major contributor to his own demise. As Macintyre notes, he came 'pounding after the convoy at high speed', creating a bow wave that was spotted by lookouts on *Walker*'s bridge. Crash-diving, Schepke avoided being rammed by *Walker* but was then forced to the surface and suffered the same fate from *Vanoc*. *Vanoc* was one of the first ships fitted with Type 271 shipboard centimetric radar, which gave her captain a clear indication of Schepke's position and speed, enabling him to reach *U-100* in half a minute.[37]

As *Vanoc* hove to and picked up survivors from *U-100*, *Walker* circled to protect her sister ship. Meanwhile, Kretschmer, all torpedoes fired, had slipped astern and was circling while making ready to sail for home. Kretschmer left the bridge in charge of a junior officer and went below. The officer on watch then spotted the silhouettes of *Walker* and *Vanoc*. Instead of remaining on the surface and easing away unseen, he ordered an immediate crash dive. As *U-99* plunged below the waves, she was picked up by *Walker*'s asdic and the destroyer attacked, a well-delivered pattern of depth charges inflicting such damage on the boat that Kretschmer was forced to surface.[38]

Losing three such 'aces' was a severe blow to the *U-bootwaffe*. They had accounted for the loss of ninety-one ships, including a battleship and three auxiliary warships, totalling 572,191grt, damaged another eighteen and had even captured a ship. Their loss had a considerable effect as their operational skills were outstanding and few who followed could match them.[39] Moreover, their fate proved the inherent effectiveness of the convoy system. Their boats had come to the convoy and, although OB293 lost three ships sunk and four damaged, losing Prien's experience, skill and leadership made this a pyrrhic victory for the *U-bootwaffe*. When Schepke and Kretschmer were lost on the night of 17 March it was a clear signal that the escorts were becoming much more effective and that the day of the individual 'ace' was over. Hereafter, it would be a battle between wolfpacks and escort groups, a new phase in the Battle of the Atlantic. For the Germans the 'Happy Time' had passed, although the Americans were to offer up a second 'Happy Time' in their own waters.

At this time also Churchill issued a directive stating that, in view of various German statements, it had to be assumed that the Battle of the Atlantic had begun. He went on to note that the next four months 'should enable us to defeat the attempt to strangle our food supplies and our connection with the United States'. The prime minister set a series of priorities:

1. We must take the offensive against the U-boat and the Focke-Wulf wherever we can and whenever we can. The U-boat at sea must be hunted, and the U-boat in the building yard or in the dock must be bombed. The Focke-Wulf and other bombers employed against our shipping must be attacked in the air and in their nests.
2. Extreme priority will be given to fitting out ships to catapult, or otherwise launch, fighter aircraft against bombers attacking our shipping. Proposals should be made within a week.
3. All the measures approved and now in train for the concentrations of the Coastal Command upon the north-western approaches, and their assistance on the east coast by Fighter and Bomber Commands, will be pressed forward ... .[40]

Thus was born the War Cabinet's Battle of the Atlantic Committee which, from 19 March 1941, met on a weekly basis under the chairmanship of Churchill himself.

March 1941 was not then seen as a positively significant period by the Admiralty or the government. The loss of merchant ships had reached over 500,000 tons for the first time since June 1940, making the month's immediate significance negative. Dönitz was unhappy at losing five of his boats, 20 per cent of his then operational force, the deaths of two 'aces' and the capture of a third. Moreover, as Barnett points out, the contrast between the organization of command, control and communications of the opposing forces could hardly have been greater. Dönitz commanded from a cramped bunker at Kerneval in Brittany with a staff of only six submariner officers and the Luftwaffe officer commanding KG40. British levels of co-operation between sea and air forces had improved immeasurably with Coastal Command coming under operational control of the Admiralty on 15 February 1941. At many levels, close links for speedy exchange of information had been established, although at the operational level much still needed to be done. An aircraft supporting a convoy could not report sighting a U-boat by radio directly to the escort commander but had to radio a report 'in a code not used by the naval escorts, and on an air force wavelength'. When the receiving station passed the message to the Admiralty it had then to be passed to the escort commander, by which time the report might be of little value, a problem that could be exacerbated by even a minor navigational error on the part of the airmen or the sailors.

However, there was close co-operation between No.15 Group of Coastal Command which, as already noted, shared a joint headquarters with the C-in-C Western Approaches, and the Royal Navy. At the strategic level, overseeing operational command, was the Battle of the Atlantic Committee, chaired by Churchill, with the naval and air chiefs and a council of eminent scientists and advisers; it would later have American and Commonwealth representation. 'Dönitz enjoyed no such backing at all. And the course of the year [1941] was to bring forth another British advantage, one sensed by Dönitz in the very operational pattern of the struggle, yet remaining for him a mystery the secret of which he could not plumb'.[41]

What Dönitz sensed was that his foes had very good intelligence about the operations of the Kriegsmarine and its *U-bootwaffe*. He was correct, although his thinking was along the lines of traditional intelligence gathering, i.e. espionage. While aware that the Allies could obtain information from radio intercepts he seems not to have appreciated just how widespread this could be, and the effectiveness of direction-finding was not appreciated fully by the Kriegsmarine at this stage. It was known that intercepting radio transmissions could allow the detecting station to calculate the bearing of the transmitting ship or U-boat, but it was believed that this was possible only through shore-based units; it was not appreciated that the equipment could be fitted on a small ship. In fact, the Germans thought that the results from such surveillance were too inaccurate to matter. 'Wishful thinking ... played a part in this belief; for any restriction of the use of radio struck at the roots of the wolfpack tactic' although 'half-hearted efforts to reduce the amount' of radio traffic were made in June 1941 through a standing order.[42]

Of course, there was no awareness that Bletchley Park was deciphering Enigma transmissions. However, Dönitz's sense that something was wrong led him to order that the four-rotor Enigma machine should replace the three-rotor machine then in use. The work of Bletchley Park's code-breakers was critical in the final Allied success and was aided in no small way by the shroud of secrecy maintained around the entire Ultra organization, a shroud that lasted until almost thirty years after the war. Thus Dönitz knew before his death in 1980 how his communications had been compromised and that his 'sense' had been correct. Suhren records how one auxiliary ship commander, Kapitän zur See Rogge, had, in conversation with Dönitz 'let slip the suggestion that our [Enigma] code might not be watertight. Dönitz reacted very strongly ...; "It's absolutely impossible, so it can't have happened."[43] It seems that Dönitz was convinced that Enigma was unbreakable, although Suhren comments that any commander 'always needs to prevent rumours like this spreading' as the effects on morale could have been incalculable.

Chapter Six

Fritz Julius Lemp sank the *Athenia* on 3 September 1939. At that time he commanded the Type VIIA *U-30* with which he remained for another year before taking command of the Type IXB *U-110*. Lemp, promoted to *kapitänleutnant* on 1 October 1939, and awarded the Knight's Cross on 14 August 1940, sank nineteen ships, totalling almost 100,000 tons. He was involved in the action in which both Schepke and Kretschmer were lost, having spotted HX112 and signalled the other U-boats; *U-110* damaged a tanker in the convoy.[1]

On 9 May 1941 Lemp's was one of a group of seven attacking OB318 in broad daylight, out of range of aircraft. Lemp sank *Bengore Head* and *Esmond* but the escorts reacted quickly and depth-charged *U-110*, forcing her to surface close to the destroyers *Bulldog* and *Broadway* and the corvette *Aubretia*. Lemp ordered his crew to abandon ship.[2] They took to the water but several were in obvious difficulties, including Georg Hügel, the radioman who had confirmed *Athenia*'s identity. Hügel was convinced he was about to die when Lemp grasped him and swam with him to safety, the rescued man being helped onto one of the British ships. According to Hügel, his captain, who had already rescued at least one other seaman, left him to help yet another drowning man, but disappeared.[3] Accounts of Lemp's death differ: some have him shot while trying to destroy the Enigma machine and codebooks or resisting the boarding party, while at least one suggests that he chose to drown rather than surrender. Hügel's testimony would indicate that Lemp died a hero. With Lemp's death that small cohort of officers who had commanded U-boats at the beginning of the war passed into history.[4]

The capture of *U-110* was a huge boost to British intelligence. Only two days earlier the Royal Navy had taken the weather ship *München* and her Enigma machine, enabling Bletchley Park to read the June Enigma traffic 'practically currently'.[5] *U-110* yielded an even richer trove with the special settings for the high-grade 'Officers signals', the U-boat short signals codebook, or *Kurzsignalheft*, and weather codebooks, or *Wetterkurzschlüssel*;

the *Kurzsignale* code was designed for short standardized messages, their speed intended to defeat direction-finding (D/F) equipment. It appeared that Lemp had disposed of the *Heimische Gewässer* (Home Waters) settings (known to the Germans as HYDRA and to Bletchley Park as Dolphin), the main cipher for U-boats and surface ships in home waters, including the Atlantic but, on 28 June, a second weather ship, *Lauenburg*, was captured, complete with *Heimische* settings. Bletchley could then read the July home waters' traffic almost as it was transmitted. Hinsley, the official historian of British intelligence, has this to say:

> By the beginning of August [Bletchley Park] had finally established its mastery over the Home Waters settings, ... which enabled it to read the whole of the traffic for the rest of the war except for occasional days in the second half of 1941 with little delay. The maximum delay was 72 hours and the normal delay was much less, often only a few hours.[6]

Interestingly, that delay of 'only a few hours' is reduced to 'within an hour of transmission' only eight pages later. As far as effective operational use of the deciphered material is concerned the difference between 'a few hours' and one hour could have been very significant.

The sequence of events leading to this intelligence coup has long been a hidden turning point of the Battle of the Atlantic. Capturing the weather ships and *U-110* (taken in tow, it was later scuttled but the Germans believed that it had sunk quickly) emphasized the importance of operational intelligence: its critical role became more and more evident as intercepted Enigma signals could lead to quick reaction on the ocean. This also allowed the Submarine Tracking Room to build an almost encyclopaedic picture of the *U-bootwaffe*. Boat by boat, that picture was created: boat pennant numbers, commanders' names, boat types, details of training in the Baltic and working up, deployment to operational ports, patrol cycles, and even refitting and leave arrangements. Terraine comments: 'Dönitz would have been astounded – and appalled'.

The German historian Professor Jürgen Rohwer considers that, from mid-1941 onwards, by a very cautious estimate the Submarine Tracking Room of the Admiralty, using 'Ultra' decrypts, re-routed the convoys so cleverly around the German 'Wolfpacks' that about 300 ships were saved by avoiding battles. They seem to me more decisive to the outcome of the Battle (of the Atlantic) than the U-boats sunk in the convoy battles of 1943 or in the Bay offensives.[7]

Rohwer is not only a historian of international repute but also served in the Kriegsmarine between 1942 and 1945, although not as a submariner.

The Submarine Tracking Room, officially Naval Intelligence Division (NID) 8(S), was part of the Operational Intelligence Centre and the hub of the anti-submarine war. In 1939 it was headed by Paymaster Commander E. W. C. Thring, a former Room 40 man, who was over sixty when he took over the job. By the end of 1940 Thring's health was suffering. He needed to stand down, but not before his successor was chosen. Thring's choice was a civilian who had offered his services to the Royal Navy in 1939. Rodger Winn was a barrister 'whose first ambition had been to serve in the Royal Navy, but who had been prevented from doing so by poliomyelitis which left him with a twisted back and a limp'.[8] Winn had thought that he might be useful in interrogating prisoners but he was sent to the Tracking Room where, under Thring's tutelage, he displayed outstanding flair for the work, able to see in U-boat operations patterns that were invaluable, especially at times when Ultra was blind. Commissioned in the RNVR, Rodger Winn was one of the most important figures in the Allied victory in the Atlantic.

A study of the importance of signals intelligence, SigInt, shows immediately how the Allied organization was so much better than the German. Hinsley captures the value of Bletchley Park when writing of 'the importance of concentrating all cryptanalytical effort in one place'. He added that Bletchley Park emphasized 'the wisdom of attacking all codes and cyphers, even the ostensibly insignificant'.[9] As well as its work on Enigma, Bletchley Park had broken other German ciphers in early 1941, including one used only for a short time between Berlin and overseas naval attachés regarding supply ships, a new mercantile marine code, codes for light-ships, air-sea rescue and naval/air operations, the meteorological code, and *Werft*, a dockyards cipher.

The last two, while seemingly of lesser importance, proved valuable since some of them were subsequently passed on by Enigma.

Terraine is surely correct in describing Bletchley Park's successes in 1941 as being equal to 'a major victory at sea'.[10] Dönitz's sense that Britain had something Germany did not have was correct. That 'something' was a co-ordinated approach to SigInt unparalleled in Germany. There may have been luck at times – there is truth in Napoleon's aphorism about lucky generals – but the scientific developments at Bletchley Park, the company of geniuses gathered there in the national interest, and their dedication all gave Britain an advantage never to be lost.

Applying the intelligence gathered by Bletchley Park and NID enabled ships to perform to their maximum, an effect multiplied by the efforts of the intelligence experts, but their training and preparation were critical basic factors. Since escorting convoys demanded a large commitment of ships and personnel, and Kriegsmarine surface ships remained a threat, the Royal Navy in 1939 did not have the resources, either in ships or men, to deal with all it was asked to do. Men could be conscripted in large numbers, and given *basic* training in a matter of months, but ships could not be built quickly. Since the threat of war had been present for some time, the Navy had prepared to recall reservists, of whom there were about 80,000 in January 1939, while a Reserve Fleet was maintained, 'consisting, in general, of the older ships ... which were maintained in serviceable condition but were not fully manned, [and] could only be prepared for service by calling up a proportion of the reserves'.[11]

On 26 May 1939 the first 15,000 reservists were called up to man the Reserve Fleet which, composed largely of Great War-vintage S, V and W-class destroyers, was to be 'brought forward to readiness for service' on 15 June.[12] However, an immense task remained. While dockyards worked apace to build new ships, the training organization had to expand to handle the large influx of conscripts and volunteers who would join when war began.

Following basic training, recruits selected for specialist roles moved to trade-training establishments. However, successfully completing a course did not mean that a man was a skilled operator or tradesman. Experience was critical. An asdic operator, for example, had often to rely on his senses and experience to distinguish a genuine return from a false one – many marine phenomena could lead an inexperienced operator to 'cry wolf'. Experience was also important for officers commanding escort ships. While this could only be gained on active service, an exhaustive training programme was devised to give escort ship officers, and their crews, the best possible preparation.

Coupled with the training programme was the development of anti-submarine tactics, which took on a momentum of its own in 1942, to which we shall return. In the meantime, let us look at another remarkable officer, Vice Admiral Sir Gilbert Stephenson KBE CB CMG, 'The Terror of Tobermory', who, in Lord Mountbatten's words, 'made such a vital impact on the Battle of the Atlantic in "working-up" green ships' companies of Escort and Anti-Submarine vessels'.[13]

Stephenson, known as 'Puggy', had retired in 1929 but was appointed a commodore in the Royal Naval Reserve in September 1939, serving as a convoy commodore in the first four months of war. Thereafter he had two posts, neither of which came to pass due to circumstances. Eventually he was given another job – he had all three at one point. This was the most important one and made a major contribution to eventual Allied victory in the Atlantic.

Stephenson was told by Admiral Sir Dudley Pound that he was to establish a working-up base for Allied escort ships at Quiberon Bay near Lorient to train both British and French personnel. The fortunes of war nullified this plan as Lorient became a Kriegsmarine port when France fell.[14] However, training escort vessels was critical and a suitable alternative base was identified in the UK: Tobermory – *Mary's Well* in Gaelic – on the Isle of Mull on Scotland's west coast. Stephenson found a suitable headquarters ship which was converted to become HMS *Western Isles*, Western Approaches Command's Anti-Submarine Training School. While Lieutenant Commander Reginald Palmer oversaw the conversion, Stephenson was involved in the Dunkirk evacuation, taking charge of the la Panne area and distinguishing himself in the following days.

Why Tobermory? The existing school at Portland was stretched fully and the fall of France meant its location was no longer suitable. Since it could not be expanded, all anti-submarine training was transferred to Scotland. The school moved to Dunoon in Argyllshire while a second establishment was set up at Campbeltown and experimental work went to Fairlie in Ayrshire. However, the most important development was the establishment of HMS *Western Isles*. On 12 July 1940 Stephenson was appointed to command the new school.[15]

Once established, Stephenson had to develop 'a refresher course of a week or ten days in new weapons and tactics to vessels of destroyer class and under, after long periods at sea'.[16] The task facing him and his small staff was much more complex since many ships arrived on which a majority of officers and ratings had never been to sea; others had as few as three with sea-going experience. Most had never worked in a team before and were not attuned to the discipline of shipboard teamwork. Thus the task facing Stephenson's team was much greater than that envisaged by the Admiralty, where it had been imagined that HMS *Western Isles* had only to work up 'ships already commissioned, with crews who were fully disciplined and accustomed to working together'. In reality they had to be 'taught the ABC of everything' and Stephenson found that he had to devise new methods.[17]

The Admiralty could hardly have chosen a more appropriate officer. Although born in 1878, Stephenson showed the vigour and agility of a man two decades younger. His mind was sharp and rarely could anyone get the better of him. With impressive and inspiring energy, he demanded much of his charges, and much was given. When a ship failed to meet his standards, he might threaten the vessel with an additional week at Tobermory, and was not 'beyond removing a captain or first lieutenant he thought not equal to the task'.[18] Although he had no authority for such action, officers he removed usually remained removed.

The programme was hectic. In addition to normal classes, Stephenson was keen on throwing in hypothetical 'Emergency' exercises, requiring immediate response. Stephenson or one of his staff might come on board and tell the captain that his vessel was not only sinking but on fire, and to engage hostile aircraft with his guns while preparing to fire depth charges. To add to the confusion, Stephenson would then add that all electrical power had been lost and the ship's officers, except the captain, had been killed. At this point,

'Improvise, my boy, improvise,' the Commodore would shout cheerfully, while lighting a thunderflash from his pocket and flinging it down behind anyone who was not moving quickly enough.[19]

Occasionally, someone might outwit Stephenson. One such occasion occurred while testing the crew of a trawler. He told a leading seaman, a gun-crew member, that he was dead and should lie down. The rating obeyed, but some minutes later Stephenson saw the 'dead' man on his feet at his duty station. Brusquely he informed the rating, 'I said you're dead!' This prompted the reply, 'Dead or alive, my place is at this gun.'

The Commodore's reaction? 'Full marks.' And a young RNVR officer was commended for his response when the Commodore came into the wardroom one day and said to him: 'There's a fire on the quarterdeck!' To which the officer replied: 'Do you mean to say, sir, you've done nothing about it but come down here and tell me!'[20]

Such alarums and excursions added a charge of energy to days that, although generally quiet, were busy and full of hard work for all. A 'typical' day began early; as the sun rose or even before, classes left their ships for instruction aboard HMS *Western Isles*. Subjects included topics such as 'Aircraft Recognition', 'Anti-Submarine Drills' and 'Spotting and Reporting'. Those remaining on board visiting escort ships would also be under instruction 'and sweating over gun and depth charge drills, Asdic, Communications, and many other exercises'. At the same time officers had to demonstrate the ability to draw up elaborate Fighting Instructions as well as routine Standing and Departmental orders. And at any time Stephenson, or one of his directing staff, could throw in an 'Emergency' exercise to be dealt with quickly and effectively.

Training at Tobermory was rigorous and highly professional and, short of active service, excellent preparation for an escort crew going to sea for the first time. The course at HMS *Western Isles* transformed a group of raw officers and seamen into a fighting team, capable of making their ship an effective and deadly weapons system with which to wage war on the U-boats. Not only did the base train Royal Navy ships and crews, it also trained those from Allied nations. In June 1943, Commodore Gilbert Stephenson was knighted for his work at Tobermory and, in 1948, was admitted to *la Légion d'honneur*, the rosette of which was presented to him by the French president.

Although he earned the soubriquet 'the Terror of Tobermory' Stephenson was no martinet but an officer who understood how to get the best from men. He cared for his staff and for the crews of visiting ships and ensured their welfare. Among other aspects of his care, he arranged with the minister in Tobermory for staff to attend church services while the minister's wife was persuaded to organize a group of volunteer ladies to run a canteen; she also established a laundry service for the base and involved some of the staff in a choir. This was not the work of an ogre but of a professional, very competent officer, an outstanding judge and trainer of men whose contribution to the Battle of the Atlantic deserves full recognition.

Gilbert Roberts had been discharged in 1938 on falling ill with tuberculosis. When war broke out he volunteered for service but was told that he would not be accepted 'for general service ... in view of the nature of [his] illness'. However, in March 1940 the Admiralty recalled him to duty as a commander (retired). Not until January 1942 was he appointed to the post in which he, too, would influence the Battle of the Atlantic. One of Churchill's aides, Admiral Usborne, and the Second Sea Lord, Sir Charles Little, called Roberts to a briefing in the Admiralty for a new job. The briefing was to the point:

> unless something was done to sway the Battle of the Atlantic in the Allies' favour, the war would be lost simply because vital food and war supplies were being sunk faster than replacements could be built; that thousands of trained seamen were being lost – in short the survival of Britain and her Allies was in doubt.[21]

Roberts learned that Churchill had sent Usborne to visit Western Approaches Command and Admiral Sir Percy Noble, the C-in-C, who 'was suffering under the appalling lack of escorts with which to protect the convoys'. When Usborne reported back it was decided that a tactical unit should be established at Liverpool to devise anti-submarine tactics and train escort commanders 'in the most efficient manner in which to protect the convoys with the small resources ... available'. Following the briefing, Usborne took Roberts to meet Churchill who gave him a simple brief: 'Find out what is happening in the Atlantic, find ways of getting the convoys through *and* sink the U-boats'.[22]

Simple the brief may have been, but its execution was more complex. However, yet again, it appears that the right man had been selected. Gilbert Roberts, born in 1900, joined the Royal Navy as an officer cadet in September 1913. Going to sea with his term-mates in the battleship *Hibernia* just before war broke out in 1914, the young Roberts became interested in gunnery, later specializing as a gunnery officer. On being commissioned, he joined the battleship *Collingwood* but later moved to destroyers. After the war he was sent to university and studied physics and German. His interwar service included some time in submarines, and his career progressed until he received his own command, the destroyer *Fearless*, in December 1937. Along the way he had taken the Long Gunnery Course and served two years on the Tactical School staff.

While commanding *Fearless* Roberts became ill with tuberculosis and was discharged. However, the exigencies of war saw him recalled to help escort commanders not only to outwit the U-boats, but to sink them. His first meeting with Noble was disconcerting. He found the C–in–C unenthusiastic and with little idea of what Roberts' task was. Noble said that he had a war to fight and that Roberts could carry on as he liked. The C–in–C seems to have judged Roberts as a gunnery specialist, leaving him with the suggestion that he might run 'occasional courses of half a dozen Reserve officers'. Usborne had suggested a tactical school and had initiated work on converting the entire top floor of one end of the Exchange Building into such a school with Roberts allocated eight rooms.

Faced with Noble's indifference, Roberts began establishing the Western Approaches Training Unit (WATU). The chief of staff at Derby House, Commodore Mansfield, suggested appointing as chief signalman Chief Yeoman Bernard Rayner, who had served at the Tactical School. This Roberts did and Mansfield also gave him two lieutenant commanders, two Women's Royal Naval Service (WRNS, or Wrens) officers and four WRNS ratings, who could type. With this small group Roberts started his school.

Before organizing courses, Roberts realized that he needed information which could be provided only by escort commanders. He wanted to learn about what really happened when a U-boat attacked a convoy and a merchantman was sunk. Commander Howard-Johnston, the Anti-Submarine Staff Officer in Derby House, suggested that he could see escort commanders as they came into Liverpool. Roberts demurred. Liverpool was only one escort base. Groups were also operating out of Greenock in Scotland and Londonderry in Northern Ireland. Roberts was allowed to interview officers from all three. These were generally commanders and when he met them Roberts outlined his objective, explaining that he needed their help. Each was asked the same question:

'When you are with a convoy at night and a ship is torpedoed, what do you do?' They all talked about 'going to action stations'; 'increasing speed'; and so on but really the answer was *nothing*! As it was explained, 'Well, what *can* you do?' There was one exception, Commander Walker … He explained that he had a counter-attack which all his group did together. On the order 'Buttercup'[23] by radio, all escorts would turn *outward*, increase to full speed, fire starshell for twenty minutes, and then return to station. Walker had in fact sunk two U-boats by this tactic while escorting convoy HG76 … Roberts took details from escort commanders of various U-boat attacks, thanked them and returned to derelict empty rooms.[24]

At this point it is worth digressing to consider the events of the previous December and Walker's achievement. HG76, of thirty-two merchant ships, had sailed from Gibraltar in December 1941. The commodore was Vice Admiral Sir Raymond Fitzmaurice and Walker was senior officer, or commander, of its escort, 36th Escort Group. Initially there was air cover from Gibraltar; a Sunderland spotted a U-boat on the first evening at sea. Next morning HMAS *Nestor* made asdic contact with *U-127*, which was engaged and destroyed. *U-127* was part of a group assembled by Dönitz to attack the convoy but with a specific order to give special attention to HMS *Audacity*, the first escort carrier, which was with HG76. *Audacity* had been the German cargo ship *Hannover*, but was captured by the Royal Navy in

1940 and converted to an escort carrier capable of operating a squadron of eight Grumman Martlet fighters, although six was the normal complement. (These were known as Wildcats in US service; the Royal Navy later adopted the American name.) Since it was intended that *Audacity* should protect convoys on the Gibraltar run, she carried fighters rather than anti-submarine aircraft as Luftwaffe aircraft were perceived as the greatest danger.[25]

On this occasion, the squadron on *Audacity*, No.802 Naval Air Squadron (NAS), could deploy only four aircraft. When HG76 passed out of range of air cover from Gibraltar, the Martlets patrolled to look for U-boats, and provide cover against Condors. On the morning of 17 December a surfaced U-boat was spotted, but a counter-attack by a corvette was unsuccessful. Shortly before 1.00pm HMS *Stanley* spotted another boat and Walker ordered a Martlet to attack. However, the boat's AA fire brought it down, killing Sub-Lieutenant Graham Fletcher. But surface escorts were already shelling the boat and caused such damage that the crew was forced to abandon ship. *U-131* sank at 1.30pm. One crewman later claimed that *U-131* had spent the night inside the convoy, acting as the wolfpack's homing unit.[26]

Next day *Stanley* sank *U-434* with depth charges, the boat surfacing long enough for the crew to abandon her. When two Condors were picked up by *Audacity*'s radar a Martlet intercepted them but the fighter's guns jammed and the bombers escaped. Another U-boat was on the surface just after dusk, presaging further attacks.

True to form, the U-boats struck again. Their first victim was *Stanley* which was hit by a torpedo and blew up with only twenty-five survivors. *Stanley*, one of the ex-US Navy destroyers, had just reported a sighting when she was hit. HMS *Stork*, Walker's ship, was nearby and obtained an asdic contact before dropping depth charges. The boat was forced to the surface and rammed by *Stork*, which dropped a second pattern of charges, set for shallow detonation. Part of the damage to *Stork* was to her asdic dome, which left her 'blind' thereafter. The boat, *U-574*, was destroyed. Two Condors joined the fray, one being shot down by Sub-Lieutenant Eric 'Winkle' Brown in a head-on attack, the other damaged. In a further air attack that afternoon, another pilot, Sub-Lieutenant Sleigh, followed Brown's example by attacking head-on. He actually hit the Condor but survived, with its wireless aerial wrapped around his tail wheel. After a quiet night another Condor appeared early on the 20th but was chased off, while a Martlet spotted two surfaced U-boats in the afternoon; both dived quickly. More sightings were reported on the morning of 21 December. Walker felt that the net was closing in, despite the work of No.802 NAS's tired airmen; only three fighters remained serviceable.[27]

That evening, his last patrol back on deck, Commander Douglas MacKendrick took *Audacity* out of the convoy, his normal practice at night. This time it had fatal consequences since no escort ships could be spared to defend *Audacity* during the night. Although MacKendrick and Walker held the same rank, the latter was junior in the Navy List and could not give his fellow officer an order. Moreover, this was Walker's first escort group command. At 8.30pm a ship at the rear of the convoy was torpedoed. Immediately the escorts began firing starshells, lighting up the surface for miles around and exposing clearly the silhouette of *Audacity* to the commander of *U-751*. Kapitänleutnant Gerhard Bigalk's first torpedo struck *Audacity* at 8.37. The carrier began settling by the stern and Bigalk struck her twice more with torpedoes. A massive explosion ensued, tearing the ship in two. She went down at 10.10pm. Many of the crew, including MacKendrick, perished when aircraft on the deck crashed into the sea.[28]

Walker's ships exacted vengeance for *Audacity* less than three hours later when *Deptford* accounted for *U-567*. Although the U-boats had taken the prize they were told to get, the price had been very high with five boats lost, prompting Dönitz to break off the operation.

A number of websites attribute the development of sophisticated anti-U-boat tactics to Walker. These include Uboat.net which comments to that effect about his time commanding 36th Escort Group. That and other websites and writers also comment that many consider the defence of HG76 the first real convoy escort victory of the war. It is difficult to justify this conclusion. Dönitz may have lost five U-boats, four against the convoy itself and another before the wolfpack made contact, but the cost to HG76 had been high with *Audacity*, *Stanley* and two merchant ships, one British and one Norwegian, lost. The encounter might best be described as a pyrrhic victory.

But were Walker's tactics really innovative? Although Roberts noted that he was the only exception to the 'well, what can you do?' school, his actions defending HG76 suggest that his policy was an orderly variation on the 'nothing' that Roberts considered others were doing. In one sense he can be held at least partially responsible for the loss of *Audacity* as starshells lit up the sea and sky, giving Bigalk a clear view of her. Significantly, Fitzmaurice's report, although praising Walker, notes that, after the sinking of *Audacity*, 'I ordered no more snowflakes to be fired in convoy'.[29]

As we look further at the work of Gilbert Roberts it will become clear that his was the analytical brain that devised sophisticated anti-submarine tactics and that it was to him, rather than Walker, that the escort force owed its increasing professionalism and effectiveness. That Roberts has been consigned to history's shadows while Walker stands in its full glare may be attributed to the Liberty Valance factor: 'When the legend becomes fact, print the legend'.

Roberts' approach was analytical, as befitted a gunnery expert who had served in the Tactical School. As he examined the circumstances of attacks on convoys he realized that the answer to the problem of how effectively to counter U-boats lay not with the moves made by escort commanders but with those of the submarine commanders. Lieutenant Commander Higham, who had been on one of the escort ships for HG76, told Roberts that the escorts were informed that 'the U-boat would fire torpedoes from outside the ring of escorts'. This was the received wisdom on which escort officers worked, that the danger came from without. It did not ring true to Roberts. He considered the moves Walker had made when a torpedo struck a ship in the convoy: he had ordered all his ships to fan outward at full speed, firing starshell outward, and, after twenty minutes, if no submarine was detected, return to the convoy. This led Roberts to examine several incidents in which merchantmen in convoy had been torpedoed. What struck him was a glaring incongruity: the U-boats were said to be outside the escort ring and yet ships in centre columns were being hit.

That incongruity prompted Roberts to ring the office of the Flag Officer Submarines in London to speak to an old friend, the chief of staff, Captain Ian Macintyre (a kinsman of Captain Donald Macintyre). However, Sir Max Horton, the Flag Officer himself, answered. Roberts introduced himself, explained his role and asked Horton, an experienced submariner, if he would answer a few questions. Horton agreed and Roberts asked if he would take his submarine into a convoy to fire his torpedoes.

The answer was brief and very clear: 'Of course, it is the only way of pressing home an attack.' The second question: 'What is the range of the U-boat's electric torpedoes?' The answer: '5,400 yards. Does this help you?' 'Very much, sir, thank you,' and the conversation was over.[30]

This put a very different complexion on the problem Roberts was trying to resolve. By this stage CPO Rayner, chief signalman at WATU, had improvised the training unit from canvas, wood, string and chalk. The staff had undergone training in laying out plots on the floor and tactical situations had been studied as part of the training for the personnel, including the Wrens, one of whom had joined straight from school, arriving *sans* uniform. On the training unit floor painters had marked parallel lines ten inches apart, with each separation representing a mile; there was also space for plotting tables and view screens. Twenty-four tactical players could participate in a floor exercise, which could be used for three discrete plots. Wooden models were used, each with a pin on its mast with a miniature flag representing the type of vessel: a corvette had the letter P and a frigate L. The number of masts on a model defined the ship's size, smaller vessels being single-masted while cruisers and heavier had two masts. The view screens, canvas on a wooden frame with a vision slit, represented the view a student would have from an escort's bridge. Wren staff could adjust the apertures of the screens so that 'different players saw their own positions relating to the convoy and any attack or defensive manoeuvre'. [31] It was simple and basic, yet effective.

Using the floor, Roberts, Rayner, and Wrens Jean Laidlaw and Janet O'Kell worked on a new plot of HG76 taking account of Horton's advice. This was done when other staff had left for the night. The convoy was laid down with escorts in the normal night disposition; this was still a time of scarcity and the usual strength was six ships (although HG76 had had a stronger escort) with nocturnal deployment, usually, one in front, one behind and two on either flank, with ships about 5,000 yards from the convoy. That gap between escorts and the body of the convoy confirmed that an attacking U-boat would be in among the merchant ships since the maximum running distance of their torpedoes was 5,400 yards. With that as a 'known' it was a reasonable assumption that a U-boat commander would want to be within about half that distance to ensure success.

Roberts placed a model U-boat within the columns of the convoy, which stretched across the equivalent of six miles. He and his staff then examined how the boat might have infiltrated the convoy. There were only four possibilities:

The submarine had entered from the front. While this was possible, the combined speeds of the convoy and U-boat, about or in excess of 20 knots, would have created problems for the captain since it would have been difficult to see in the dark, and errors in handling could have caused a collision.

The submarine had dived and then surfaced in the middle of the convoy. Again this was possible, but a boat breaking the surface in the hours of darkness would have created a significant splash of white water. Roberts and his team considered this approach less likely than the first.

The submarine had come in from a flank. However, this meant a high risk of collision, especially during darkness, as well as the distinct possibility of being spotted by lookouts. For those reasons this was considered least likely.

The submarine had come in from astern. If the boat was travelling at 12 knots and the convoy at 7, its overtaking speed would be only 5 knots. However, a 12-knot approach would reduce both bow wave and wash and the chances of being spotted by a lookout, most of whom would be watching forward and to the flanks. Although this approach would be slower, it would also be safer and was considered the most likely way for a U-boat captain to insinuate his boat into a convoy.[32]

Applying these findings to a fresh study of Walker's sinking of *U-574* in HG76, to the question 'where was the submarine in relation to the convoy?' the answer was clear: *U-574* had been behind, on the same course; the time had been after midnight. *Stork* had not killed the U-boat that had just destroyed *Stanley*; it had caught and sunk another infiltrating from astern to join the attack. Walker's outward fanning move with its starshell display had produced a lucky kill.

Schepke had been spotted making just such an approach on 17 March 1941 but his approach seems not to have been considered a standard operating procedure. Had the Admiralty considered that such a tactic was being used regularly, countermeasures could have been adopted. As it was, German captains all too often had a clear run into convoys because of this lapse.

Studying the episode more closely, Roberts considered the next obvious question: how would a U-boat that had just sunk a merchantman in the middle of a convoy escape? Naturally, his first move would be to dive. But would he move away at submerged speed? This seemed unlikely: he might be detected by asdic and, submerged, could not hope to outrun an escort. Roberts' conclusion was that the captain would dive to a safe depth, close down his boat and stay silent, allowing the convoy to pass over. Then he would surface and follow, ready for another attack should the opportunity present itself. Such opportunity was likely if the night was still young.

Playing this tactic out on the tactical school floor, Roberts quickly devised a simple, logical and effective countermeasure. If a ship within a convoy was torpedoed a standard word of command would be passed to the escorts. On this command all ships, except that at the front, would turn immediately at maximum speed to line up abreast about two miles *behind* the convoy. With their speed reduced to that of the convoy, they would then begin an asdic sweep, likened to a giant 'trawl' behind a fishing boat that would 'sweep' everything in front into the trawl. They would net the U-boat. Having played out the tactic three times, Roberts and his staff knew they had an effective solution.

Roberts and Rayner translated the countermeasure into the language of operational instructions, cleared the tactical floor and left a message with the duty officer that Roberts would like to see the C-in-C at the earliest opportunity. Later that morning, Sir Percy Noble and his staff, including Howard-Johnston, the Anti-Submarine Staff Officer, appeared. Although Noble appeared sceptical at first, the demonstration, in which Roberts and his staff plotted a convoy across the tactical floor, demonstrating the current means of countering a submarine attack, before plotting HG76 and Walker's reaction as well as Howard-Johnston's escort technique, was convincing. Having cleared the floor, Roberts explained that the tactics then in use were based on the false belief that U-boats attacked from outside the convoy. By this stage all scepticism had gone. Roberts outlined the basic facts that merchantmen were being sunk anywhere in a convoy, outwards from the centre columns, proving the attackers were inside. This argument was underpinned by the fact that a U-boat torpedo's maximum range was only 5,400 yards, with an average firing distance, in Roberts' view, of about half that distance.

Another demonstration followed. With a convoy laid out, Roberts moved the U-boat model into its columns and indicated that it had torpedoed a merchant ship. As Wrens moved the convoy forward, other staff moved the escorts into their countering positions, behind the convoy, in line abreast, to 'trawl' the intruder as he emerged. Such was the clarity and impact of the demonstration that Noble was, for the first, enthusiastic about what the school was doing. Howard-Johnston congratulated Roberts and his staff and seemed happy as a schoolboy. Noble asked Roberts for a name for the tactic. He was told that it was 'Raspberry', as suggested by Third Officer Jean Laidlaw who had described it as a 'raspberry' to Hitler, 'raspberry' being the term for a noise denoting derision or rejection.

Thus was born 'Raspberry', the first of a series of anti-U-boat tactical 'fruits'. Howard-Johnston was told to have printers produce a detailed description – the operational instruction Roberts and Rayner had prepared – so that 'Raspberry' could be added to the Western Approaches Command Instructions (WACIs) as soon as possible. Noble also told Roberts that he was promoted to acting captain immediately and that a signal would be sent to the Admiralty 'that the first investigations of your tactical school show a cardinal error in our anti-submarine thinking and that a new immediate and concentrated counter-attack would be signalled to the fleet in twenty-four hours'.

Roberts was also told that Noble wanted to see him often in Derby House's Operations Room. He had been accepted, as was the value of his school. No more would there be any reluctance in answering requests from Roberts. He could be assured of full and enthusiastic co-operation and support and that became especially true when WATU's first detailed anti-submarine tactic proved a major success. WATU would go from strength to strength with a duplicate being established at HMS *Ferret*, the Londonderry base. The work of another pensioned-off naval officer proved a further critical factor in wresting the advantage from the U-boats.

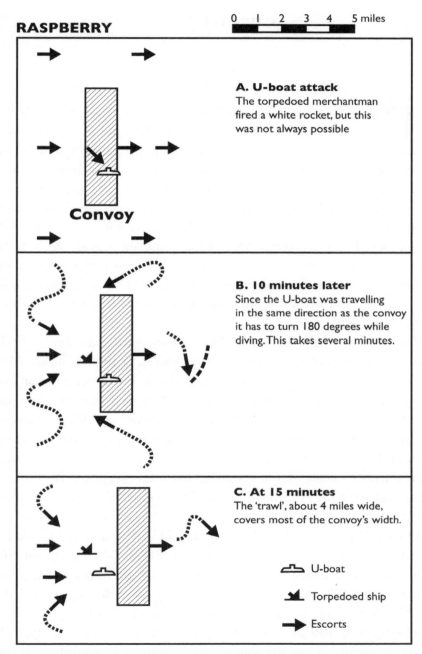

Figure 7: The 'Raspberry' tactic was the first devised by Robert's Western Approaches Tactical Unit.

Chapter Seven

The U-boat losses in early-1941, especially those of March when Prien, Schepke and Kretschmer were lost, proved that the escorts could counter-attack effectively and that co-operation between ships and aircraft was improving steadily. Although U-boats continued taking their toll of convoys, those losses forced them to move farther west, out of reach, hopefully, of UK-based surface escorts. By April Dönitz's boats were operating within 500 miles of the Canadian coast, which led to the basing of escort groups and Coastal Command squadrons in Iceland to cover convoys from the outward limit of UK-based escorts to the coast of Greenland. Although the war was entering its twentieth month, only a few escorts could make the full transatlantic trip with capacity to combat U-boats en route.

That deployment to Iceland was but one measure taken during 1941 to improve convoy support. While we have looked at the significant March convoy battles, the *Bismarck* episode and HG76 in December, it is also worth taking an overview of developments during the year. The period from mid-March to 31 December 1941, Hessler's third phase, saw Dönitz attempting to shift the operational balance in his favour. Early in this period his main force still consisted of about a dozen boats in the North Atlantic but, by June, thirty-five boats were at sea, all but ten in the North and West Atlantic; a group of six in the Freetown-Cape Verde area sank thirty-two ships during May.[1]

From 1 March to 31 May U-boats sank 142 ships, almost 818,000 tons, the majority – ninety-nine vessels, about 600,000 tons – being British. Ships accounted for by enemy aircraft, surface vessels and mines added another 256, of which 179 were lost to air attack. The overall loss was 412 ships (1,691,499 tons), the worst three months of the war to date.[2]

The Royal Canadian Navy (RCN), a small coastal force in 1939, had expanded greatly – Canadian shipyards were building Flower-class corvettes, and Tribal-class destroyers had been ordered – and had based its available destroyers and anti–submarine vessels at St John's in Newfoundland, not then part of Canada. This concentration of Canadian naval vessels, the Newfoundland Escort Force (NEF), provided escorts to Iceland. Groups were formed on the same basis as those in Western Approaches Command, usually a destroyer with two or three corvettes.[3] Sir Percy Noble observed that 'the RCN solved the problem of the North Atlantic convoys'.[4] While Canadian ships may not have been the complete solution, they were a very valuable part of it, one that would grow to pre-eminence.

The greatest problem facing Western Approaches Command, and which the Canadians helped resolve, was providing end-to-end escorts. Lack of suitable ships had meant convoys sailing with a minimal escort of an elderly battleship, such as *Ramillies*, an armed merchant cruiser, such as *Jervis Bay*, or a small escort of light ships at either end of the crossing. Since most small ships lacked the endurance to accompany a convoy from west to east or vice versa, much effort had been expended in improving existing ships, mainly by removing non-essential equipment and fittings and adding additional fuel tanks. Some V- and W-class destroyers, which were inherently short-ranged, underwent such modifications; with torpedo tubes, a forward gun mounting and a boiler room removed, they could carry extra depth charges and fuel, while a Hedgehog replaced the gun mounting.

Until the longer-legged frigates entered service, such improvisation was essential but, since most convoys included at least one tanker, there was an obvious solution: refuel at sea. In September 1941 Western Approaches Command began trials to prove the viability of such refuelling. When

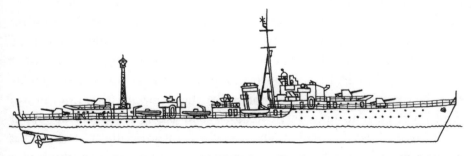

Figure 8: W-class destroyer, prior to modification. The forward gun turret (A gun) was replaced by a Hedgehog as part of the modification process.

those proved successful, this became a standard practice that increased the escorts' endurance, allowing them to remain with a convoy for the entire voyage.[5] As a result, an ocean escort would take over from the local escort that accompanied the convoy from its assembly point and shepherd it across the Atlantic, handing over to another local escort to see the convoy into port. This also gave greater flexibility in routeing and, allied with operational intelligence, added another weapon to the Admiralty in ensuring their safe arrival.

As we have seen, Coastal Command received its first Catalinas in early 1941. Some were operational in April, a month in which Coastal aircraft flew a million miles on convoy duties and another 200,000 on anti–submarine patrols.[6] However, aircraft were still of reduced value during the hours of darkness. Although ASV allowed an aeroplane to detect a surfaced U-boat, contact was lost as the gap closed with the airmen 'blind' in the final mile of the attack, unable to see the target. Dropping flares was an interim answer but, since a flare would light up only the immediate area, attacking aircraft were compelled to release a series of flares until the U–boat was spotted and then circle to attack, giving the boat time to dive. A more sophisticated variation was a time–delayed flare fired from a buoy dropped by the aircraft, allowing the aircraft more time to circle; the U-boat would be shown in silhouette as the attack was made. A much more effective solution came from the brain of a Great War RNAS pilot who had rejoined the RAF in September 1930 and was a staff officer in Coastal Command headquarters. Wing Commander Humphrey de Verde Leigh had talked with a colleague involved in 'special duties' – development of ASV – about the problem of attacking a surfaced U-boat at night. Having considered the problem carefully, Leigh believed a powerful forward–pointing searchlight under the aircraft to be the solution. The light could be switched on and focused as the plane approached the U-boat, illuminating the submarine so quickly that the commander would be deprived of the chance to dive. Bowhill had issued a circular to units in September 1940 asking personnel to submit any 'bright ideas' that they might have for combatting the U-boats. That circular included the comment, 'For instance, somebody may think of a new way of killing U-boats at night – a very difficult problem'. It prompted

Leigh to submit a paper entitled 'Proposal for Attacking Enemy Submarines by Night' in which he suggested fitting a 90cm searchlight in the nose or underside of a Wellington.

Leigh proposed the Wellington since several, already modified to detonate magnetic mines from the air, had been fitted with an auxiliary generator which could power the searchlight. The proposal was received well; Bowhill lent his support, commenting that, since 'our shipping losses from submarine action are running in the neighbourhood of 200,000 tons per month, the matter is so urgent that no possible means of countering this must be neglected ...'.

Scientists at the Royal Aircraft Establishment at Farnborough, thinking that the 90cm light would not fit a Wellington turret, proposed a smaller lamp, or a towed-flare scheme, trials of which had been carried out in 1928. Neither Leigh nor his superiors thought the towed flares viable. Given permission to work fulltime on his idea, Leigh substituted the 61cm (24-inch) naval searchlight for the Anti-Aircraft Command 60cm unit. The naval light could fit into a retractable mounting lowered from the aperture for a belly-mounted gun in the Wellington, with a Frazer Nash hydraulic system directing it accurately in angle and elevation. The light's heat demanded an effective cooling and fume-dispersal system, which Leigh also designed, to draw air through an under-fuselage scoop and pass it via 'a cleverly designed labyrinth of holes' on the mounting to cool the light while fumes were extracted via a rotating cowl that the aircraft's slipstream kept pointing rearwards.

In March 1941 the prototype Leigh Light was fitted in a Wellington. When flight trials proved successful the aircraft was also fitted with ASV so that both devices could be tested against a submarine. Carried out from RAF Limavady against HM Submarine *H-31*, the first trial was not successful, due to the operator switching the light off prematurely. The next trial, on 4 May, was a success; Leigh himself operated the light. Subsequent trials left Royal Navy personnel very enthusiastic about the concept.

The aircraft was not heard by the submarine until it [the submarine] had been illuminated, and was able to dive and attack down the beam for 27 seconds before being pulled out at 600 feet. This effort was most impressive, [and] ... this weapon would be invaluable in attacking U-boats on the surface at night .... [7]

The Leigh Light was not ordered immediately. Another project had been under development, the Helmore Light, also named for the RAF officer whose idea it was. Developed for fighters, fitted in the nose of a Douglas Havoc and known as the Turbinlite, it was not successful and was overtaken by the arrival of higher-performance night fighters. Nonetheless, Joubert, who succeeded Bowhill in June, had seriously considered rejecting the Leigh Light:

When I first took over at Coastal Command, having been so closely associated with the Helmore Light, I thought it might be given a general application by being used against U-boats as well. I thought that its wide beam and great illuminating power would be valuable. I therefore gave instructions that Squadron Leader Leigh was to return to his duties as Assistant Personnel Officer. After some months I found ... that I had made a mistake. ... the Helmore Light was unnecessarily brilliant for use against U-boats and otherwise unsuitable. ... Leigh's light was preferable for use against the U-boat, and [I] decided to drop the Helmore Light and concentrate on the Leigh Light.[8]

Joubert's prevarication meant a two-month delay. When Leigh resumed work in August he made some modifications before the definitive version entered production; it would be mid-1942 before Leigh Light-equipped Wellingtons became operational. Lights would also be fitted to other aircraft such as the Catalina and the Liberator. The light's introduction was remarkable since it came from the work of a man outside the normal circle from which such technical innovation could be expected. Doubtless, the many hours that Leigh had spent in the air on anti-submarine duties in the Great War had focused his thinking.

Dönitz's wolfpacks continued claiming victims. They might not have found the hunting as easy as it had been earlier but could still occasionally maul convoys. In April a boat shadowing SC26 called up another seven. Of twenty-two merchantmen in the convoy, ten were sunk and three damaged. Also damaged was the AMC HMS *Worcestershire*. *Worcestershire* was fortunate; *U-74* had fired her last two torpedoes at the AMC but only the second struck. The ten ships lost from SC26 accounted for almost a quarter of the forty-one lost during April.[9]

Co-operation between the Admiralty and Coastal Command led to a study of the deployment of aircraft supporting convoys. Hitherto, this had been close escort, with the aircraft operating 'like the surface escorts, in a fairly constant position close to the convoy'. This led to some friction between seamen and airmen, with the latter regarding the Navy as over-eager to fire on aircraft.

If you got too near a convoy, the Navy – either they weren't too good at aircraft recognition or else they just played on the safe side – but they would shoot off at you. In fact, I was out in a destroyer in the Atlantic – they used to come and fly with us, the escort commanders, and we used to go on their ships occasionally for experience. One day one of our aircraft got rather close to this ship and the commander said to me ... 'I should open fire on that aircraft.' I said, 'Sir, what about your aircraft recognition?' 'Well,' he said, 'he's within fifteen hundred yards and he shouldn't be there. I'm entitled to open fire on him.'[10]

Although co-operation between the Submarine Tracking Room and Coastal Command Headquarters was very good, the two services were not yet fully integrated but this took another step forward with a change in operational practice in spring 1941. The close escort tactic gave way to one taking full advantage 'of the speed and mobility of aircraft to sweep ahead of and around convoys'. In April this new policy was tested and, found to be more effective, implemented for general use on 9 May. The new *modus operandi* for aircraft also reduced the possibilities of a friendly plane being downed by gunfire from a British warship.[11]

German aircraft remained a major threat to merchant shipping: in April 1941 air attack accounted for the loss of 116 ships, almost three times the forty-three sunk by U-boats; in tonnage the ratio was not quite so great with 323,454 tons lost to aircraft against 249,375 to submarines. Churchill dubbed the Condor the 'scourge of the Atlantic' but other aircraft were involved in anti-shipping operations, especially against coastal convoys along Britain's east coast. To defend merchant ships against air attacks, many were equipped with anti-aircraft guns manned by Royal Artillery detachments. Eventually, six Maritime Regiments Royal Artillery were formed; their gunners served in all theatres of the naval war, participating in 3,500 actions 'from long drawn out convoy battles to sudden brief encounters'. The Maritime Royal Artillery even adopted its own motto, *Intrepide per Oceanos Mundi* (Fearless through the oceans of the world). From an initial complement of 500 light machine guns, Lewis and Bren guns on anti-aircraft mounts, merchant ships were eventually equipped with 'Bofors 40mm light AA guns, Oerlikon 20mm guns and, for the defence of Atlantic convoys, at least 100 3-inch AA guns, ... transferred to the Admiralty on Churchill's orders at the end of 1941'.[12]

The best defence against aircraft was recognized as being fighters. Coastal Command had some long-range fighter squadrons, equipped with Bristol Blenheims, supplemented by other squadrons on loan from Fighter and Bomber Commands. The Blenheim, and its successors, the Bristol Beaufighter and de Havilland Mosquito, could not support convoys in mid-ocean, nor did the Royal Navy have aircraft carriers available for the task, although a new carrier class, the escort carrier, was planned (the first was *Audacity* which entered service in June 1941). A stop-gap measure was implemented in the form of fighters catapulted from ships. This involved single-seat fighters launched from either fighter-catapult (FC) ships, merchant ships commissioned by the Royal Navy in April 1941, manned by naval personnel and flying the White Ensign, or catapult-armed merchant (CAM) ships carrying normal cargoes and flying the Red Ensign. FC-ships carried either a Fairey Fulmar two-seater naval fighter or a Hawker Sea Hurricane Mark IA, known as a 'Hurricat'; CAM-ships generally carried Hurricanes.[13]

Trials took place off Belfast and the first CAM-ship, the *Michael E.*, sailed with OB327 on 28 May. *Michael E.* was sunk by *U-108* on 2 June and had no opportunity to launch its Hurricane. *Michael E.* was the only Royal Navy-sponsored CAM-ship, the remainder being sponsored by the RAF, which created a Merchant Ship Fighter Unit (MSFU) at RAF Speke, Liverpool,

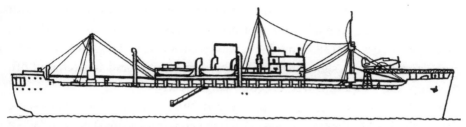

Figure 9: The CAM-ship SS *Empire Faith*, showing a Hurricat on her catapult.

on 5 May. Having completed his mission, the pilot had to fly to a shore base, if one was within range, 'ditch' his machine alongside a ship, or bale out and wait to be picked up.[14]

The first success by a 'Hurricat' came on 3 August when HMS *Maplin*'s shot down a Condor some 400 miles from land. Another eight CAM-ship aircraft were launched between then and the withdrawal of Hurricats from Atlantic convoys a year later; no launches were possible in the foul conditions of January and February 1942. Of nine combat launches, only one aircraft recovered to a shore base, in the USSR.[15] In one case, a pilot,

Figure 10: A Hurricat is blasted off over the bows of a CAM-ship.

Flying Officer John B. Kendal, died from injuries received while baling out of his Hurricane. Kendal, who shot down a Junkers Ju88 and chased off a Blohm und Voss BV138 flying boat, was Mentioned in Despatches.[16] With nine enemy aircraft shot down by CAM-ship fighters and four chased off, this stop-gap weapon proved exceptionally effective.[17]

The FC- and CAM-ships had served their purpose, although some operated with Mediterranean and Freetown convoys for another year. While HMS *Audacity* sailed with Gibraltar convoys from summer 1941, and the first escort carrier accompanied a convoy to Russia that winter, it would be spring 1943 before escort carriers joined Atlantic convoys. Meanwhile another improvised carrier would become available. The MAC-ship, carrying three or four Swordfish biplanes, was an adapted merchant ship. Unlike escort carriers, MAC-ships were never HM ships but operated as Merchant Navy vessels with a detachment of FAA personnel to fly, service and control the Swordfish.

> MAC-ships were always tankers or grain ships because these ships loaded and discharged cargo by means of a pipeline, with no hatches to open. The tankers could carry three Swordfish while the grain ships could carry four as it was possible to convert one of the holds aft into a small hangar .... Once the superstructure of these ships had been cut down and converted into an island on the starboard side, with their boiler uptakes diverted to the island, a flight deck could be laid over their holds. The grain ships had a shorter flight deck, at between 413 and 424 feet, than the 460 feet of the tankers, but the extra length of the tanker deck was no advantage as it was offset by having aircraft parked on the deck, reducing the take-off run.[18]

MAC-ships served a double role by carrying much of their intended cargo: a tanker MAC-ship could take 90 per cent of its normal capacity, since only a small part of that was used to store aviation fuel, whereas grain ships, having lost one hold as a hangar, had less capacity for grain.

The Fairey Swordfish looked like a relic from the First World War. An open-cockpit biplane, known affectionately as the 'Stringbag' and designed as a torpedo, spotter and reconnaissance aircraft, it entered service in 1936 when

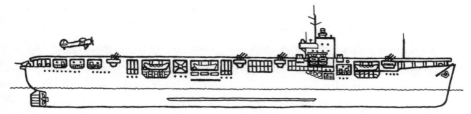

Figure 11: A Swordfish lands on the deck of a MAC-ship. These improvised mini-aircraft-carriers played a valuable role in forcing U-boats to remain submerged.

the RAF still controlled the FAA. The Royal Navy took over the service in mid-1939; by then the Swordfish, considered obsolescent, was to be replaced with an updated biplane called the Albacore, another product of the Fairey company that looked like a Swordfish with an enclosed cockpit. However, the Swordfish proved so adaptable that it outlived the Albacore, which could not perform some of the roles discharged by the venerable Stringbag.

With a 690hp Bristol Pegasus engine, the Swordfish had a three-man crew of pilot, observer and radio operator/rear gunner, a maximum speed of 143mph fully loaded, excellent endurance of five and a half hours and a range of over 500 miles. Moreover, take-off and stalling speeds were such that it could fly off a carrier without the vessel turning into wind; more than one Swordfish took off from a carrier at anchor. It was suited ideally to escort carrier operations and the even smaller MAC-ships, especially as it could be fitted with RATO (rocket-assisted take-off). Designed to carry a torpedo, the Swordfish had no difficulty carrying depth charges and, later in the war, was fitted with a battery of eight 60lb rockets. It could be equipped with ASV, something impossible with the Albacore. Rugged and stable, it was ideal for the carrier-borne anti-submarine role.

Although escort carriers preceded MAC-ships into service, the original intention was that MAC-ships should enter service first. Wragg argues that, with hindsight, 'it seems almost criminal' that MAC-ships were not available until 1943 when conversions might have taken place shortly after the outbreak of war.

The reason ... was that too few at the Admiralty believed that the concept would work. The Naval Air Division convinced itself that

12-knot ships would be too slow to operate aircraft. The Director of Naval Construction felt that it would take more than a year just to design such ships, obviously expecting everything to be just right! The Admiralty and the Ministry of War Transport agreed that it would be far too dangerous for aircraft to land and take-off on a steel flight deck running over tanks containing thousands of tons of highly inflammable fuel.[19]

Left to bureaucrats, MAC-ships might never have existed. However, the Director of Merchant Shipbuilding, Sir James Lithgow, had a more practical attitude, suggesting that two planned ships could be converted 'without undue delay' if the Admiralty agreed not to interfere. As a result, in June 1942 work began on converting the grain ships *Empire MacAlpine* and *Empire MacAndrew*. Conversion of ten more had begun by October. Although a programme for thirty-two MAC-ships was planned, this was reduced to nineteen as escort carriers became available.[20]

By mid-1941 Coastal Command's Catalinas were the longest-ranging aircraft available but machines with even greater endurance were needed to provide cover far out into the Atlantic. For that role, the American B-24 Liberator, also built by Consolidated, was the best aeroplane available and Coastal Command craved Liberators. In 1940 France had ordered 139 B-24s, to be designated LB-30, the first production order for Consolidated's new four-engined bomber as the United States Army Air Corps (USAAC) had shown little interest. France collapsed before any were delivered and the UK took over the order, most of the LB-30s being assigned to RAF Ferry Command for transatlantic services; they were considered unsuitable for combat, a view the USAAC shared. However, some twenty ex-USAAC YB-24s became the first to see active service with the RAF. Fitted with powered gun turrets, self-sealing fuel tanks, some armour and a 31-inch 'plug' in the forward fuselage to create more crew space, these went to Coastal Command as Liberator GR Is; as with several other US-produced aircraft, the B-24 was given its name by the RAF. The GR I's armament was increased by fitting four 20mm cannon in an under-nose 'gunpack'. Additional fuel tankage was provided, increasing endurance to some sixteen hours.[21]

No.120 Squadron re-formed at RAF Nutts Corner in County Antrim on 2 June 1941 as Coastal's first Liberator unit.[22] The squadron received nine GR Is and, after training and familiarization, became operational in September, flying its first anti-submarine patrols on the 20th. Commanding 120 was the highly experienced Wing Commander V. H. A. McBratney, known as 'Mac', an Irishman who had already formed and commanded a Canadian Catalina squadron in Coastal Command, No.413. Among his pilots was a fellow Irishman, Terence Malcolm Bulloch, from nearby Lisburn, who had flown the Liberator on transatlantic flights. Bulloch had twice made return journeys across the ocean in Liberators, which he had also crossed in B-17 Flying Fortresses. Needless to say, he was recruited by McBratney to assist in training other pilots as the squadron also had to absorb and train personnel, including ASV operators, to fill out the crews.[23] The early ASV – Mark II in the first Liberators – was difficult to operate:

> the device was regarded with such secrecy that the absolute minimum of training was given to the non-commissioned aircrew … detailed to operate them. As also, it was 'next to impossible' to gain much intelligence from these sets when flying over the heavy seas of the North Atlantic, due to the clutter that filled the tiny viewing screen given back by echoes from the large waves and heaving rollers, it is no wonder that they contributed little to the locating of U-boats.[24]

However, Bulloch had a sergeant wireless-operator/air gunner (WOP/AG) who 'seemed to grasp how to get the best out of the ASV aboard' and 'soon became expert at distinguishing between the more solid return "blips" from ships etc. and the constant flickering returns from the seas below'.[25] Sergeant 'Ginger' Turner was in Bulloch's crew when, on 22 October 1941, they spotted their first U-boat on Bulloch's fourth sweep over the Atlantic. They also met and fought a series of skirmishes with a Focke-Wulf Condor, the two machines clashing over a period of some hours; the German aircraft sustained no visible damage while the Liberator was struck in an engine by one round; another passed through a propeller blade.[27]

Then available only in small numbers, the Liberator would become a significant element in the Allied campaign in the Atlantic, having been designed for an intercontinental range. Although it was to take Boeing's B-29 and Consolidated's B-32 and B-36 to achieve fully that aim, the B-24 was the longest-ranged Allied aircraft in 1941, defined as a VLR (very long range) machine when modified for Coastal Command use. Modifications to RAF Liberators produced even more effective machines in the course of the war. While some sources claim that the Liberator closed the mid-Atlantic Gap this is not accurate: even the Liberator did not have the endurance to provide full cover for convoys across the gap. The real solution to that problem came from the escort carriers and the even more basic MAC-ships.

The Liberator GR I was followed by the GR II, which equated to the USAAF's B-24D, of which 140 were purchased by the UK (although some were requisitioned by the USAAF following Pearl Harbor). These, and the original deliveries, were made against British and French orders, but subsequent B-24s were provided under Lend-Lease.[28] By war's end No.120 Squadron would be the RAF's most successful anti-submarine unit with Bulloch its, and Coastal Command's, most successful pilot; No.120 accounted for fourteen U-boats, with another three shared and eight damaged; Bulloch accounted for four boats, although his total was probably higher.

With American aircraft in Coastal Command service – Hudsons, Catalinas and Liberators – and former US Navy warships and US Coast Guard cutters in Royal Navy service, an increasing United States' influence in the war may be seen. That influence was much greater than the supply of equipment and weapons. Although neutral, the United States government, and especially President Roosevelt, was disposed to supporting the Allies. Strict interpretation of neutrality would have prevented any American assistance since US law forbade American companies selling war matériel to a belligerent nation. At this time several US companies had received orders from the UK, France and Belgium for military equipment, including Hudsons from Lockheed and PBY-4s and B-24s from Consolidated. Roosevelt wanted to help the Allies as much as possible without upsetting Congress or US public opinion.

As well as failing to ban the sale of military equipment to the Allies, Roosevelt's government declared a 'Western Hemisphere Neutrality Zone' in October 1939, an extension of the Monroe Doctrine which warned any

European nation that attempts to interfere in the American continents would result in intervention by the United States. The Neutrality Zone regulations banned belligerent ships from a sea area out to 300 miles from the shores of the Americas, excluding Canada and European colonies. Roosevelt hoped that US Navy patrolling of this area would ease the Royal Navy's burden, allowing British ships to be deployed elsewhere on convoy duties, but the real effect was negligible.[29]

In November the Neutrality Act was revised to become much more favourable to the Allies. The embargo on US companies supplying military equipment to belligerents was superseded by regulations allowing trade on a cash–and–carry basis.[30] In revising the law thus, it appeared that the United States intended to be evenhanded and would trade with Germany on the same basis as the UK or France. This impression was intentional, but the cash–and–carry condition meant that Germany could not benefit. Since the Atlantic sea lanes were closed to German shipping by British and French ships, only the Allies could benefit, although much that was purchased – and paid for at the factory gate – was lost to the customer whenever a merchant ship was sunk en route to Europe. In such cases the sole beneficiaries were the companies producing the goods.

Both the United Kingdom and France had established purchasing commissions in the United States before war began and the money they spent helped American companies to increase production and gear up for further orders. Between the creation of the British commission in 1938 and late-1940, the United Kingdom expended almost all its gold and dollar reserves in purchasing equipment, principally aircraft, from the United States. When Belgium, France and Norway were overrun, their orders were taken over by Britain which then had to pay for the products ordered by her allies. No longer was the United Kingdom the rich state it had once been. Churchill's ancestor, the Duke of Marlborough, had dominated the Grand Alliance against Louis XIV of France because Britain was the richest partner, a situation also true for Pitt in the Seven Years' War and the Younger Pitt in the wars against revolutionary France and Napoleon. This had even been the case in the First World War, but that conflict had drained Britain's resources while this new war was pushing the country towards bankruptcy.

On 21 August 1940, just when the Battle of Britain was approaching its crisis, the Chancellor of the Exchequer ... warned the Cabinet that the total cost of munitions, raw materials, and industrial equipment to be bought in North America over the next twelve months would amount to $3,200 million, while our total remaining gold and dollar reserves came to less than $2,000 million. Britain would therefore exhaust her reserves by December 1940, unable any longer to pay for the dollar goods – oil, foodstuffs, raw materials, technology – on which her war effort, indeed her national life itself, depended. So even if Britain could survive the immediate threat of a German invasion she would be unable to carry the war much beyond New Year 1941.[31]

Facing a crisis of a magnitude no British statesman had faced before, Churchill saw the United States as Britain's lifeline and convinced Roosevelt that Britain was a sound bet through personal diplomacy and his insight into American thinking, inherited from his American mother. While Roosevelt was undoubtedly influenced by the economic advantages of supplying Britain, and was therefore pro-British, if only for pragmatic reasons, it was Churchill who drew the United States closer and closer to the Allies until the Japanese attack on Pearl Harbor, and the lack of strategic vision of both Hitler and Mussolini, brought America fully into the war in December 1941. By then, however, the United States was already a belligerent in the Atlantic.

Britain's gold and dollar reserves, the fuel that stoked American industry almost to a war footing, were all but exhausted. Yet Churchill believed that Roosevelt would help the United Kingdom remain in the war. The US government, having already introduced conscription – the 'draft' in American parlance – for the first time in peacetime and increased the defence budget from $2 billion to $10 billion dollars, appeared to be much more amenable to continued, and increasing, support of Britain. Churchill pressed Roosevelt on this but the latter's ability to manoeuvre was restricted severely by the Neutrality Acts, which prevented his government from offering credit on the sales of war matériel, or lending money to a belligerent.

Roosevelt believed that Britain and the Commonwealth were fighting for the survival of civilization and that America had a moral duty to help. He also believed that most American voters agreed; in his own words, 'there can be no reasoning with incendiary bombs'. His solution to the conundrum was to provide matériel to Britain and her allies without charge, on condition that such matériel was returned to the United States at the end of the war; any matériel destroyed would be written off. The scheme devised by Roosevelt became known as Lend-Lease or, in the language of legislators, An Act to Further Promote the Defense of the United States.[32]

In December 1940 Roosevelt had proclaimed the United States to be the 'arsenal of democracy' as he proposed selling arms and munitions to the UK and Canada.[33] Although most Americans saw the war as a European conflict, opinion changed as growing numbers recognized that funding Britain's war effort helped American industry and workers, although they preferred that the United States should remain neutral.

By February 1941 the *New York Times* was reporting the findings of a Gallup poll indicating that 54 per cent of Americans favoured unequivocally the proposed Lend-Lease scheme; another 15 per cent backed the concept provided it did not lead to American involvement, or the British gave some security for what was received. Only 22 per cent were opposed completely. In terms of political allegiances, the majority, 69 per cent, who favoured Lend-Lease unconditionally, were Democrats; only 38 per cent of Republicans favoured it.[34]

In Congress, opposition was strongest amongst isolationist Republicans, who considered that this could be 'the longest step this nation has yet taken toward direct involvement in the war abroad'. The vote in the House of Representatives was passed by 260 votes to 165, with 238 Democrats in support against only two dozen Republicans.[35] The bill passed the Senate a month later with a similar breakdown in voting: forty-nine Democrats supported it, but only ten Republicans.[36]

Two days after Senate approval, Roosevelt signed it into law. The president was thereby authorized to 'sell, transfer title, exchange, lease, lend, or otherwise dispose of, to any such government [whose defence the President deems vital to the defence of the United States] any defense article'. A month later China was included in the beneficiary nations, followed by the Soviet Union in October, four months after the German invasion.[37]

Barnett notes that Churchill had 'gradually turned the President into a colleague – an ally in spirit if not yet in fact'. In this subtle process the prime minister had been assisted greatly by Roosevelt's friend Harry Hopkins, the president's personal emissary in the UK, a man whom Churchill, on his arrival in January 1941, considered 'an envoy of supreme importance to our life'.[38] The introduction of Lend–Lease

> ensured that Great Britain could go on importing the foodstuffs, the oil, the raw materials, the technology and military equipment for which she could no longer pay. From now until the end of the conflict, Lend–Lease would cover more than half the United Kingdom's balance-of-payments deficit, signifying that Britain's war effort, indeed her very national life itself, would be underwritten by America's wealth and industrial power.[39]

With the introduction of Lend-Lease, the United States abandoned completely its neutrality stance. Isolationists who had predicted that this was a step towards American involvement in the war would be proved right before the year was out. But other measures taken by Roosevelt marked further steps along the path to war.

In April an agreement between the UK and the USA allowed US Navy ships and US aircraft to carry out sweeps along convoy routes and in critical areas of the North Atlantic, shadowing and reporting any Axis vessels. However, US Navy vessels were not to take offensive action. Three months later, US Army troops relieved British and Canadian troops in Iceland. August brought the Atlantic Charter, later the basis for the United Nations' charter, following the meeting between Churchill and Roosevelt at Placentia Bay in Newfoundland. This led to further development of American policy, including defining 'the final destruction of the Nazi tyranny' as an aim of US policy. On his return from Argentia, Churchill reported to the cabinet that 'The President had said that he would wage war but not declare it, and that he would become more and more provocative'.[40] Subsequent events were to show that this was no idle comment.

In September American ships and aircraft were ordered to engage and destroy any surface raiders threatening or attacking shipping between North America and Iceland while the United States undertook to escort the faster convoys in the western Atlantic, to the westward of a line down the meridian of 10 degrees West to latitude 65 degrees North, thence to position 5300N x 2600W and thence down the meridian of 26 degrees West. The details of the individual convoy air and surface escorts were to be worked out by the respective staffs of the three countries concerned ...[41]

The United States had become involved ever more deeply to the extent that it might be argued that the country had declared war on Germany; Roosevelt's policy of waging war but not declaring it was reality.

The first major incident involving a US Navy ship and a U–boat occurred on 4 September when a Coastal Command aircraft signalled the American destroyer *Greer* that a German submarine was 'lying athwart her course about ten miles ahead'. Having identified the boat on asdic (sonar to the US Navy) the *Greer* began tracking it and maintained contact with *U-652* for over three hours. The pilot of the British aeroplane then enquired if *Greer* intended to attack the boat and, when the answer was in the negative, dropped a stick of four depth charges before leaving to refuel. Not long after this attack, *U-652* fired a single torpedo at the *Greer,* the boat's commander, Oberleutnant Georg-Werner Fraatz, presumably believing that the destroyer had dropped the depth charges. *Greer* retaliated with depth charges and Fraatz fired another torpedo. 'Unable to re-establish sound contact, *Greer* discontinued the search at 1416 and resumed course for Iceland'.[42] From then onward the undeclared war intensified. On 11 September, in a radio broadcast, Roosevelt described *U-652*'s attack on the USS *Greer* as piracy and proclaimed that 'From now on, if German or Italian vessels of war enter waters the protection of which is necessary for American defence, they do so at their own risk'.[43]

Days before the *Greer* 'incident', on 1 September, Admiral Ernest King, head of the US Navy, issued a new operational plan providing the rationale for US ships or aircraft engaging German or Italian naval vessels in the Western Atlantic. Cinclant [Commander-in-Chief Atlantic] Op. Plan 7 laid down that 'Naval vessels in the North Atlantic were ... required specifically to operate under war conditions, and to darken ship when east of Cape Breton Island'.[44] On the day King's order was promulgated, Roosevelt made his Labour Day broadcast and declared his government's intention to 'do everything in our power to crush Hitler and his Nazi forces'. He warned that defeat of the United Kingdom and her allies would leave the United States with an impossible situation, since the US Navy 'cannot now, or in the future, maintain the freedom of the seas against all the rest of the world'.[45]

Since it could be argued that escorting convoys was 'a combat duty', the US government adopted a theory that convoys were being escorted between two United States bases to support US troops in Argentia and Iceland, rather than to any belligerent country. However, a proviso used before, 'shipping of any nationality which might join', allowed Allied vessels to avail of United States naval protection. The Admiralty and the Navy Department in Washington agreed that a US Navy escort group from Argentia should relieve a Royal Canadian Navy escort at a designated western ocean meeting place off Newfoundland, and, except for Iceland-bound ships, hand over the convoy to a Royal Navy escort at an agreed mid-ocean meeting point, or 'Momp', where the US escort either picked up a westbound convoy, or peeled off to take Iceland-bound ships to Reykjavik. In this way, the US Navy assumed responsibility for the transatlantic route between the meridians of Newfoundland and Iceland.[46]

Mid-ocean meeting points were established south of Iceland between 26 and 22W. To the east would operate Royal Navy escort groups while US Navy groups would protect HX and ON convoys; RCN escort groups, 'augmented as necessary by Royal Navy vessels undertook the slow SC and ONS convoys'.[47]

In October the destroyer USS *Kearny* was torpedoed by *U-568*. This was not an unprovoked attack. *U-568* was with a wolfpack that attacked convoy SC48 and overwhelmed the escort. *Kearny* and three other US destroyers of Task Unit 4.1.4 were detached from supporting ON24 to provide assistance. On reaching SC48, the American ships dropped depth charges, continuing to do so throughout the night. However, at about 4.15am on 17 October, *U-568* fired four torpedoes at an American destroyer which, the boat's captain reported, was struck by one of the projectiles, broke in two and sank. He had targeted and hit *Kearny* which did not sink, although damaged badly. *Kearny*'s captain, Commander Anthony Danis, was unable to send a distress signal for thirty minutes as his ship had lost power. Eleven crewmen were killed and twenty-two wounded. Danis got *Kearny* underway and limped at 10 knots to Iceland, escorted by *Greer* and *Monssen*, for emergency repairs alongside the repair ship USS *Vulcan* before returning to Boston for permanent repairs.[48]

A week after this attack, five US Navy destroyers of Escort Group 4.1.3 sailed from Argentia to escort HX156; one was the 1920-vintage USS *Reuben James*, whose captain was Lieutenant Commander H. L. Edwards. On 31 October the convoy was south of Iceland and about 600 miles west of Ireland. Only one escort, USS *Niblack*, covering the rear of the convoy, was equipped with radar. The *Reuben James* was positioned about 2,000 yards on the port beam of the convoy centre as day was breaking.

The convoy was not zig-zagging, and the destroyers may not all have been patrolling their stations. *Reuben James* was turning to investigate a strong direction-finding bearing when a torpedo from *U-552* struck. The resulting explosion probably ignited the forward magazine, blowing off the fore part of the destroyer as far aft as her fourth stack. For about five minutes, the rear section remained afloat but, as it went down, depth charges exploded, killing men in the water. Only forty-five of the ship's company of about 160 were rescued by other escorts; no officers survived.[49]

The other escorts, *Benson*, *Hilary P. Jones*, *Niblack* and *Tarbell*, conducted a vigorous asdic search for the U-boat but with no success. Next day, however, the British 6th Escort Group, which was relieving the US ships, surprised two U-boats trailing on their port beam and engaged them with gunfire, forcing both to dive. One was probably *U-552* as Rohwer and Hummelchen note this boat, and *U-567*, making unsuccessful torpedo attacks on HX156 on 1 November and also maintaining contact until the 3rd.[50] *Reuben James* was the only ship lost from convoy HX156. In one sense the destroyer had performed her duty by protecting the merchantmen.

The USS *Reuben James* has the sad distinction of being the first US warship sunk in the Second World War, her loss described by Morison as 'a deliberate act in the undeclared state of war that existed between the United States and Germany'. Morison also notes that seven American merchant ships were sunk from a variety of causes before the Japanese attacked Pearl Harbor.[51] His comment on an 'undeclared state of war' describes accurately the United States' position at the time. Escorting convoys was an act of belligerence. Attacking German submarines cannot be described as anything other than being at war.

Ultra had been important in routeing convoys to avoid U-boats during July and August. So successful was this that, during August, UK imports reached almost a million tons each week. As recently as May, no fewer than fifty-seven ships had been lost from North Atlantic convoys. The figure dropped to twenty-two in August. The threat from Coastal Command aircraft was increasing, and becoming more effective, while more ships were available for escort groups, which were working better as teams. The overall effect persuaded Dönitz to move his boats eastward, closer to the British Isles, where shipping density was greater. More boats were also deployed against Gibraltar convoys with one outbound convoy, OG71, stalked all the way from west of Ireland to the latitude of Lisbon by aircraft and U-boats. Ten ships from OG71, including two escorts, were lost to U-boats in a battle raging over three nights.[52]

Although there had been something of a lull during July and August, with few boats being sunk and few effective attacks on convoys, Dönitz had 198 boats in commission at the end of August with eighty operational. Against this, escort numbers were increasing steadily and Coastal's effectiveness was to take a great stride forward with the introduction of air-dropped depth charges for land-based planes.

September 1941 witnessed heavy convoy losses with fifty-three ships, over 200,000 tons, sunk by U-boats. Following lack of success in the Western Approaches during July and August, Dönitz pushed his boats farther west, where they would not be constantly scanning the skies. The Admiralty believed that at least a dozen were in the Western Atlantic. Their effectiveness was demonstrated when SC42, of sixty-four ships, was attacked by the Markgraf wolfpack of fourteen boats, which increased to nineteen during the five days of battle. However, this battle also demonstrated the effectiveness of the measures implemented to protect convoys.[53]

Markgraf had been operating south-west of Iceland since August but Ultra had allowed the re-routeing of several convoys. When the group's patrol line failed to find any prey, U-boat headquarters dispersed it over a greater area. The signal to the group was intercepted and decrypted by Ultra, but exact positions of its boats were not known. While it was possible to re-route another three convoys, SC42's room for manoeuvre was restricted by a storm and the ice barrier. On 9 September the convoy was sighted by *U-85*.

U-85 launched an immediate unsuccessful attack but reported the convoy's location. Other boats converged to join the attack. During the night *U-81*, *U-82* and *U-432* each sank a ship. *U-652* attacked two ships, the tanker *Tahchee* and the *Baron Pentland*, damaging both. Two men of the *Baron Pentland* were killed and the master gave the order to abandon ship. Although her back was broken she remained afloat, thanks to a cargo of timber, but was torpedoed and sunk by *U-372* on the 19th.

Markgraf continued menacing the convoy on 10 September, with *U-432* maintaining contact. *U-85* made two daylight attacks, sinking one ship, but was attacked by the destroyer HMCS *Skeena* and the corvette HMCS *Alberni*. Damaged severely, her captain was compelled to make for base in France for repairs.[54]

There was an interesting incident during the 10th involving *U-501* and two Canadian corvettes, *Chambly* and *Moosejaw*, which had been at sea on a 'shake-down' cruise when they were ordered to reinforce SC42's escort, 24th Escort Group. Seeing rockets fired during a night attack they altered course and, within forty minutes, had asdic contact. *Chambly* attacked with a depth-charge pattern that forced *U-501* to the surface close to *Moosejaw*. When the latter put her engines astern, the U-boat was practically alongside and men with their hands up could be seen on the conning-tower. *U-501*'s captain, Forster, jumped aboard the corvette and others were preparing to follow when *Moosejaw* sheered off. Minus her captain, *U-501* made off quickly, with crewmen manning their gun. *Moosejaw* turned to ram, struck the boat a glancing blow and opened fire. The crew abandoned ship. Although *U-501* was boarded, she sank soon afterwards. Forster's excuse for abandoning was the unlikely one that he intended to demand that his crew be saved. This was the first U-boat to surrender to Royal Canadian Navy ships. Neither *Chambly* nor *Moosejaw* had seen action before.[55]

Twenty-fourth Escort Group was really still only a collection of a destroyer and three corvettes with little experience as a group. Although the senior officer, Commander J. C. Hibbard RCN, was 'an experienced and skilful destroyer captain' and his ship, *Skeena*, was a 'well-equipped and fairly modern destroyer', the corvettes *Alberni*, *Kenogami* and *Orillia* 'had been recently commissioned, their crews hastily trained, and sent to sea lacking experience'.[56] 'No one [had] really expected EG 24 to do as well as it did, and the corvettes sent out to help surprised *U-501* near the convoy and destroyed it'.[57]

Markgraf continued attacking with 'wave after wave of U-boats' working their way into the convoy and sinking more ships: *U-82* sank three and damaged another while *U-432* and *U-433* sank one each. *U-207* also sank two and, after the main battle was over, *U-202*, with no previous success, torpedoed and sank the merchantman damaged by *U-82*.

The escort was reinforced further on the 11th when three corvettes and a trawler, diverted from HX147, joined EG 24; these were HMCS *Wetaskewin*, HM Ships *Mimosa* and *Gladiolus* and HM Trawler *Buttermere*. The British 2nd Escort Group (B2) also arrived, diverted from ON13; B2 included five destroyers: *Douglas*, *Veteran*, *Leamington*, *Saladin* and *Skate*. *Veteran* and *Leamington* sank *U-207* and daytime air cover kept the U-boats down although *U-432* maintained contact with the convoy. *U-652* made an unsuccessful attack while *U-105* sank a ship sailing independently.

The reinforced escort kept the pack at bay during the night with only *U-43* and *U-84* targeting ships but missing with their torpedoes. On the 12th and 13th the strength of the escort and air cover made things very difficult for the U-boats while heavy seas and poor visibility added so much to those difficulties that attack was impossible. *U-552* joined on the 14th but was the last to have contact with the convoy before the operation was ended. Two days later, however, as we have seen, the ship damaged by *U-82* was sunk, bringing total losses from SC42 to sixteen ships sunk and four damaged, a loss rate of 25 per cent.

The battle for SC42 proved once again the value of a strong escort and good air cover. Milner comments that 'The Germans later confessed that they found the escort "surprisingly strong" despite the distance from support'. One almost immediate result was that the Admiralty asked the Royal Canadian Navy to increase the group size in the NEF from four ships to six. This the Canadians were able to do, thanks to the US Navy taking over the HX convoys. However, the Admiralty request indicated a lack of faith in the ability of the Royal Canadian Navy and would lead to convoys in the autumn being reinforced by RN and USN escorts.[58]

On page 109 the behaviour of the commander of *U-501* in abandoning his boat was described. This had been the second example of diminishing morale on the part of *U-bootwaffe* personnel, the first having been provided by the commander of *U-570*, Kapitänleutnant Hans-Joachim Rahmlow. Rahmlow had taken command on 15 May 1941 and commenced a war patrol on 1 August. While on the surface south of Iceland on 27 August, *U-570* was spotted by a Hudson of No.269 Squadron. Unaware of this, Rahmlow dived and the Hudson dropped smoke markers. Two hours later, another Hudson from 269, Squadron Leader J. H. Thompson's machine, sighted *U-570* surfacing. Attacking as Rahmlow attempted to crash dive, Thompson dropped four depth charges, the explosions from which caused some panic amongst the boat's crew, although damage was not serious. Rahmlow was neither a Prien nor a Kretschmer, who would have maintained discipline and made good their escape. Convinced of defeat, and fearful of chlorine gas, he ordered his men to don lifejackets and surfaced. As crewmen appeared on deck, the Hudson sent a signal requesting surface vessels. Rahmlow was in no mood for a fight and some judicious machine-gunning ensured that the boat's anti-aircraft weapons remained silent. A white flag, actually Rahmlow's shirt, was waved as the Hudson circled her prize.[59]

Subsequently a flying boat from Iceland took over until HM Trawler *Kingston Agate* arrived and warned Rahmlow not to scuttle his boat. Other trawlers joined *Kingston Agate* as did a destroyer, a prize crew boarded the boat, whose crew was taken off, and *U-570* was towed to Iceland. How little damage she had sustained may be gleaned from the fact that, with a skeleton Royal Navy crew, she was soon on her way to Britain to be commissioned as HM Submarine *Graph*. Although the Enigma machine and codebooks had been destroyed, *U-570* still yielded considerable technical information, including the fact that she could dive to 600 feet.[60]

Neither Forster nor Rahmlow had shown much fight, surrendering with almost indecent haste. Their behaviour cannot have inspired Dönitz with any great faith in the new generation of commanders, although the captain of *U-111*, sunk south-west of Tenerife after a gun battle with HM Trawler *Lady Shirley* on 4 October would have sustained his hope. Kapitänleutnant Wilhelm Kleinschmidt was one of eight members of his crew to die in the battle that followed *Lady Shirley* forcing *U-111* to surface with depth charges.[61]

U-boats enjoyed some respite of an unwelcome variety in the last three months of 1941 as exceptionally bad weather in the North Atlantic scattered convoys and made it almost impossible to sight and engage targets. Such weather was also difficult for escorts and for Coastal Command. In those three months, only sixty-nine ships were lost to U-boats, thirty-two in October, twelve in November and twenty-five in December. Against this, nine U-boats were believed sunk in December, from a total, according to the Admiralty, of fifty-three boats for the year. In fact, ten were lost in December, including one rammed by an Italian submarine in the Mediterranean. All but two of the others were sunk by warships, the exceptions being one sunk by aircraft and another shared between aircraft and surface ships. The Admiralty figure for the year was optimistic: German records show only thirty-five boats lost in 1941.[62]

On 11 December 1941, following the Japanese attack on Pearl Harbor, Germany and Italy declared war on the United States, bringing the weight of the US Navy into the Atlantic battle and prompting Churchill to comment that Britain could not now lose the war. It seemed as if the *U-bootwaffe* faced overwhelming odds, even though there were some 260 boats available with about a score of new boats being delivered each month, a figure that fell to an average of thirteen in January, February and March 1942, partially due to extreme cold in the shipyards.[63] Nonetheless, U-boat crews were to find themselves with an unexpected second 'Happy Time' in the early months of 1942 off the coast of the United States.

Chapter Eight

Hessler brackets the fourth phase of the Battle of the Atlantic between January and July 1942. The United States' entry into the war not only marked this phase's beginning, but also gave the *U-bootwaffe* a new hunting ground, the eastern seaboard of America, which became, in one German prisoner's words, 'the U-boats' paradise'. By the time it was pitched into war, the United States was much better prepared than it might otherwise have been without Roosevelt's stealthy determination to fit his country and its armed forces for war. British, French and Belgian treasure had helped American industry achieve production levels that would enable the country to go to war with better-equipped forces that were prepared for active service.

Roosevelt had not been alone in wanting the USA to be ready for war. Admiral Harold Stark, Chief of Naval Operations, and General George Marshall, Chief of Staff of the US Army, were of like mind, as were the Secretaries of State, War and the Navy. The US Navy, especially, realized the extent of the German threat in the Atlantic, command of which had 'hitherto been shared by Britain and America'. As a result, 'those responsible for safeguarding American interests decided, in June 1940, that plans for a full, armed cooperation with the British Commonwealth must be prepared without further delay.'[1] Aware of the scale of the disaster that befell Belgian forces due to their king's scrupulous neutrality forbidding them to discuss defence measures with their French counterparts, they were determined to avoid such a fate for the United States.[2]

On 12 July 1940, following the collapse of France, and Italy's declaration of war, Admiral Stark delegated his deputy, Rear Admiral Robert L. Ghormley, to lead a group of senior military officers to the United Kingdom for 'exploratory conversations' with the British Chiefs of Staff. Ghormley arrived in London on 15 August, accompanied by Major General George V. Strong, Marshall's deputy, and Major General D. C. Emmons, of the Army Air Forces. They were to report to Roosevelt whether England [sic] could hold out; for this was the period of her greatest danger, when she stood alone against the Nazi fury. Senator Pickering's toast of 1810 – 'The world's last hope – Britain's fast-anchored Isle' – had again become a reality. The British Chiefs of Staff showed the Americans their plan for continuing the war; and the Royal Air Force demonstrated with its radar-directed Spitfires that the air blitz could be defeated.[3]*

The mission returned convinced that Britain would hold out, Strong and Emmons reporting to Marshall that the UK was not to be conquered.[4] (The US ambassador to the UK, Joseph P. Kennedy, father of a future president, had a different view; his anti-British views saw him having to resign in November 1940.)

Ghormley, reporting from 'the laboratory of war', remained in Britain when his compatriots returned to Washington. He believed that the United States could learn from British experience and his reports to Stark helped lead the latter to recommend that the United States should increase the strength of both the army and navy. Roosevelt was urged to 'authorize Army and Navy representatives immediately to enter upon an exhaustive series of secret staff conversations with the British, from which definite plans and agreements to promote unity of effort against the Axis and Japan could emerge'.[5]

Those staff conversations continued into 1941 when Rear Admiral Arthur LeR. Bristol Jnr was charged with organizing a support force for escort duties in the Atlantic and was appointed Commander Support Force on 26 February. In March Bristol's chief of staff, Captain Louis Denfeld, accompanied by an airman and a civil engineer 'visited the British Isles ... to select bases from which both surface ships and aircraft of the United States Navy might operate'.[6] (The term 'British Isles' indicates that the party visited Ireland, where they tried to obtain the use of Lough Swilly in County Donegal but de Valera refused. A visit by Colonel William J. 'Wild

---

* Morison goes on to note that 15 September was the 'day of the great fall [autumn] turkey shoot' when RAF fighters shot down 187 German bombers, a figure now known to have been greatly overestimated.

Bill' Donovan, a well-known Irish–American soldier, also failed to change de Valera's mind, although he himself was American born.)

While the Denfeld party was in Liverpool conferring with Sir Percy Noble that city was twice bombed heavily. Since it seemed that the Luftwaffe might bomb the US Navy 'out of one pair of bases, two were selected: Gare Loch, on the Clyde, for destroyers, together with Loch Ryan at the entrance of the firth for naval aircraft; Londonderry for destroyers with Lough Erne in County Fermanagh for aircraft'.[7] The Scottish sites were undeveloped but those in Northern Ireland were already in use by the Royal Navy and Royal Air Force. Some $50 million in Lend-Lease money was allocated to the bases, an American company was awarded the building contract, and the shipping of materials, in British ships 'since it was still illegal for American vessels to enter war zones', began in June.[8]

Meanwhile, Bristol's Support Force initiated intensive anti–submarine warfare training and, on 20 March, Roosevelt was told that US ships would soon be ready to escort convoys to the United Kingdom. Secretary of the Navy Knox planned a force of twenty-seven destroyers, four Catalina squadrons and minesweepers and tenders to deploy to Lough Foyle and Lough Erne in mid-September with about 15,000 US Army personnel to protect and service the bases. Before the first personnel landed in Northern Ireland, there was a change of plan; from mid-June it was decided that the Support Force should concentrate on the Argentia–Iceland sector. As yet Roosevelt did not want US ships to be seen escorting combat troops and many convoys from North America carried Canadian troops. He considered that escorting merchant ships was another matter 'since the entire U-boat warfare on merchant ships, as conducted by Germany, was contrary to international law and treaty obligations'.[9]

In spite of this change of plan, the US Navy base at Londonderry went ahead and was commissioned officially on 5 February 1942 as Naval Operating Base (NOB) Londonderry.[10] The flying-boat base at Lough Erne never came to fruition; the partially-built facilities were handed over to the RAF. New facilities had been added to the Royal Navy's jetty at Lisahally (a Gaelic name, meaning, appropriately, 'the fort of the fleet') near Londonderry, and in the city. US Navy and Coast Guard vessels would join Royal Navy ships, as would Royal Canadian Navy ships as the RCN expanded to become the dominant element of the escort force in the latter phase of the war. Interestingly, Admiralty files suggest that the Londonderry base could have been handed over to the US Navy entirely but, with the expansion at Lisahally, there was sufficient more space for all.[11] By mid-1943 Londonderry was home to more escorts than Liverpool and Greenock combined. Noble described it as 'the best Escort Base that we possess, and it is the nearest to the field of action'.[12]

The Newfoundland Escort Force, 'a milestone in Canadian naval history', was established in May 1941 with Commodore Leonard Warren Murray commanding it from 15 June.[13] The Royal Canadian Navy had been a force of a dozen small ships at the start of the war but had grown to be strong enough to assume the convoy escort role in the relatively safe western Atlantic waters, the overstretched Royal Navy gladly delegating this responsibility. Canadian pride required that Canadian ships be formed into Canadian groups, wherein lay a weakness: corvettes and other small ships could be built and equipped faster than crews could be trained to man them effectively. 'Though the lesson that ill-trained escorts were no match for U-boats had been learnt from harsh experience, the relative quiet on the western portion of the convoy route during the summer had made it seem a fair risk to employ newly commissioned ships and weak, newly-formed groups in that area.'[14]

With ships being commissioned faster than crews could be trained, the Canadian training system was under almost intolerable strain. Commander James Douglas 'Chummy' Prentice had the seemingly Sisyphean task of working up the RCN's new ships and overseeing escort groups.[15] Circumstances dictated that the RCN did not have a scheme comparable to HMS *Western Isles*.

With the establishment of the Newfoundland Escort Force, RCN destroyers operating from Halifax and UK ports were assigned to it. Each Canadian group was to include five corvettes, although destroyers added more muscle to some groups, as we have seen with EG24 in the SC42 battle, so that the usual early form was two or three corvettes with a destroyer; this followed Western Approaches Command policy even though Canadian groups were still weak. Since RCN corvettes had not been intended initially for oceanic escort work, these were not being modified, as were their RN counterparts, with extended forecastle, heavier armament and improved bridge; their magnetic compasses meant they also had to make do with an obsolete asdic – Type123A; RN corvettes had gyrocompasses allowing the use of more modern equipment. The switch to oceanic work rather than inshore patrolling had unfortunate and uncomfortable consequences for Canadian crews. In 1941 the RCN solution was to make frigates, initially described as 'twin-screw' corvettes, its priority, but these would take two years to build. As a result, the service had to order improved Flowers in 1942.[16] The NEF's first encounter with U-boats occurred on 23 June 1941 when the destroyer *Ottawa* and the corvettes *Chambly*, *Collingwood* and *Orillia*, escorting HX133, engaged *U-203*. Lack of training and inadequate equipment became evident as communications broke down. RN ships arrived to deal with the attackers but six ships were lost to them, although two U-boats, *U-556* and *U-651*, were claimed by the British ships.[17] Although dispiriting, this salutary lesson was one on which the RCN would build.

The Argentia conference and the Atlantic Charter had an almost immediate effect on the NEF. With the US Navy taking over responsibility for HX and ON convoys between Newfoundland and Iceland, the RCN looked after the SC and ONS slow convoys in the same sector. However, the US Navy would also assume operational control of the north-west Atlantic, a control vested in an American admiral at Argentia, initially designated Commander Support Force but later to become Commander Task Force 4 (TF-4) and, subsequently, Commander Task Force 24 (TF-24). In this change in operational command Canadian authorities had no say: it was agreed between the UK and US governments. Thus Canada, a nation at war, had to place a substantial element of its armed forces under control of a nation that remained neutral. Doubtless, the measure was intended to draw the United States closer to a state of war.

The agreement also severed the embryonic RCN escort fleet from the steadying influence of Western Approaches Command. The USN took no proprietary interest in the Canadian navy or its operational efficiency, and after September 1941 (when the arrangements went into effect) NEF and the burgeoning RCN were beyond any effective British control.[18]

There was, however, a positive dividend: the new system added the strength of the fifty US destroyers of Support Force to that of NEF, reducing the operational burden. The opportunity arose of creating a training group for escort crews, but increasing enemy pressure made this almost impossible during autumn 1941.[19] When Murray planned to re-establish it in December, he was thwarted again by enemy action, this time from Japan. Redeployment of US ships to the Pacific gave the RCN a much greater task in the Atlantic and led to the role 'for which it would always be remembered'.[20]

As the fourth phase of the Battle of the Atlantic opened, the Royal Navy was concentrated east of Iceland while the Royal Canadian and US Navies covered the western Atlantic, although the Americans were looking over their shoulders at the Pacific. With 260 boats available to him, and new boats being commissioned, Dönitz ought to have been happy. The opposite was the case: Hitler had committed another strategic blunder in October by ordering U-boats into the Mediterranean to boost the *Regia Marina*'s efforts to seize control of the central basin. When *U-81* sank the aircraft carrier *Ark Royal* on 13 November, followed by *U-331*'s sinking of the battleship *Barham* on the 25th and *U-557*'s success against the cruiser *Galatea* on 14 December, it seemed as if the reduction of strength in the Atlantic might be worthwhile. Dönitz did not agree, writing that he had only ninety-one operational boats on 1 January 1942, of which twenty-three were in the Mediterranean; these are described later as 'the most effective part of the U-boat arm'. A further three boats were 'under orders from Naval High Command' to join those in the Mediterranean, while six were stationed west of Gibraltar and four along the coast of Norway. This left him with fifty-five boats available, of which '60 per cent were in dockyard hands undergoing repairs prolonged by shortage of labour'.[21]

Although he protested against the Mediterranean deployment, Dönitz was overruled. His view was that the battle against British 'vital lines of communication across the Atlantic' was the Kriegsmarine's most important task, from which forces should be withdrawn only 'if a state of real emergency arose, and even then only to the extent required to deal with the emergency'.[22]

Dönitz believed that eliminating Malta was key to the Mediterranean problem with air power having more to contribute than U-boats while only the minimum number of boats should have been withdrawn from the Atlantic. That the Atlantic was denuded of boats, with operations suspended for almost two months 'was, in my opinion, completely unjustifiable'.[23]

Anticipating the United States entering the war, Dönitz had asked for early warning of such an occurrence so that he could deploy boats off the east coast to take 'full advantage ... of the element of surprise to strike a real blow in waters in which anti-submarine defences were still weak'. This was not to be as even Hitler was taken by surprise by the Japanese attack on Pearl Harbor on 7 December. Two days later Dönitz sought permission for the release of twelve U-boats for operations off the American coast[24] and Hitler lifted all restrictions on U-boat operations against US ships or in the American security zone. U-boat Command was confident that a dozen boats off the American coast would take a heavy toll since those waters had been untouched by war and ships sailed independently in them. Since the Royal and US Navies had been co-operating and exchanging information it was inevitable that there would be some anti-submarine defences, but, as the US Navy had little operational experience, it was believed that such defences would not be effective, and U-boats would find conditions at least as favourable as those in British waters earlier in the war.[25]

Dönitz could deploy only six boats since OKM refused his request to withdraw six Type IXCs from the Mediterranean, an area for which they were inherently unsuited. Left with but six submarines, he found that only five were ready to sail between 16 and 25 December, although he was filled with admiration for their crews' enthusiasm. They had 'sacrificed many of the amenities of their living quarters ... to make room for the larger quantities of stores, spare parts and other expendable articles which an increase in the radius of action demanded'.[26] Life on a U-boat was never comfortable; life on the boats that sailed for America was even less so.

One commander, Kapitänleutnant Reinhard 'Teddy' Suhren of *U-564*, comments that 'America seemed about as far off as the Moon, between 3,000 and 4,000 nautical miles away', which required a longer arm than the older submarines possessed. Suhren's boat would join the campaign with the second wave.[27]

> From an exchange of blows at a distance it soon developed into close combat, reaching all the way ... from the St Lawrence to the Caribbean. We had enormous success. In ... January alone, only a handful of submarines were responsible for sinking some sixty-two ships [the true figure was lower: forty-six]. The submarines could be counted on the fingers of two hands. Among the Kommandants were, for instance, Hardegen, Topp and Zapp, all 'beating their drum'.[28]

Small in number they may have been but that first wave caused consternation and havoc on the western side of the Atlantic. Their first victim was not an American ship but the British *Cyclops*, sailing independently on a regular coastal route. Its sinking by Kapitänleutnant Reinhard Hardegen's *U-123* on 12 January 1942 was 'the beginning of a holocaust of shipping such as had never before been seen'.[29] Although *Cyclops* was outside the U-boats' designated operational area they had been given permission to attack vessels of over 10,000 tons encountered en route; *Cyclops* was 9,076 tons.

U-123's attack took place two days before the campaign off the eastern seaboard began officially. The next two weeks of Operation PAUKENSCHLAG (Drumbeat) were fruitful for Hardegen: *U-123* sank nine ships totalling 53,173 tons, bringing a congratulatory message from Dönitz on 20 January: *'An den Paukenschläger Hardegen. Bravo! Gut gepaukt. Dönitz'* (For the drumbeater Hardegen. Well done! Good beating. Dönitz) More than a message of congratulations was in the offing: on the 23rd Hardegen was told by radio that he had been awarded the Knight's Cross. Hardegen decided to report successes in verse, which did not impress Dönitz. Suhren writes of his reaction when first hearing such a report: 'you've really put your foot in it now', but the security aspect of this radio traffic seems to have been unappreciated. Hardegen was not the only commander taking a heavy toll of shipping in American waters: Zapp in *U-66* sank five ships, including an ore-laden freighter and two tankers; Kals in *U-130* sank three tankers and a freighter; and the other two boats had similar success.[30]

The first phase was 'a complete success'.

The U-boats found that conditions there were almost exactly those of normal peacetime. The coast was not blacked out, and the towns were a blaze of bright lights. The lights, both in lighthouses and on buoys, shone forth, though perhaps a little less brightly than usual. Shipping followed the normal peacetime routes and carried the normal lights.[31]

Local communities had not dimmed waterfront lights, nor did the military authorities require them to do so until three months after the campaign began. A proposal to adopt 'this obvious defence measure' caused protests that the 'tourist season would be ruined' from Atlantic City to southern Florida. Miami and its suburbs contributed six miles of lighting against which southbound shipping was silhouetted. 'Ships were sunk and seamen drowned in order that the citizenry might enjoy business and pleasure as usual.' On 18 April 1942 the Eastern Sea Frontier commander finally ordered the dousing of waterfront lights while the Army's Eastern Defense Command ordered a strict dim-out on 18 May.[32]

Most surprisingly to U-boat commanders, and to Dönitz, it seemed that very few anti-submarine measures were in place. Existing patrols were lacking experience and single destroyers patrolled shipping lanes 'with such regularity that the U-boats were quickly able to work out the timetable being followed'.[33]

On 2 January 1942 OKM released for Atlantic operations all the new Type VIIC boats that had been intended for the Mediterranean. Dönitz immediately ordered them across the Atlantic. In the meantime OKM was trying to increase the number of boats by attempting to 'prevent dockyard and shipbuilding workers being called up for the army' since their efforts were needed for the building and maintenance of U-boats.[34] Additional boats would allow the campaign in American waters to be continued and intensified, as would the introduction of Type XIV supply boats, known as *Milchkühe* (milk cows).

The first Type XIV was *U-459*, commissioned on 15 November 1941, which departed on its maiden patrol on 29 March 1942, commanded by Kapitänleutnant Georg von Wilamowitz-Möllendorf (at forty-eight, one of the oldest U-boat commanders). Their role was to re-supply the Type VIIs and IXs with stores and ammunition. *U-459* was 'a clumsy great boat of nearly 1,700 tons. As she was not intended for offensive purposes, she carried no torpedo armament and mounted only AA guns for her own protection'.[35] These soon became priority targets for the Allies, as, in the campaign in American waters, the *Milchkühe* had a valuable role, allowing the smaller Type VIICs to operate so far from home. *U-459* was followed by *U-460* and *U-116*; these three supplied fuel oil to twenty of the thirty-seven attack boats in the Caribbean over three months.[36] With *Milchkühe* stationed some 600 miles off New York, it was possible for Type VIICs to replenish in relative safety from air attack. However, the operational life of the Type XIVs was short: better ASV and more extensive Allied air coverage led to their eventual demise; the last was sunk in June 1944.[37]

Between the sinking of *Cyclops* and 31 January no fewer than forty-six merchantmen were lost in the North Atlantic, of which forty had been sailing independently west of 40W, mostly off the American coast. February saw sixty-five ships lost in American waters (the total for the entire North Atlantic was seventy-one), rising to eighty-six in March with another sixty-nine going down in April.[38] The reduction in April when, according to the Admiralty account, seventy-five ships were sunk, six more than Macintyre notes, was not due to any countermeasures but to 'the melancholy expedient of curtailing sailings' and a reduction in U-boat numbers in the area.[39] April also saw the first U-boat sunk in American waters when, on the 14th, *U-85* was caught in shallow water in early-morning darkness off Cape Hatteras, North Carolina, by the USS *Roper*.[40] Engaged with gunfire the boat remained on the surface. When her commander gave the order to abandon ship, perhaps half the crew took to the water before she started sinking. All died when *Roper* dropped eleven depth charges on the stricken boat.[41]

The toll of merchant shipping rose again in May with 111 ships sunk, followed by another 121 in June. Then, almost as suddenly as it had begun, the havoc was over. In July the loss rate was nearly nothing with 'almost total immunity in the areas where previously the sea had been littered with burning and sinking ships'.[42]

One simple factor caused this great change: convoys had been introduced from Canada to the Gulf of Mexico. U-boats now worked mainly at night, spending their days on the bottom, using their high surface speed to catch their targets, chosen to obtain the best possible tonnage return; shortage of torpedoes meant that ships were often gunned. A high percentage of tankers went up in flames and people in coastal towns could watch ships sinking, burning and exploding. Almost nightly battles kept them awake, and their hospitals filled with maimed and burned survivors.[43]

Even while Roosevelt was deploying US vessels as convoy escorts in his 'undeclared war' against Germany, shipping along America's east coast had been unmolested. Now it had become a war zone with every ship, especially tankers, a target. It seemed that the US Navy had ignored the lessons of the First World War, when the importance of convoy had been learnt at such terrible cost, and the experience so far in this war of the British. The Royal Navy's experience in modern anti-submarine warfare, gained at great cost since 1939, had been made available freely to the United States Navy. Thus it seems that the events of early-1942 and the scale of German success in Operation PAUKENSCHLAG ought never to have happened. Not only were those losses tragic, they were avoidable, but no steps had been taken to institute a convoy system on America's eastern seaboard, 'along which ran the densest and most valuable stream of shipping in the world ..., carrying cargoes of cotton, sugar, oil, iron, steel and bauxite'.[44]

Responsibility for the failure to begin convoys when U-boats first appeared in American waters rested with Admiral Ernest King. Commander of the Atlantic Fleet before being promoted to Commander-in-Chief US Fleet, King was subsequently also appointed Chief of Naval Operations. However, the official historian of the United States Navy in the Second World War, Professor Samuel Eliot Morison, does not hold King responsible for this failure. Indeed, Morison, while outlining the debates leading to the introduction of convoys, notes that Admiral Adolphus 'Dolly' Andrews, commanding the Eastern Sea Frontier, 'Knowing that a convoy without adequate protection is worse than none ... decided that convoys were *then* inadvisable'.[45] *Then* was February to April 1942. However, Andrews oversaw a partial convoy system dubbed the 'Bucket Brigade' with ships steaming from port to port during daylight hours and taking refuge in harbours at night; these had a makeshift escort of local craft of little value. When Andrews had seven Atlantic Fleet destroyers assigned in February he used them not to protect convoys but to patrol the sea lanes and hunt for U-boats that had betrayed their positions by sinking merchant ships. Not surprisingly, these tactics proved fruitless.

Had Andrews' meagre forces been used to escort convoys, however 'inadequately', 'experience elsewhere shows that a U-boat would have been unlikely to sink more than one or two ships, probably at the expense of most of her torpedoes. The Admiral's contention that a "convoy without adequate protection is worse than none" cannot therefore be accepted.'[46]

The United States found itself short of aircraft and surface ships, due to the heavy commitment in the Pacific and so, in February, two dozen Royal Navy anti-submarine trawlers were sent to assist under US command and 'These rugged little coal-burners, manned with tough, aggressive former merchant seamen, were a great help in the Eastern and Gulf Sea Frontiers'. Ten corvettes were handed over to the US Navy.[47] However, the RAF refused to release to the US some American-built bombers that were ready to be flown to Britain. The US Navy and Army Air Forces included modern aircraft, such as the Catalina, in their squadrons although there were also many obsolescent machines, including the Douglas B-18 Bolo, a bomber based on the DC-2 airliner; two B-18s at Miami were described as 'practically falling apart'.[48] (Some B-18s also served with the Royal Canadian Air Force, where they were known as Digbys.)

As well as striking against the Americans, U-boats were attacking Britain as many of the ships sunk off the US coast were bound for, or carrying cargoes destined for, the UK. This was especially true of tankers since much of Britain's oil came from the Americas. With the Mediterranean closed, oil from the Persian Gulf had to be transported around the Cape of Good Hope, facing interdiction from Japanese ships and submarines in the Indian Ocean, as well as German and Italian boats in the South Atlantic. The Japanese had occupied Borneo and the Dutch East Indies, stopping all oil from those sources. Britain had to rely on oil from the west: tankers carried supplies from Aruba, Curaçao, and the Gulfs of Mexico and Venezuela. All this fuel passed out in a 'stream of tankers ... [from] the Caribbean and Gulf of Mexico and up the east coast of the United States before voyaging across the Atlantic in convoy'.[49] Should the U-boats sever that critical lifeline at or close to its source, then they could gift victory in the Battle of the Atlantic to the Axis. Hitler never recognized that possibility.

The onslaught in the Caribbean reduced in scale during March due to a shortage of the larger U-boats, since only the Type IXs could operate there without support. Attacks off the US coast continued until the convoys began, while the introduction of *Milchkühe* allowed Type VIIs to work in the Caribbean. In mid-May the first convoy ran between Hampton Roads and Key West but it took time for the system to become fully effective and losses rose in June to over 600,000 tons, the highest monthly figure until then. As convoys and countermeasures became more effective, U-boats moved to areas where convoys were less likely, such as the Gulf of Mexico and the Caribbean. (One even ventured to the Gulf of St Lawrence, torpedoing two ships; another mined Chesapeake Bay.)[50]

Eventually the American convoy system became so sophisticated that it was possible for a ship to sail under escort from the UK to New York and thence to the oil ports in the Gulf of Mexico or the Caribbean. But the U-boat offensive off the Americas, the 'second Happy Time', saw huge losses of merchantmen: between 12 January and mid-July 1942 the Allies lost 495 ships, totalling over 2,500,000 tons. Of that total, more than a million tons represented tankers, of which 142 were lost. In the first seven months of 1942, the *U-bootwaffe* lost thirty-three boats;[51] the Admiralty claimed forty-two German and Italian boats lost from all causes.[52]

Operations off the Americas had another outcome. Mexico and Brazil declared war on Germany. Mexico's declaration followed the sinking of two tankers carrying oil to US ports. The *Potrero del Llano* was sunk off Fowey Rocks near Miami on 13 May by Suhren in *U-564*, the *Faja de Oro* on its return

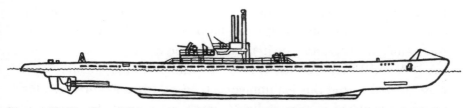

Figure 12: The Type IX long-range U-boat, of which 193 were commissioned. The most successful of these were the IXBs but only fourteen were commissioned.

voyage from Marcus Hook, Pennsylvania to Tampico.[53] Both were sailing under the Mexican flag and *Potrero del Llano* 'was brilliantly illuminated', indicating clearly her neutral status.[54] Suhren makes no mention of whether the tanker was illuminated when he attacked, simply listing her with two other vessels 'to name but a few'.[55] The Mexican government declared war on Germany on 1 June.

Dönitz pays much more attention to Brazil than Mexico in his *Memoirs*. Brazil had been friendly towards Germany until 27 January 1942 when she broke off diplomatic relations. Between then and April U-boats sank seven Brazilian ships. Dönitz considered that they were justified in so doing 'under the rules of the Prize Ordinance' as captains were unable to establish their neutral identity and the blacked-out ships had been following zig-zag courses, with 'some of them armed and some painted grey' while none had carried any flag or sign of neutral identity.[56]

Dönitz further claims that Brazilian ships began mounting guns until 'their whole merchant navy was armed', prompting an OKM order that South American ships known to be armed would be attacked without warning, except for Argentinean and Chilean vessels. In late-May Brazil announced that Brazilian aircraft had attacked U-boats, and would continue doing so. Since the Brazilians had initiated a state of undeclared war, U-boats were permitted to attack Brazilian-flagged vessels from 4 July 1942.[57] On 15 June Hitler agreed with Raeder that 'a real U-boat blitz against Brazil' would be launched and ten boats were despatched in early-July, accompanied by *U-460*, a *Milchkuh*, which allowed the boats to remain longer on station. Brazil's formal declaration of war was made on 22 August.[58] Roskill's summary puts Dönitz's account into a broader perspective: although Brazil had shown herself favourably disposed to the Allies,

> the Germans brought its active hostility on themselves by typically callous actions. Brazilian ships had been sunk by U-boats at various times since the beginning of 1942, and tension had been rising. But on the 16th and 17th of August 1942 *U-507* sank five in rapid succession close off Bahia, and this led immediately to a declaration of war. This may be considered an outstanding example not only of the Germans' political ineptitude, but of their lack of strategic insight.[59]

The Brazilian government had earlier – 11 December 1941 – allowed the US Navy to station flying boats at Natal while the Brazilian navy had co-operated with the US Navy before the German attack. After the declaration of war, Brazilian forces worked even more closely with their US counterparts and Brazilian naval officers received training in anti-submarine warfare in the United States while an attack trainer was provided for both navies in Recife; suitable vessels were donated to the Brazilian navy by the United States. Brazil later sent an expeditionary force, an infantry division, to Italy where it served as part of Fifth (US) Army; a Brazilian air force fighter squadron also served there under USAAF command. For her part, Mexico provided a fighter squadron to support USAAF operations in the Pacific war.

During the sustained campaign in the western Atlantic and Caribbean, the offensive against Atlantic convoys continued on a much-reduced scale under less-experienced commanders. With better countermeasures and more escort ships with well-trained crews, the U-boats were largely ineffective, markedly so during March when nineteen ocean convoys reached the UK without losing a single ship; 450 ships had sailed in those convoys. Three U-boats had been lost during the month, including *U-587* to ships of B2 south-west of Ireland.[60]

The loss of *U-587* was particularly significant. Korvettenkapitän Ulrich Borcherdt's Type VIIC was returning from operations off Canada, where it had sunk five ships, when convoy WS17, a fast troop convoy outbound to North Africa and India (it would split into WS17A and WS17B at Durban), was sighted. Borcherdt reported the convoy's location but his signal was detected and his position fixed by the escort. HMS *Leamington*, detached to attack the U-boat, passed it by but, on her return, spotted *U-587* which had just made a second radio report. With HM Ships *Aldenham*, *Grove* and *Volunteer*, *Leamington* attacked with depth charges and *U-587* was sunk, becoming the first boat detected and fixed by onboard HF/DF.[61]

Two U-boats lost in March were sunk in the Barents Sea, one by German mines and the other by HMS *Sharpshooter*. *U-585* and *U-655* had deployed against convoys to Russia, the *U-bootwaffe*'s main effort after the American offensive. Convoys to Russia had begun in August 1941, following the German invasion of the Soviet Union. Although the first was codenamed

Operation DERVISH, subsequent convoys were numbered in the PQ (outbound) and QP (return) series until September 1942 and in the JW (outbound) and RA series from December 1942 until 1945. Since evasive routeing was impossible due to the ice barrier, and there was no darkness during the summer months, protection for the convoys became a task for the Home Fleet. U-boat operations were difficult, again due to the ice, but there was also a threat from surface ships, especially the battleship *Tirpitz* and battle-cruiser *Scharnhorst*, both based in Norway, as well as from the Luftwaffe. All this led to Russian convoys being escorted by capital ships of the Home Fleet, usually supported by a fleet carrier cruising between Iceland and Spitzbergen to provide air cover. Two RAF Hampden torpedo-bomber squadrons were stationed in northern Russia, on call to attack German surface ships, while a flight of Catalinas was also deployed to a Russian base for anti-submarine operations.

A new anti-submarine weapon, a forward-firing spigot mortar, was fitted to some escort ships in January 1942. Known as Hedgehog because of its spiky appearance with twenty-four 'bristles' slanted forwards at 45 degrees, it fired a salvo of twenty-four small bombs ahead of an attacking ship.[62] A weapon on the same principle, known as a howitzer, had been developed during the First World War, but had fired only a single large charge. The idea was to overcome a disadvantage of the depth charge, an attacking ship losing contact before it was directly above the target as it came within asdic's minimum range. This resulted from the merging of the outgoing sound pulse and return echo, which meant that depth charges would be fired when the ship was 'blind'. U-boat commanders became skilled at making sharp movements during this 'dead time'. One way to overcome the problem was for escorts to operate in pairs, with one maintaining asdic contact to ensure that the second could make an accurate attack. Since this was not always possible operationally, Hedgehog was devised.

Lieutenant Commander Evelyn Chavasse, Senior Officer of B6 and captain of HMS *Broadway*, was impressed by Hedgehog.

This weapon obviously had great advantages over depth charges dropped from the stern (which we also carried), and as far as I know,

Jerry never rumbled to the idea of our lobbing bombs *ahead* at them, instead of making the old-fashioned type of attack, in which the attacking ship had to pass, with noisily threshing propellers, over the U-boat, giving it a very good chance of dodging, before the depth charges were dropped. With the Hedgehog or the [later] Squid, they never knew what hit them.[63]

The weapon, developed by the Directorate of Miscellaneous Weapons Development, was based on the Army's Blacker 'Bombard'. From the inventive mind of Lieutenant Colonel Stewart Blacker of the Royal Artillery, it was adapted for shipborne use by Major Millis Jefferis' team which had introduced the Bombard. Hedgehog's bombs were fired in an arc, to land in an ellipse some 120 by 140 feet across and about 250 yards ahead of the ship. Initially on a fixed mounting, a gyro-stabilized mounting was later introduced to prevent accuracy being affected by pitching and rolling.[64]

Hedgehog was 'ripple fired' from four cradles, each having six launcher spigots. The firing sequence ensured that all the bombs would land at much the same time, with minimum stress on the mounting, obviating the need for deck reinforcing. Bombs exploded only on contact so that an unsuccessful attack did not hide a submarine from asdic as with an unsuccessful depth-charge attack. Following a depth-charge explosion, it could take some fifteen minutes before the sea settled sufficiently for asdic to again become effective. Nor did Hedgehog bombs need to be set for depth. As the submarine commander had no warning of an attack, he had no time for evasive manoeuvres. One or two direct hits could sink a U-boat, whereas many depth charges were needed to inflict damage sufficient to do so; a depth charge exploding some distance from the target had much of its energy absorbed by the water between it and the boat.[65] (Some 240 depth charges were dropped without success on *U-427* by two escorts on 29 April 1945.)[66] Hedgehog's disadvantages were few: unlike depth charges it could not cause cumulative damage, and did not have the same psychological effect on a submarine crew as a depth-charge attack.

Although 'a weapon of precision and a great advance on the depth charge' it took time for crews to gain confidence in Hedgehog. In the meantime another major technological development was being fitted to ships, a new and much more effective radar system, based on the work of British physicists John Randall, Harry Boot and James Sayers, who had developed the cavity magnetron. This allowed the production of centimetric radar and more accurate direction of the detecting beam by a small paraboloid reflector. On 21 February 1940 the equipment had been tested and GEC had produced the first sealed magnetrons by June. These were also suitable for aircraft, as we have seen, but first priority for an airborne radar remained on equipment for night-fighters and development was concentrated on a 10-centimetre AI set.[67]

However, the new development came to the attention of the Royal Navy and two officers, Captains B. R. Willett and C. E. Horton, were given a demonstration in the autumn that showed that the ground-based experimental equipment could track ships. Trials with HM Submarine *Usk* followed on 11 November in which the submarine was tracked at seven miles. After fine tuning of the equipment and defining the antennae, a cylindrical paraboloid section was arrived at for installation on ships with the first fully-engineered 10-centimetre set, Type 271 radar, installed in the corvette HMS *Orchis* by March 1941.[68] Sea trials in April indicated that the radar could detect a surfaced submarine at 4,000 to 5,000 yards, between two to three miles; the periscope of a submerged boat was detected at distances between 1,100 and 1,500 yards. By July twenty-five corvettes were equipped with Type 271 and by the end of the year 100 sets had been produced and fifty ships equipped. On 16 November the sinking of *U-433* east of Gibraltar by HMS *Marigold* was attributed to the new radar which, by May 1942, was fitted in 236 ships.

Although 10-centimetre radar for use in aircraft, AI Mark VII, entered service in night fighters in March 1941 it was August before the fully-engineered AI Mark VIII followed. However, development of the ASV version was slow, even though trials against HM Submarines *Sea Lion* in April 1941 and *Sokol* in August had shown its effectiveness. Not until December was an experimental set flown. With Ferranti working on the production version, known as ASVS, in summer 1942, it looked as if the new radar would soon be in Coastal Command service but Bomber Command's demands again took precedence and Ferranti was told, on 30 September, to stop work on ASVS. Why? A ground-mapping centimetric radar, H2S, was being developed for

Bomber Command. Similar to ASVS, H2S was closer to production and had been highly successful in trials. Problems remained, including whether to use a cavity magnetron or a klystron for microwave power, with fears that a cavity magnetron in a bomber would fall into German hands. The dilemma was resolved by the klystron simply not being able to produce the necessary power; the cavity magnetron had to be used. By December some two dozen four-engined bombers, Halifaxes and Stirlings, carried H2S. Bomber Command had once again helped deny Coastal a vital tool. It would be 1943 before ASVS, by then known as ASV Mark III, was operational.[69]

The fourth phase of the Battle of the Atlantic ended on 31 July 1942 by which time Allied navies were developing closer operational working practices. Morison notes that convoy escort duty in 1941–42 'did more to cement good feeling among the three Navies concerned, and their merchant marines, than years of speechmaking and good-willing.'[70]

US Naval Operating Base Londonderry was a busy terminus for what US sailors dubbed 'the Londonderry Ferry' (RN and RCN personnel called it the 'Newfie-Derry Ferry'). US ships had begun using Londonderry in January, escorting troop and merchant convoys. The first US soldiers to arrive in the UK arrived in Londonderry on 26 January from convoy NA1, of two British merchant ships and two Royal Navy escorts. Destroyers previously based in Iceland started using the base which 'was most welcome' in almost all respects, although Londonderry, 'a stronghold of strict Irish Presbyterians, offered bluejackets slight recreation on the Sabbath, but seemed like Cony Island after Reykjavik'. Compared with Iceland's barren wastes the Irish countryside was heaven. Repair facilities were also superior as Londonderry was already an important Royal Navy base, and the main British centre for anti-submarine training. American gunners found the British 'dome teacher', in which they were trained to use anti-aircraft guns in a planetarium-like setting, of great value. So, too, were the 'tame submarines' on which escort vessels practised day and night attacks. 'A destroyer's stay in port was so arranged that the last two days before sailing were given up to anti-submarine training. This system allowed time for upkeep and recreation and sent sailors out on escort duty with fresh knowledge of the actual sound and appearance of a submarine under various conditions.'[71]

Morison also noted a rapid improvement in air cover in early spring 1942. Commander Paul R. Heineman's report on HX183 in early April noted that 'air escort on both ends of journey was very satisfactory'. A US Navy aeroplane off Newfoundland had helped locate the convoy and provided information on ships, their course, speed and distance ahead, and also visibility, while almost continuous air escort was present on 12, 13 and 14 April, and reply, as well as signalling, were very prompt and effective.[72]

Of US Navy-escorted convoys that crossed the Atlantic in early 1942, only one suffered heavy loss. ONS67 (ON67 according to Morison), thirty-five ships in eight columns, left the UK for North America and picked up its ocean escort of the US Ships *Edison*, *Nicholson*, *Lea* and *Bernadou*, under Commander A. C. Murdaugh, south of Iceland. HMCS *Algoma*, from the local escort group, remained with the convoy, which included a rescue ship, the SS *Toward*. It was *Toward*, equipped with HF/DF, that picked up a U-boat's signal in the late afternoon of 21 February, following which the USS *Lea* searched along the bearing but returned less than an hour later without making contact. *Lea*'s search was too short, for at 3.05am next day two ships were torpedoed. *Nicholson*, the sole US ship with working radar, and *Toward* rescued survivors as the convoy continued. Two destroyers swept out to fifteen miles abeam and ten miles astern to keep any U-boats down. That night was uneventful, although the next proved the convoy was being shadowed.

Between 12.30 and 6.45am on the 24th two attacks were made and four ships torpedoed, two of which sank. Later that day *Toward* reported two suspicious signals on her HF/DF and *Lea* and *Nicholson* sped off along the bearing, the latter spotting two surfaced U-boats about fifteen to twenty miles off. Murdaugh signalled the Chief of Naval Operations for permission to disperse, but almost seven hours passed before permission was granted. The convoy then changed course by 68 degrees. *Edison* made a sound contact off the convoy's starboard front and sighted a diving U-boat. Depth-charge attacks were made but after *Edison* was back on station she spotted another boat, about 200 yards away; the boat dived before the destroyer could engage. No further contact was made but *Edison* patrolled fruitlessly between the convoy and where the boat had submerged for some hours. Eight ships, a total of 54,750 tons, were lost to a group of six U-boats; two were damaged.

No further attacks occurred but the escort had learned several important lessons: the value of radar for anti-submarine operations; the need for active, aggressive patrolling; the urgent need for a definite doctrine for depth-charge attacks; and more effective training in following up underwater sound contacts. Murdaugh's group had not lacked aggression, but his officers had been lacking in their attack technique. Experience and further training would improve and hone the skills of the US Navy groups with the 'tame submarines' at Londonderry helping the process.[73]

The presence of *Toward* merits elaboration. Since the institution of the convoy system the rear ships had been detailed to perform rescue work whenever possible. However, there were frequent instances of masters of other ships ignoring orders to remain with the convoy to aid stricken comrades. This led to further sinkings and additional loss of life since ships generally came to a standstill to bring survivors aboard. As a result, in 1941, special rescue ships were fitted out. Macintyre reminds us that this 'innovation' was 'actually a lesson from the First World War re-learnt'.[74] They sailed at the stern of convoys to be on hand to remain with a torpedoed ship to rescue survivors, staying in the danger area while the convoy took evasive action and sailed on. Since it was important to offer as small a target as possible, ships assigned to the task had to be 'small, handy and relatively fast', requirements met only by the small ships of the coastal companies, or railway company steamers, with passenger accommodation. Manned practically entirely from the Merchant Navy, they braved the worst winter gales of the North Atlantic, and were often in action with enemy aircraft. Until June 1945 twenty-nine rescue ships covered 2,250,000 miles on 796 convoy voyages, saving the lives of about 4,200 British and Allied seamen.[75]

As well as HF/DF equipment, rescue ships included accommodation for survivors, a Royal Naval surgeon and a well-staffed sick bay, plus new rescue gear, including a large net to pick up incapacitated survivors. *Toward*, which sailed with HX183, belonged to the Clyde Shipping Company and was the first rescue ship. She was followed by the SS *Rathlin* and then by another twenty-seven such ships. When rescue ships were not available their task could be assigned to a converted trawler or ocean-going tug.[76]

Commander Heineman, in his report on HX183 in April 1942, was very appreciative of the air cover provided. Outside the mid–Atlantic gap, where no aircraft could give adequate protection, HX183 had been supported off Newfoundland by US Navy aircraft from Argentia on the early stages of its journey. On the final leg Heineman noted the almost continuous air escort from 12 to 14 April. The convoy was not troubled by U-boats, something to which air support would have contributed. By this time, Allied air bases were established firmly in Newfoundland, Iceland, Northern Ireland and Scotland's Western Isles.

The US Navy operated flying boats and land planes from Naval Air Station (NAS) Argentia, which came into operation during 1941. Aircraft from NAS Argentia provided the first cover for HX183, and for many other convoys, while the ships remained within range. On the final three days of the convoy's transit, air cover would have come from any of a number of bases –Sunderlands from RAF Lough Erne, Hudsons from RAF Limavady, Liberators from RAF Nutts Corner and, possibly, Hudsons from RAF Tiree in the Western Isles, although No.224 Squadron only began moving in to Tiree on the 12th.

The Sunderlands at RAF Lough Erne (originally RAF Castle Archdale, a name re-adopted in January 1943) were operated by No.201 Squadron, which had arrived from Sullom Voe in the Shetland Islands in August 1941. At the time of HX183's journey, No.201 was the sole operational squadron at Lough Erne, the Catalinas of No.240 Squadron having left for the Far East in March. Lough Erne's aircraft were the closest of any Coastal unit to the north-western approaches. There was, however, one drawback to their location: to reach the Atlantic, they had to fly over a four-mile strip of land in County Donegal, in neutral Ireland. Since it was felt that de Valera's government might raise objections to this, an approach was made by the UK representative in Dublin, Sir John Maffey, for permission to cross both the short neck of land and the three miles of Irish territorial waters to reach their patrol areas. The alternative was a detour towards Lough Foyle, adding over 200 miles to every patrol and costing about two hours. The Irish government agreed and the 'Donegal Corridor' was born. Aircraft 'had to keep to the northern boundary of Rathlin O'Beirne Island, Carrigan Head, Saint John's Point and Pettigoe and to the southern boundary of Inishmurray and the south bank of Lough Melvin'. De Valera, a stickler for protocol, informed the German representative in Dublin of the Donegal Corridor Agreement, but 'made it clear that the flight path was to be used only for air–sea-rescue missions for planes or vessels in distress, regardless of their country of origin'.[77] Needless to say, the Germans were aware of its true purpose. (The corridor is commemorated by plaques on Ballyshannon Bridge, in County Donegal, and at Belleek, in County Fermanagh.) The Irish government also permitted an air–sea-rescue vessel, HM Trawler *Robert Hastie*, to be stationed in Killybegs harbour in Donegal. Strangely, no similar agreement was sought for aircraft from airfields in County Londonderry which often flew over County Donegal.

While Heineman was impressed with the aerial support given to HX183, Coastal Command's chiefs and the Royal Navy were concerned about the command's strength. With the appointment of Air Marshal Arthur Harris as AOC-in-C of Bomber Command on 23 February 1942 even more problems were in store. Harris, with a single-minded belief in the efficacy of strategic bombing and almost virulent opposition to any dilution of the bombing effort, saw the provision of four-engined bombers to Coastal Command as a dilution; he even described the command as an obstacle to victory.

When Bowhill handed over to Sir Philip Joubert in June 1941 the strength of Coastal Command stood at thirty-five squadrons with 582 aircraft, about twice the number on 3 September 1939. However, the real indicator of effective strength was the number of aircraft ready for operations on any day; this was only about half that figure of 582 machines. Bowhill had argued for new types: Mosquitoes to replace Hudsons for operations off the enemy coast; Beaufighters to supersede Blenheims, and true long-range machines for anti-submarine warfare to replace the mix of Hudsons, Whitleys and Wellingtons in service, all of which were stop-gaps.[78] The true situation was even worse: front-line strength owed much to 'the loan of seven squadrons from other commands, with aircraft unsuited to the maritime role, and with a daily average availability of 298 aircraft'.[79]

On assuming command, Joubert re-assessed the command's needs, leading him to state a requirement for 838 aircraft at home and in the Atlantic, to include all purposes: anti-invasion reconnaissance and strikes against enemy shipping, maritime reconnaissance and anti-submarine warfare.[80] These were to be disposed in sixty-three and a half squadrons.[81] The response was disappointing. In October Churchill proposed transferring Coastal Command's bombers to Bomber Command. When Sir Dudley Pound made his objections known, the prime minister postponed a decision until the new year. Roskill writes that 'All the new long-range bombers were meanwhile being allocated to Bomber Command [while] prospects for deliveries of new flying boats ... were also very bad.'[82] To add to the Admiralty's and Joubert's frustration, the Air Ministry then set its face against the expansion scheme.

In January 1942 Admiralty concerns about Coastal Command's effectiveness were increasing. The daily number of aircraft ready for operations had reduced still further, to about 156, and Joubert renewed efforts to obtain modern long-range machines. On 1 December 1941 the effective strength was eighteen Catalinas, nine Sunderlands, twenty Whitleys and 170 Hudsons – plus 120 strike aircraft (twenty Beaufort bombers, forty Beaufighters and sixty Beaufort torpedo-bombers) as well as sixty Blenheim long-range fighters.[83] However, the Chief of the Air Staff, Air Chief Marshal Sir Charles Portal, another firm believer in strategic bombing, believed that all four-engined bombers should go to Bomber Command.

> Plainly the clash between the rival purposes of bombing Germany or helping to sink the U-boats and to bring the convoys safely home had now reached a point where the matter had to be weighed and decided by the Cabinet and the Defence Committee.[84]

The dispute continued, although in January 1942 No.220 Squadron began converting to the American four-engined Boeing B-17 Fortress. Bomber Command had operated some B-17s as daylight bombers but found them unsuitable and the remaining Fortresses were handed over to Coastal. No.220 became operational from its new base at RAF Nutts Corner on 29 April 1942. More Fortresses would follow.

In late-1941 the Royal Navy had suffered severe losses in all theatres, including the new Far Eastern theatre when HM Ships *Repulse* and *Prince of Wales* had been lost to Japanese naval bombers in December. As maritime operations stretched across the globe, with new commitments such as the Russian convoys, combating the Japanese navy in the Indian Ocean and the increasing pace of operations in the Atlantic, the early months of 1942 became some of the most tense and worrying of the war. Pound commented in March, 'if we lose the war at sea we lose the war'. Amidst all the strain and worry, Admiralty thinking turned to one factor where, it seemed, some immediate improvement might be expected: obtaining more long-range aircraft for Coastal Command while 'accepting the inevitable decline in our bombing offensive against Germany'.[86]

An Air Ministry paper to the Cabinet in March started what Pound called 'The Battle of the Air', a months-long tussle between Admiralty and Air Ministry over allocating long-range aircraft. The Admiralty argued that if merchant shipping losses, especially in tankers, caused overall tonnage available to fall beneath the minimum needed to sustain essential imports then the United Kingdom would lose the war. It pointed out that the Americans were then suffering 'frightful losses' in tankers. In response the Air Ministry agreed with the Admiralty estimate of its need for long-range aircraft, accepting that it was 'incumbent on us to do our utmost to meet'. Indeed, the airmen stated that 'provided deliveries from American production reached the planned totals, they would all be met by the end of the year'.[87] However, this meant that Coastal Command would remain very much understrength in such aircraft for the first half of 1942.

> The Admiralty's needs would, therefore, be met 'in quantity though not in time'. This was perhaps rather chilly comfort to the department which was responsible for protecting the country's merchant shipping, and knew that it was disappearing at a rate which would render it inadequate within a very definite period of time. The help of the RAF might well be coming. But would it come in time?[88]

The Air Ministry would not transfer bombers to long-range maritime reconnaissance duties until they were fitted with radar, without which they would be ineffective. However, prioritizing Bomber Command's H2S over ASVS was causing the shortage of radar sets. In the meantime, the Air Ministry considered that Bomber Command's most important contribution to defeating the *U-bootwaffe* was bombing German industrial centres.

In March Coastal lost three precious squadrons of Catalinas on transfer to the Indian Ocean to protect shipping against Japanese attack. With a trickle of B-17 Fortresses and B-24 Liberators arriving under Lend–Lease, discussion in London focused on their allocation. The unfortunate Joubert found himself being 'kicked by the Admiralty for not asking enough and blamed by the Air Ministry for demanding impossibilities'. The argument even grew to include the War Office. Harris' arrival as AOC-in-C Bomber Command did nothing to alleviate the situation since he claimed all four-engined aircraft as his own; in spite of this, Bomber Command made little use of the Fortress or Liberator, with those that did serve with it used for electronic warfare duties; most Liberators were transferred to the Middle East and Mediterranean as bombers.

While this argument continued, Coastal Command patrolled the ocean. New airfields were coming into use: in June No.220 Squadron with its Fortresses moved to RAF Ballykelly in County Londonderry from Nutts Corner; No.206 Squadron formed with Hudsons at RAF Benbecula in the Western Isles at the end of June; RAF Killadeas in County Fermanagh – part of the planned US Naval Air Station – became operational as a Coastal Command station in July but was home to a training unit; and RAF Tiree opened for operations in April.

In the first seven months of 1942 the *U-bootwaffe* lost thirty-three boats, including twelve in July, the same number as in the first sixteen months of the war and only two fewer than in 1941. Thus the year had not been a good one for the U-boats, although the successes of the second 'Happy Time' provided a counterbalance. Worse was to come; the toll for the year rose to eighty-six boats, more than between 3 September 1939 and 31 December 1941. There was 'increasing anxiety' during the first half of 1942, in spite of the successes off the American coast, and Dönitz felt that 'irretrievable time had been lost'. After almost thirty months of war, the *U-bootwaffe* had only a small fraction of the boats needed to achieve the necessary rate of sinking of Allied merchantmen. U-boat strength remained far short of what Dönitz had demanded in 1939.[89]

There had been problems with completing new U-boats and training crews, due largely to the extremely cold winter months of 1941–42, during

miral Sir Percy Noble forged
e weapon that defeated the
bootwaffe. (*UK Government
icial/public domain*)

Efficient and ruthless,
Grand Admiral Karl Dönitz
commanded the *U-bootwaffe*
and, later, the Kriegsmarine.
(*UK Government official/public
domain*)

Sir Max Horton accepted the
surrender of the *U-bootwaffe*.
(*UK Government official/public
domain*)

miral Leonard Murray,
in-C Canadian North-West
antic, the only Canadian
eatre commander of the war.
ARA)

Fleet Admiral Ernest King, the
US Navy's chief, who transformed
command and control of US
Navy anti-submarine operations.
(*NARA*)

ptain Rodger Winn's
derstanding of the
bootwaffe made him one of
e most important figures in
e Battle. (*UK Government
cial/public domain*)

Captain Philip Ruck-Keene,
NOIC, Londonderry, identified
and opened the westernmost
escort base, on the River Foyle,
in 1940. (*Author's collection*)

Commander James D.
'Chummy' Prentice did much
to shape Royal Canadian Navy
anti-submarine and escort
doctrine in 1941-42. (*NARA*)

Air Marshal Sir Frederick Bowhill, AOC-in-C Coastal Command, 1937-41, a former merchant seaman. (*UK Government official/public domain*)

Air Marshal Sir Philip Joubert de la Ferté initiated operations against U-boats crossing the Bay of Biscay. (*UK Government official/public domain*)

Air Marshal Sir John Slessor intensified the Battle of the Bay (*UK Government official/public domain*)

Air Chief Marshal Sir William Sholto Douglas, the final wartime AOC-in-C Coastal Command. (*UK Government official/public domain*)

Squadron Leader Terence Malcolm Bulloch developed new tactics to attack U-boats. (*Ulster Aviation Society, via Ernie Cromie*)

Commander Peter Gretton, commander of B7 escort group was one of the Royal Navy's most successful U-boat hunter (*Author's collection*)

Captain Donald Macintyre commanded B5 escort group which accounted for *U-100* and *U-99*, commanded by Schepke and Kretschmer. (*UK Government official/public domain*)

Commander Evelyn H. Chavasse, commander of C2 escort group, claimed the first sinking of a U-boat by Hedgehog. (*Author's collection*)

A convoy assembles in Bedford Basin, Halifax. A local escort will see it out into the Atlantic where an ocean escort will take over to shepherd the merchantmen across the ocean. (*Library & Archives Canada, MIKAN 3194308*)

eath and destruction: orpedo finds its target d another merchant ip is sunk. (*NARA*)

Force multiplier: extending the Royal Navy jetty at Lisahally on the River Foyle in County Londonderry. The Londonderry/ Lisahally base, HMS *Ferret*, became the largest and most important for escorts with over 130 oceangoing ships at its peak. (*Author's collection*)

The backbone of the escort groups was the Flower-class corvette. Canadian-built Flower HMCS *Pictou* is escorting a convoy in this photograph. (*Ken Macpherson/ Naval Museum of Alberta*)

Initially described as twin-screw corvettes, River-class frigates were excellent escort ships. K428 HMS *Waveney* was commissioned in September 1942. Seven nations operated the 151 Rivers built. (*UK Government official/public domain*)

HMS *Skate*, a First World War veteran R-class destroyer, was the oldest destroyer used by the Royal Navy during the Second World War, which she survived, having seen extensive convoy escort service. (*UK Government official/ public domain*)

Commissioned in 1933, HMS *Duncan*, a D-class destroyer, saw considerable wartime service. After a refit, she joined B7 escort group under Peter Gretton and led the group when it was 'given a run' as a support group. *Duncan* is pictured steaming into Londonderry at the end of that 'run' on 5 November, having covered 6,700 miles, refuelled at sea six times and replenished her depth charges at sea. B6 sank three U-boats while supporting several convoys in which no merchantmen were lost. (*UK Government official/public domain*)

ae Rivers were followed by the ꜱch-class frigates, based on the ull of the River but with increased ꜱeer and flare. Their armament cluded the new Squid ahead-ᵣowing mortars. Up-to-date ꜱdar and HF/DF made Lochs, ch as K391 HMS *Loch Killin*, ꜳmidable opponents for the -*bootwaffe*. (*UK Government ficial/public domain*)

The US Navy introduced destroyer escorts (DEs) for convoy escort work. DE250, USS *Hurst*, an Edsall-class DE, made a dozen return crossings of the Atlantic without seeing any action. In 2014 this ship was still in service with the Mexican Navy as a training vessel. DEs supplied to the Royal Navy were classified as Captain-class frigates. (*Author's collection*)

HMS *Sabre* appears to be under tow in this image but was being refuelled from a tanker in the convoy she was escorting. Trials had proved the efficacy of this operation, thereby allowing escorts to remain with convoys for their entire passage. (*UK Government official/public domain*)

HMS *Western Isles* at Tobermory, the Royal Navy's training school for escort ship crews, was established by Vice Admiral Sir Gilbert Stephenson, the 'Terror of Tobermory'. Lord Mountbatten praised the school for its contribution to the Battle of the Atlantic by 'working up' green ships' companies into well-drilled crews. (*UK Government official/public domain*)

As well as HMS *Western Isles*, Western Approaches Training Unit (WATU) in Liverpool, brainchild of Captain Gilbert Roberts, made a vital contribution through developing tactics and training anti-submarine officers, some of whom are being trained at WATU in this photograph. (*UK Government official/public domain*)

aptain 'Johnny' Walker developed some of his own tactics, including the 'creeping attack' (p.217).
ommanding 2nd Support Group, Walker was the most successful anti-submarine officer. He died of
troke in July 1944. Bareheaded and wearing a duffel coat, he takes a bearing on the bridge of HMS
arling. (*UK Government official/public domain*)

om 1941 specially-equipped rescue ships were included in most convoys. A total of twenty-nine rescue
ips, such as that on station in this convoy, saved the lives of about 4,200 Allied seamen. (*Author's
'lection*)

RAF Coastal Command was an important element of the operational strategy to defeat the *U-bootwaffe*. Unfortunately, when war broke out the Command was the Cinderella of the RAF and had insufficient aircraft, and few suitable for the task. Some Supermarine Stranraer biplane flying boats, such as this machine of No.228 Squadron, remained in service and continued with operational units until early-1941. (*UK Government official/public domain*)

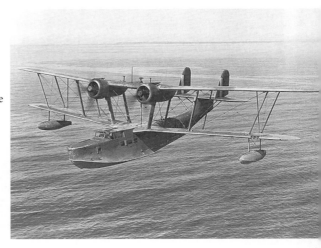

The Short Sunderland flying boat first entered service in 1938 but there were not enough when war broke out. Well-armed and with good endurance, the Sunderland played a valuable role in the Battle of the Atlantic but the RAF was frustrated by the failure of Short Brothers' factory in Belfast to meet their production schedule. This Royal Canadian Air Force Sunderland from RAF Castle Archdale is fitted with ASV II radar indicated by the antenna array atop the fuselage. (*Library & Archives Canada*)

The RAF's first Lockheed Hudsons were delivered in 1939. Some 200 had been ordered off the drawing board and proved a valuable addition to Coastal Command's inventory, being used for maritime reconnaissance and anti-submarine duties. In August 1941 a Hudson from Iceland attacked *U-570*, causing the boat to surrender. The Hudson, which also served with other Allied air forces, including the USAAF, was followed into service by the Lockheed Ventura. (*NARA*)

Consolidated Catalina over Gibraltar. Long-range aircraft were essential for Coastal Command and PBY-5 flying boats were ordered before the war but did not enter service until 1941. A Catalina from RAF Lough Erne in County Fermanagh spotted the *Bismarck* in May 1941, leading to the sinking of the German battleship. Catalinas, with longer range than Sunderlands, were invaluable in the U-boat war. The RCAF developed a very-long-range version; in Canadian service the Catalina was known as the Canso. (*UK Government official/ public domain*)

eing Fortress GR Is, unsuitable
Bomber Command operations,
re passed to Coastal and used for
ritime reconnaissance and anti-
marine duties. This Fortress I from
F Ballykelly is escorting a convoy.
K *Government official/public domain*)

Fortress GR IIs were also used by Coastal Command. ASV aerials are visible under the wings and in the nose of this No.206 Squadron machine on Benbecula. (*UK Government official/public domain*)

ckers Wellington bombers were also
ed by Coastal Command. This Mk
V of No.38 Squadron, fitted with
V III radar in the bulge under its
se, is escorting surrendered U-boats
the Northern Irish coast in 1945.
uthor's collection)

The greatest boon to Coastal
Command was the Consolidated
B-24 Liberator, a small number
of which, converted for anti-
submarine duties, equipped the
newly-re-formed No.120 Squadron
at RAF Aldergrove, County Antrim,
in June 1941. With ASV II, a six-
cannon gunpack under the fuselage
and extra fuel capacity, these had
such exceptional endurance that
they were dubbed 'very long range'
(VLR). Although many more
Liberators were supplied to Coastal
Command, none could equal the
range of the GR Is. (*Ulster Aviation
Society, via Ernie Cromie*)

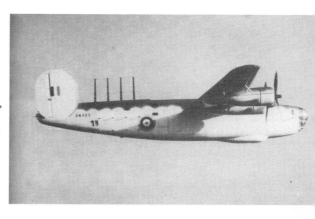

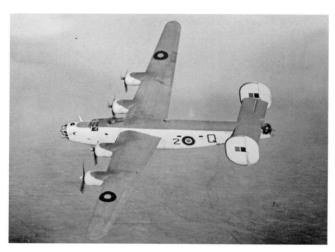

A Liberator GR V of No.86
Squadron from RAF Ballykelly. T
GR V was a long-range machine
but could not match the sixteen-
hour endurance of the GR I. It wa
equipped with the later ASV III
radar. (*Author's collection*)

The US Navy also operated
Liberators from UK bases. This
PB4Y-1 of VB-103, part of Fleet Air
Wing 7 (FAW-7), known as 'Calvert
& Coke', was lost on 12 November
1943 in a battle with *U-508*, which
was also lost with all hands. FAW-7
was based at RAF Dunkeswell in
Devon. The US Navy adopted the
white camouflage scheme developed
by Coastal Command's Operational
Research Unit under Professor
Paddy Blackett. (*NARA*)

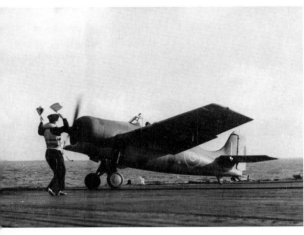

The ideal answer to providing air cover for convoys was accompanying aircraft carriers but this did not become possible generally until mid-1943. In 1941 proof of the value of such support came from the first escort carrier, HMS *Audacity*, on Gibraltar convoys. With the greater menace the Focke Wulf Condor, *Audacity* carried Grumman Wildcat fighters, then known as Martlets in the Fleet Air Arm. This Martlet of No.811 NAS had just landed on HMS *Biter* after shooting down a Ju290. (*UK Government official/public domain*)

combat U-boats British escort carriers and the smaller MAC-ships carried Fairey Swordfish bombers, equipped with ASV III and depth charges. The Swordfish later introduced rockets, launch rails for which may be seen under the lower wings of this aircraft. (*Author's collection*)

From its escort carriers the US Navy operated the Grumman TBF Avenger, the largest single-engine aircraft of the war. Equipped with ASV, Avengers could carry depth charges and the Mark 24 mine or homing torpedo. (*NARA*)

Left: The improvised nature of th[e] escort carrier is clear from this v[iew] of HMS *Archer*. A Long Island-class CVE, and sole example of t[he] class in the Royal Navy, she was commanded initially by Captain Conolly Abel Smith who later commanded 5th Support Group. *Archer* could carry up to fifteen aircraft. (*NARA*)

Right: As senior officer of 5th Support Group, Abel Smith commanded HMS *Biter*, seen from a Swordfish as it leaves the flight deck. With No.811 NAS embarked, her complement of aircraft was usually nine Swordfish and three Martlets/Wildcats. As well as convoy escort duties, *Biter* supported the Operation TORCH landings in North-West Africa in November 1942. (*UK Government official/public domain*)

Left: The MAC-ship *Rapana*, a tanker converted to carry three Swordfish as well as most of its cargo of oil. MAC-ships converte[d] from grain carriers could carry fo[ur] Swordfish in a hangar provided b[y] converting three holds. Unlike esc[ort] carriers, MAC-ships were manne[d] by Merchant Navy crews and were never Royal Navy ships. (*UK Government official/public domai[n]*)

Right: The USS *Bogue*, the first US Navy CVE, and name ship of her class. With her air group of Avengers and Wildcats and screen of destroyers, *Bogue* sank thirteen U-boats, earning a Presidential Unit Citation. After VE Day, she was transferred to the Pacific. (*NARA*)

6 June 1944 the hunter-killer group led by the USS *Guadalcanal*, commanded by Captain Daniel lery, detected *U-505* returning to base after an eighty-day patrol off West Africa. A combined ration by aircraft and destroyers led to *U-505* becoming the first enemy warship taken by the US Navy the high seas since 1815. *Guadalcanal* received a Presidential Unit Citation, the officer commanding boarding party the Medal of Honor and Gallery the Legion of Merit. *U-505*, subsequently operated by US Navy as the USS *Nemo*, is today on display at Chicago's Museum of Science and Industry. (*NARA*)

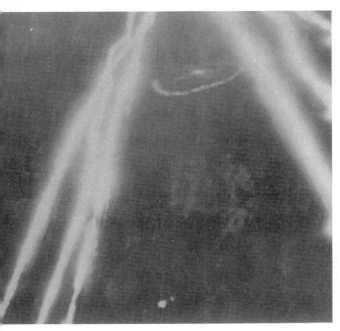

U-boat under attack by a Leigh Light-equipped Coastal Command aircraft. The introduction of this powerful searchlight to ASV-equipped machines eroded the sense of safety that U-boats had enjoyed during the hours of darkness. (*UK Government official/public domain*)

Depth charges being loaded on the Flower-class corvette HMS *Dianthus* in Londonderry. Better detonation pistols, more effective explosives and improved launch systems, made depth charges more deadly as the war progressed. (*Author's collection*)

Hedgehog was developed to supplement depth charges by firing an array of small mortars ahead of the ship. It had the advantage of not creating an explosion except through a direct hit and thus the boat being attacked had no idea that rounds had been fired. (*UK Government official/public domain*)

Crewmen from HMCS *Kootenay* watch as a Hedgehog salvo splashes into the water ahead of the corvette. (*Library & Archives Canada*)

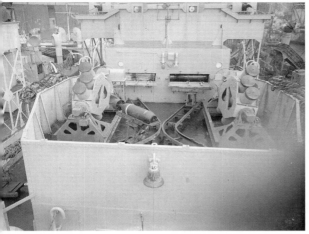

The next development was Squid, a multi-barrelled depth-charge mortar, a successful weapon that remained in service long after the war. This double-Squid installation is on HMS *Loch Fada*. HMS *Loch Killin* sank the first U-boat destroyed by a Squid – *U-333* on 31 July 1944. In fifty attacks, seventeen U-boats were sunk by Squid. (*UK Government official/public domain*)

10 September 1941 HMCS *ambly* achieved the Royal nadian Navy's first sinking of a boat, *U-501*. For their actions hat engagement, Mate A. F. kard (left) was Mentioned in spatches and Chief Engine om Artificer W. Spence received Distinguished Service Medal. *brary & Archives Canada, KAN 3576697*)

RAF Bomber Command and the USAAF carried out attacks on U-boat pens in France but only when construction was complete. Little damage was done, as shown by this image of the pens at Brest after a raid. (*NARA*)

Raids on shipyards where U-boats were constructed had more success, although off-site prefabricat[ion] reduced their effect. British soldiers patrol the shipyard at Hamburg in May 1945 with three Type X boats on the slips. (*UK Government official/public domain*)

This grave in Londonderry City Cemetery of an unknown sailor of HMS *Redmill*, killed when his ship was torpedoed by *U-1105* off Sligo Bay on 27 April 1945, is the final resting place of one of the last British seamen killed in the war against the U-boats. Coated in rubber tiles, *U-1105* was an early 'stealth' vessel, known as the 'Black Panther' to her crew. (*Author's photo*)

In the former Ebrington Barracks in Londonde[rry,] this statue of the Universal Sailor, commemorat[ing] all who lost their lives in the Battle of the Atlan[tic,] was unveiled by HRH Prince Michael of Kent, Honorary Rear Admiral of the Royal Naval Reserve, in May 2013. (*Author's photo*) which the Baltic ports and the southern part of the Baltic Sea froze over. This precluded any proper training while the shipyards were also affected by the cold, and production fell. Rather than twenty new boats becoming operational each month there were only thirteen on average for January, February and March. This did not improve with the spring, the average for April, May and June dropping as low as ten, a result of the lost training months. Only sixty-nine new boats entered service in the first six months of 1942, of which twenty-six were diverted to Norwegian waters and two to the Mediterranean.

With twelve boats lost in the Atlantic between January and June added to those diverted, the addition of sixty-nine new boats only strengthened by twenty-nine the force in the Atlantic. On 1 July Dönitz had 101 boats in the Atlantic, of which, on average, fifty-nine were at sea each day and forty-two in port. Moreover, of those at sea, only nineteen were on operations; the remainder were either sailing to operational areas or returning home. He was frustrated by the situation, especially it seems a 'request' from Hitler to divert a group to oppose a possible Allied landing in the Azores and Madeira in June. On this occasion OKM supported Dönitz and Hitler's request was withdrawn.

Dönitz's frustration is illustrated by an entry in U-boat Command's War Diary on 15 April 1942:

I am therefore of the opinion that tonnage must be sought in those localities where, from the point of view of U-boat operations, it can most readily be found, and where, from the point of view of keeping down our own losses, it can most easily be destroyed. It is infinitely more important to sink ships where and when we can than to sacrifice aggregate sinkings in order to concentrate on sinkings in any particular locality. Imports to America are just as important, in my view, as imports to Britain, and I therefore believe that the focal point of our operations must remain, as before, in the area off the east coast of America for as long as the strength of anti-submarine defences and the prospects of U-boat successes remain approximately as they are at the present moment.[90]

Dönitz's belief in a focused effort provides an interesting parallel to that of those in the Royal Navy who had argued for the convoy system.

In his favour in mid-1942, Dönitz had the fact that the Admiralty was routeing convoys by the shortest route along the great circle. He attributed this to 'British obstinacy' but when he wrote his *Memoirs* he knew that the true reason had been 'a dearth of escort vessels and of fuel oil'; there was real concern in Britain that stocks of fuel were reducing to danger levels. This routeing applied to transatlantic convoys and those to and from Sierra Leone which made the U-boats' task easier. One further reason for this may have been, as Suhren points out, an advantage the *U-bootwaffe* enjoyed at this time:

> During the trip to Florida we already had in use a code-machine (the 'Enigma') that was fitted with four rotors. It was superior to the previous three-rotor version, and caused the Allies a complete black-out for at least six months: in other words it made it impossible for them to read the coded messages ... exchanged between submarine command and the submarines themselves.[91]

This was the 'Shark' code, which Bletchley Park's cryptanalysts were working hard to crack. They received another fortunate gift in the form of a four-rotor Enigma machine recovered from *U-559* in the Mediterranean. On 30 October a Sunderland of No.230 Squadron had detected the boat on ASV but *U-559* had dived. However, ships of the 12th Destroyer Flotilla raced to the scene and bombarded the submarine's last-known location with depth charges. HMS *Petard* had an asdic return indicating that the boat was at a depth of 500 feet. Eventually, through using soap to delay the charges exploding, *U-559* was forced to surface and surrender; its crew, who had counted 288 explosions during their ordeal, were taken off. Since the crippled boat did not sink immediately, Lieutenant Anthony Fasson and two men, Able Seaman Colin Grazier and Boy Seaman Thomas Brown, swam across and began a search, recovering codebooks and a four-rotor Enigma machine. Unaware of the significance of their find, they passed these to men who had crossed in a whaler. Fasson and Grazier continued their search while Brown remained in the conning tower to make further handovers. Without warning, *U-559* sank. Brown jumped clear, but Fasson and Grazier were lost.

When the significance of their finds was realized Fasson and Grazier were recommended for the Victoria Cross but, since their actions were not in the *presence* of the enemy, each received a posthumous George Cross. Brown, who was only sixteen, received the George Medal. The codebooks included the boat's *Wetterkurzschlüssel* and *Kurzsignalheft*, which, with the new Enigma machine, were a boon to Bletchley's cryptanalysts, allowing them to work out the possibilities for the fourth rotor. By 13 December translated U-boat signals were again being passed to the Submarine Tracking Room. The advantage of the four-rotor Enigma had been removed.[92]

During 1942 the Allies had lost over 7.7 million tons of shipping worldwide including 5,471,222 tons in the North Atlantic. However, the renewed ability to decipher Enigma messages paid a dividend as that month saw the lowest losses in the North Atlantic during 1942, although worsening weather may have contributed. Even so, December's losses, at 262,135 tons and forty-six ships, was almost half of November's 508,707 tons and eighty-three ships.

Chapter Nine

Although 1942 had been the worst year for losses to U-boats, there had been developments that indicated a better future, although that was not clear at the time when too many advantages seemed to lie with the enemy. The Allies had achieved a series of victories since June that proved to be the pivot on which the war swung in their favour. The United States Navy's victory at Midway was first, followed by Eighth Army's at El Alamein in November, leading to the destruction of all Axis forces in North Africa the following May, and the defeat of Paulus' German Sixth Army at Stalingrad in February 1943. To these may be added the Battle of the Atlantic, even though its very worst months came in early 1943.

Losses in December 1942 would have been higher had it not been for a single Liberator of No.120 Squadron from Iceland. HX217 and SC111 were en route to Britain, on parallel courses about twenty-five miles apart when a U-boat spotted them on 1 December. The sighting was reported to U-boat headquarters, now moved to Paris to avoid attack by British commandos, and twenty-two boats were ordered to target HX217 which further observation showed on a more northerly course; faster convoys were considered to carry more valuable cargoes. On 7 December two Liberators were despatched from Reykjavik to provide air cover but one returned with engine problems. The other found the convoy and remained with it for six hours.

Next day, at 1.37am, *U-600* torpedoed and sank a straggler. Later that day, Terry Bulloch, commanding 120's Reykjavik detachment, took off in Liberator AM921, the machine that had suffered engine trouble the previous day, to escort HX217, although he had been flying for most of the past two days. On a sweep on the 6th (according to Bulloch's log this was on the 5th) he had encountered foul weather that forced a diversion to Northern Ireland, whence he returned on the 7th. Squadron Leader Desmond Isted was to follow in another Liberator. Bulloch's navigator, Michael Layton, a Canadian, the oldest member of his crew, was 'one of the few men whom the Bull trusted implicitly'. An outstanding navigator, Layton 'true to form, located HX217 without delay' as dawn broke. Bulloch began scanning for signs of U-boat activity while Ginger Turner concentrated on his ASV screen.[1]

At 11.30am Bulloch's remarkable eyesight detected a surfaced U-boat, picking out the firmer line of its wake from the many white slashes on the ocean while flying through a hailstorm. Bulloch, known as 'Hawkeye', called his crew to action stations, and dived to attack. Usually a U-boat crew spotted an aircraft first, but not in this case. As the boat began diving, the Liberator was in the final stages of its attack. In the bomb bay were eight 250lb depth charges, filled with Torpex, a new and more powerful explosive then coming into service. Bulloch chose to drop six charges, timed to fall with fifty feet between each.

The attack was a copybook one. All six depth charges were seen by the WOP/AG ... to explode ... around the U-boat just as it dived. Nos.3 and 4 apparently fell right alongside the fast disappearing grey hull as it slid under the waves with its stern protruding at an angle of about 30 degrees. Layton was also in a position to see well and with his usual precision had noted these details. If the hydrostatic fuses had triggered the firing pins at the pre-set depth (25 or 50 feet), then damage or destruction seemed assured. Almost at once there was visible evidence of this. A metal object, estimated by Layton to be about six feet in length, came hurtling into the air and rose to ... about 50 feet. ... After this had settled back ... with a big splash, further eruptions came from below. These were quite separate from the depth-charge explosions. A great upheaval of water, dome-shaped, rose to several feet, followed by a rapid spread of dark brown oil. Later still, the crew aloft saw pieces of yellow planking float to the surface and ... a large flock of gulls appeared wheeling around excitedly and diving down to feast upon something edible below.[2]

U-611 had been destroyed on its first operational patrol. Its commander, Kapitänleutnant Nikolaus von Jacobs' relative inexperience probably contributed to his fate.[3]

Bulloch's two remaining depth charges were expended shortly after this when two U-boats were spotted travelling on the surface about 300 yards apart some twenty miles from the convoy. They were trying to catch up with HX217 but had to dive on spotting the Liberator. One was quick to crash dive but the second, which appeared to be trailing oil, had only disappeared as AM921 attacked. Both depth charges fell about 200 feet ahead of the spot where she had dived and exploded 'just above where the conning tower was likely to have been'.[4] Another upheaval of water followed about fifty feet ahead of the first explosions but no evidence of damage was seen, or found by surface vessels – a corvette had confirmed the earlier kill. Nonetheless, two U-boats had been forced down where their speed was reduced well below the convoy's, and they became blind.

Although his depth charges were gone, Bulloch remained with the convoy since the presence of an aircraft would force any U-boat to submerge. And that is exactly what happened. A fourth U-boat was spotted and Bulloch once again went to action stations. With no depth charges left, he used his 20mm cannon, although the rounds could not penetrate the U-boat's hull but would have produced a frightening sound inside the boat. The cannon had just been reloaded when yet another U-boat was spotted and attacked, forcing it to crash dive. As if five boats were not enough, a sixth was spotted and engaged, the U-boat captains clearly having imagined themselves to be in an area where no aircraft were operating. There followed a seventh, and an eighth. By the end of his patrol Bulloch had sunk one U-boat, possibly damaged a second and forced six down.

When Isted relieved Bulloch, he tracked down another five U-boats. With ten depth charges onboard he unleashed nine on the first target and one on his third. The results were inconclusive but another five boats were removed from the equation. This was a unique episode in Coastal Command's history: the forcing down of twelve boats, and the sinking of another, contributed to the fact that no more than three ships were lost from HX217, only two of them actually in convoy: one was sunk in the early hours of the 8th while the second was sunk the following morning.[5]

Including the loss of the straggler, HX217 lost 20,229 tons.[6] Bulloch had given a convincing demonstration of the effectiveness of Coastal Command's aircraft. Until May 1942 the Command had sunk only nine U-boats but from June 1942 the picture changed considerably and, by May 1945, more than

200 boats had been destroyed by its aircraft. This episode also represented the conflation of several important factors.

One factor was the introduction of Torpex, 30 per cent more powerful than the Amatol used previously. Depth charges began to be filled with Torpex in April with the first reaching Coastal stations by the end of the month.[7] (Torpex was also used in Hedgehog warheads.) The depth charges were much improved and Coastal aircraft were provided with 250lb charges suitable for air dropping; with a 170lb bursting charge they fitted existing 250lb bomb racks. A new detonation pistol (Mark XIIIQ) allowed the charge to be set to explode at a depth of thirty-four feet. Ideally, this should have been twenty-five feet. Radio altimeters were on their way, and work on new bombsights was in progress while radio telephones (R/T) were being introduced for use between escorts and aircraft.

The recommendation for twenty-five feet as the ideal depth for an air-dropped depth charge to explode was the result of operational research, the speciality of a group of British scientists including such luminaries as Patrick 'Paddy' Blackett (later Lord Blackett), the 'father of operational research', Solly Zuckerman (later Baron Zuckerman) and Conrad Hal Waddington. They were among some 1,000 men and women conducting operational research in the United Kingdom during the war; the Army alone employed 200 operational research scientists.[8]

Blackett had worked for the Royal Aircraft Establishment at Farnborough where he established a team, the 'Circus', that helped reduce from over 20,000 in summer 1940 to 4,000 in 1941 the number of anti-aircraft shells needed to down a hostile plane.[9] General Sir Frederick 'Tim' Pile, GOC-in-C of Anti-Aircraft Command, had persuaded A. V. Hill to send Blackett to AA Command where he 'started ... an organization that eventually took over the scientific research of the Army'. Pile considered Blackett

an ideal man for the job. He spoke his mind clearly, and was always ready to admit the fact that the most desirable things sometimes may be inadvisable. He soon started Operational Research in a large way, and when he found that radar was too tricky for the ordinary man he began collecting all sorts of scientists, and a school was started at Petersham to train them. ...

> Blackett passed on from us to the Admiralty when the U-boat menace
> needed something doing to it.[10]

One of Bowhill's last significant decisions led to Blackett's transfer to the Admiralty. Some three months before leaving Coastal Command, Bowhill had brought Blackett in as Scientific Adviser, a move that 'was the beginning of the Command's long, imaginative and productive alliance with the world of science'.[11] Thus, when Joubert returned as AOC-in-C, he had the makings of the Operational Research Unit (ORU) that would initiate major and important changes in Coastal Command's operations. As well as continuing the campaign for more aircraft, especially VLR machines, and the introduction of centimetric radar, Joubert sought to improve the efficiency and effectiveness of the command and the ORU was a major element in so doing; not only Blackett but four Fellows of the Royal Society were to be associated with it – Sir John Kendrew, Professor Evan James Williams, Professor Conrad Hal Waddington and Professor J. M. Robertson.

Since research depends on the availability of relevant information and operational research on information about the roles and procedures of aircrew engaged against U-boats, the work of another individual, Captain Dudley Vivian Peyton-Ward RN, the Royal Navy's liaison officer at Coastal Command, was vital to the ORU's work. Joubert was only in post a short time when Peyton-Ward, in addition to his routine duties, began

> writing up each individual sighting and attack on U-boats as they took
> place, using every scrap of first-hand evidence obtainable and analyzing
> the probable result from all the data available. Whenever possible the
> attacking crews came to the Headquarters which enabled personal
> corroboration, discussion of detail and practical experience to be
> effected while the event was still fresh.[12]

Peyton-Ward thus produced much of the raw data needed by ORU. Collaborating with the Submarine Tracking Room, he continued his task until the war ended, becoming an authority on aircraft in anti-submarine operations. Not surprisingly, he also wrote, for the Royal Navy, an official history of the RAF in the maritime war.

Among ORU's results was the adoption of a new camouflage scheme for Coastal's aircraft. These had been finished in the scheme used for bombers, with upper surfaces in a pattern of dark green and dark earth and undersurfaces in 'night black', although the latter had been changed to 'sky' for Blenheim fighters, Sunderlands and other flying boats, in June and August 1940.[13] Even with sky undersides, the scheme did not provide effective over-water camouflage. ORU established that, for an ASV II-equipped aircraft, complete cloud cover was a major advantage, a finding that would, or should, have been obvious to all. It was then discovered that, unless the cloud base was low, a U-boat would have time to crash dive when an aircraft emerged from the clouds. As a Type VIIC needed at least twenty seconds to dive it could be well below the waves before an attack could be made.[14]

The new problem was to make the aircraft more difficult to see from ... the U-boat. After various experiments in camouflage it was discovered that plain white on all sides and undersurfaces of the aircraft gave a remarkable degree of invisibility in the cloud and sky conditions generally prevalent in northern latitudes. This white camouflage, with certain refinements resulting from scientific investigation, remained the standard colour of anti-U-boat aircraft throughout the rest of the war. Thus started in the summer of 1941 the familiar 'White Crows' of Coastal Command.[15]

Calculations showed that a white aircraft had a 30 per cent greater chance of catching a U-boat on the surface than one with the earlier camouflage scheme. Since concurrent improvements made it difficult to analyze the results of the camouflage change alone, there was no specific proof that the new scheme worked better but Blackett notes that ORU was confident that the 'White Crows' contributed to Coastal Command's improved rate of sinkings in the second half of 1942.[16] It was the realization that a U-boat needed only twenty seconds to dive to safety that led to the recommendation of a twenty-five-feet detonation for air-dropped depth charges. Blackett records that Professor Williams carried out this research work in 1941. Such charges had been set to explode at 100 feet on the basis that a U-boat could reach that depth in the two minutes between sighting an aircraft and an attack, but Williams spotted the fallacy underlying this belief through an analysis of attacks. A U-boat sighting an aircraft two minutes before the depth charges could be dropped would have been out of sight for so long when the attack was made as to eliminate almost completely any chance of success. On the other hand, should the boat have been caught by surprise with the attack emerging from cloud or rain, or coming under cover of darkness, there would be little doubt that it could be delivered *accurately* since the target would be either on the surface or submerging. Therein lay the problem of the existing procedure; the charges would detonate almost 100 feet below the boat, producing little more than discomfort for the crew. Peyton-Ward's work provided the data for Williams' work which showed that only attacks made on 'a still visible U-boat or within fifteen seconds of disappearance' had led to destruction of, or damage to, boats. Of boats attacked only 35 per cent had been wholly or partially visible when the charges were dropped; another 15 per cent had been out of sight for under fifteen seconds. About half of all attacks had been on almost invulnerable targets.

Adjusting detonation pistol setting to twenty-five feet would ensure a much more effective depth charge when used against a U-boat caught by surprise, classified as a Class A target; the U-boat with a two-minute warning could be ignored since any charges dropped against it would almost certainly be wasted.[17]

In spite of recent innovations, by September 1941 all that Coastal Command had to show for 'long weary hours of flying were the incalculable (but clearly substantial) 'Scarecrow' effects, *U-570* captured and three kills shared with surface vessels' plus an estimated ten or a dozen boats damaged badly in 245 attacks.[18] With air-dropped depth charges finally available, this discouraging picture called for further work by ORU to identify any fundamental changes that might be made in operational procedures to improve results.

When the French Atlantic ports had been taken over, Dönitz recognized their vulnerability to air attack. In an October 1940 meeting with Hitler, the dictator authorized constructing concrete shelters for the U-boats at their new ports. Days later Dönitz was visited by Dr Fritz Todt, the minister for armaments and munitions and head of the Todt Organization, to 'settle priorities, types and numbers of U-boat pens to be built in the various bases'.[19]

Work began at Lorient and la Pallice where, by the end of 1941, all boats were under shelter. The mammoth task was carried out in an 'astoundingly short space of time' with pens at Brest and St Nazaire complete by mid-1942 and those in Bordeaux finished not long after. This huge project was completed with, to Dönitz's surprise, virtually no interference from the British, who preferred to bomb German cities. Had the pens been attacked while under construction behind watertight caissons, much damage could have been done. 'Once the U-boats were in their concrete pens, it was too late.'[20]

That the pens were not bombed while under construction was one of the Air Staff's most serious errors. Once complete, it was too late to attack them; their thick reinforced concrete was immune to any bomb in Bomber Command's inventory. Middlebrook and Everitt describe the construction of the shelters as 'one of the finest investments the Germans made during the war'.[21] While considerations for French civilians' safety played a part in the failure to act while the pens were being built, in early 1943 the War Cabinet decided to bomb the towns housing the U-boat bases, and nearby industrial works, 'as a result of the recent serious increase in the menace of the U-boat operations'.[22]

Those raids reduced the residential quarters of the ports to ruins, but had no effect on the U-boat repair facilities. Only once did a heavy bomb all but penetrate the roof of a pen; but that was a roof that had yet to receive its planned reinforcement. Although the roof was damaged severely, there was no further damage to the pens.[23]

The first target was Lorient, which was hit on nine occasions in January and February and laid waste. U-boat operations were unaffected. St Nazaire suffered on the night of 28 February/1 March and again on two occasions in late March.[24] These raids served no strategic purpose and had no effect on U-boat operations. Had similar effort been put into bombing the pens as they were being built the result might have been more noticeable.

Although U-boats were safe in their pens 'they found themselves hard pressed by enemy aircraft as soon as they emerged into the Bay of Biscay'. With the many demands on the Luftwaffe from home defence to the Mediterranean to the Russian front, Göring's airmen had failed to gain command of the air in the coastal area off the bases, giving Coastal Command the opportunity to attack boats crossing the Bay.[25]

Joubert, keen that Coastal should undertake offensive operations, initiated an offensive in the Bay in June 1941. In the early stages of what became known as the First Bay Offensive there seemed to be few positive results from strengthened air patrols. While there may not have been sinkings, the U-boats were forced to cross underwater; when crossing at night they could do so on the surface as there was little chance of air attack. Although about three in four Coastal aircraft were fitted with ASV II, the majority of detections were visual. In theory the majority should have been ASV detections. During August and September seventy-seven U-boats were sighted, but only thirteen by ASV detection.

To examine what was wrong with ASV in its operational setting, Joubert formed a working party which found the main problem to be poor equipment serviceability. Since the equipment was a wartime creation, with the stress and pressure of time that implied, parts were often in short supply, as was test equipment. Moreover, no ground technician training programme existed while, in the aircraft, another set of problems pertained. Bulloch's ASV operator, Ginger Turner, was a *rarum avis* indeed: nobody really seemed to want to be an ASV operator and most who did so, usually the navigator or a wireless operator such as Turner, also had their usual roles. In addition, the operator's position was usually an afterthought, 'poorly designed and uncomfortable' and therefore not something to attract aircrew to the role. A Whitley ASV operator's position was midway down the cramped fuselage where he had to sit on 'the closed lid of the aircraft's lavatory'.[26]

Joubert acted quickly, initiating training programmes for ground technicians and aircrew, as well as improving the flow of spares and test equipment. The role of ASV operator became that of the wireless operator, with an additional crewman included to share the burden. Improving the ASV operator's position in aircraft was more problematical with existing machines, but the AOC-in-C ensured that 'those in future aircraft types would be much better'.[27]

Joubert's quick response was typical of his style of leadership, fitting in with the practice of 'Sunday Soviets' at the Telecommunications Research Establishment at Swanage where senior officers involved with the operational use of radar met scientists working on existing equipment and developing new systems. Other interested parties, including government ministers and junior officers who had to operate the equipment, also attended and 'on more than one occasion a senior officer had "his ears pinned back" by an over-enthusiastic junior'.[28] The Sunday Soviets helped bring the reality of operational service to the scientists, who could be hypnotized by their own subjects, and permitted users of the equipment to obtain helpful advice on getting the best from their systems. Senior officers also learned how new systems worked in harsh practice and of any organizational weaknesses. The improvements for ASV technicians and operators were a clear indication of the effectiveness of a system such as the Sunday Soviets, an information 'loop' with no counterpart in Kriegsmarine practice.

On 30 November 1941 Bletchley Park detected a U-boat outward bound in the Bay of Biscay. Having been told where to look, a Whitley of No.502 Squadron, from St Eval in Cornwall, made for the general area. The ASV operator detected a surfaced U-boat, *U-206*, at five miles, an attack was made, *U-206* was destroyed, the air-dropped depth charges performing as intended.[29] (However, Uboat.net ascribes the boat's loss to an air-laid mine in a British minefield, as does Nesbit.) This action, while Joubert's working party was at its studies, demonstrated what could be achieved with ASV, showing clearly how Ultra decrypts could be employed operationally. *U-206* was the first boat destroyed solely by a Coastal aircraft.

Mention has already been made of the nighttime sinking of a U-boat by a Fleet Air Arm Swordfish, of No.812 NAS, which occurred three weeks after the sinking of *U-206* and was also attributable to ASV detection. The victim was *U-451* which was trying to pass through the Straits of Gibraltar in darkness. When the signal was lost in sea clutter, the operator continued guiding his pilot on the existing heading until the boat's wake was spotted. *U-206* had also been heading for the Straits when 502 Squadron's Whitley found her.

This first offensive in the Bay of Biscay was continued until late in the year. Overall results were not as impressive as hoped for, especially as attacks were made in daylight. In the ninety-one days of the September–November period, aircraft flew a daily average of forty hours but reported only thirty-one sightings, resulting in twenty-eight attacks in 3,600 flying hours. In only five attacks was it considered that a boat had suffered damage sufficient to force its return to base.

December saw only four sightings, including three at night, prompting Peyton-Ward to note that this emphasized the need for an efficient method of night attack.[30] As ten U-boats were lost in December, it may be that the reduced number of sightings in the Bay was partly attributable to there being fewer boats.

The first Biscay offensive may have been short on tangible results in the shape of kills, but Dönitz emphasizes that it was on the journey across the Bay that 'the boats found themselves exposed to the greatest danger'. He believed that this was where the greatest concentration of hostile aircraft was and mentions 'constant air attacks' on the bases.[31] Although Joubert's offensive had not produced the hoped-for dividend, it had created a precedent that would be followed as the Battle of the Bay took on a life of its own. Coastal Command continued harassing U-boats in the Bay, although only two were damaged, for the loss of six aircraft, between 1 January and 31 May 1942 when 5,041 hours were flown.

In Chapter Seven we examined the development and operational use of the Leigh Light. At the time of the first Bay offensive the light was not in operational use and it was June 1942 before No.172 Squadron's Leigh Light-equipped aircraft began patrols. Formed at RAF Chivenor, North Devon, from the Leigh Light Flight,[32] the squadron had a handful of Wellingtons fitted with the new equipment and 'crews trained in the difficult and precise flying necessary to use the system'[33] and began operations with it on the night of 3/4 June, finding and attacking two U-boats.[34]

The first was a *Regia Marina* boat, *Luigi Torelli*, from la Pallice. Squadron Leader Jeaffreson Gresswell, who had taken part in the Leigh Light trials, was piloting Wellington VIII 'F' when his ASV operator picked up the boat at over six miles. The operating procedure was to lower the light and descend to 250 feet, switching it on a mile from the target. However, when the operator, Pilot Officer Triggs, did so, there was no sign of the boat. Adjusting the beam both up and down brought a fleeting glimpse of the

Luigi Torelli for Triggs and Gresswell. The Wellington was too high, the altimeter having been set on the basis of a forecast pressure that put the machine 100 feet higher than intended. Meanwhile, *Tenente di Vascello* Augusto Migliorini and his crew, assuming that any aircraft displaying such a bright light in the area was friendly, fired identification flares of red, green and white. These had exactly the opposite effect to that intended. Gresswell knew these were not Royal Naval identification signals – British submarines used floating candles. The Italian boat had signalled its exact position. A second attack was made, with the altimeter corrected, the light was switched on a mile from the target, the submarine was pinpointed, the nose gunner sprayed it with machine-gun fire and Gresswell dropped to sixty feet before releasing four 250lb depth charges at thirty-five-foot intervals.

The depth charges exploded beneath the *Luigi Torelli*, causing severe damage. With steering gear damaged, gyrocompass wrecked and a small fire onboard, Migliorini had no option but to return to France. However, he ran aground in fog on rocks and was towed off into a Spanish harbour which he had to leave within a day to avoid internment. Although Migliorini left for France, his boat's purgatory was not over. Crawling slowly off the coast, the submarine was spotted by a Sunderland of No.10 Squadron Royal Australian Air Force (RAAF).

As the Sunderland came in to attack, *Luigi Torelli*'s crew manned the deck gun and machine guns. Although two crewmen were wounded and some damage done to the aeroplane, the attack was pressed home and eight more 250lb depth charges straddled the boat. But the submarine was not hit mortally. Then another Sunderland from No.10 Squadron RAAF attacked. Once again, the submarine's crew fought back, and, once again, the attacking Sunderland was hit and damaged. But the flying boat pressed home its attack and another eight 250lb depth charges plummeted down towards *Luigi Torelli*. The submarine seemed to lift out of the water, but survived the attack, albeit with its diesel engines stopped. When the engineers coaxed them back to life, Migliorini had no choice but to make for the nearest port, Santander in Spain. Listing and limping, *Luigi Torelli* was run onto a sandbank close to Santander's main pier and interned by the Spanish authorities.[35-36]*

Between the attacks on *Luigi Torelli* and 23 June, three U-boats were attacked and damaged in the Bay by two Sunderlands of No.10 Squadron and a Whitley of No.58 Squadron.[37] Two, setting out on patrols, were forced to return; the third was nearing the end of a patrol. It seemed that the depth charges were still not functioning properly, although they had hydrostatic pistols designed to detonate at twenty-five feet. Tests indicated that the charges hit the water hard before sinking quickly and pulling down a large air bubble that delayed the pistol's action by slowing the entry of water. The solution was relatively simple: the convex nose of the charges was replaced with a concave one and a new tail, designed to separate on impact, fitted. With these modifications the charges sank broadside on rather than nose first and at a much slower rate.

The redesigned depth charges with the 'genuine twenty-five foot setting' would take a few months to come into general service, and during this time other submarines survived attacks that would otherwise have been lethal.[38]

As a result of the unsuccessful first attack on *Luigi Torelli*, No.172 Squadron Wellingtons were fitted urgently with radio altimeters which 'bounced'

---

* The *Luigi Torelli* story did not end there. A month later the crew was ordered to man their boat as she was being towed into Santander's inner basin for permanent repairs before being taken over by the Spanish navy. During the tow, an engine was started and the crew made a bolt for freedom with two Spaniards on board. The two men, one a senior naval officer, were allowed to transfer to a nearby fishing boat and the submarine made for Bordeaux without interruption by Coastal Command. In 1943 *Luigi Torelli* sailed to the Far East with a cargo of German military equipment, including radar sets, and personnel for the Japanese; Colonel Satake Kinjo, a telecommunications officer, was also aboard, returning from training in Germany. When the new Italian government agreed an armistice with the Allies, *Luigi Torelli* was taken over by the Kriegsmarine as *UIT-25*. When Germany surrendered in May 1945 the Imperial Japanese Navy became the boat's new owners. As *I-604*, *Luigi Torelli* fell into American hands on Japan's surrender. She was scuttled by the US Navy in April 1946, an ignominious end for a vessel with a remarkable history.

radio beams off the surface and made possible an accurate attack run-in for a Leigh Light–equipped aircraft.[39]

On 5 July *U-502*, returning from the Caribbean, was crossing the Bay under cover of darkness when it was detected and attacked by a Leigh-Light Wellington. When the water had settled after the explosions of the depth charges, a dirty growing patch of oil signalled the end of the boat. The Wellington was commanded by Pilot Officer Wiley B. Howell, an American who had joined the RAF before the United States entered the war.[40] Eight days later, Howell followed up with another successful attack in which a U-boat was damaged badly and put out of action for several months. Although the crew opened fire on the Wellington, their aim was poor due to glare from the light. Four depth charges exploded close to *U-159*, causing severe damage; the boat limped into Lorient twelve hours later.[41]

Dönitz and his commanders had identified 'an increasing number of surprise attacks by day' over the Bay. Observing strengthened British air patrolling and what appeared to be faster aircraft they had assumed that attacks 'would occur on bright, moonlight nights'. This new pattern of surprise daytime attacks was strange and it seemed unlikely that there had been a general lack of alertness. This gave rise to a suspicion that the aircraft had located the U-boat beforehand and had taken up attacking positions while out of sight, a suspicion confirmed in June when boats in the Bay were attacked from the air on a dark night. In one case a 'searchlight had suddenly been flashed on at a range of 1,000 or 2,000 yards and had at once picked up the U-boat'. Bombs had then been dropped. During the month three boats suffered severe damage in the Bay in such attacks and, unable to submerge, had to return to base.[42]

While the 'searchlight' had not 'at once picked up' the *Luigi Torelli* the appearance of this new weapon of war was a surprise, confirming the suspicion that British aircraft had some form of detection equipment.

Worse still, for Dönitz, was the much broader threat to operations. Predicated on boats operating on the surface where they had the speed to match and overtake convoys, these operations were imperilled. The culmination of *U-bootwaffe* operational doctrine was the wolfpack tactic which 'we had evolved' but this might no longer be possible where Allied air cover was strong. Should 'two maritime powers' be able to maintain a constant air patrol in all sea areas, say, over the whole of the Atlantic, then the mobility of the U-boats would vanish and their system of joint surface attacks would be defeated.[43]

This unwelcome development demanded countermeasures. An immediate response was to seek air cover for the Bay and Dönitz, with the authority of OKM, flew to *Oberkommando der Luftwaffe* (OKL) headquarters and to Rominten to meet Göring. As a result, twenty-four Ju88C6s were transferred to Atlantic Air Command as heavy fighters to deal with Coastal Command aircraft. Dönitz also ordered boats to remain submerged while crossing the Bay by day or night, surfacing only to recharge batteries. Should a boat be surprised on the surface, by day or by *'das verdammte Licht'* (that damned [Leigh] Light), each was to be fitted with four 8mm machine guns for anti-aircraft defence, a temporary expedient 'pending the drawing up of plans which would permit the mounting of heavier AA weapons'.[44]

Another defensive countermeasure was introduced from August 1942, a radar warning receiver to pick up signals from airborne ASV sets. A year before, a Wellington fitted with ASV I had fallen into German hands in North Africa and its radar was examined by German scientists, who fitted it in a Focke-Wulf Condor for flight trials.[45] Since ASV I operated on the 1.5-metre wavelength, the Germans were able to design and build a detector.[46] Known as FuMB 1 Metox 600, this was manufactured by the French company Metox in the German-occupied zone of France. Since it also picked up signals from a Luftwaffe transmitter about twenty-five miles (forty kilometres) away at Bordeaux it had to be modified for operational use. A crude antenna was devised, made of five pieces of wood in a cruciform shape, with wires wrapped around it. Installed in a bracket in the conning tower it could be rotated manually and became known as the 'Biscay Cross'. Picking up transmissions from an airborne ASV set, Metox could give a commander sufficient warning to dive before the aircraft crew made a visual sighting. Ironically, although the Germans had known about it for some time, ASV had not been considered a serious threat.[47]

Early warning of an ASV-equipped aircraft gave U-boats a tactical advantage but was not a complete answer since the number of submarines lost to aircraft between 1 August and 31 December was twenty-five, plus two shared with surface vessels, almost half the fifty-four lost in that period.

Metox was also used against the Germans in an example of psychological warfare that may have been the initiative of a captured airman, taken prisoner after the introduction of ASV III, which was undetectable by Metox. At that time, the Germans, unaware of the new radar, were concerned about the cause of so many air attacks on U-boats. Since Metox emitted a weak signal, the prisoner told his captors that their latest problems were due to transmissions by Metox being picked up by Coastal Command aircraft. When tests proved this possible, the Germans accepted the story. At the time they were about to introduce a successor to Metox that could detect centimetric signals, but the new equipment, Naxos, was delayed by some months as a result of this hoax.[48]

Joubert ordered constant patrols in the inner Bay 'by Leigh Light Wellingtons supplemented by other aircraft dropping flares periodically'. Daytime patrols continued, but with ASV switched on only once every quarter hour, and then for only fifteen seconds, although in good visibility U-boats might be sighted with the naked eye. An attempt to carry out long-range patrols as far as 15W was also planned.[49] These measures were unsuccessful and the offensive ended as winter began, but would later resume and intensify.

As well as these defensive methods, Dönitz also considered that further impetus ought to be given to developing a new type of U-boat with high underwater speed. Such a boat had been designed before the war by a young engineer, Dr Hellmuth Walter. Working at the Germaniawerft shipyard in Kiel, Walter proposed a revolutionary submarine powered by stabilized hydrogen peroxide (Perhydrol). With smaller and lighter engines than the conventional diesel/electric combination, this boat would not have to spend long hours on the surface recharging batteries. Moreover, it would be able to travel underwater at 30 knots and on the surface at 26 knots. Walter put his ideas before the naval command in 1934 but they were rejected.

Three years later Walter presented his proposal to Dönitz who was sufficiently impressed to have a research vessel, the *V-80*, based on Walter's design, ordered. When the *V-80* was tested it proved capable of over 23 knots submerged, leading to real interest from OKM but its trials and completion had been postponed repeatedly since 1939. This was due to 'lack of means', but also to the priority given to building quickly as many conventional boats as possible and to OKM's doubts about the *V-80*'s operational value.[50]

Although Dönitz was enthused about Walter's designs, none of the eleven boats completed ever saw action. One, *U-794*, reached 24 knots underwater in the Bay of Danzig in March 1944, witnessed by five admirals, including Dönitz. At much the same time, however, contracts for further Walter boats were cancelled in favour of the Type XXI, which used increased battery power rather than a turbine to achieve 17 knots submerged. Type XXIs were ordered and built but none saw operational service.

Of other technological innovations underway for the *U-bootwaffe*, the most important was the *Schnorchel*, which allowed a submerged submarine to take in air from above the surface. Although a defensive measure, to reduce the risk of air attack, the schnorkel (this spelling will be used hereafter) also increased operational effectiveness, turning *submersibles* into true *submarines*, able to remain submerged for long periods.

The first patent for a schnorkel was taken out by a Clyde-based shipyard during the First World War[51] but the Admiralty saw no need for it and it was left to the Italian navy to test a similar device in the 1920s. Although intended for operational use, the system was scrapped in 1937 by the head of the submarine arm, Rear Admiral Antonio Legnani. The schnorkel story passed to the Royal Netherlands Navy and a 'sniffer' device designed by Commander Jan Jacob Wichers. Fitted to a few submarines that could travel underwater on their diesel engines, this drew in air through a breather tube. Two such boats were captured by the Germans when they overran The Netherlands in 1940 (others escaped to Britain where the schnorkels were

Figure 13: The Type XXI U-boat. Fast both underwater and surfaced, the XXI was able to remain submerged for lengthy periods, thanks to the schnorkel equipment.

removed) but the Kriegsmarine saw the device only as a means of refreshing the air in a submarine, not for running diesel engines underwater. No operational advantage for it was identified by them until 1943.[52]

Dönitz suggests that the schnorkel was the outcome of Walter's work, arising from the 'demand for a one-hundred-per-cent under-water vessel of high speed, or at least of sufficiently high speed for its tactical employment' and that it was Walter's 'air intake and expulsion apparatus, which ...was later given the name of "Schnorchel".'[53] In fact it was the Dutch device that German engineers fitted to U-boats, although it was Walter who suggested it be adapted; two of Walter's engineers, Ulrich Gabler and Heinrich Heep, redesigned the equipment for North Atlantic waters. Subsequently, Dönitz writes that 'in the meanwhile the Schnorchel had been perfected, tested, and pronounced ready for operational use'. This is misleading since the Germans had great difficulty in making it work. Knowing the Italians had developed the schnorkel before the Dutch, although the latter's version owed nothing to the *Regia Marina*'s, the Germans 'also sought to interview the developer of the Italian schnorkel, Pericle Ferretti, in 1943'; in Italy the device was initially called the Ferretti instrument, later becoming the ML instrument. By then, however, Ferretti had retired to become a professor of engineering. Although Italy was still Germany's ally, Ferretti had no wish to help the Germans and, on learning that they wanted to contact him, changed his identity and went into hiding.[54]

The fate of the first two schnorkel-fitted U-boats to sail confirms that Gabler and Heep had no easy task. Neither boat returned, although the second, *U-575*, did transmit 'an enthusiastic signal', but warned that the schnorkel ought not to be used during a hunt because nothing could be heard through the hydrophones with the diesels running. However, *U-667* returned from patrol, including nine consecutive days submerged.[55]

Schnorkels were retro-fitted to Type VIICs and IXCs and designed into the structure of new vessels such as the Types XXI and XXIII. However, it would be 1944 before it became operational, at least in part thanks to *Professore* Ferretti's disappearing act.

Dönitz admits frankly that, in the second half of 1942, the Allies had gained the tactical upper hand with effective countermeasures that had removed much of the U-boats' 'primary tactical advantages of concealment and surprise'. These advantages could be restored only by some revolutionary developments in basic design.[56]

Meanwhile the Allies were proceeding and succeeding by evolutionary design. By late-1942 many British escorts were fitted with HF/DF equipment, known popularly as Huff Duff. German command and control practice meant that U-boats communicated regularly with headquarters by high-frequency (short-wave) radio with even the shortest transmission detectable by shipboard HF/DF. As already noted, most rescue ships were similarly equipped. When the HF/DF set's fluorescent screen lit up with a bright point of light, the escort commander was alerted to the presence of a U-boat. However, a signal on one set did not allow much more than the bearing of the transmitting boat to be ascertained, although an experienced operator could often estimate the distance from which the signal emanated by its strength and quality. When cross bearings were available, either from shore stations or other shipboard HF/DF sets some distance apart, the position of the U-boat could be fixed. Even with only a line of bearing an escort could be despatched to search along that line, forcing the boat to dive and lose the convoy, or even to hunt down and destroy it. Combined with centimetric Type 271 radar the escort groups had an operational advantage over the wolfpacks since the radio traffic to concentrate a pack could betray the position of every individual boat while radar stripped away the cover of darkness or fog.

Unfortunately, the RCN was operating at a great disadvantage as Canadian escorts were not being fitted with HF/DF on the same scale as British, and nor did they have Type 271 radar. Canadian escorts lacked a modern radar to detect a surfaced U-boat at night, relying on a Canadian version of the British Type 286, operating on the 1.5-metre wavelength. As Milner comments this 'was good for locating ships or Newfoundland, but nearly useless for a low-lying U-boat'. He adds that 'Canadian reliance on a 1.5 metre set became a source of weakness in crucial ways' by autumn 1942.[57]

In July Sir Dudley Pound considered 'that another turning point in the U-boat war is approaching'. The pressure in the western Atlantic would persuade Dönitz that operations there would soon not be worth the risk. Pound noted that Dönitz deployed three U-boats in the eastern Atlantic for every one he sent to the western end of the ocean and that he could pit four or five times the strength of boats against a convoy in eastern waters compared to one in the west. A major concern for Pound, should U-boats renew the mid-Atlantic campaign, was that the Royal Navy had sent reinforcements to the US Navy, thus stretching escort resources 'just when attacks on our Arctic convoys were increasing'. Dönitz confirmed Pound's thinking in a radio broadcast on 27 July when he warned the German public that his forces 'would suffer heavier losses', indicating to the Admiralty that Atlantic convoys were to be targeted again.[58]

We have already touched on this renewed offensive in mid-Atlantic but some significant events during this period have not been mentioned, including the establishment of the first support group under Commander Frederic J. 'Johnnie' Walker. Styled 20th Escort Group, it included ten flotilla vessels with an oiler. Its creation was a bold move since there were still not enough escort ships but it was felt that such a group could alleviate pressure on convoy escort groups by being available to attack lurking wolfpacks. Although some of the group sailed on 22 September to reinforce ONS132's escort, Walker's ships were not given much opportunity to work as a team due to the need to provide escorts for the convoys sailing for North Africa as part of Operation TORCH, the Allied landings in French North-West Africa in early-November. TORCH also delayed the deployment on convoy duties of the first escort carriers, which were diverted to protect the expeditionary forces. At this time also work began on the first MAC-ships.

Among ships sunk by U-boats in late-1942 was the troopship *Laconia*. On 12 September *U-156* spotted and torpedoed the liner south of the equator. On board were almost 1,800 Italian prisoners en route to PoW camps. When the boat's commander, Kapitänleutnant Werner Hartenstein, who had intended to take prisoner *Laconia*'s senior officers, saw the many survivors in the water, he began a rescue operation, calling on other U-boats to join him. He broadcast his intention on open channels and flew a Red Cross flag. Sailing with his foredeck crowded with survivors and towing lifeboats, Hartenstein was attacked by an American B-24. The aircraft's crew had reported that *U-156* was carrying survivors and flying the Red Cross but were ordered to attack anyway. Many on *U-156* were killed and Hartenstein had to crash dive, the Americans claiming to have sunk her.[59] (*U-156* was sunk in March 1943.)

This incident prompted Dönitz to issue an order, known as the 'Laconia order', instructing commanders not to rescue survivors from sunken ships. At his trial for war crimes at Nuremberg this was claimed to be a violation of the 1936 Protocol, although he had never ordered killing survivors. However, the International Tribunal did not accept this argument.

Paradoxically, the *Laconia* incident allowed a large British troop convoy, making for the Cape of Good Hope, to put considerable distance between itself and a wolfpack that may have intercepted it had it not been diverted to assist Hartenstein's operation.[60] Subsequently, when Operation TORCH was launched, Dönitz ordered a concentration against the convoys but, although some valuable ships were sunk, U-boat losses were severe with three sunk and six damaged badly to the west of Gibraltar; those in the Mediterranean also suffered. At the end of November a redeployment westward, intended to attack troop and supply convoys coming directly from the United States to north African ports, was also unsuccessful.

By the end of 1942 the Royal Navy's escort force was being strengthened by the River-class frigates, the first of which, HMS *Rother*, had been commissioned in April. With a speed of 20 knots, armed with a Hedgehog and up to 150 depth charges, the Rivers had been designed for ocean escort anti-submarine work, and their arrival allowed some older destroyers to be withdrawn. Originally they were to have been called super-corvettes but the name 'frigate' was revived, although their roles were not those of Nelson's frigates. Frigates were larger than the corvettes, at 1,370 tons, with a ship's company of 140 officers and men. More comfortable than corvettes, nine had been launched by the end of June 1942; another twenty-eight from yards in Britain and Canada followed before the end of the year.[61]

In all, 151 were built and served with seven wartime Allied navies. Although simple in construction, the time taken to design, build and introduce them to service emphasized the truth of Jellicoe's warning in 1929, when Churchill was chancellor of the exchequer, that 'war experience showed that the fast vessels needed for anti-submarine convoy escort cannot be hurriedly improvised'.[62]

With the River-class frigates entering service, fitted with Type 271 radar and HF/DF, the threat to the U-boats was increased. The only criticism

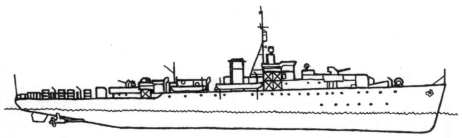

Figure 14: HMS *Mourne*, one of the River-class frigates which entered service from 1942.

of the Rivers, and the subsequent Loch class, was that there were never enough; that was especially true in 1942.

Irrespective of the types of ships included, escort groups were now becoming effective teams through the policy of keeping a group of vessels together to create a strong tactical unit. In addition, senior officers commanding the groups and the captains of individual ships had been able to develop their operational expertise and an instinct for what U-boat commanders might attempt. And with Torpex-filled depth charges, capable of being set to detonate at 500 feet, they had even more chance of destroying a boat once it had been detected.

As 1942 drew to an end, Sir Percy Noble handed over command of Western Approaches Command to Admiral Sir Max Horton. Noble went to Washington to succeed Admiral Sir Andrew Cunningham who had been appointed as Naval Commander of the Allied expeditionary force to North Africa. Horton, a submariner with considerable experience from the First World War, would take the excellent command that Noble had forged and hone it into a war-winning weapon.

There was no living officer who better understood the U-boat commander's mind, nor could more surely anticipate what his reactions to our countermeasures would be. Though the British submarine service to a man deplored his departure from its headquarters, all knew that he had been called to carry even greater responsibilities, and in a crisis which was becoming ever more plain. With his knowledge and insight, his ruthless determination and driving energy, he was without doubt the right man to pit against Dönitz.[63]

Chapter Ten

In the dying days of December, Russia-bound convoy JW51B was attacked by German surface ships, including the 'pocket battleship' *Lützow* and heavy cruiser *Hipper*, but the attackers were repelled by the Home Fleet escort which included heavy ships. The Kriegsmarine ships' performance was poor: they failed to press home their attack, indicating a lack of morale, in spite of a sound battle plan in which each heavy ship, escorted by three destroyers, was to make separate attacks. However, the senior officers remained constrained by Hitler's insistence on taking no risks by engaging with enemy forces of equal or greater strength.[1]

The German attack was defeated and Captain Robert St Vincent Sherbrooke of HMS *Onslow*, commanding the destroyer escort, was awarded the Victoria Cross. Hitler was outraged by the outcome, ignoring the fact that his instruction had much to do with the failure of his ships. He sent for Raeder and demanded that he make plans to pay off all the large ships. Rather than oversee the neutralization of the fleet he had done so much to build, Raeder resigned. In his place Hitler appointed Dönitz.[2]

In spite of his belief that U-boats could win the war on their own, Dönitz realized the wisdom of Raeder's argument for a balanced fleet and, being in the Führer's favour, was able to persuade Hitler not to lay up the surface fleet. As commander of the Kriegsmarine he was now much better placed to obtain what he needed for the *U-bootwaffe* by using his good standing with Hitler in the prosecution of the war against the convoys.

Taking over command of the Kriegsmarine on 30 January, Dönitz also retained close control of the *U-bootwaffe*. He remained Flag Officer Submarines for two reasons: he believed the personnel relied on him, and that there was no senior officer with his knowledge or experience of submarines. Thus he had the U-boat staff incorporated into OKM as Section II of the Naval Staff with Konteradmiral Godt as Flag Officer, or *Führer der U-boote*, and Fregattenkapitän Gunter Hessler at Godt's side. U-boat headquarters left Paris for the Hotel am Steinplatz in Berlin's Charlottenburg.[3]

Dönitz now had the strongest U-boat fleet yet: he lists 164 boats in the Atlantic, twenty-four in the Mediterranean, twenty-one in the Arctic and three in the Black Sea. During December he had maintained a daily average of ninety-eight boats in the Atlantic, with thirty-nine in the operational area and the balance either returning from or sailing towards that area. Dönitz had asked Hitler to release the boats in the Arctic and the dictator had agreed that all but six should leave for the Atlantic, bringing the strength there to 179 boats. That formidable force posed a great threat, perhaps the greatest yet, to the convoys.[4]

As already noted, the North Atlantic weather had been very stormy in the closing months of 1942. January brought no improvement, Dönitz describing conditions with the phrase 'the elements seemed to rage in uncontrolled fury' while Western Approaches Command's war diary noted that the first two weeks had 'been marked by a further succession of Southerly gales'. It also commented that:

> During the first fortnight of the New Year U-boat activity against North Atlantic Convoys has been quiet, but it seems very probable that the enemy is even more strongly pursuing the policy of concentrated attacks on isolated convoys, followed by comparative lulls whilst re-grouping his forces.[5]

Conditions on a U-boat on the surface can only be imagined. Those on an escort ship were only slightly better. However, writes Dönitz, the weather alone could not have been the reason why, during the first two weeks, U-boats failed to find four convoys that they deployed to target. This led Dönitz and his staff to believe that something fundamental had occurred in the British command. Hitherto, convoys had been routed in a 'very conservative manner' but this had changed and they seemed to be dispersed over a much greater area. When he wrote his *Memoirs* Dönitz had come to believe that this was due to Horton's assumption of command in Liverpool but the Admiralty had introduced new ciphers in December (just as Bletchley Park was again able to read Enigma signals), which *B-Dienst* was unable to read, thus giving the British a temporary operational intelligence advantage. Other factors included an end to the immediate fear that UK oil supplies were running dangerously low, which had been one reason for the more rigid routeing system. (The situation had not changed overnight but a new twenty-day cycle of forty-ship convoys of tankers direct from Aruba in the Dutch West Indies was to be instigated.) In addition, the escort system had changed with the changeover at Iceland no longer standard procedure. The new procedure was for a local escort to protect the assembly of a convoy, take it out to sea and hand over to the ocean escort to protect it across the Atlantic where a local escort would come out, meet the convoy and shepherd it on the last stage of its journey as the ocean escort made its way into Londonderry. This had become possible through refuelling at sea, which was now operational practice with over 140 commercial tankers equipped with the hoses and ancillary gear needed to transfer fuel. Circumstances ensured that two dozen tankers performed half the fuelling done during the war. In two and a half years, 350,000 tons of fuel were transferred in all weathers up to a full gale. 'The performance of all who served in those tankers was outstanding.'[6] Commander (Eng.) R. R. Shorto DSC had been appointed to the staff of Commodore Simpson at Londonderry in January 1942 with one of his duties being 'oiling at sea'.[7] Macintyre notes that this solved the problem of maintaining a full-strength escort for the entire crossing.

Although air cover was increasing there remained a gap south of Greenland where convoys could not be supported by land-based aircraft and where Dönitz hoped to take a heavy toll of merchantmen. During 1942 the Germans estimated that they had sunk 7,000,000 tons of shipping, close to the target Dönitz had set and which he believed would bring the UK to its knees. The actual tonnage sunk by U-boats that year had been 6,266,215 tons (1,160 ships) but other weapons had brought the totals to 7,790,697 tons and 1,664 ships.[8] Allied shipyards had produced slightly more than 7,000,000 tons of new shipping. Thus another million tons had been added on the deficit side of the balance for the Allies since September 1939 and British imports had fallen below 34,000,000 tons, a one-third reduction on 1939 figures. It was clear to the Admiralty that 'the Battle of the Convoy Routes was still to be decided, that the enemy had greater strength than ever before, and that the crisis in the long-drawn struggle was near'. The *U-bootwaffe* had achieved much in 1942 with a considerably lower strength than Dönitz had hoped for since a monthly average of only seventeen new boats had entered service rather than the planned twenty. Even so, he had begun the year with 249 boats of which ninety-one were operational and, in spite of losing eighty-seven (plus twenty-two Italian), had 393 boats at the end, 212 of them operational,[9] no fewer than 179 of which were available for Atlantic operations.

Having missed the four targeted convoys, the North Atlantic wolfpacks had a lean month in which only one ship from HX222 was lost, that being the sole convoy attacked. However, Dönitz knew that there was prey to the south and deployed a group (Delphin) across the great circle route from New York to the Canary Islands. After some days with no sightings, a group of tankers was spotted and Delphin converged for an attack on convoy TM1, from Trinidad to Gibraltar. In Roskill's words the convoy was 'cut to pieces' between 9 and 11 January; only two of nine tankers survived to reach Gibraltar. Since TM1 was carrying fuel oil for Allied forces in French North-West Africa, the commander of Fifth Panzer Army in Tunisia, Colonel General Jürgen von Arnim, sent Dönitz a telegram of congratulations.[10]

January may have been a lean month for U-boats, with only fifteen ships sunk, but that changed in February. The Admiralty's Monthly Anti-Submarine report noted that 'a bolder and more reckless strategy is now characteristic of the enemy. The tempo is quickening and the critical phase of the U-boat war in the Atlantic cannot long be postponed'.[11] During February thirty-four ships were sunk in convoys, or 14 per cent of ships in the convoys attacked. However, the U-boats had also lost heavily with, according to Macintyre, twelve sunk in the Atlantic. Total losses for February were actually eighteen, with survivors from only four boats. Aircraft were responsible for destroying seven boats and shared in the sinking of another two.

HX224 was attacked on 2 and 3 February with two ships torpedoed and sunk; a third, a tanker, which had straggled, was also sunk. From the straggler, U-632 picked up a survivor who told the boat's crew that a large slow convoy, SC118, was following on the same route. The information confirmed a B-Dienst intercept and allowed no fewer than twenty-one U-boats to concentrate against the unfortunate convoy; these included thirteen from the Pfeil wolfpack, five from the Haudegen pack and two that had been engaged against HX224. (B-Dienst had been rendered ineffective for a time from early-

December due to the Admiralty's new ciphers, but German cryptanalysts had broken those by early-February.)[12] SC118, sixty-three merchant ships with ten escorts, came under attack between 4 and 9 February. At one stage the convoy split but was re-formed the following morning. Air support was called up and there was a furious running battle between air and surface escorts on one hand and U-boats on the other. Roskill considers that at least three quarters of the attackers came under depth-charge attack at some stage; three U-boats were sunk while another two sustained serious damage. One lesson from this battle was that 'even continuous escort by long-range aircraft in daylight could not prevent some enemies catching up and attacking the convoys during the long winter nights'. As a result it was decided to fit Fortresses and Liberators with Leigh Lights as soon as possible. Another lesson emphasized the value of trained escort groups. SC118's escort had been reinforced by US Coast Guard cutters from Iceland so that there were twelve escorts with it at the height of the battle, twice the strength of a normal group. However, the reinforcements were unable to make an effective contribution 'because they lacked training as part of an integrated group' and such training was more important than raw numbers.[13] A further lesson came from the great expenditure of depth charges during the lengthy, furious battle. It was decided that merchant ships should carry stocks of depth charges with which to replenish escorts. In addition, Roskill notes that this battle added more weight to the arguments 'in favour of support groups being used to reinforce threatened convoys' and quotes Horton who described such groups as 'vital to ensure reasonable safety'.[14]

By mid-February Dönitz had four groups either formed or forming to interdict the North Atlantic routes. Their next target was ONS165, which was located, close to the end of its journey, about 350 miles off Newfoundland. Two merchant ships were sunk but *U-201* and *U-69* were sunk on 17 February by HM Ships *Fame* and *Viscount* respectively.[15] Both destroyers had sunk two other U-boats during attacks on SC104 the previous October, *Fame* destroying *U-353* while *Viscount* had rammed and sunk *U-661*. That these two ships had each destroyed two U-boats gives a clear example of what a well-trained escort group could do. *Fame* was relatively modern, having been completed in 1935 while *Viscount* had entered service in March 1918: the V and Ws were still giving sterling service.

The U-boats had more to show for their next attack, launched on ONS166 which was picked up by *B-Dienst* early on its voyage. Escorting ONS166 was Commander Heineman's A3 group, which included the USCG Cutters *Spencer* and *Campbell*, four Canadian corvettes, *Chilliwack*, *Dauphin*, *Rosthern* and *Trillium* and the British corvette *Dianthus*. Although both cutters were fitted with Type 271 radar and HF/DF, the Canadian corvettes, lacking these refinements, were at a disadvantage. Of forty-nine ships in ONS166, fourteen (85,000 tons) were sunk and seven damaged.[16] Only one U-boat was lost from the nineteen that harried the convoy for five days across 1,100 miles of ocean. That boat, *U-623*, fell victim to a Liberator of No.120 Squadron west-south-west of Ireland.[17]

The attacks on ONS165 and ONS166 were followed by one on ONS167. Two ships were sunk, both by *U-664*. These attacks were all made possible by the presence of two *Milchkühe*, *U-460* and *U-462*, north of the Azores, which refuelled and replenished twenty-seven operational boats between 21 February and 5 March.

January's merchantman losses had been low with only thirty-seven ships (203,128 tons) sunk by U-boats from an overall loss of fifty ships totalling just over 250,000 tons. However, February had seen the toll rise to sixty-three ships and 359,328 tons. Bad as February had been, March was even worse. In the worst month since November 1942, U-boats claimed 108 ships (627,377 tons) while enemy aircraft added another dozen (65,623 tons) to the list. There was now no doubting the level of the crisis. With a daily average of 116 boats at sea during March, almost fifty in operational areas, it seemed to those in the Tracking Room that the prediction made in January by the Anti-Submarine Warfare Division of a 'potentially annihilating superiority' might be about to come true.[18] Dönitz's preferred operational deployment within the air gap saw two groups waiting north-east of Newfoundland, at the gap's western edge, a further two at its eastern extremity south-west of Iceland and another west of Gibraltar, placed to interdict convoys from North America to the Mediterranean. Although *B-Dienst* had provided routeing details for an eastbound and a westbound convoy, and the boats of the two groups north-east of Newfoundland were waiting for one or both, stormy weather with much reduced visibility allowed both convoys to pass unnoticed. However, on 6 March, SC121 was spotted and reported.

Seventeen boats were ordered to attack. This wolfpack, now called Westmark, found easy victims as atrocious weather conditions had splintered the convoy's cohesion, causing many ships to straggle. U-boat headquarters then directed another nine boats to join Westmark; these became wolfpack Ostmark. In the ensuing ravaging of the convoy fourteen ships were sunk and one damaged while two LCTs (landing–craft, tanks) were lost with the ships carrying them. From a convoy of fifty-nine ships this was a loss rate of almost 25 per cent. Once again the escort was Heineman's A3, this time including the USCGC *Spencer*, the destroyer USS *Greer*, the RCN corvettes *Dauphin*, *Rosthern* and *Trillium* and the RN corvette *Dianthus*. SS *Melrose Abbey* was also in the convoy as the rescue ship. A3 had taken over the convoy only days after handing over ONS166, giving the escorts no opportunity for repairs to equipment or ships. Nonetheless they fought a hard fight and were reinforced by the destroyer USS *Babbitt* and the USCGCs *Bibb* and *Ingham* and HM Ships *Mallow* and *Campion*. A Liberator from No.120 Squadron also joined the battle, forcing boats to keep down.[19] Most ships sunk were stragglers, a vindication of the convoy system at least, but it was clear that more such battles would have an adverse effect on merchant sailors' morale.

While SC121 was enduring its purgatory, another U-boat group had spotted HX228 south-west of Iceland. Wolfpack Neuland attacked the sixty-ship convoy on 10 March, its thirteen boats joined by another six. Against them were pitted the ships of a mixed British–Polish–Free French escort group; the senior officer was Commander Arthur 'Harry' Tait DSO in the destroyer *Harvester*; the group included HM Ships *Escapade*, *Narcissus* and *Orchis*, the Polish destroyers ORP *Garland* and ORP *Burza* and the Free French *Aconit*, *Renoncule* and *Roselys*. Also with the convoy was the first US Navy support group, the escort carrier USS *Bogue* and the destroyers *Belknap* and *Osmond*.

The wolfpack made its first attacks on the evening of the 10th when two ships were sunk and a third damaged by *U-221* which was counter-attacked by escorts and forced to withdraw damaged. Two more ships were torpedoed, and sank, one damaging the attacking boat, *U-757*, as she exploded. Next morning *Harvester* spotted *U-444* and attacked the boat before she could dive. Engaging *U-444* with gunfire, *Harvester* rammed the submarine but damaged her propellers in the process. Initially it was thought that *U-444* had been sunk but the boat was later spotted on the surface and finished off by *Aconit*. Meanwhile *Harvester* had picked up survivors from a sunken merchant ship and one from *U-444*. Making to rejoin the convoy her engines stopped and, lying dead in the water, she was torpedoed by *U-432*. *Harvester* was lost with 149 lives including Commander Tait. *Aconit* then avenged *Harvester*, picking up *U-432* at periscope depth and blowing the boat to the surface before sinking her with gunfire. *Aconit* rescued men from *U-432*, *Harvester*, the sunken merchantman and the man from *U-444*.[20]

HX228 lost six merchant ships and *Harvester* while two U-boats had been sunk. Two merchant ships were damaged. The USS *Bogue* was unable to play any part as foul weather prevented air operations. One result of the loss of *Harvester* was that the Admiralty 'officially discouraged' the ramming tactic.[21]

The Bletchley Park cryptanalysts had encountered problems in February, leading to a spell of 'blank' days between the 8th and the 17th, followed by more from 10 March that would have horrendous consequences for convoys as B-*Dienst* was reading the Admiralty signals and knew the routes planned for convoys while the Ultra team was temporarily blind. Thus B-*Dienst* was able to inform U-boat headquarters of the routeing instructions for two convoys due to sail from New York: SC122 and HX229. The latter was actually split in two, one having the suffix A after its code; the full complement of seventy-five ships was divided into one of thirty-seven and another of thirty-eight.[22] (Convoyweb.org.uk shows higher numbers in both convoys, although some of these were only with the convoy for part of the journey.)

Had the convoy sailed as constituted originally its escort force might have numbered eleven ships but only five were assigned to HX229 and six to HX229A. The first of these was simply a group gathered from different escort groups with all the problems inherent therein. Having withdrawn boats from the attacks on earlier UK-bound convoys, Dönitz used them to reinforce the wolfpack Raubgraf (Robber Baron) against SC122 and HX229 and HX229A; the reinforcing boats formed two wolfpacks, Stürmer and Dränger (Stormer and Thruster), in north-south patrol lines.

The presence of the U-boats was betrayed by an attack on 13 March which sank a merchantman and alerted the Convoy and Routeing team in

Washington. Reports of several detections and attacks by escorts gave a good indication of the position of the line of U-boats and SC122 and HX229 were diverted south of the wolfpack while HX229A, having rounded Newfoundland, was sent northerly to sail west of the waiting U-boats. The new instructions for SC122 and HX229 were decrypted and passed to Konteradmiral Godt some hours after transmission, but Godt had no information on HX229A's new route. With this information he redeployed the boats, although a gale had blown up, causing problems for both convoys and U-boats. The new plan was for Raubgraf and the Stürmer/Dränger boats to converge on SC122. First contact was made by *U-653*, heading for home low on fuel and torpedoes, which found herself in the midst of a convoy, dived and allowed the ships to pass over before resurfacing to trail the convoy and send out regular signals for the other boats. At U-boat headquarters it was believed that *U-653* had contacted SC122 but the boat had encountered HX229.

All the Raubgraf boats and ten from the Stürmer and Dränger groups were ordered to converge on the convoy that *U-653* was shadowing. An additional baker's dozen of boats, some arriving from their home ports, some returning from rendezvous with *Milchkühe*, were ordered to join. In all, more than forty boats were converging on HX229, which U-boat headquarters still believed to be SC122, a convoy that had slipped the net, if only briefly. However, all the attackers did not reach HX229 at the same time. Had they done so, the escort could have been swamped in a co-ordinated assault. HF/DF had betrayed the U-boats' presence to the escort and Lieutenant Commander John Luther, the senior officer, expected an attack, but had only three ships as one of his destroyers had been despatched to hunt along the bearing of an HF/DF signal. As it was, the first boats to reach HX229 on 16 March waited until dark before attacking. Nine boats torpedoed and sank eight ships during the night. Luther ordered his ships to carry out a 'Raspberry' but without firing starshell since the moon gave enough light. Due to the absence of a rescue ship, the escorts were kept busy picking up survivors and, at times, the convoy was all but undefended.

Not long after midnight, *U-338* found SC122 and torpedoed four ships. Additional boats were ordered to join this attack, although German records refer to the two engagements as one battle. On the 17th Liberators from

Nos.86 and120 Squadrons, from Aldergrove and Reykjavik respectively, surprised shadowing U-boats, forcing them down. However, U-boats still managed to sink another five ships, two from HX229 and three from SC122, as the battle continued; the Liberators were at extreme distance from their bases and near their prudent limits of endurance (PLE). Next day Liberators again patrolled into the battle area but could not find HX229, which lost another two ships; a further vessel from SC122 was destroyed while a straggler was torpedoed and sunk in the wake of the convoys. Fighting continued into the 19th when a Liberator sank *U-384*. Only one ship was sunk that day, the SS *Matthew Luckenbach* which had left HX229 to steam for England at best speed but had the misfortune to sail into the nest of U-boats assailing SC122 and be torpedoed by *U-523*. Dönitz notes that air cover was continuous from 17 March – not entirely true – and that surface escorts were also reinforced while weather conditions hampered the U-boats. Nearly all his boats suffered damage from depth charges or bombs with two damaged badly. That evening the boats were ordered to break off. Fourteen ships, including the straggler, had been sunk and six damaged.[23]

The losses had been heavy but the German claim of thirty-two ships and an escort destroyer sunk was an exaggeration: twenty-two merchantmen had been lost but no escorts; Dönitz claims twenty-one merchant ships, but adds an escort. U-boat Command's war diary describes the battle as 'so far the best result obtained in a convoy battle, the more gratifying as almost 50 per cent of the boats took part in it'.[24] While the 'fog of battle' may explain some exaggeration, including the claimed sinking of a destroyer, the assertion that this was 'the best result' in a convoy battle must have been obviously false at the time. Roskill notes that the commodore of HX229, a man with great experience in Atlantic convoy work, included in his report that 'apart from U-boat attacks the voyage was fairly average'.[25] For the Germans, in terms of effort expended and boats deployed, the number of sinkings was poor, even if the war diary claim were true (only 11 per cent of the ships in convoys). This is especially so as some U-boats were deploying a new torpedo, *Federapparat-Torpedo*, or FAT, which, in theory, ought to have led to more sinkings. Designed specifically for attacks on convoys, these ran a straight course for a predetermined distance before making a half-turn to come back through the convoy's columns. Although the first boat to attack HX229 had fired three FATs only one hit a ship. Padfield suggests that this may have been 'because the convoy made a fortuitous alteration [of course] as he fired'.[26] It had only been with the introduction of the new magnetic pistol in December 1942 that the effectiveness of *U-bootwaffe* torpedoes became better than those used in the First World War.[27]

As already noted, March saw the loss of 120 ships totalling almost 700,000 tons, the majority – 108 vessels and 627,377 tons – to U-boat action. Since the beginning of the year 208 ships had been lost to the *U-bootwaffe*, a total of 1,189,833 tons. We have seen Dönitz's war diary claim of a 'best result' which he repeats in his *Memoirs* as the 'greatest success' against a convoy while quoting the Admiralty comment at the end of 1943 that 'the Germans never came so near to disrupting communication between the New World and the Old as in the first twenty days of March 1943' as vindication of his claim. He quotes Roskill:

> Nor can one yet look back on that month without feeling something approaching horror over the losses we suffered. In the first ten days, in all waters, we lost forty-one ships; in the second ten days fifty-six. More than half a million tons of shipping was lost in those twenty days; and, what made the losses so much more serious than the bare figures can indicate, was that nearly two-thirds of the ships sunk during the month were sunk in convoy. 'It appeared possible' wrote the Naval Staff after the crisis had passed, 'that we should not be able to continue [to regard] convoy as an effective system of defence'. It had, during three-and-a-half years of war, slowly become the lynchpin of our maritime strategy. Where could the Admiralty turn if the convoy system had lost its effectiveness? They did not know; but they must have felt, though no one admitted it, that defeat then stared them in the face.[28]

Dönitz was being selective in quoting Roskill, especially as he omitted the next line of the paragraph:

> Apart from the indomitable spirit of the seamen and airmen engaged in the battle, it was the advent of the Support Groups, the Escort

Carriers and the Very Long Range Aircraft which turned the tables on the U-boats – and did so with astonishing rapidity.[29]

Sir Max Horton felt no sense of impending defeat in March 1943, instead writing to his friend Rear Admiral Reginald B. Darke DSO, on the 23rd, that 'although the last week has been one of the blackest on the sea, so far as this job is concerned, I am really hopeful'.[30] Horton had cause to be hopeful. He knew that the hard work in training, in obtaining the resources required to defeat the U-boats, in developing technological devices and in intelligence successes were all about to mesh together. He knew also of the fundamental weaknesses of the Kriegsmarine and its *U-bootwaffe*. And, most recently, he knew of the decisions made at the Atlantic Convoy Conference in Washington. The conference, including British, US and Canadian representatives, could not have been more timely. It had reached several important decisions, some of which would be implemented almost immediately, but had also focused minds at the highest level on convoy protection. The attacks on HX229 could hardly have been timed better had Dönitz set out to give maximum support at the highest level to Allied naval and air commanders waging the Battle of the Atlantic.

At the Symbol Conference in Casablanca in January 1943 Allied leaders decided to hold an additional conference to plan strategy for the Battle of the Atlantic as they had agreed that 'defeat of the U-boat must remain a first charge on the resources of the United Nations'.[31] As a result, the Atlantic Convoy Conference was convened in Washington on 1 March. Those attending were not the highest naval and air commanders, but representatives who would report back to the Combined Chiefs of Staff. Admiral Sir Percy Noble, head of the Admiralty delegation in Washington, a man well versed in the problems facing convoys and their escorts, led the UK delegation, which included Vice Admiral Sir Henry Moore, Pound's deputy, Rear Admiral Jack Mansfield, of the Admiralty's Trade Division, and Air Marshal Sir Albert Durston, senior air staff officer at Coastal Command, representing the AOC-in-C; Durston had been AOC No.18 Group of Coastal until the end of 1942. The Royal Canadian Navy was represented by Rear Admiral Victor-Gabriel Brodeur, senior Canadian naval officer in Washington.[32] Admiral Ernest King, Chief of Naval Operations, hosted the conference and led the US Navy delegation, assisted by his deputy, Admiral Richard S. Edwards. Following his opening remarks, King handed over to Edwards to chair the proceedings. King stated his belief that:

> convoying is 'not only the best way to protect Allied shipping but the *only* way. 'A ship saved,' he emphasized, 'is worth two built.' The 'safe and timely' arrival of convoys should continue to be the guiding strategic principle; hunter-killer operations secondary.[33]

The Admiralty would have preferred one overall commander in the battle but King opposed such an idea, in all probability because he believed that the British, with greater experience in such warfare and deepest interest in the outcome, would have claimed the post. That there was no British push for such an appointment, with Horton the obvious candidate, was due to the fear that an American might be appointed and the UK lose control of the battle for its very survival.

An early shock for British and Canadian representatives came when the Americans made clear their wish to withdraw completely from escort duties on the HX/ON and SC/ONS convoys; although HX and ON codes continued in use, New York had become the departure/arrival point from 1 September 1942. The American proposal seems to have been based on King's dislike of mixed-nationality escorts and a desire to concentrate USN ships on the more southerly convoys serving US forces in the Mediterranean. Whatever the reason, British representatives were surprised by King's proposal, although US Navy and Coast Guard escorts accounted for only two in every hundred such vessels in the North Atlantic.[34]

Discussion led to an agreement that the US Navy would take over the tanker convoys between the Dutch West Indies and the UK, compensating for the increased British and Canadian commitment in the North Atlantic. The Americans would also place the *Bogue* support group under Admiralty control to work with North Atlantic convoys. With the UK and Canada taking 'complete charge of all convoys running between Britain and New York, or ports north of the latter', Canada would create a new naval command to exercise control in the Western Atlantic, west of 47W. This became North-West Atlantic Command, or Canadian North-West Atlantic, and its first

C-in-C was Rear Admiral Leonard Murray RCN. The Americans were not enthusiastic about this, although the Canadians had been pushing for some time for authority commensurate with Canada's commitment to the battle. Until now, and except for Canadian territorial waters (then only twelve miles offshore), the Royal Canadian Navy was under command and control of US Navy Task Force 24. The Americans were opposed to any discrete theatre command for the Canadians, arguing disingenuously, or naively, or both, that:

the RCN lacked the expertise to exercise the command and control functions required of independent command. Canadians gently reminded them that Commander Task Force 24 had learned his duties from [then Commodore] Murray in 1941.[35]

It was agreed that, from 1 April, the 'Chop Line' (*Ch*ange of *Op*erational control) would be the 47th Meridian. However, long-range aircraft, irrespective of nationality, would operate to their PLE, and support groups would also move wherever needed 'under the general strategic control of the command to which they belonged'.[36] Other changes included new convoy cycles and more long-range aircraft in Newfoundland, a nominal total of forty-eight (four squadrons). More ships were to be fitted with HF/DF, corvettes that the RCN had lent to the US Navy for the Caribbean were to be returned, corvettes deployed for Operation TORCH made their way home and six older Royal Navy fleet destroyers were transferred to Canada. Those half dozen destroyers were *Decoy*, *Express*, *Fortune*, *Foxhound*, *Griffin* and *Hero* which became *Kootenay*, *Gatineau*, *Saskatchewan*, *Qu'Appelle*, *Ottawa* and *Chaudière* respectively.[37] They provided a useful boost to Royal Canadian Navy strength; the first River-class frigates were also arriving.

Roskill notes that Canadian responsibilities included:

Independently-sailed troopships and also merchantmen plying between Canadian, Newfoundland and British ports ... . It will thus be seen how the Royal Canadian Navy, having started the war with such very small strength, and having so long shared with the Royal Navy the heat and burden of the Atlantic Battle, now came into full partnership in controlling the forces deployed in this vast theatre.[38]

That 'heat and burden' had honed the professionalism of the Canadian crews and:

> the groups had made major improvements in early 1943. They were thoroughly trained and re-equipped, and through February and March successfully escorted convoys to North Africa. During one of these operations, *Shelliac* sank *U-87* off Portugal.[39]

For a time in early 1943 the groups that had been worked hardest in the North Atlantic had been based in the United Kingdom to rest and train and have their ships repaired and updated; many corvettes were fitted with Type 271 radar. 'In particular, the RCN personnel were able to benefit from individual and group training in all aspects of anti-submarine warfare from expert and experienced instructors.'[40] Canadian escort groups were strengthened by inclusion of Royal Navy ships while most had British senior officers assigned. The Canadian 2nd Escort Group (C2) included two RN Town-class destroyers, *Broadway* and *Sherwood*, the River-class frigate *Lagan*, two Flower-class corvettes, *Primrose* and *Snowdrop*, the French *Savorgnan de Brazza* and three RCN ships, *Drumheller*, *Morden* and *Chambly*, although HMCS *St Croix* could replace *Sherwood*. Commanded since April 1942 by an Irishman, Lieutenant Commander Evelyn H. Chavasse DSC, a cousin of Noel Chavasse VC and Bar MC, the group would play a major part in one of the convoys marking the point at which the Battle of the Atlantic turned decisively against the U-boats.[41]

A new Area Combined Headquarters, paralleling Derby House, built in Halifax for naval and air operations staff, opened on 17 July. Murray had already taken command of Canadian North-West Atlantic on 30 April. As Milner emphasizes, this marked a milestone in the history of both Canada and the RCN: the North-West Atlantic was the only independent theatre of operations in the Second World War commanded by a Canadian.[42] RCN training facilities at Nova Scotia and Quebec were also expanding and produced a flow of highly trained sailors, the signals school at Quebec turning out skilled signalmen, a necessity for the burgeoning force and a critical element in the coming battle.

Keen to improve the effectiveness of its escort force even more, the RCN considered options for reinforcing groups and concluded that a small fleet of auxiliary carriers, converted from merchant hulls with a full-length flight deck, hangar space and about twenty aircraft, was needed. On 6 April the directors of operations and plans reported that 'It is probable that Air will be the decisive factor in the "Battle of the Atlantic"' and recommended a Canadian equivalent of the FAA with four escort carriers, allowing one to operate with each escort group. This recommendation, agreed by the Naval Staff, was passed to the Naval Board, which stated that 'all anti-U-boat phases of air operations' should be pursued. This echoed Brodeur's statement at the opening of the Washington Conference that the Royal Canadian Navy would support any plan to 'destroy the present submarine menace' in the Atlantic.[43]

Padfield stresses that the 'really pressing problem' accepted by those attending the conference was how to close the air gap.[44] Although the problem was recognized by all, there was no agreed solution. Politics, in the service sense, threatened resolution with services differing on priorities and competition between theatres. The Pacific loomed large in King's mind and, although he had seventy-one VLR Liberators in a reconnaissance role there, he had none on the eastern seaboard of North America. Coastal Command still had only the VLR Liberators of No.120 Squadron, split between Ballykelly and Reykjavik (the entire squadron would move to Iceland in April, as part of the agreed solution to the air-gap problem) and the Royal Canadian Air Force had none. Coastal also had a squadron of unconverted Liberator GR IIIs, which moved from Thorney Island to Aldergrove in March.

It seemed incredible to [the British and Canadians] that King could have so disregarded the Casablanca recommendation and indeed the primary strategy for the war as to employ his entire Liberator force on non-urgent missions in the Pacific; moreover, he maintained continuous and largely fruitless anti-submarine patrols over the Caribbean and Gulf Frontiers. These were regarded largely as training flights for pilots who might not have been equal to the fogs and storms off Newfoundland and Greenland. Yet that is where the convoys were beset by the U-boats.[45]

King and his staff argued that aircraft to close the gap could be diverted from the strategic bombing campaign in Europe which, in his view, was of little value. Neither the US Army Air Forces' senior officers involved in that campaign, nor the British Air Staff were likely to agree – although the RAF's Lancaster would have made an ideal maritime patrol aircraft (as it did after the war when Liberators and Catalinas were returned). While seeing the faults in the air forces' deployments and operations in Europe, King failed signally to see that 'his own concentration on the Pacific at this crisis in the Atlantic was an equally costly, more dangerous and even less comprehensible misuse of air power'.[46]

The convoy battles during March turned many eyes towards the U-boat menace. One man whom King could not ignore was Roosevelt who demanded to know where the US Navy's Liberators 'were operating at the time when the recent heavy losses in the Atlantic were suffered'. Roosevelt was aware of the recent report from the Allied Anti-Submarine Survey Board referring to 'totally inadequate' air cover in the North Atlantic and of the fact that, at Casablanca, the Combined Chiefs had recommended that eighty VLR aircraft be allocated to cover the air gap south of Greenland. Moreover, the board had pointed out that '*not one* VLR aircraft was to be found at any Allied air base west of Iceland'. The machines on Iceland were from the detachment of No.120 Squadron based there since September 1942.[47]

The reaction to Roosevelt's question was prompt.

The result was that the Americans agreed that 255 Liberators (seventy-five from the US Army Air Forces, sixty from the US Navy and 120 from British allocations) should be provided for the North Atlantic. This could not, of course, take effect at once, and the full benefits were not felt until the next phase. At the end of March we had twenty VLR aircraft operational, and by mid-April the maximum was only forty-one – all of them flown by British crews.[48]

The VLR aircraft referred to were the Liberators of No.120 Squadron and the machines of No.59 Squadron which had converted from the Fortress II to the Liberator V, on which it became operational in March; in May No.59 Squadron moved to Northern Ireland. No.86 Squadron also converted to the Liberator

V at this time, beginning anti-submarine patrols from Aldergrove. Although the nominal strength of the VLR Liberator units was fifty-four aircraft, only forty were held by squadrons on 1 March (when No.59 was converting) while the figure for aeroplanes available for operations on that date was twenty-six.[49]

Clay Blair asserts that the number of VLR and long-range anti-submarine aircraft available 'was far more impressive than is depicted in most accounts'.[50] By looking at the five Allied squadrons operating Liberators in March 1943, Blair concludes that there were 'sixty-odd' B-24s.[51] This assumes that each squadron had 'the standard twelve' machines.[52] While this may have been the case with the two USAAF squadrons in his total, RAF squadrons were a different story. Blair describes No.224 Squadron as having twelve VLR Liberators whereas it had six machines on strength, of which only two were available; not all six were VLR. Likewise, he writes, 'By March 1943, the whole of Terence Bulloch's pioneering RAF Squadron 120, comprised of a dozen to fifteen Liberators had deployed [to Iceland]'. In fact, the squadron maintained a detachment of seven Liberators on Iceland from September 1942. Of those seven, only three were available. The remainder of the squadron was still based in Northern Ireland during March but moved to Iceland in mid-April.[53] Although 120 had a nominal strength of fourteen aircraft, with eleven available, not all were VLR machines as replacement aircraft were either Liberator IIs or IIIs; the Mark II was not modified for VLR work and the III, while having additional fuel capacity was not, in Bulloch's view, as capable as the Liberator I.[54] (Simons notes that the Mark III's range was only 1,680 miles compared to the 1,800 of the II and the 2,400 of the I.[55] Nor was Bulloch the commander of No.120 as Blair seems to think. Blair's conclusion that the shortage of VLR machines has been exaggerated by historians can, therefore, be dismissed. As Spooner comments, the practical strength of a squadron might be only half its theoretical strength (up to twenty-four machines).[56]

In spite of their satisfaction with the battle of 17 to 19 March, the Germans were concerned about the intelligence on which the Admiralty seemed to be operating. Their failure to find convoys in the first weeks of the year had led to an investigation of possible sources from which the British were able to work out where U-boats were. There was sufficient evidence to indicate that the Admiralty had excellent intelligence on *U-bootwaffe* operations which disturbed Dönitz and his staff.

After examining all possibilities they concluded that there was no evidence of treachery, and that their cyphers were secure. Our successes must, they considered, be achieved by constant search and patrolling by radar-equipped aircraft. On their own side they were still deriving great benefit from the daily 'U-boat situation' and convoy-control signals sent by the Commander-in-Chief, Western Approaches, or the Admiralty; and such successes as they achieved in intercepting our convoys were largely brought about through the undoubted efficiency of the German wireless intelligence service.[57]

The belief that Admiralty intelligence was based on a British 'wide use of and superiority in radar, and the efficiency of ... air patrols' led to an order being issued to U-boat commanders on 5 March ordering them to dive for thirty minutes as soon as they became aware of radar transmissions. Aware also that the escorts were now stronger and that many convoys had an outer screen of escorts as well as an inner – this being made possible by refuelling from tankers in the convoys – U-boat command also began developing new tactics to counter these changes. The convoy battles of February and March were testimony to those efforts.[58]

What the Germans did not know was that their Enigma ciphers were completely secure for a period during March and that the Allies were concerned that Bletchley Park might be unable to decrypt four-rotor Enigma signals for several months. It was Bletchley Park cryptanalysts who made this dire prediction, having learned from one decrypt that a new short signal codebook was to be introduced for weather reports from 10 March, superseding the book recovered from *U-559* the previous October. This could have fatal consequences for the Ultra team. Although *U-559* had been using a four-rotor Enigma, its fourth rotor had been set in neutral since the Short Weather Book and Short Signal Book had only three-rotor settings because not all boats had received the four-rotor machine. However, with supply of the new machine complete, on 8 March Dönitz sent a signal ordering boats to begin using the fourth rotor at midnight. The grim news was passed to Pound on 9 March.

it seemed that the worst had happened. On the 9th, Admiral Edelsten, Assistant Chief of Staff (U-boat and Trade) reported ... that what had so long been feared had now occurred and that the Tracking Room was likely to be 'blind' for a considerable period, perhaps for months.[59]

As we have seen SC122 and HX229A were attacked by three wolfpacks while many more boats were in the Atlantic. Without accurate and up-to-date knowledge of the locations of U-boats it had been impossible to divert convoys to avoid their concentrations.

The knowledge that the Tracking Room was 'blind' while Bletchley Park tackled the problem seized the minds of those at the Washington conference. Delegates believed that the code-breakers would lose four-rotor Enigma for several months and perhaps longer. But the 'blind' spell lasted only ten days.

In one of the great intelligence feats of the war, British codebreakers at Bletchley Park, who had sixty three-rotor bombes on line, broke back into four-rotor Enigma on 19 March. The official intelligence historian wrote that in the 112 days from 10 March to 30 June, the British read four-rotor Enigma for 90 days, or 80 per cent of the time.[60]

Beesly is not quite so enthusiastic, writing that 'although the flow of Special Intelligence continued with no greater interruptions than those to which it had been subjected since December ... those interruptions were themselves serious'. Nonetheless, the codebreakers' work was outstanding. Delays in cracking the daily changes in Enigma settings varied between three and seven days, which might not have been a major concern had it not been 'for the superb efficiency of the *B-Dienst*, who frequently, but not invariably, were able to supply Dönitz with decrypts of our signals diverting convoys in time for him to move the U-boats across the new track of the convoy concerned,' as had happened with SC122 and HX229A.[61] However, Beesly does note that this was not always the case, as Rohwer pointed out that of 175 Allied signals to convoys in the North Atlantic over twenty days in March 1943 only ten were decrypted in time for Dönitz to take effective action.[62]

Another area in which Allied intelligence officers erred greatly was in estimating U-boat construction during 1943. On 1 March they produced an estimate of 613 boats in commission by the end of the year. Believing that the Kriegsmarine would commission 320 new boats during 1943, while Allied action would only destroy 124, they concluded that the net gain of 196 boats, added to 417 believed to be in commission on 1 January 1943, would give Dönitz 613 boats by 31 December. However, estimates for 'kills' proved very inaccurate. Allied successes against the U-boats increased greatly during the year and the Atlantic force decreased in strength rather than increasing.

While the intelligence war rumbled on, the war over, on and under the waves was changing. In addition to the reinforcement of the VLR Liberator force, thanks to Roosevelt's goading of King, more ships were joining the escort forces and the concept of support groups was taking operational shape. Mention has already been made of the first Royal Navy support group, 20th Escort Group, under Walker, and the US Navy support group, built around the *Bogue*. However, Walker's group had been sidelined due to the need for ships to escort the TORCH convoys but the *Bogue* group had sailed with SC121 before taking SC123 under its wing. In between these two sailings, HX230 had a sailing uninterrupted by U-boat attacks. On the other hand, it seemed as if the weather was determined to make enough difficulties for the convoy as:

> Once again a storm of such violence as to warrant classification as a hurricane raged around the embattled convoys. [HX230 and the corresponding westbound convoy] Even the normally stormy North Atlantic excelled itself in the weather which it provided throughout this winter and early spring. Storm succeeded storm, and ships were often overwhelmed by the mere violence of the elements. True, the weather handicapped the U-boats, but our escorts and aircraft suffered as much and more; the convoyed ships were forced to scatter and straggle, and so fell easy victims to the pursuers when the weather abated.[63]

The sole ship from HX230 to fall victim to a U-boat had indeed straggled. An American Liberty ship fell behind with engine trouble on 28 March and was torpedoed shortly before midnight on the 29th by *U-610*. Seven of the crew of fifty-seven swam to a landing craft that had broken free from the wreck; picked up by HMS *Shikari* of B21, they were taken to Londonderry. *U-610*, commanded by Kapitänleutnant Walter Freiherr von Freyberg-

Eisenberg-Allmendingen, was sunk in October by a Sunderland of No.423 Squadron RCAF from RAF Castle Archdale.[64]

Weather conditions were the second biggest threat to convoys. Roskill notes that 'the Commodore's ship of one convoy capsized, and was lost with all hands'.[65] Some ships disappeared without trace and several Liberty ships broke in two and sank before engineering changes eliminated the cause of the fractures.

The Washington Conference had approved the creation of support groups, known as hunter-killer groups in the US Navy. But the Royal Navy's support groups were already forming at the time of the conference with 1st Support Group under Commander Godfrey Brewer, followed by Walker's 2nd Support Group. (Officially styled Escort Groups, to avoid confusion the term Support Group will be used in this account.) A typical order of battle for a support group included about six ships: Brewer's included the Egret-class sloop *Pelican*, the former US Coast Guard cutter *Sennen*, and the River-class frigates *Rother*, *Spey*, *Wear* and *Jed* while Walker's consisted entirely of sloops: *Cygnet*, *Starling*, *Wren*, *Kite*, *Whimbrel*, *Wild Goose* and *Woodpecker*. By 1 April Horton had five such groups under his command. Those already detailed were composed of experienced ships and crews of Western Approaches Command, while 3rd and 4th Support Groups included destroyers on loan from the Home Fleet and 5th included the escort carrier *Biter* with three destroyers.[66]

Both the US Navy's *Bogue* group and Captain James A. McCoy's B3 (*Offa*, *Obedient*, *Oribi*, *Orwell* and *Onslaught*) helped ensure safe passages for SC123 and HX230. The *Bogue* group saw SC123 to a position about 175 miles south-east of Cape Farewell where 3rd Support Group joined to shepherd the convoy safely through the zone where U-boats were positioned before moving to aid HX230. The escorts' HF/DF allowed them to find the reporting U-boat and force it down, so that 'a hole was punched in the [U-boat patrol] line and the convoy passed safely through'.[67]

With *Biter* in 5th Support Group and *Bogue* operating in a similar role the escort carriers added their contribution. As well as *Biter*, two other escort carriers joined Western Approaches Command in March, *Archer* and *Dasher*. Tragically *Dasher* suffered an internal fuel explosion and sank on 27 March while returning to the Clyde with engine problems from a convoy escort task. Before joining Western Approaches Command, both *Biter* and *Dasher* had taken part in Operation TORCH. The *Dasher* tragedy notwithstanding, escort carriers played an important role in the battle against the U-boats, just as their predecessor, *Audacity*, had shown they could do.

As well as the formation of support groups, there were now sufficient escort ships to increase the size of groups, which rose from an average of five and a half ships to seven and a half. Moreover, time could also be spared between voyages for some intensive training.

The training Canadian groups had undertaken in the United Kingdom was that of the programme devised for Royal Navy crews and commanding officers of ships, especially at Tobermory and WATU. This regime had been enhanced by Horton who, to the theoretical work of WATU, added a spell of practical sea work to demonstrate the lessons learnt. For this practical course the 'classroom' was the millionaire Sir T. O. M. Sopwith's private yacht, *Philante* (a play on the name of his wife Phyllis and his first initial: Phil and T), which the philanthropist had gifted to the nation. Commanded initially by Commander Joe Baker-Cresswell and later Captain Robin Durnford-Slater, HMS *Philante* had a staff of specialist veteran anti-submarine officers (both Baker-Cresswell and Durnford-Slater were experienced anti-submarine commanders) and a number of submarines were attached for training purposes. *Philante* would move from base to base – Greenock to Londonderry to Liverpool as well as Belfast and Larne – to train with escort groups preparing to put to sea. These groups were given intensive practice under the watchful eye of *Philante*'s staff and, in this way, 'the quality of the escort groups was raised and kept at a high level'.[68]

King also established a new US Navy command to oversee all anti-submarine activities. On 1 May he submitted a report to the Chiefs of Staff.

> It is arranged to set up immediately ... an anti-submarine command to be known as the Tenth Fleet.
>
> The headquarters ... will consist of all existing anti-submarine activities of US Fleet headquarters, which will be transferred intact to the Commander Tenth Fleet. Such additional officers will be assigned

to the Tenth Fleet as are necessary ..., in the same manner as any other major command. In addition, a research-statistical analysis group will be set up composed of civilian scientists, headed by Dr Vannever Bush.

The Commander Tenth Fleet is to exercise direct control over all Atlantic Sea Frontiers, using sea frontier commanders as task force commanders. He is to control allocation of anti-submarine forces to all commands in the Atlantic, including the Atlantic Fleet, and is to re-allocate forces from time to time, as the situation requires. In order to insure quick and effective action to meet the needs of the changing anti-submarine situation, the Commander Tenth Fleet is to be given control of all LR and VLR aircraft, and certain groups of units of auxiliary carriers, escort ships and submarines which he will allocate to reënforce task forces which need help, or to employment as 'killer groups' under his operational direction in appropriate circumstances.[69]

For the post of Commander Tenth Fleet King did not look far. He appointed himself, adding to his many other responsibilities, but gave the job of chief of staff to Rear Admiral Low, 'a tough, conscientious, intelligent and hardworking officer'. In spite of its title, Tenth Fleet had no ships; it was a co-ordinating headquarters for all US anti-submarine 'activities', including operations, training, research and intelligence. It had an Operations Division, an Anti-Submarine Measures Division, a Convoy and Routeing Division and a Civilian Scientific Council, 'a typical brainchild' of King who 'believed in using existing units rather than creating new ones, and whose capacity for responsibility was immense'.[70] Perhaps the best summary of its value comes from Padfield who writes, 'After it became operational towards the end of May 1943, the Tenth Fleet was to prove as formidable as the previous US command structure had been flawed'.[71]

There had been another change of commander in the UK before the Washington Conference began when Sir Phillip Joubert was succeeded by Air Marshal John 'Jack' Slessor, who assumed command of Coastal Command on 5 February 1943. Slessor would hold the post for almost a year; he was knighted in June 1943. Acknowledging the work of his predecessors,

Slessor 'made no appreciable change in policy but opted in anti-submarine warfare for the emphasis to be on 'the trunk of the tree', the transit route for U-boats through the Bay. However, he did not lose sight of the need to counter concentrations of U-boats in the areas through which convoys sailed and so his policy was to 'consider both areas according to operational conditions and requirements'.[72] Thus his term in office would see a revival and intensification of the Battle of the Bay.

However, there was still the threat to the Atlantic convoys which seemed to be reaching a climax in March and, moreover, swinging in the Germans' favour. In the Anti-U-boat Committee the Admiralty stated a requirement for additional Coastal Command aircraft for the Bay of Biscay, setting down a figure of 190, and asked that the U-boat bases and pens be subjected to continuous bombing. This latter proposal was opposed by the Air Ministry since it would reduce the bomber offensive against Germany. The Air Ministry pointed out that recent bombing of Lorient and St Nazaire had been ineffective, in spite of 10,000 tons of bombs. Sir Charles Portal allowed that he could increase patrols in the Bay of Biscay by about seventy aircraft by lending machines to Coastal Command and redeploying some of its forces. Portal also agreed to ask the Americans for more radar-fitted aircraft for an 'all-out offensive ... in the Bay of Biscay' in July.[73]

In spite of Portal's undertakings, the effect of the March crisis was a re-opening of the 'Battle of the Air'. The Admiralty believed that Allied grand strategy depended on defeating the U-boats and Professor Blackett, now Chief of Operational Research at the Admiralty, agreed: 'The people of Britain can tighten their belts but our armies cannot be let down by failure to provide equipment, guns and tanks. This means ships and more ships, and safe escort for them.' As well as bombing the Biscay ports, the Admiralty wanted more VLR aircraft to close the air gap, the rapid introduction of escort carriers and use of bases in the Azores. (The Azores, a group of islands in the Atlantic, some 850 miles west of Portugal and 1,200 miles south-east of Newfoundland, are a Portuguese autonomous region. Portugal, although neutral, was England's – not Britain's – oldest ally and it was felt that the Portuguese government, although Fascist in nature, would allow Allied bases there; Churchill told parliament that he would use the 1373 Anglo-Portuguese Treaty on which to base an agreement with Salazar's government.) The Air Staff argued that the persistent use of heavy bombers against strategic targets in Germany was the prerequisite for victory.

> Against that the Admiralty argued that the art of grand strategy was to employ all our forces in furtherance of a common aim, that the accepted aim was the strategic offensive by all arms into Europe, and that the destruction of the U-boats was the necessary prelude to the successful mounting and maintenance of our offensive plans.[74]

Neither side won the argument. The result was a compromise that satisfied Admiralty needs, albeit more slowly than their lordships would have wished, while the bombing offensive continued. The subject still excites debate and Roskill added his personal view in the official history:

> this writer's view is that in the early spring of 1943 we had a very narrow escape from defeat in the Atlantic; and that, had we suffered such a defeat, history would have judged that the main cause had been the lack of two more squadrons of very long range aircraft for convoy escort duties.[75]

Meanwhile the battle on the convoy routes and the offensive in the Bay continued. Most U-boats engaged in the March battles had exhausted their fuel and weapons and returned to base. As April opened Dönitz writes of a 'U-boat vacuum', adding that it was the middle of the month before another large group, Meise, was operating north-east of Cape Race, Newfoundland. Roskill writes of this group being north-west of Cape Race at the beginning of the month, but that was another group which intercepted HX231, escorted by Commander Peter Gretton's B7. Although many boats were undergoing repair, Dönitz had 207 in the Atlantic from a fleet of 423, to which twenty-seven new boats were being added each month.[76]

Eleven boats were involved in the attack on HX231, a convoy of sixty-one ships,* which sailed from New York on 25 March. Gretton's escort group

---

* The authoritative website www.convoyweb.org.uk lists sixty-seven ships in the convoy. However, of the ships listed, six either turned back or travelled only as far as Halifax.

included the old V-class destroyer *Vidette*, the frigate *Tay*, from which he commanded as it was the sole escort fitted with HF/DF, and five Flower-class corvettes: *Alisma, Loosestrife, Pink* and *Snowflake*; all escorts 'had their asdic and radar sets in full working order'.[77] There was no rescue ship. First contact with the enemy was made two hours before dark on 4 April, a Sunday. Three boats were spotted on the horizon and HF/DF picked up signals from several more.[78]

Twenty-two of the ships were tankers while several others carried explosives. Shortly after darkness fell, Gretton ordered a change of course, designed to confuse the wolfpack, forcing some to attack sooner than planned and others later.

> The prospects were certainly grim and the escort commander's chief hope had to lie in good drill and efficient teamwork as a means of reducing the number of ships to be sunk. He could not count upon being able to stop attacks.[79]

It was the good drill and efficient teamwork of B7 that won out, combined with Gretton's leadership and experience. Not for nothing does Macintyre describe B7 as 'one of the First Division teams'.[80] That night two ships were torpedoed and damaged by *U-635*. Both vessels were sunk by *U-630* next day. A third ship was sunk on the 5th. These were the only ships lost in the convoy, but a straggler and two ships that broke, or 'romped', when the first U-boat attacked were also sunk. Of the attackers, *U-635* was despatched by a Liberator of No.120 Squadron on the 5th, and *U-632* by one of No.86 Squadron's Liberators next day.[81]

Only a well-trained, experienced escort group with effective air cover could have defeated the determined assault on HX231. B7 was reinforced during the most critical days of the battle by the arrival of Captain Scott-Moncrieff's 4th Support Group and the combination of two veteran groups with strong air cover gave the advantage to the convoy. The next convoy, HX232, lost four ships, two to *U-563*, as it followed the northerly route.[82]

HX233 followed what Dönitz describes as an 'unusually southerly' course, taking it about 400 miles north of the Azores, presumably to avoid a concentration on the northerly routes; another group of four boats, making for their operational areas independently, was sent to intercept. All four came up to the convoy, one after another, within twenty-four hours, but the escorts detected them on radar and attacked with depth charges. One ship was damaged by *U-628* on 17 April and sunk by *U-226* the next day. With the escort, a mixed group led by Commander Paul Heineman, reinforced by 3rd Support Group and the weather favouring the warships, the U-boats withdrew. *U-175* was depth-charged to the surface and sunk by gunfire from the USCGC *Spencer*, having been boarded before sinking.

HX234 sailed on 12 April and used the northerly route where it was attacked, losing two ships sunk and a third damaged. It also had a powerful escort, B4 being reinforced by 4th Support Group and no fewer than twenty-one ships deploying to protect the forty-six merchantmen between North America and Britain. The outward-bound convoys ONS3 and 4 were also attacked. (The designation of this series was started afresh during March with ONS1.) Two ships from ONS3 were sunk but none from ONS4. However, two U-boats were sunk, *U-191* by HMS *Hesperus* of B2 and *U-203*, shared by a Swordfish of No.811 NAS from *Biter* of 5th Support Group and *Pathfinder*. In both instances the U-boats destroyed were those that had detected the convoy. *U-203*'s signals were detected by HF/DF, her location fixed by the close escort before being forced down by the Swordfish and finished off by *Pathfinder*, one of *Biter*'s screen.[83]

April 1943 was, therefore, not a good month for the U-boats but neither Dönitz nor any of his commanders could have realized how dramatically the strategic situation would change in the next month. They certainly did not notice that 'the first real signs that the tide of victory had set in the Allies' favour' had been evident in the final week of April. Perhaps Elliot had it right when he wrote that 'April is the cruellest month'. More cruelty was to be visited on the U-boats before the month was out. Ironically, Goebbels, the German propaganda minister, chose April to announce that 'In the U-boat war we have England by the throat'.

Chapter Eleven

Before examining the May convoy battles, it is worth noting another result of the ORU's work. (Blackett had become Director, Naval Operational Research.) It was appreciated that the number of escort ships with a convoy reduced the loss rate and that air cover of about eight hours a day decreased ship losses by a third.[1] However:

> Since it was by no means safe to rely on the increase of air support to stop the crippling ship losses of the autumn of 1942, an energetic search was made for some other measures which could be put into operation quickly. Detailed attention was given, therefore, to the organizational aspects of the Atlantic convoy system. Perhaps some alteration in the organization of the convoys might conceivably improve the situation.[2]

Hitherto, organization of convoys and escorts had been 'a matter of chance'. The Admiralty had defined some broad principles, including the belief that large convoys were more dangerous and that, therefore, the optimum was about forty vessels. Sixty was the maximum and larger convoys were not permitted. A rough guide to escort numbers was also in place; known as the $3 + N/10$ rule, this stipulated a minimum of three escort vessels for a very small convoy with an additional ship for every ten merchantmen in the convoy: a convoy of twenty would have the minimum three escorts plus two; in this case the value of N was twenty. Likewise, the largest convoy, of sixty, would have nine escorts: three plus six, the value of N.

The basic assumption was that every convoy, irrespective of size, was equally safe or, at least, likely to suffer the same percentage rate of loss. Where the $3 + N/10$ rule originated, no one seemed to know, but Blackett points out that it 'could be shown to be not consistent with the view that small convoys were safer than large'. That inconsistency is demonstrated by his theoretical example of running three twenty-ship convoys, each with the five escorts of the $3 + N/10$ rule, against pooling those convoys and their escorts. By applying the rule, a sixty-ship convoy should enjoy only a nine-ship escort whereas pooling the three convoys and their escorts would produce an escort of fifteen.

Examination of records of ships lost in differing-sized convoys over the previous two years showed clearly, and surprisingly, that larger convoys had suffered relatively smaller losses.

> The figures were startling. Dividing convoys into those smaller and those larger than forty ships, it was found that the smaller convoys, with an average size of thirty-two ships, had suffered an average loss of 2.5 per cent, whereas the large convoys with an average size of fifty-four ships, had suffered only a loss of 1.1 per cent. Thus large convoys appeared to be in fact over twice as safe as small convoys.[3]

Although the calculations appeared reliable, Blackett knew that the Admiralty would be reluctant to introduce larger convoys, and so ORU began gathering evidence to strengthen the case for a change. Accounts by captured U-boat personnel proved very enlightening, and after several weeks of intensive work sufficient evidence had been gathered. It was discovered that the chances of any individual merchantman being sunk during any voyage depended on three factors:

> (a) the chance that the convoy in which it sailed would be sighted; (b) the chance that, having sighted the convoy, a U-boat would penetrate the screen of escort vessels around it; and (c) the chance that when a U-boat had penetrated the screen the merchant ship would be sunk. It was found: (a) that the chance of a convoy being sighted was nearly the same for large and small convoys; (b) that the chance that a U-boat would penetrate the screen depended only on the linear density of escorts, that is, on the number of escort vessels for each mile of perimeter to be defended; and (c) that when a U-boat did penetrate the screen, the number of merchant ships sunk was the same for both large and small convoys – simply because there were always more than enough targets.[4]

The researchers concluded that, given the same linear escort strength, the same *absolute* number of sinkings could be expected, irrespective of convoy size, and the *percentage* of losses would be inversely proportional to size. Thus the number of convoys sighted should be reduced by decreasing the number of convoys run, which could be achieved by increasing convoy size. After 'some weeks of earnest argument' new orders were issued in spring 1943; before long convoys of up to a hundred ships were crossing the Atlantic.[5]

Coastal Command was receiving ASV III for its aircraft towards the end of 1942 and aircraft so fitted became operational early in 1943. Terence Bulloch, who was resting from operations, took part in testing ASV III and was impressed with its quality which 'was many times easier to interpret and presented the information in a readily acceptable form, the Planned Position Indicator'.[6] ASV III's beams could not be detected by Metox and so the advantage conferred by that equipment waned. Boats crossing the Bay by night had felt much safer with Metox to warn of the presence of an ASV II–equipped aircraft, but, once again, they found themselves being attacked without warning. Surfaced U–boats elsewhere were taken by surprise when a Coastal Command aircraft appeared from low clouds. Although U–boats had been fitted with anti–aircraft armament, the conning tower and deck of a submarine was not a steady gun platform, but U–boats that fought it out on the surface could inflict serious damage, often bringing down aircraft.

With more VLR and LR aircraft available, the air gap was being reduced steadily. The advent of escort carriers and MAC-ships finally removed it completely. During May the *U-bootwaffe* would learn that there was no safe area in the North Atlantic. Land-based aircraft and flying boats operated from Newfoundland, Iceland and Northern Ireland, and the US Navy had opened bases in Greenland, from which some B-24s could operate in favourable conditions; the Greenland Fleet Air Group included detached elements of US Navy squadrons which, in April 1943, included two PBY-5A Catalinas from HQ Squadron Fleet Air Wing 7, and three Lockheed Venturas and three Catalinas from VB-126.[7] Coastal Command disposed almost thirty squadrons, including four-engined Liberators, Halifaxes, Fortresses and Sunderlands, and twin-engined Catalinas, Wellingtons,

Whitleys and Hudsons. The Handley Page Halifax was one of Bomber Command's 'heavies' but some had been lent to Coastal and proved excellent long-range aircraft.

Some of these aircraft were called into action again in support of B7 which, having fought HX231 through to the UK, left Londonderry to escort ONS5 to North America. The convoy, forty-two ships, left Liverpool on 21 April with B7 joining next day. HMS *Duncan*, Gretton's own ship, was back and he also had *Tay* and the corvettes *Loosestrife*, *Pink*, *Snowflake* and *Sunflower*. Although *Vidette* remained with the group, she had sailed earlier for Iceland to escort three ships joining the convoy. As well as two rescue trawlers, *Northern Gem* and *Northern Spray*, there were two tankers to refuel escorts; one would prove of no use since its hose system was canvas rather than rubber. Initially the voyage was uneventful but for the weather, which was so bad that two ships collided with one making for Iceland for repairs.[8]

Apart from a false alarm on the 24th there were no signs of U-boats until four days later when HF/DF intercepted a signal from straight ahead and close to the convoy. In between, in the afternoon of the 24th, a Fortress from Benbecula-based No.206 Squadron attacked and sank *U-710*, which was lying ahead of the convoy on its course.[9] It appeared that ONS5 might escape interception but the boat from which the signal was heard on the 28th proved to be *U-650*, which shadowed the convoy all day, awaiting another fourteen boats which had been ordered to join her and attack that night. With inclement weather preventing aircraft interdicting the gathering wolfpack, it became obvious that a battle loomed.[10]

The other boats being called up were *U-533*, *U-386*, *U-231*, *U-532*, *U-378*, *U-192*, *U-258*, *U-552*, *U-954*, *U-648*, *U-209*, *U-413* and *U-710*, forming the Star wolfpack, which included the boats of the former Meise group and six that had deployed with Meise two days earlier. They had been patrolling between Iceland and Greenland, just south of the amended course Western Approaches Command had advised the convoy to take that morning, a course intended to keep the convoy as far as possible from known U-boat concentrations. Oberleutnant Ernst von Witzendorff, of *U-650*, could only see six ships and, from his sighting report, U-boat headquarters assumed that he had spotted part of ONS6, which had yet to leave Liverpool. Since von Witzendorff was forced to submerge several times by Catalinas of VP-84 from Iceland, his failure to see more ships can be understood. Nonetheless his signal brought four boats to join him that day; escorts attacked the U-boats that night.[11]

HMS *Sunflower* depth-charged *U-386*, damaging her, while *U-532* and *U-650*, having launched torpedoes at *Snowflake* and *Duncan*, were also depth-charged. During the 29th *U-532* was attacked again, this time by *Tay*, while *U-258*, in a daytime attack, sank an American merchantman and *U-528*, damaged by a Catalina of VP-84, had to make for home. Both *U-386* and *U-532* sustained such serious damage that they also had to break off. The destroyer *Oribi* was ordered to leave SC127 to augment B7 while 3rd Support Group, with the destroyers *Offa*, *Impulsive*, *Penn* and *Panther* under Captain James McCoy DSO, an Irishman with an Italian wife, was ordered from St John's to support ONS5. The weather was so bad that McCoy's group had difficulty finding the convoy and did not make contact until 8.00pm on 2 May.[12]

With poor weather and reduced visibility on 30 April and 1 May, the U-boats lost contact after an unsuccessful night attack by *U-192*. Conditions were such that the convoy had to heave to in gale-force 10 winds, which resulted in some ships becoming separated from the main body; escorts could not refuel due to heavy seas, the threat from icebergs, and pack ice. Six ships straggled, but *Northern Spray* tried to keep them together, while a further half dozen were gathered together to be shepherded by HMS *Pink*.[13]

After 3rd Support Group joined, the convoy came out of the ice but scattered widely. Had the weather been good the stragglers would have fallen victim to U-boats but these had also suffered and had been ordered to break off operations late on the 1st.[14] On the 3rd *Duncan*, short of fuel and with another gale raging, had to make for St John's and Lieutenant Commander Sherwood of *Tay* assumed the duties of senior officer B7. Next day, two of McCoy's group, *Penn* and *Panther*, had to leave to refill their tanks. Western Approaches Command then ordered 1st Support Group to reinforce the escort; this group, under Commander Godfrey Brewer, included the sloop HMS *Pelican*, the cutter *Sennen* and four Rivers, *Rother*, *Spey*, *Wear* and *Jed*.[15]

German attention switched for a time to SC128 with boats of the Star and Specht groups forming a patrol line across its expected route. This patrol line, Fink, was augmented by another, Amsel, formed by boats newly-arrived from France and further divided into Amsel 1 to 4. In total, more than forty boats deployed. The German plan was foiled, thanks to an Ultra decrypt that allowed SC128 to be re-routed away from the waiting wolfpacks. Allied aircraft also deployed and a Royal Canadian Air Force Canso (the RCAF name for the Catalina) attacked and damaged *U-209*; another Canso damaged *U-438*. *U-209* subsequently disappeared and may have sunk as a result of the damage. At the time a Canso was believed to have sunk *U-630*[16] but this boat was actually destroyed by *Vidette* on 6 May.[17]

While SC128 escaped the planned ambush, ONS5 ran into the concentration, meeting the patrol line from the other side. Weather conditions meant that the convoy had only progressed by twenty miles. When *U-628* made its sighting report the Fink and Amsel 1 and 2 groups were ordered to attack ONS5. 'The real battle was joined after dark on the 4th'.[18] By then the weather had improved, allowing some thirty ships to re-assemble. *Pink* and *Northern Spray* were still escorting stragglers, one of which, the SS *Lorient*, became the first victim of the renewed assault. *Lorient* was torpedoed and sunk by *U-125* which was destroyed two days later by gunfire from *Snowflake*, having been rammed by *Oribi*.[19]

That night *Oribi*, *Snowflake* and *Vidette* depth-charged and damaged three boats, which withdrew, although *U-514* resumed its patrol some days later. The U-boats pressed home their attacks with *U-707* attacking from the front, diving under, passing below, and attacking and sinking a straggler. *U-628* penetrated the screen to fire five torpedoes at five targets but only damaged a single ship, which the same U-boat subsequently finished off. At much the same time, *U-264* made a similar attack with five torpedoes, four of which found targets: the American *West Maximus* and the British *Harperley* were sunk. After that *U-358* fired three torpedoes sinking *Bristol City* and *Wentworth*.[20]

Attacks continued next day. Dönitz had taken command, exhorting his commanders to seize any opportunity. Serial submerged daylight attacks followed, putting considerable pressure on the escorts. *U-638* sank the steamer *Dolius* but, hunted down by *Sunflower* and *Loosestrife*, was sunk by the latter. Another multiple-torpedo attack, by *U-266*, claimed three ships with four projectiles, the Norwegian *Bonde* and the British *Gharinda* and

Selvistan. *Offa* damaged *U-266* which was sunk ten days later by a Halifax of No.58 Squadron. An American steamer from the stragglers with *Pink* was torpedoed by *U-584* in the afternoon while *Pink* was engaging *U-358*, which had made the first attack on the stragglers, thus allowing *U-584* a clear run. *U-358* had to return to France.[21]

That evening a Liberator of No.120 Squadron from Iceland spent a short time overhead but was at the limit of its endurance and could not loiter, even though it was a VLR machine.[22] Undeterred by the Liberator, the U-boats continued gathering. Before the light faded *Tay* had spotted seven boats but there were no fewer than fifteen already in contact. Dönitz continued encouraging commanders to greater efforts as he 'anticipated that the night would bring some hard fighting, but also considerable success'.[23]

With the escorts running low on depth charges, it threatened to be a very bad night. However, as evening was falling, ONS5 sailed into a thick fogbank, which worked to the advantage of the escorts and merchantmen since the former could still find the U-boats with their radar, which Metox could not detect. Nonetheless, attacks continued throughout the night, about twenty-four being made from every direction except ahead, before the attackers eased off at 4.20am on the 6th. In a very confused situation the escorts, well trained and very experienced, had gained the upper hand. Dönitz's headquarters' war diary reads:

> A golden opportunity had thus been ruined by fog; no further success was scored by any U-boat. During this fog period alone fifteen boats were attacked with depth charges and six of them were located by destroyers, surprised on the surface and engaged with gunfire. The lack of any means of counteracting this radar location undoubtedly left the boats in an inferior and, indeed, hopeless position.[24]

Seven U-boats were lost, including *U-531* and *U-630*, both sunk by *Vidette*. *Loosestrife* depth-charged *U-575* without success before obtaining a radar fix on *U-192*. As the corvette loomed out of the mist at about 500 yards, the U-boat launched two torpedoes at her, both of which missed. A pattern of depth charges, set for shallow detonation, destroyed the still-surfaced submarine. *Snowflake* chased off *U-107* with depth charges before beginning a search for another four boats that had appeared on her radar. While *Snowflake* was engaging some of those with gunfire, *Oribi* appeared from the fog and rammed *U-125* which the corvette then sank with gunfire. *Offa*, which had made five attacks before midnight, damaged *U-223* with gunfire and depth charges. Also damaged was *U-533* but both escaped destruction; *U-223* was damaged again on the 11th when she was depth-charged to the surface by *Hesperus* which then rammed her; she survived the encounter and limped home. While escorts and U-boats were fighting, Brewer's 1st Support Group arrived and joined in the fray. *Pelican* found *U-438* by radar and closed to within 300 yards before being spotted. The boat crash-dived too late as a fusillade of shallow-set depth charges sent her to the bottom. Meanwhile *Sennen* raced to join *Pink* and her charges, en route attacking both *U-650* and *U-575* with depth charges and Hedgehog. Neither sustained serious damage. *Spey* fell into station behind the convoy and drove off *U-634* with gunfire; the boat was hit by two rounds but not damaged seriously.[25]

Success, let alone 'considerable success', had eluded Dönitz. When he realized the scale of his losses he called off the engagement. Although twelve merchantmen had been sunk, not including the vessel on 29 April, he 'regarded this convoy battle as a defeat'. He writes that the 10-centimetre radar with which the escorts were equipped had 'a direct and extremely adverse effect on the fighting of the individual U-boat'. For the Royal Navy, the ONS5 battle was remarkable in that most defensive work had been done by surface escorts who, in spite of what looked like overwhelming numbers, fought off a very large wolfpack; in all, as many as fifty-five U-boats deployed against ONS5. The US Navy Intelligence Service estimated that, on the evening of 5 May, fifteen boats were in contact with the convoy while another ten to fifteen were no more than fifteen nautical miles away. Captain James McCoy stated that 'the convoy was threatened with annihilation'.[26] ONS5 was also memorable as the last time so many merchant ships were lost in convoy.

Dönitz had not given up the fight and when *B-Dienst* provided details of the next two eastbound convoys, HX237 and SC129, he ordered thirty-six U-boats to attack. The convoys were to take more southerly routes, passing not far from the Azores. HX237 was protected by C2 under Lieutenant

Commander Evelyn Chavasse DSC, which included HM Ships *Broadway*, *Lagan* and *Primrose* and HM Canadian Ships *Chambly*, *Drumheller* and *Morden* with HM Trawler *Vizalma* and a tug. Thus half of this RCN group was made up of British ships and the Irish Chavasse was a Royal Navy officer. For its journey across the Atlantic HX237's escort was reinforced by 5th Support Group with *Biter* and the destroyers *Opportune*, *Obdurate* and *Pathfinder*; commanding the group was Captain Conolly Abel Smith, whose maternal grandfather was the Irish VC John Augustus Connolly.[27]

At first Abel Smith refused to place his carrier within the convoy from where his destroyers could 'reinforce the very sketchy close screen' and act as a striking force. Instead, he planned to operate between twenty to fifty miles from the convoy.[28] That was not the only friction that Chavasse had to face at the start of the journey:

On 6 May C2 ... sailed from St John's [although] the *Vizalma*, the tug and one merchant ship sailed late to intercept, and *Biter* and his boys sailed from Argentia. The usual thing happened, as so often in May: fog closed down. The convoy itself, unknown to me, became almost completely scattered and disorganized ..., and we had the greatest difficulty in finding it. Most of the Local Escort had lost touch, and the situation was most confused. Homing on to them by radar was useless, and we had to resort to a lot of chatter by R/T (radio/telephone) in an effort to make contact. No doubt U-boats were avidly listening and licking their chops in anticipation ...; and in fact I was rebuked from shore for using too much wireless. But there was no alternative. At dusk on the 6th we did find a few ships of the Western Local Escort ... but no convoy, and throughout the night we chugged along together on convoy course and speed.

As dawn broke, on the 7th, the weather was clearer. The *Biter*, who was to the northward of us, put up an air search, found the convoy, and signalled to me a course to steer, which turned out to be wildly wrong. I put all my ships on an extended screen at visual distance from each other and, by the greatest good fortune, the ship at the extreme end of the screen sighted the convoy on a totally different bearing. ... By afternoon we were in touch.[29]

Abel Smith's refusal to bring the support group, including *Biter*, into the convoy was causing problems. On 8 May, a slightly misty day, *Biter* flew off aircraft which failed to find the convoy 'and were therefore quite useless' to Chavasse in detecting and reporting U-boats since the Swordfish crews did not know the convoy's position. Since the position of *Biter* and her destroyers relative to the convoy had not been established, the carrier could not be used to 'fix' any high-frequency signals that might be intercepted. With deteriorating weather on the 9th, *Biter* was unable to fly off any aircraft. That was the day the first U-boat appeared. At the time *Broadway* was refuelling.

> *Broadway* received what was called a 'close-range B-bar', in other words a wireless transmission from a U-boat, dead astern of the convoy, and not far away. We were temporarily connected by hosepipe to the tanker, and while we were hastily disengaging I ordered *Primrose*, who was stationed astern of the convoy, to search and, if possible, attack. At the same time I informed *Biter*, but she could not do anything useful, as she didn't know where we were. *Primrose*, however, actually spotted the U-boat, which hastily dived, but she did not make asdic contact and she later regained her station on the screen astern of the convoy.[30]

By this stage, the Admiralty had recognized the folly of *Biter* operating so far from the convoy and, on 10 May, Abel Smith was told to take 5th Support Group into the convoy, placing himself under the orders of the escort commander. The commodore made space for the ships in the heart of HX237. From that point on, 'we never looked back' as *Biter* did magnificent work, flying off aircraft in spite of foul weather and never once refusing a request to send aircraft out on a sortie; the carrier's embarked unit was No.811 NAS, with a mix of Swordfish bombers and Wildcat fighters, still known as Martlets in British service. In a series of 'superb feats of sea-plus-airmanship in the most difficult conditions imaginable', *Biter* made a tremendous contribution to the safety of HX237. C2 and Abel Smith's group had become that most valuable asset, a co-ordinated team as Swordfish kept watch over the seas around the convoy while the fleet destroyers, each capable of over 30 knots, chased down any submarine spotted near the merchantmen and C2, 'perhaps a little more experienced in these matters', provided the final close protection.[31]

Almost as soon as the support and escort groups came together 'things began to happen thick and fast'. The boat sighted by *Primrose* had been the spotter and others were answering her call. More HF/DF detections indicated a build-up and it became clear that a wolfpack was gathering, principally to the north. Acting on HF/DF information, Chavasse asked *Biter* to carry out searches with the Swordfish backed up by destroyers. A number of U-boats stayed on the surface when spotted and opened fire, wounding a Swordfish pilot in one engagement, but, when a destroyer appeared, the boats submerged hastily.

I don't think that any of the destroyers got in asdic contact with a submerged U-boat, but they probably kept them well down by plastering the area with depth charges. At least one can say that these tactics prevented the U-boats from concentrating, or even getting near the convoy, which at this stage was never closely threatened.[32]

Information from the Admiralty indicated that at least six U-boats were gathering to attack and Chavasse was told that, as soon as the convoy was within range, shore-based aircraft would be despatched to operate under his orders. Although night attacks were expected, none occurred; night-flying was not possible from *Biter*.

On the 12th the convoy was within range of shore-based aircraft and a Liberator, which had attacked and damaged a U-boat, reported the engagement to Chavasse, adding that the boat lay on the surface, some distance off the port beam. However, the Liberator had not previously contacted the convoy and, probably due to a navigational error, and reports of other U-boats in the area, provided an inaccurate position for the stricken boat. Although two destroyers of 5th Support Group were sent to finish off the U-boat, their quest was unsuccessful. With the third of Abel Smith's destroyers carrying out a search astern, only C2's ships were available to protect the merchantmen. At this juncture one of *Biter*'s aircraft, returning low on fuel, spotted a surfaced U-boat about six miles ahead of the convoy.

This was dangerous. I told the Commodore to turn ... ninety degrees to starboard, and as *Broadway* was the nearest and fastest of the Close Escort, I abandoned my position, and increased to 29 knots to attack, calling *Lagan* to follow me at her full speed of 20 knots. I handed over command of the escort to young Lieutenant [Philip] Kitto in the *Primrose*, the senior corvette captain.

Meanwhile the [Swordfish] had attacked with depth charges and possibly damaged the U-boat, which dived. There followed a piece of copy-book co-operation between us in *Broadway* and the aircraft. The latter dropped a smoke marker on the spot where the U-boat had dived, and flew back to the convoy. I told the pilot by radio/telephone which [was] my ship, and he circled and flew over me, waving cheerfully, and led me in a beeline to the smoke marker, which I duly sighted right ahead. Reducing speed I almost immediately got firm asdic contact, and the hunt was on. The convoy steamed steadily away from us, with little *Primrose* in charge. For once the weather was good.[33]

The fix allowed Chavasse to make a Hedgehog attack. However, no rounds struck the boat, which would have been unaware of the attack, allowing *Lagan* to drop a pattern of depth charges. The boat survived and a prolonged hunt began. *U-89* had dived to 400 feet, Korvettenkapitän Dietrich Lohmann, an experienced submariner, using all his skills to avoid being caught in the bombardment. The boat 'twisted and turned like a snake in ecstasy' as both ships strove to keep contact.

Finally the lot happened to fall on *Broadway*. A salvo of bombs from our hedgehog soared beautifully into the air, ... splashed in a neat circle 250 yards ahead of us, and then, after the usual anxious pause, we were at last rewarded with a lovely bang. We had hit her fair and square.[34]

Chavasse sent *Lagan* back to the convoy but remained at the scene because he 'desperately wanted to make sure' the U-boat had sunk. There had been many Hedgehog attacks on boats, some apparently successful 'with a nice bang as one or more of the bombs had struck' the boat, but never any proof that a U-boat had been sunk. As a result confidence in Hedgehog was diminishing. *Broadway* waited over the scene of the attack for more than an hour until, with the convoy disappearing over the horizon, patience paid off and wreckage began surfacing.

> We didn't get much, but quite enough to satisfy ourselves: part of an electrical control panel with switches tallied in German, a rather dirty cotton singlet embroidered with an eagle and swastika, and a much-darned sock with the owner's name-tape in German ... but without his foot inside. The crew of *U–89* were now lying in 1,700 fathoms. May they rest in peace.[35]

This was the first Hedgehog attack to produce proof positive that a U-boat had been destroyed and the news caused morale to rise in Hedgehog-equipped ships. But the 'safe and timely arrival' of HX237 had not yet been achieved. There were still troubled waters to traverse, although the end of the battle was close.

Next morning a Sunderland from No.423 Squadron RCAF at RAF Castle Archdale spotted and attacked a U–boat 'uncomfortably close' to the convoy on its starboard side. The U-boat fought back and the Sunderland shadowed it for about twenty minutes, firing some 2,000 rounds and taking one hit. *Drumheller* forced the boat to dive with gunfire, after which the Sunderland dropped two depth charges. A Swordfish from *Biter* then dropped smoke markers and *Drumheller*, having made asdic contact, attacked with depth charges. With the boat immobilized, *Lagan* delivered the coup de grace. It was believed that the victim was *U–456* but she had been sunk the day before by *Opportune*, having been damaged by a Liberator of No.86 Squadron. The boat despatched by *Drumheller* and *Lagan* was actually *U–753*. Uboat.net suggests that *U–753* perished due to the captain's decision to dive to avoid capture.[36]

This was the final act in HX237's battle:

> Just as we felt we were getting into our stride, *Biter* and her destroyers were withdrawn to assist another convoy in peril. Simultaneously, any survivors of 'our' wolfpack evidently decided to give it up as a bad job, and an unearthly silence descended over our stretch of the Atlantic,

which for the past five days had been almost deafening with German and British radio.[37]

Lieutenant Commander Chavasse ordered C2 to Splice the Main Brace. Three U-boats had been destroyed and no ship in the convoy had been lost, although three stragglers were. Gretton writes that one of *Biter*'s Swordfish was shot down, but this was probably an aircraft that failed to return. (Losses such as this led to an order that Swordfish should fly in pairs.) The convoy was delivered safely to Britain and C2 made for Londonderry. Subsequently Chavasse was awarded the DSO for:

good services during an A/S hunt on 12th May, 1943, which, after several setbacks, resulted in the destruction of an enemy submarine. Lieutenant Commander Chavasse has been favourably commented upon on several occasions in the past for his keenness and enthusiasm and it is evident that the result of his zeal has been to keep his ship's company in a high state of efficiency.[38]

This recommendation, from Commodore George 'Shrimp' Simpson, Commodore (D) Western Approaches, was endorsed by Horton who added that Chavasse's command and control of C2, his co-ordination of HF/DF intelligence and excellent use of aircraft 'all contributed to the safe and timely arrival of the convoy with relatively light losses and considerable loss and damage to the enemy'.[39]

As C2 continued to Londonderry, 5th Support Group, which Western Approaches Command had withdrawn from HX237 once it was safely under shore-based air cover, was about to add its considerable muscle to the escort for SC129, then crossing the Atlantic under threat from a wolfpack. A small convoy of twenty-four ships, SC129 included a rescue ship and an escort oiler and was protected by B2, commanded by Commander Donald Macintyre. The group included Macintyre's ship, the destroyer HMS *Hesperus*, the modified W-class destroyer *Whitehall*, the frigate *Spey*, the corvettes *Campanula*, *Clematis*, *Gentian*, *Heather* and *Sweetbriar* and the ASW trawlers *Lady Madeleine* and *Sapper*. It was a strong and well-balanced escort, particularly as *Biter*'s No.811 NAS could provide almost continuous daytime air cover.

Macintyre was under no illusions about the journey. He knew that the Battle of the Atlantic was reaching its climax since 'an unprecedented number of U-boats' had been operating in the ocean for two months, forcing convoys to fight their way through. 'We were therefore on tip-toe in anticipation of the encounter we knew must come. There was no longer any possibility of evading the U-boats – they were too thick for that.'[40]

B2's crews were on full alert with close attention being paid to HF/DF sets, including that in the rescue ship, whose operators were sometimes more skilful than those of the warships. On the afternoon of 11 May, six days after B2 had sailed, the HF/DF operators heard their first U-boat signals, although Macintyre's operator considered that the boats were not close. Since 'I had learnt to trust implicitly in 'B-Bar's' estimates and up to date he had never been wrong', Macintyre accepted this judgement. *Whitehall* and *Clematis* were sent to sweep the horizon but found nothing. Then, at 6.00pm, in broad daylight, two ships were torpedoed. Both sank rapidly, all but two of their crewmen being picked up by the rescue ship, or an escort. *U-402*, which had torpedoed them, eluded the escorts.[41]

For Macintyre it was a particularly galling experience, the first time in his nine months commanding B2 that a ship had been lost in a convoy under his protection – and that by a U-boat penetrating the convoy in daylight. Next day, however, *Hesperus* pinpointed and sank *U-186*. On the 14th a Halifax of No.58 Squadron accounted for *U-266*, a sinking attributed initially to a homing torpedo from a Liberator of No.86 Squadron which had actually attacked *U-403* without causing damage. *Hesperus* also damaged *U-223*. In his book *U-boat Killer*, Macintyre recounts the battle between *Hesperus* and *U-223*, giving the German side of the story as far as possible, including the fact that, despite serious damage, her captain managed to get back to St Nazaire, a twelve-day voyage.[42]

From HX237 and SC129 three dozen U-boats had sunk only five ships, three of which were not in convoy when attacked, for the loss of five of their number. Escort commanders had noticed that 'there were clear signs that attacks were being pressed home with less determination' and the same held true for the next convoys to cross the ocean.[43] ON184, with C1 and the

American 6th Support Group, including the *Bogue*, lost no ships. HX239, with B3 and 4th Support Group, plus the escort carrier *Archer*, had a similar experience. Two of *Bogue*'s Avengers sank *U-569* with depth charges while one of No.819 NAS's Swordfish from *Archer* accounted for *U-752* using air-launched rockets, a new weapon recently added to the Fleet Air Arm's inventory. Surfacing to gain speed, the U-boat began shadowing the convoy. One of *Archer*'s Swordfish, flown by Sub-Lieutenant H. Horrocks RNVR, had spotted the periscope and used cloud cover to approach undetected to within 300 yards. Although *U-752* tried to crash dive, it was too late and a rocket pierced the pressure hull. Unable to dive, the boat fought it out on the surface but a Martlet from *Archer* swept *U-752*'s bridge with her guns, killing the captain and several crewmen. In a hopeless situation, the engineer officer flooded the tanks and the submarine sank. Apart from *Biter*'s success, this was the first time aircraft from a British escort carrier were responsible for sinking a U-boat. It was also the first time a rocket was fired operationally by any of the Western Allies. The projectile, with a solid head weighing 25lb, was fired from about 600 yards and at a suitable angle. It could penetrate both the outer and inner plating of a submarine's pressure hull.[44]

Three of 819's Swordfish had been fitted with rockets only two months after their use against submarines had been first suggested,[45] an exceptionally speedy introduction to service for a new weapon.

While HX238 had a trouble-free passage, the same could not be said of SC130, escorted by Gretton's B7 group, which had barely recovered from the westbound battle around ONS5.[46] SC130 left Halifax on 11 May and, as well as B7, had 1st Support Group protecting it; the Canadian corvette HMCS *Kitchener* was detached from the local escort to join B7, which was a ship short. B7 met the convoy on the 14th when, during the handover of papers, Gretton informed the commodore that he was due to be married soon after his scheduled arrival in Londonderry. The commodore, Captain H. C. C. Forsyth RD, agreed that the convoy would maintain or, if possible, improve upon its rated speed. Although no fewer than four wolfpacks were sent to attack, not a single ship was lost. All attacks were repelled, the attackers losing heavily as they assailed the convoy between the 15th and 20th. A Liberator of No.120 Squadron, flown by Flight Sergeant Shores, attacked *U-731*, forcing her and five other boats to dive; subsequently, one of these, *U-952*, was damaged by depth charges from *Tay*. *U-954* was sunk by depth charges from *Sennen* and *Tay* while *Duncan* damaged *U-707* with Hedgehog. Peter Dönitz, the 21-year-old younger son of Admiral Dönitz, was among the dead of *U-954*. Another Liberator from No.120 Squadron, with *Vidette*, forced a further six boats down, while two more Liberators from the squadron did likewise with groups of four and two boats, three of which were bombed. *Jed* and *Spey* drove off the final spotter and a Liberator from 120 sank *U-258*. In all, five boats were lost, the others being *U-209*, sunk by *Jed* and *Sennen*, and *U-273* by a Hudson of No.269 Squadron; *U-381*, believed to have been sunk by *Duncan* and *Snowflake*, had fallen victim to an unknown cause.[47]

SC130 survived intact through the presence of daytime air cover during the critical period, although there was no carrier with the convoy, the assistance of 1st Support Group 'and the discipline of the convoy which executed numerous emergency turns with the precision of a battle fleet'.[48] Peter Gretton got to the altar in time, where he and his bride were married before the Reverend Willie Devine MC CdG, Catholic chaplain to the Londonderry Escort Force.[49]

Dönitz now finally admitted that his boats were losing in the Atlantic. Recognizing the skill of the escort and support groups, the continuous air cover available, and the fact that most long-range aircraft were 'equipped with the new radar', he accepted that large-scale operations in the Atlantic could resume only if it proved possible to increase substantially the *U-bootwaffe*'s fighting power. Dönitz decided to withdraw his boats from the North Atlantic, issuing an order on the 24th that they should move with 'the utmost caution' south-west of the Azores. 'We had lost the Battle of the Atlantic.'[50]

May was the bloodiest month for the U-boats with forty-one lost. Added to the sixteen lost in April, this underlined the folly of continuing with the campaign as it had been fought until then. New weapons or new tactics, or a combination of both, were essential to continue the fight with any hope of success. And yet it is almost incredible that not until this point was a Naval Headquarters scientific directorate established with its most urgent task being the production of a new search receiver operating on a wider range of frequencies to detect Allied locating signals and so provide more timely warning of attack.

Other weapons were being developed; Dönitz sought the support of Albert Speer, Minister of Armaments and War Production, to accelerate work on the next generation of torpedo. Speer's co-operation ensured that deliveries of the acoustic torpedo began in August 1943 rather than the projected date of autumn 1944. Meanwhile, schnorkel equipment was being fitted to existing boats and designed into new boats although no schnorkel-equipped boats would be in service until 1944. However, Germany was lagging well behind in the development of weaponry and technology in comparison to the Allies.

The accounts in this chapter of the convoy battles of spring 1943 indicate some of the advances the Allies had already made. Evelyn Chavasse's comments about talking to other ships by radio telephone and communicating directly with Coastal Command aircraft marked an important feature of operations at this stage. Similar comments were made by Commander Martin James Evans, senior officer of B3 in *Keppel*, who reported that air coverage from both sides of the Atlantic was good, as was 'visual and telephonic communication ... and no time was wasted in passing to aircraft the particular patrol that was required'.[51] The American VHF radio telephones allowed speedier and clearer communication between ships which, combined with the ability to speak directly to the pilot of an aircraft, made co-operation between sea and air units much more effective; the R/T system was known as Talk Between Ships (TBS).[52] Some U-boats sunk in recent months had been destroyed by ships and planes acting in concert; this included shore-based Coastal machines and carrier-based FAA and USN aircraft. The small escort carriers, known as 'Woolworth carriers' in the Royal Navy, and MAC-ships would prove invaluable, as shown by the comment from *Keppel*'s captain that 'HMS *Archer* more than filled the thirty-six hour gap between the departure of the last aircraft from Newfoundland and the arrival of the first home-based aircraft'.[53]

ASV III made Coastal Command aircraft even more deadly, an effect further intensified by the new weapons available to the aeroplanes fighting the U-boats. We have noted the fitting of rocket rails to Fleet Air Arm

Swordfish, which had required replacing their fabric-covered lower wings with metal-skinned undersides. In addition, Swordfish were also adapted to carry ASV III, the machines fitted with this and rockets being Swordfish Mark II, which also had a more powerful engine. The later Swordfish Mark III had ASV XI which could detect a ship or, in good conditions, a surfaced U-boat at a range of twenty-five miles and, in calm sea conditions, a schnorkel at up to five miles.[54]

In the account of the passage of SC129 reference was made to a No.86 Squadron Liberator using a homing torpedo. Although unsuccessful that attack represented another increment in the battle. The 'homing', or acoustic, torpedo was an American innovation, known officially as the Mark 24 Mine to conceal its true nature, which entered US Navy service in March 1943 and was also supplied to the UK and Canada. With a warhead of 92lb of HBX (High Blast Explosive), derived from Torpex, the weapon, weighing 680 pounds, had a preset circular search pattern when dropped into the water. Once its hydrophones detected a signal, the homing guidance system took over. With a speed of 12 knots, the torpedo could not overtake a surfaced submarine but could catch a submerged boat. Also known as Fido, Wandering Willie or Wandering Annie, its first kill was achieved in mid-May, two months after its entry to service. On 12 May a Liberator of No.86 Squadron launched a Mark 24 at *U-456* which damaged the boat severely and probably contributed to its subsequent sinking by HMS *Opportune* (see page 204). Two days later a US Navy Catalina of VP-84 sank *U-640* with a Mark 24.[55]

Horton continued paying close attention to training with many more escort group officers undertaking courses on *Philante*. He was also aware of the expanding needs of the Fleet Air Arm in its anti-submarine role. Thus on 1 May 1943 two RAF stations in County Londonderry, close to HMS *Ferret*, RAF Eglinton and RAF Maydown, its satellite, were handed over on loan to the Admiralty, being commissioned two weeks later as 'stone frigates'. Eglinton became HMS *Gannet*, a base for the formation and training of fighter squadrons, while Maydown became HMS *Shrike*, the home for No.836 NAS, the pool, or parent, squadron for the MAC-ships then entering service.[56] Although the Admiralty had intended to make HMS *Gadwall* (Belfast) the headquarters for MAC-ship flights, it was decided that Maydown would be more suitable.[57] HMS *Shrike,* or RNAS Maydown, later became home to the Dutch No.860 NAS, operating Swordfish from MAC-ships. Eventually *Shrike* was the base for about 100 Swordfish; No.744 NAS re-formed there to train MAC-ship Swordfish crews.[58] Swordfish would land on a MAC-ship as it steamed off Ireland's north coast on its westbound voyage. Nearing the end of the return journey the Swordfish would fly off and return to *Shrike.* In between, the crews may have been involved in action against U-boats, in which some aircraft may have been lost, or simply spent the voyage flying ahead of and over the convoy, forcing submarines to remain submerged. The Swordfish played an important part in ensuring the safety of convoys. It was these flimsy-looking biplanes rather than the large robust land planes that closed completely the mid-Atlantic air gap.

Another factor in expanding Allied air cover was the Portuguese government's agreement to allow British aircraft to operate from the Azores. In Operation ALACRITY British forces landed in the Azores in October, to pre-empt an anticipated German invasion, and an air base was established at Lajes, known as RAF Lages; US Navy aircraft also operated from there.[59] North of the Azores three British escort carriers worked with convoys, while US Navy carriers 'continued their good work south of the Azores'.[60]

Although many writers have chosen to define May 1943 as the 'end' of the battle, it still had many months to run and would not conclude until the end of the European war.[61] However, the battle against the U-boats from June 1943 until May 1945 was of a quite different complexion to its first forty-five months, although there continued to be action in the Atlantic as Dönitz still hoped that new types of U-boat, new weapons and new technology would help him defeat the Allies.

Of the operational situation at the beginning of June, the Admiralty noted that the boats had been 'virtually withdrawn' from North Atlantic convoy routes. Small numbers continued operating off the coast of Brazil, off Freetown and in the Mozambique Channel, areas where they were immune from shore-based aircraft. About eighty boats were at sea, sinking twenty ships (about 96,000 tons) during June for the loss of seventeen of their own number. The Allied shipping tonnage lost was the lowest since November 1941.

Hessler defines the sixth period of the battle as June, July and August 1943, three months of much action in areas as varied as the waters off West Africa and the Bay of Biscay. During June U-boats were sighted in the calm weather belt, the Horse Latitudes, between 500 and 700 miles south-west of the Azores. They were concentrating against US convoys to North Africa, an increasingly important route following the Axis capitulation in Tunisia and the impending Allied landings in Sicily, Operation HUSKY. This was one area where U-boats had operated with the same impunity from shore-based aircraft as they had done far to the north in the mid-Atlantic gap. On 26 May Dönitz ordered seventeen boats to form a north-south line along the forty-third meridian between latitudes 32 and 39N, straddling 'an Atlantic highway teeming with valuable targets' of US ships carrying troops, fuel and equipment to North Africa.[62] If Group Trutz hoped to have a field day attacking slow merchantmen, they were mistaken. With fast escorts and escort carriers, the US Navy was well prepared to protect troop convoys. As soon as Group Trutz was detected 'it became the victim of an anti-submarine offensive unique for the rapidity with which tactical innovations were introduced'.[63]

Once again U-boats became prey to carrier-borne aircraft. USS *Bogue*, which had already served in the North Atlantic, was assigned to support UGS9 and, on 5 and 12 June, its aircraft accounted for *U-217* and *U-118*. (The Avenger bombers of VC-9 were exceptionally capable aircraft. With a three-man crew, the Avenger, the war's largest single-engined aircraft, which had first seen service in the Battle of Midway in June 1942, was easy to fly and carried a heavy payload. In the ASW role it was radar-equipped and carried depth charges.) Perhaps more significantly than these two sinkings, on 4 June, an Avenger, flown by Ensign Edward R. Hodgson, saved a convoy of LCIs (landing craft, infantry) from attack by bombing and forcing down *U-603*.[64]

Bogue was joined in protecting North Africa convoys by two sister ships, *Card* and *Core*, and the Sangamon-class *Santee*. In what Morison describes as the 'Azores Happy Hunting Ground' in July and August they wrought havoc, with a series of U-boat kills, the result of 'a tactical transition: the evolution of the close-support escort carrier group into a roving convoy support group, and finally into an independent hunter-killer group'.[65]

During July the *Core* and *Santee* groups sank *U-487*, a *Milchkuh*, as well as *U-67*, *U-160*, *U-509* and *U-43*, and damaged *U-373*. *U-509* was sunk by a Fido from an Avenger of VC-29 from *Santee*, after a Wildcat had forced the boat down; Dönitz sent a signal to his commanders on 5 August warning them of 'new, more dangerous bombs' being used by the Allies and adding, 'Do not report too much bad news, so as to depress the other boats; every radio message goes the rounds of the crew in every boat'.[66] The CVEs and their groups ensured that American convoys to Casablanca passed unscathed. One of those, UGS8A, was increased to 129 merchant vessels and nineteen escorts off Gibraltar and, covering seventy square miles of sea, became the largest convoy by tonnage in history to that point. It did not retain the distinction long, however; the Royal Canadian Navy escorted the 167 ships of HXS300 safely across the Atlantic in August 1944.[67]

The Battle of the Bay was causing the U-boats more grief. Coastal Command's offensive, reinforced by US Navy aircraft from August, was conducted by No.19 Group, under Air Vice-Marshal Geoffrey Bromet, but with Sir John Slessor showing a keen interest. Slessor regarded this offensive to be one of the most important of the war. Taking up the concept from Joubert, he had added even more emphasis. Likening the deployment of U-boats against Atlantic convoys as a tree, he described their routes across Biscay as the trunk, the best place in which to attack the tree, since U-boats were bound to be concentrated there; the 'trunk' measured 300 by 120 miles. One advantage for Coastal in such operations was that they could be conducted by aircraft from bases in south-western Britain that were less likely to be affected adversely by weather conditions than those farther north.[68]

When Slessor succeeded Joubert in February an offensive, Operation GONDOLA, was underway, which from 4 to 16 February, saw Coastal and US Army Air Forces' units interdicting U-boats crossing the Bay. Two USAAF B-24 squadrons, on loan to Coastal, equipped with SCR517, the American name for ASV III, were deployed and it was a Liberator of No.2 US Squadron that was believed to have achieved the only kill in 300 sorties, during which only nineteen boats were sighted and eight attacks made. Although the Liberator was credited with sinking *U-519*, it had actually attacked and damaged *U-752*, which was returning to base. *U-752* was sunk by a Swordfish from HMS *Archer* on 23 May; *U-519* had gone missing on 31 January.[69]

With ASV III fitted to their Leigh–Light–equipped Wellingtons, both No.172 Squadron RAF and No.407 Squadron RCAF operated over the Bay in March. One of 172's Wellingtons found and attacked *U-333* during the night of 4/5 March. Although taken by surprise, *U-333* fought back and shot down the Wellington, which had dropped its depth charges, two of them hitting the boat; one shattered without detonating while the second bounced off. The aircraft had sunk *U-268* on 19 February.[70] *U-333* would become the first victim of the Squid anti-submarine mortar in July 1944.

The next phase, Operation ENCLOSE, began on 20 March. When it ended, on the 28th, twenty-six sightings had resulted in fifteen attacks with no sinkings. One kill had been claimed by a Wellington of No.172 Squadron, but this was *U-665*, which was sunk west of Ireland by a Whitley of No.10 Operational Training Unit. No.172's plane had attacked *U-448* without causing damage.[71] ENCLOSE II produced a similar result with another kill claim for 172, this time for *U-376*, but the Wellington had attacked and damaged *U-465*. Then followed Operation DERANGE in which Bromet deployed some seventy ASV III-equipped Wellingtons, Liberators and Halifaxes. This also produced no kills, the one boat lost during the operation, *U-526*, falling victim to mines. It might seem that the offensive was wasted effort but there was undoubtedly an effect on U-boat crew morale, especially at stages when they might otherwise have expected to be able to relax to some degree.[72]

Against the morale effects on the U-boat crews should be measured similar effects on aircrews. When the *Official History of the War at Sea* was written it was believed that ten U-boats had been sunk in the Bay between 1 January 1941 and 30 April 1943 with the cost to Coastal Command of 170 machines; 148 were lost between 1 June 1942 and 30 April 1943. The aircraft had flown 80,443 hours, losing seventeen machines for every U-boat sunk. However, the true number of U-boats lost was only four, making the overall total since January 1941 five. Thus the ratio of aircraft to U-boats lost was really thirty-four to one. Had this been known at the time, the effect on morale can but be imagined.

In June Coastal Command returned in strength to operations in Biscay as Ultra confirmed Dönitz's change of strategy. However, there were also changes in how the boats passed through the Bay; night-time passage was to be submerged in groups, but by day they were to travel on the surface in groups to use combined firepower against attacking aircraft. Anti-aircraft armament on boats was strengthened and one, *U-441*, was converted to be an aircraft trap, renamed *U-Flak-1*, with her 88mm deck gun replaced by two 'bandstands', one forward and one aft of the conning tower; the boat mounted two four-barrelled 20mm guns and a single 37mm gun, plus several MG42 machine guns. Crew complement was increased to sixty-seven, including a doctor and some scientists, the latter to investigate Allied detection methods. Another two boats were converted to this role but it was realized quickly that these were not the answer. That realization came when *U-Flak-1* was attacked by three Coastal Command Beaufighters on 12 July. Armed with four nose-mounted 20mm cannon and six .303-inch machine guns in the wings, a Beaufighter was a lethal opponent. The three pilots, from No.248 Squadron at RAF Predannack, used speed, firepower and their numbers to outfight the flak-boat. Attacking from various directions, they overpowered the gunners, one burst of fire virtually wiping them out. Casualties included most of the officers and it was left to the surgeon to order a dive and return to port. Dönitz acknowledged that this encounter proved that a U-boat was 'a poor weapon with which to fight aircraft' and, as a result, no further modifications were made; *U-Flak-1* resumed her former identity as *U-441*.[73]

Coastal Command continued attacking boats on the surface. Slessor's orders were emphatic: should a U-boat be prepared to fight it out on the surface, aircraft were to do likewise 'even in the face of heavy opposition'.

A scientist asked him one day what would happen when the U-boats' anti-aircraft weapons forced our aircraft up, and reminded him how in 1940 we had made the Luftwaffe abandon low attacks on our convoys by using far less lethal weapons than those now being fitted in the U-boats. Slessor replied 'the one thing we want to see is the U-boat on the surface. We shall not be forced up.' It was precisely in that spirit that the Coastal Command aircrews were now sweeping the Bay.[74]

At this time 5th Support Group, commanded by Captain Horace Bayliss, now with the escort carrier *Archer*, was added to the forces arrayed against boats in the Bay. Bayliss' group also included four destroyers and three corvettes with HMS *Glasgow*, a cruiser, in support.[75] This was not all as three Canadian destroyers were patrolling the area. On 24 July a No.172 Squadron Wellington sighted and attacked *U-459*, one of the *Milchkühe*. Although the Wellington surprised the boat, it met intense and accurate fire. Flying Officer William Jennings, from Devon, lost control and the aircraft slammed into the U-boat. The tail gunner was the only survivor; his turret sheered away and landed in the water close to an inflated dinghy. *U-459* lost most of its AA guns while several gunners were killed. Three unexploded depth charges were found on deck as wreckage was being cleared; these were rolled overboard but one exploded, damaging the steering gear and the stern compartments. Another Wellington, from No.547 Squadron, based at RAF Davidstow Moor in Cornwall, later machine gunned *U-459* and dropped depth charges that inflicted more damage. At that stage Korvettenkapitän Georg von Wilamovitz-Möllendorf ordered his men to abandon ship; he remained with the vessel which he scuttled. Forty-one of his crew and the first Wellington's tail gunner were picked up by the Polish destroyer *Orkan*.[76] Flying Officer Jennings was Mentioned in Despatches.[77]

Two other boats were sunk by aircraft on 28 and 29 July. *U-404* was attacked by three Liberators in succession, two American and one British. The crew fought back when the boat resurfaced to find its first antagonist waiting. All three Liberators were damaged by AA fire, the worst being that of No.224 Squadron, which got back to St Eval only after dumping its guns and all loose equipment. Next day a Wellington from No.172 sank *U-614*. Added to the toll taken by the US Navy carrier-borne aircraft already mentioned, the U-boats were suffering grievously, but more was to follow. In the closing days of July, eleven boats sailed from the French ports for their patrol areas. Two were *Milchkühe*, *U-461* and *462*, which Dönitz was especially keen to see safely in the ocean and to which he assigned an escort, *U-504*. The boats were sighted and in a series of attacks by Coastal Command, an American Liberator and ships of 2nd Support Group, all were sunk although the episode indicated some problems in navigation and communications, prompting Coastal Command Headquarters to emphasize the need for 'the most careful training' in these subjects.[78]

Aircraft operating over the Bay also had to contend with German machines, especially Junkers 88 fighters. Beaufighters were deployed to counter the 88s but in some cases the heavy aircraft had to fight it out with Luftwaffe fighters. One such combat occurred on 2 June when a Sunderland III of No.461 Squadron RAAF was attacked by eight Ju88s, and shot down three 88s and damaged three more. The Sunderland's pilot, Flight Lieutenant Colin Walker, was injured, one crewman was killed and others suffered serious injury but the aircraft returned to base at Pembroke Dock. It had been searching for a missing KLM/BOAC passenger plane that had been shot down by the Luftwaffe the day before. Among the missing was the actor Leslie Howard and it is believed that the Germans thought Churchill might have been on the DC-3. It is also possible that the attack on the Sunderland was prompted by a belief that it was being used by Churchill.[79]

Walker's support group demonstrated new tactics during these operations. By spring 1943 it had been found that U-boats were diving to 600 feet and more, which meant they could not be detected by asdic at close range. Captain Walker had devised a countermeasure, the 'creeping attack': the U-boat was stalked at low speed by a directing ship on the flank which kept constant asdic touch at about 1,500 yards while an attacking ship was guided slowly over the boat's position. When the bearings and ranges of U-boat and attacking ship coincided, the latter dropped depth charges by signal over and along the target's path. This eliminated the last-minute speed increase by the attacker which, detected by the U-boat's hydrophones, warned of imminent attack and allowed evasion. Attacks now came unheralded. Walker used the method for the first time on 1 June 1943, sinking *U-202*.[80]

The Allied offensive in the Bay led to the U-boats abandoning the practice of travelling on the surface in daylight. Fewer boats were making the passage and tended to hug the north coast of Spain, even slipping inside that country's territorial waters. This area was at extreme range for UK-based aircraft, especially long-range fighters, while the Bay was now patrolled by more Luftwaffe machines. In spite of air patrols off the Spanish coast, using British and US aircraft from both Gibraltar and Morocco, and between Cape Finisterre and Cape Ortegal, the latter in concert with naval escort groups, there were few positive results. A Gibraltar-based Wellington from

No.179 Squadron scored the first success in August when, on the 24th, the Leigh-Light-equipped machine sank *U-134*, a boat that had been attacked only three days earlier by aircraft from the USS *Croatan*. The boat was intercepted near Vigo in Spain; the earlier attack had occurred off Portugal.[81]

The Luftwaffe had reinforced western France with the Heinkel He177 Greif replacing Junkers 88s. Dönitz had asked for the He177 to be deployed to protect boats crossing the Bay but the aircraft, 'Germany's biggest bomber programme' of the war, 'is remembered as possibly the most troublesome and unsatisfactory aircraft in military history'. Built to a 1938 requirement for a heavy bomber capable of dive-bombing, the designers hoped to reduce drag by using coupled engines. This was a serious mistake 'because no engines in bomber history have caught fire so often in normal cruising flight'.[82] The Avro Manchester bomber had a similar problem but Avro reworked the Manchester with four Merlin engines to produce the Lancaster. When Göring rejected Heinkel's similar proposal the Luftwaffe found itself with a plane that needed courage simply to fly in it.

As aerial combats increased in August the Luftwaffe claimed seventeen Coastal ASW aircraft and six fighters and also attacked surface vessels deployed in those waters. On the 27th a group of Allied ships – Brewer's 1st Support Group reinforced with HMCS *Athabaskan* and HMS *Grenville*, came under attack from eighteen German aircraft. Some of the attackers, Dornier Do217s, carried new weaponry under their wings. HMS *Egret* of 1st Support Group found herself the target for one of these, becoming the first ship ever sunk by a guided missile. The missile was the Henschel Hs293 radio-controlled glider-bomb which was released from its parent aircraft, whereupon its small jet engine fired and the missile was guided to its target from the plane. An Hs293 could fly at speeds between 345 and 460mph with a 1,100lb warhead.[83] Both *Egret* and *Athabaskan* were struck by missiles with *Egret* blowing up and 194 of her crew perishing. *Athabaskan*, a Canadian Tribal-class destroyer, was damaged badly but returned to service. This was not the first occasion on which Hs293s had been launched at Allied ships as, two days before, 5th Canadian Support Group had been attacked in similar fashion, with HM Ships *Landguard* and *Bideford* hit and damaged; one man was killed on *Bideford* and several others injured.[84] It was realized that intense close-range AA fire could provide effective defence against the

Hs293 and escorts quickly ensured that their AA gunners were well trained and well practised in such techniques.

After the first few days the month of August thus produced few successes to our sea and air patrols, and considerable losses were suffered by the latter. Dönitz had at least regained a large measure of safety on the Biscay transit routes, and never again did our patrols accomplish such good results as they had achieved in July [1943].[85]

The U-boats were still crossing the Bay, but submerged, surfacing only at night to recharge batteries and then only for the minimum time required.

Chapter Twelve

In July Allied shipping losses were forty-five ships (244,000 tons), higher than in June but, balanced against U-boats destroyed and increased essential imports into the UK, it 'was the better month of the two'. No attacks had been made against North Atlantic convoys, which now had regular MAC-ship support. August proved a highly significant month with the Allies sinking more U-boats than the latter sank merchantmen: twenty-four U-boats against sixteen merchant ships (86,000 tons).[1] A Canadian Sunderland of No.423 Squadron sank *U-489*, another *Milchkuh*, between the Faeroes and Iceland on the 4th, a major loss to the *U-bootwaffe* that seriously curtailed operations off the Brazilian coast. By the end of August, the campaign in Brazilian waters was abandoned. Although earlier a soft spot for U-boats, the area had become much more dangerous as US Navy ships and aircraft, from Brazil or the RAF base on Ascension Island, sank three boats in August.[2]

U-boats were also operating off West Africa. On 11 August *U-468* was spotted some 215 miles west-south-west of Bathurst by a Liberator of No.200 Squadron. The Liberator's captain, New Zealander Flying Officer Lloyd Trigg DFC, attacked immediately. The U-boat opened fire and the Liberator, hit several times, caught fire. Trigg continued, released his depth charges and damaged the boat so badly that it sank within ten minutes. However, the Liberator crashed in flames with no survivors. Seven U-boat crewmen were later rescued from the Liberator's dinghy and their account formed the basis of the citation for a posthumous Victoria Cross for Lloyd Trigg.[3]

As summer moved towards autumn, Allied troops had taken Sicily and Eighth Army landed in Italy on 3 September, followed by Fifth Army's landings six days later. Mussolini had been deposed and Marshal Badoglio's government negotiated an armistice with the Allies that took effect on 9 September. Meanwhile, the Kriegsmarine had re-evaluated the Atlantic submarine campaign, since it was only in those waters that U-boats could affect adversely the Allied build-up for the inevitable landings in France. By then the U-boats had a new torpedo, German engineers having developed an acoustic torpedo at much the same time as the US Navy had developed Fido.

The first German acoustic torpedo had been introduced in March, but the T4 *Falke* saw only limited use before being replaced with the T5 *Zaunkönig* (wren), which was faster, longer ranged and could be fitted with either magnetic or contact detonators. Known to the Royal Navy as the GNAT (German Navy Acoustic Torpedo) the Zaunkönig entered service in the autumn. It was designed to lock on to the loudest noise after it had run 400 metres but, since the loudest noise could come from the U-boat itself, the standard procedure adopted was that, following a shot from a bow tube, the boat dived immediately to sixty metres (200 feet); after a shot from a stern tube the boat maintained complete silence. It is believed that *U-972* and *U-377* were lost to their own T5s in December 1943 and January 1944. The GNAT had some early successes but the Allies, anticipating its introduction had an effective countermeasure ready. That the Allies were waiting for the Germans to introduce an acoustic torpedo is a serendipitous intelligence story dating back to 1941 when the Germans suspected that the British already had such weapons. Although there had been no British acoustic torpedo in 1941 their suspicions spurred the Germans into beginning work on an acoustic torpedo. When a prisoner reported that trials were underway, NID watched for signs of progress. These seemed to come from an Enigma decrypt in January 1943 which referred to the FAT torpedo, but the abbreviation was interpreted, wrongly, as meaning *Fernakustischtorpedo*, or long-range acoustic torpedo. Thus when the Germans produced the GNAT for use against escort ships, the countermeasure was deployed only sixteen days later.[4] U-boats carried three or four GNATs 'to destroy a fair number of escorts [before using] ordinary torpedoes for sinking the unprotected merchant ships'.[5] 'Foxer' was the codename of the countermeasure, an acoustic array of hollow metal pipes with holes drilled into them, towed about 200 yards behind the ship; water rushing through the clashing pipes created a cavitation noise greater than that from the ship's propellers. The US Navy created its own decoy, called FXR, and the Canadians the CAT (Counter-Acoustic Torpedo) which made a noise similar to a circular saw. Foxer also rendered useless the towing ship's asdic and, since it could be heard from a considerable distance, allowed U-boats to home on convoys. Since Foxer could not be used above 15 knots, its value to destroyers and other faster ships was limited. However, in Walker's group, slow speed, already part of the tactical pattern, was used to counter the GNAT.[6] Foxer was later improved so that it could be used at 20 knots.[7] Although the Germans created a new torpedo that ignored the sounds of decoys it never became operational. As Schull writes, 'the acoustic torpedo remained merely an added nuisance to the end of the war'.[8] Gilbert Roberts' team at WATU also devised the 'Stepaside' tactic for use by escorts, which proved to be another antidote to the problem.

By September the Battle of the Atlantic was into its seventh phase with Dönitz trying to regain the initiative. We have seen (page 208) that he established a Naval Scientific Operations Staff which Terraine comments was 'better late than never', but that 'it was very late indeed', and likely to concentrate on radar as Professor Küpfmüller led the organization. The operational submariner now had a direct contact with the scientists, but too late for anyone, however great his talent, to save Hitler's state from economic crisis and defeat.[9]

Ultra had indicated that U-boats were moving out again from Biscay in late August, a pattern that continued into September. The Submarine Tracking Room reported fifteen or sixteen boats outward bound on 6 September but with no indication of their destinations. A week later the numbers had increased to about twenty but commanders were observing strict radio silence. They might have been sailing to the Mediterranean or the Azores. More information came on the 20th when a signal from U-boat Command was intercepted: boats were to resume operations in 'the main battle area'. The words 'North Atlantic' might as well have been used. As if to compound the folly, the signal then described the coming operations as 'the decisive struggle', which would be executed using 'new weapons and installations ... to decimate the escort for moral effect and to denude the convoy'. The main convoy routes were to be targeted again, using GNATs to destroy the escorts, leaving the merchantmen exposed.[10]

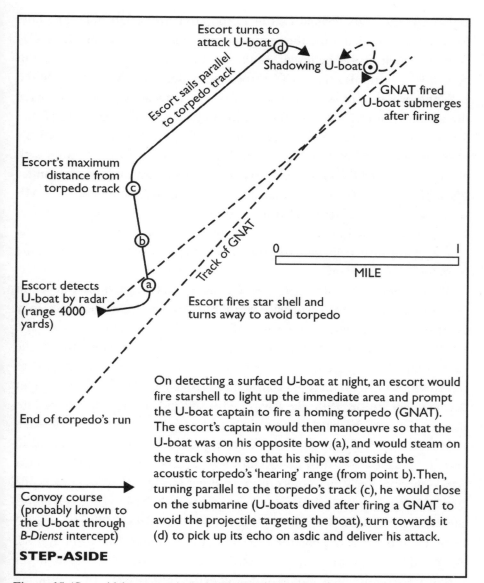

Escort turns to
attack U-boat

Shadowing U-boat

GNAT fired
U-boat submerges
after firing

Escort sails parallel
to torpedo track

Escort's maximum
distance from
torpedo track ⓒ

ⓑ

Track of GNAT

0   1

MILE

Escort detects
U-boat by radar
(range 4000
yards)

ⓐ

Escort fires star shell and
turns away to avoid torpedo

End of torpedo's run

On detecting a surfaced U-boat at night, an escort would
fire starshell to light up the immediate area and prompt
the U-boat captain to fire a homing torpedo (GNAT).
The escort's captain would then manoeuvre so that the
U-boat was on his opposite bow (a), and would steam on
the track shown so that his ship was outside the
acoustic torpedo's 'hearing' range (from point b). Then,
turning parallel to the torpedo's track (c), he would close
on the submarine (U-boats dived after firing a GNAT to
avoid the projectile targeting the boat), turn towards it
(d) to pick up its echo on asdic and deliver his attack.

Convoy course
(probably known to
the U-boat through
B-Dienst intercept)

STEP-ASIDE

Figure 15: 'Stepaside' was a tactic devised by WATU for use against the GNAT.

Twenty-one boats formed Leuthen group to patrol a 350-mile-long line. Nine were equipped with the new non-radiating Hagenuk (or *Wanz G1*) receiver which, it was believed, would not allow Allied aircraft to home in on it. These boats also carried T5 torpedoes to 'decimate the escort'. On the 19th the presence of some was known to the Tracking Room. They were threatening not one but two westbound convoys, ONS18 and ON202, the former of twenty-seven merchantmen, the latter of forty-two. ONS18's escort included the MAC-ship *Empire MacAlpine* and B3 escort group with eight ships while ON202 had C2's six ships as its escort under Commander Philip Burnett, Evelyn Chavasse having just taken command of HMS *Bentinck* as senior officer of B4. The Admiralty had also ordered 9th Support Group to leave the Bay to assist in the North Atlantic, a prescient move. As well as Swordfish from *Empire MacAlpine*, the convoys also had support from long-range aircraft.[11]

'Expectations were high at U-boat Command: a fair-sized pack in action once more, a deadly new surprise weapon, German electronic technology contributing handsomely.'[12] To cap it all, an excellent target of two convoys, almost seventy merchantmen, and a strong escort against which to test the Zaunkönig. The escort was reduced by one when HMS *Escapade* had to return following a premature explosion of Hedgehog rounds. That accident occurred late on the 19th, the day the U-boats and convoys first came into contact. Earlier, the battle's first clash had been won by the Allies when a Canadian VLR Liberator from No.10 Squadron, flying from Iceland to Gander, sank *U-341* en route to join the attackers. That night the U-boat attacks began. Early next morning two ships of ON202 were sunk while *Lagan* was hit by a GNAT; damaged so badly that she had to be towed home, she was later written off.[13] Since the convoys were so close, Horton ordered them to join up and pool their escorts. Commander Evans, in *Keppel*, described how 'the two convoys gyrated majestically round the ocean, never appearing to get much closer and watched appreciatively by a growing swarm of U-boats'.[14]

During daylight on the 20th the boats were kept away by No.120 Squadron's Liberators and excellent work by the escorts. By night the boats could move in. HMCS *St Croix* took a hit from a GNAT and was sunk an hour later by another torpedo. A GNAT also despatched HMS *Polyanthus*.

Both *St Croix*'s and *Polyanthus*'s crews were rescued by HMS *Itchen*. For the next two days the convoy was swathed in dense fog and the battle eventually ended, according to Dönitz, because of the fog. Before the battle concluded, however, the fog had cleared, allowing Liberators of No.10 Squadron RCAF to swamp the area, forcing at least two boats to withdraw and make for home. *Empire MacAlpine* managed to fly off a Swordfish, in a clear patch and, almost miraculously, the aircraft landed on again in spite of dense fog.

That night, the 22nd/23rd, the U-boats renewed their attacks, sinking four merchantmen and *Itchen*, which was struck by a GNAT. *Itchen* was still carrying the survivors from *St Croix* and *Polyanthus* and all but three of the crewmen were lost. Five merchantmen from ON202 were sunk and one damaged while one from ONS18 was lost. Uboat.net claims that ten ships were sunk and two damaged, as well as the escort vessels that were lost. Dönitz told Hitler that twelve destroyers had been sunk with the new torpedo, another three damaged, and nine merchant ships destroyed for the loss of two U-boats. He did not include *U-341* which had been some 160 miles distant.[15]

Western Approaches Command warned escort captains that acoustic torpedoes were being used against them but also told them that countermeasures would soon be available: Foxer was issued just over two weeks later.[16]

Although U-boat losses in September were eleven boats, only 43,775 tons of Allied shipping was lost in the Atlantic, from a global total of 156,419 tons. Neither Zaunkönig nor Hagenuk nor the Hs293 were going to turn the battle for the Germans. During October U-boat Command again tried wolfpack tactics, but with little success. Packs, numbering between fifteen and twenty, attempted to operate in their old stamping ground. One group, Rossbach, committed the fatal error of concentrating too close to Iceland; several boats paid the highest price for that error. Three were sunk on the 4th and 5th, *U-279* by a US Navy Lockheed Ventura of VB-128, *U-389* by a Liberator of No.120 Squadron and *U-336* by a rocket-firing Hudson of No.269 Squadron. That two were lost to a Hudson and a Ventura indicates how close to Iceland the pack was concentrating. *U-419* was one of three boats sunk on 8 October, the others being *U-610* and *U-643*, despatched, respectively, by a Liberator of No.86 Squadron, a Sunderland of No.423

Squadron RCAF and two Liberators, one each from Nos.86 and 120 Squadrons. Five days later the group had moved south where, in mid-ocean, an Avenger of VP-9 from the USS *Card* launched a Fido that killed *U-402*. An Avenger from *Core*'s VC-13 depth-charged and sank *U-470* on the 16th; the boat had been part of Rossbach until a few days earlier.[17]

One convoy targeted by U-boats was SC143 which had sailed from Halifax on 28 September with thirty-nine merchantmen and a MAC-ship. Nine escorts protected it and 10th Support Group was on call. On 8 October the Polish destroyer *Orkan* was hit by a GNAT and sank with the loss of most of her crew. An American merchantman was also sunk. Against this, *U-419*, *U-610* and *U-643* were sunk by Coastal Command aircraft. Although a Luftwaffe flying boat flew over the convoy, its attempts to 'home' the U-boats in were unsuccessful.[18]

Group Schlieffen also lost three boats to Liberators from Nos.59, 86 and 120 Squadrons on 16 and 17 October. *U-470* was attacked by two aircraft, one from 59 and the other from 120. *U-844* was also attacked by two Liberators, but shot down a machine from No.86 Squadron whose depth charges had twice failed to release (the other aircraft, from No.59 Squadron, returned to base with severe damage). *U-540* was also pounced upon by two Liberators, one from 59, the other from 120. A Liberator from No.86 Squadron also sank *U-964*, which was not assigned to a specific wolfpack, on the 17th. Although the boats moved farther west, less than 600 miles from Newfoundland, they achieved no more success, thanks to the Tracking Room's evasive routeing of convoys and the co-ordinated efforts of escort groups, support groups and aircraft from shore bases and carriers.[19]

The redoubtable Peter Gretton with B7 sailed out of Londonderry on 12 October to meet ON206, escorted by B6 under Commander Robert Currie in HMS *Fame*. Gretton had done 'a great deal of lobbying in order that we should become a support group, ... a much more interesting task than the routine work of a normal convoy escort' but it was not until October that B7 was 'allowed the privilege of one run as a support group'.[20] This 'was no ordinary period'; B7 spent twenty-five days at sea during which there were 'few dull moments'. With only five ships, as both *Tay* and *Snowflake* were refitting, B7 met ON206 on the 13th. Gretton and Currie had already discussed plans, agreeing to organize their groups into fast and slow divisions, irrespective of group, with the slow division as close escort under Currie while the fast, under Gretton, 'hared around the convoy to discourage U-boats approaching'. Tactical command, as usual, was exercised by the close escort commander. During the night of 15/16 October HMS *Vanquisher*, of B6, forced down a U-boat and next morning two boats were sunk by Liberators: *U-844* and *U-470*'s fates have already been described. *Duncan*, with survivors from *U-470* aboard, and *Vidette* kept more boats down during the night. Those had first been spotted by Commander Evelyn Chavasse's HMS *Bentinck* which opened fire, forcing them down. On the 17th, as already noted, *U-540* was sunk by aircraft. Gretton's fast division had spotted a boat on radar at dawn and forced it down although subsequent attacks produced no tangible result. 'Several days of attack had resulted in no damage to the convoy or escorts, and our first encounter had proved most satisfactory.'[21]

Having refuelled in atrocious conditions from the tanker *Roxane*, B7 left to support ONS20, which was under heavy attack from astern. The convoy was some 150 miles to the north-east. As B7 raced towards ONS20, *Sunflower* had a radar contact at 3,400 yards and sighted *U-631* at 700 yards. *U-631* dived with *Sunflower* about 300 yards away. Depth charges were dropped and the boat was blown to the surface, but dived again just before *Sunflower* made her second attack which sent *U-631* to the bottom. One ship from the convoy had been sunk but two U-boats had perished, *U-964* by a No.86 Squadron Liberator and *U-841* by HMS *Byard*, one of the new Captain-class frigates. By 20 October ONS20 was out of danger and B7 moved to support ON207.

HMS *Biter** was part of the escort for ON207 and was inside the convoy. Gretton collected the information he needed and B7 moved to its station, 100 miles to the north-north-west, which was reached early on the 23rd. In addition to B7, the convoy had Walker's 2nd Support Group deployed 'out of sight to the southward', as well as C1 in close escort. Before long the group was again engaged with a U-boat. On this occasion *Sunflower* had

---

* Roskill identifies the escort carrier as *Tracker*.[22]

suffered a radar defect that could be repaired only with a spare part that was not held on any of the ships. A message to No.15 Group brought the response that a Liberator would divert to drop the spare. Thirty minutes before he was due overhead, the pilot radioed to say that he had sighted a U-boat and B7 sped to the scene 'in time to see the splash of his explosions on the horizon'. *Duncan* and *Vidette* were first to arrive and as soon as the group had assembled Gretton deployed his ships to search for the boat. Within thirty minutes it had been detected and *Duncan* had three hits with her second Hedgehog attack. *U-274* had been destroyed.

On the 28th B7 joined ON208 with which it remained for two days before leaving to meet HX263. Leaving ON208 a U-boat was detected stalking the merchantmen and *Sunflower* made a Hedgehog attack, sinking *U-282*. The rendezvous with HX263 was made on 31 October and B7 remained with the convoy 'for several days without incident'.[23]

In the *Duncan* we had steamed 6,700 miles ... crossed the Atlantic five times ... fuelled at sea on six occasions, and ... also topped up with depth charges. On 5 November the group sailed up the River Foyle feeling very pleased with itself. The track chart of our wanderings resembled the antics of a fly drying after a dip in a bottle of ink.

The group had kept going remarkably well and all radar and asdic sets were working on return to harbour, except for *Loosestrife* whose anti-submarine dome had been ripped off by heavy seas. There had been no engine defects and we had proved that, if B7 were given a 'run' supporting, we could make a good job of it.[24]

Commander Gretton's group was at sea for twenty-five days, during most of which the Atlantic produced its customary autumn gales. Fifteen years later one of the *Duncan*'s company sent his recollections to the author. 'The conditions inside the ship' he wrote 'were almost indescribable. She often rolled between fifty and sixty degrees, and water several inches deep swirled continuously around on the mess decks. We were at "Action Stations" with scarcely a break, and no one had a stitch of dry clothing left. Towards the end we were living off little more than bully beef and ship's biscuit.'[25]

On 13 December *The Times* included an extensive article on the battles involving B7, noting the fine co-operation between air and surface escorts and quoting Horton's congratulatory signal 'describing the operations as a decisive defeat of the enemy'.

October also saw the deployment of a group of eight U-boats with Luftwaffe support against convoys on the Gibraltar route. An aircraft spotted a sixty-ship convoy (MKS28 and SL138 combined) on the 27th and the boats were ordered to move south to interdict, making contact on the 31st. The spotting boat's signals were detected by HF/DF and HMS *Whitehall* followed the bearing and, with *Geranium*, attacked and sank *U-306*. After a merchantman had been torpedoed, escorts chased down one U-boat which was damaged badly. U-boat Command then called off the attack, ordering the remaining boats to form a patrol line between Cape Finisterre and the Azores; the command war diary noted the presence of Allied aircraft on the Azores.[26]

By the time the U-boats of the Rossbach and Schlieffen groups were threatening the October convoys RAF aircraft were indeed based on the Azores. Following two years of negotiations with Salazar's government, and planning for occupation either by invitation or force, the UK government had seen Salazar's fear of German retaliation recede, but he remained unwilling to allow American forces in the Azores. This almost broke the negotiations since the Americans, whom Salazar did not trust, insisted on sharing any bases in the islands. Not until 18 August was an agreement reached: in return for military equipment and a guarantee of protection against German aggression 'we [the UK] were promised the use of air bases on Fayal and Terceira islands' from 8 October.[27]

On 30 September the British force for the Azores sailed in three small convoys, landing on 8 October, although Salazar had yet to sign a formal agreement. No.247 Group was formed under Air Vice-Marshal Bromet and an Area Combined Headquarters was established on Fayal. Bromet, who was responsible to the AOC-in-C Coastal Command, was also Commander, Combined British Forces Azores, a post he held until 1945. While maritime aircraft at Gibraltar reverted to Coastal, the Americans' Moroccan Sea

Frontier remained independent, thus preventing the extension of the new pattern for effective control of maritime aircraft over all the eastern Atlantic. Fortresses of No.206 Squadron due to land at Lagens on Terceira were delayed by bad weather at Gibraltar but nine Swordfish flew off HMS *Fencer* to the airfield and, in spite of very basic conditions, began dawn and dusk searches and carried out anti-submarine patrols until the Fortresses arrived.[28]

There was frustration in the United States where a force had been assembled for the Azores. The Americans could not understand Salazar's concerns; the Portuguese leader 'had reason to believe that once the Americans were in the Azores, they would not leave'.[29] Churchill considered this a sour note. Not until 1944 was the situation resolved to Salazar's satisfaction, and then only by the subterfuge of 'disguising [the Americans] as part of Coastal Command's No.19 Group'.[30] The Azores base was a valuable addition to the anti-U-boat campaign and, combined with the three British escort carriers and MAC-ships operating with convoys in the North Atlantic, allowed aircraft to cover the entire ocean north of 30N, while US Navy CVEs worked south of the Azores. It was yet another major blow for Dönitz.

The German admiral's second campaign had brought only more tragedy to the *U-bootwaffe*. From 2,468 merchant ships crossing the North Atlantic in sixty-four convoys, only nine had been sunk, whereas thirty-nine U-boats had been lost,[31] most by shore-based or carrier-borne aircraft, seven by warships and two by joint aircraft/ship action.[32] Dönitz was determined to persevere but began dispersing boats much more.

Dönitz's reaction to this second defeat was welcome news to the Admiralty but it caused some to believe that the battle had been won.

Such a belief, unless checked, could lead to a relaxation of our efforts and vigilance, so giving the enemy the opportunity to seize the initiative once again. The Naval Staff therefore pointed out that, in their estimate, some 300 operational U-boats still remained to the Germans [who] would probably renew the battle as soon as their improved equipment, and especially the new radar sets, were available. That these fears were not groundless is shown by the great difficulty experienced in dealing with the 'Schnorkel' U-boats when they started operating in the middle of 1944.[33]

U-boats continued operations in the North Atlantic but met the full fury of Allied response. Walker's 2nd Support Group was east of Newfoundland in early November with the escort carrier *Tracker* in foul conditions with a full gale that prevented the carrier flying off her aircraft. *Tracker* was rolling as much as 52 degrees:

> Down below a couple of Swordfish had broken adrift and were crashing from side to side like mad stallions, on a hangar deck ... awash with oil and sea water, pursued by a gang of matelots who had to secure them before they smashed up the rest of the planes.[34]

The wind dropped and died suddenly on 6 November, permitting operations against the groups of U-boats in the area. One of *Tracker*'s aircraft spotted a boat and Walker began a search. *Kite* had a radar contact and fired starshell, forcing the boat down, to be hunted by *Kite*, *Woodcock* and Walker's *Starling*. *Tracker* was ordered to move to safety, accompanied by the other two sloops. Following a depth-charge attack by *Kite*, Walker carried out a patient pursuit with *Starling*, *Kite* and *Woodcock* stalking the boat in firm asdic contact in pitch darkness. Deciding that the next attacks could wait until daylight, Walker ordered his other two ships to keep clear and continued jogging along behind the submarine for four hours.

> At dawn he ordered *Woodcock*, under Commander Clive Gwinner, to close so that he could pass instructions to him over the loud hailer. While *Starling* continued to track the U-boat, scarcely moving through the water, *Woodcock* crept in at five knots with her asdics switched off, to deliver a creeping attack with charges set deep, directed by Walker.[35]

At 7.47am 'the remains of *U-226* started to float to the surface' including a torpedo which was recovered so that experts at home could examine it. *Kite*'s captain believed this to have been 'a milch cow or a 1,200-ton supply boat' but it was a VIIC. That afternoon *Wild Goose*, also directed from *Starling*, destroyed *U-842* in another creeping attack. Roskill notes that 'no enemy had so far survived to describe the experience'.[36] Walker's procedure

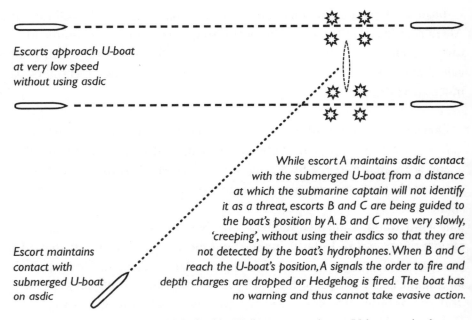

Escorts approach U-boat
at very low speed
without using asdic

Escort maintains
contact with
submerged U-boat
on asdic

While escort A maintains asdic contact
with the submerged U-boat from a distance
at which the submarine captain will not identify
it as a threat, escorts B and C are being guided to
the boat's position by A. B and C move very slowly,
'creeping', without using their asdics so that they are
not detected by the boat's hydrophones. When B and C
reach the U-boat's position, A signals the order to fire and
depth charges are dropped or Hedgehog is fired. The boat has
no warning and thus cannot take evasive action.

Figure 16: The 'creeping attack' devised by Walker was one that no U-boat survived.

was to station a 'directing ship' about 1,000 yards astern of the U-boat, to keep in contact all the time by asdic, while another ship, not using her asdic, meanwhile steamed very slowly (at perhaps five knots) up the enemy's track. The U-boat commander was thus lulled into a false sense of security; for he could only hear the comparatively distant asdic transmissions of the directing ship, and would not pick up the approach of the slowly moving attacking ship on his hydrophones. He would thus get no warning such as would enable him to take drastic avoiding action before the arrival of the depth charges.[37]

Having supported HX264, Walker's group sailed to Argentia, arriving on 12 November.[38] The U-boats remaining off Cape Farewell found themselves plagued by Allied aircraft at all hours, as did their comrades along the Gibraltar route who lost *U-707* to a Fortress of No.206 Squadron from the Azores on 9 November. *U-707* had been one of eight boats attempting to ambush MKS29A but the escort, deployed in inner and outer screens, was much too powerful and repelled all attack attempts.[39]

The North Atlantic boats were to be transferred to the Gibraltar route as Dönitz's staff realized that the Allies held all the advantages in Atlantic waters with air cover 'using location methods against which we have no warning' curtailing the mobility of the boats which, since they could no longer refuel at sea, could spend much less time on patrol. As the northern boats moved towards their new station, a Liberator of No.86 Squadron, escorting convoy HX265, spotted and sank *U-280* en route.[40]

The face of the Battle of the Atlantic was changing as U-boats once again forsook their hunting grounds. Dönitz remained convinced that the battle could be turned in Germany's favour and looked to the prospect of more new weapons and new submarines incorporating new technology to restore his fortunes. Although he had accepted that the revolutionary Walter boat could not be in production in time, there was another option. This was the 'one-hundred-per-cent underwater boat' which used some design elements of the Walter but, powered by electric motors, with a much larger bank of batteries than existing boats, could travel submerged at 18 knots for ninety minutes and maintain 12 to 14 knots for ten hours. To accommodate the batteries required for such power and endurance, the boat would be about 1,600 tons. Designated Type XXI, but also known as the *Elektroboot* because of its mass of electrical equipment, it was the hope for the future. Alongside it, a smaller boat with a 12-knot underwater speed was proposed, the Type XXIII, a 300-tonner, designed for shallow water operations in the North Sea, off the coasts of the UK, and the Mediterranean.[41]

However, the Kriegsmarine's Construction Branch could not foresee the Type XXI entering mass production until 1945 with entry into service at the end of 1946, much too late for Dönitz. An appeal to Speer brought an alternative plan. Speer had placed industrialist Otto Merker in charge of shipbuilding and Merker proposed that the new boats be built in sections at other sites before being moved to shipyards for final assembly, a method used by the American industrialist Henry Kaiser to build merchant ships. Once convinced that this would not compromise the structural integrity of the finished boats, Dönitz was in favour of it, noting that a Type XXI could thus be built in 260,000 to 300,000 man hours as against 460,000 man hours by traditional methods. Hitler approved the plan on 8 July 1943 and

Merker hoped to have the first boats ready in autumn 1944. Dönitz quotes the official instruction: 'The U-boat building programme is to maintain a monthly production of forty boats. Modifications in type are not to be allowed to cause any delay in production.'[42]

Although planning production schedules was no longer feasible in Germany, making target-setting unreliable, 181 Type XXIs and XXIIIs were commissioned between the end of June 1944 and 31 March 1945. The January–March 1945 average monthly production of twenty-six boats totalling 28,632 tons exceeded the previous best by over 6,000 tons.[43] In spite of this, the Type XXIs and XXIIIs came too late for effective use. Nor is there any guarantee that they would have turned the tide of war since the Allies were working on their own new weapons and technologies while new and better warships were coming off the slipways. Expecting the new boats, the Allies had begun devising countermeasures in anticipation of the Walter boats or other submarines with improved underwater performance. The Royal Navy submarine *Seraph* was adapted to mimic a Type XXI and used to train escorts in dealing with the new threat.

Before the war, United States Navy naval architects working on the concept of small and cheaper destroyers had produced six designs. When the US Navy showed no real interest the designs were filed until it was realized that a British specification for much-needed escort ships seemed to match very closely one of the designs, that of the Evarts-class, with diesel-electric engines. This brought an Admiralty order for fifty vessels, defined in the US as British destroyer escorts, or BDEs, later abbreviated to DEs.[44] Only six were delivered to the Royal Navy as BDEs, the remainder being retained by the US Navy. By the time the first ships were completed America was in the war and its own navy needed ships. The seventy-eight DEs transferred to the Royal Navy were either diesel-electric Evarts- or turbo-electric Buckley-class ships.

The destroyer escorts were the equivalent of the British Hunt-class destroyers with the Buckleys capable of slightly over 24 knots and the Evarts of about 20; the latter had greater endurance. Main armament was lighter than on a Hunt, consisting of three single 3-inch guns, but AA armament was good with seven or eight 20mm Oerlikon cannon; some were fitted with aft-mounted twin 40mm Bofors guns while others later received two or three additional Oerlikons instead of the Bofors. Four K–gun depth–charge throwers were carried, as well as stern dropping rails; a Mark 10 Hedgehog was fitted behind A gun. US Type SL radar was included and the British DEs received Type144 asdic equipment in the UK.[45] In British service the DEs were designated Captain–class frigates, since they did not have torpedo tubes, a standard identifier of a destroyer. The class designation indicated that each was named after a famous Royal Navy captain.[46]

Although crews of the early Captains worked up in the United States, the ships all had to put into Belfast after arrival in the UK, usually after reinforcing convoy escorts, for modifications. Intended to adapt them to Royal Navy standards, these included increased stowage for depth charges, both on deck racks and in magazines, changes in weaponry and equipment, fitting splinter–shields to the 3–inch guns and modifying shipboard communications. Domestic changes were also made, including removing ice-cream machines and dishwashers and ending the canteen messing system. Not all ships received every planned modification, however, and soldiered on with, for example, no splinter–shields for the 3–inch guns or the unpopular Mark IV mounting for Oerlikons.[47]

When the work was complete, ships were assigned to escort groups, a number of which were all DE-equipped. The Belfast-formed 1st, 3rd, 4th and 5th Groups each had three Buckleys and three Evarts while 15th was all Evarts and 21st all Buckleys. Other Captains were placed in mixed groups with older destroyers and corvettes and a few Buckleys were transferred to the Nore, Portsmouth and Devonport Commands for North Sea and Channel convoy duties, and E-boat patrols during and after Operation NEPTUNE/OVERLORD.[48]

As the first Captain-class frigates arrived in the UK, work was advanced on a development of the River-class, the Loch-class, the first of which was laid down in June 1943. Although they would not enter service until 1944, it is worth looking at their design and capabilities. Based on the hull of the Rivers, but with increased sheer and flare for better seakeeping, and modifications to allow pre-fabrication, the most significant change was the new Squid ahead-firing mortar. Squid was a three-barrelled weapon firing

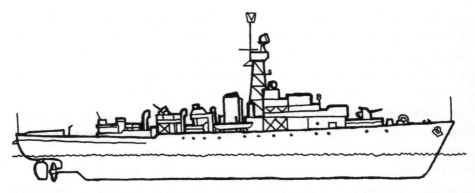

Figure 17: A Castle–class corvette. Based on the modified Flower-class vessel, the Castles had revised forecastles and bridges, as well as a different mast, and could mount a single Squid three-barrelled mortar.

depth charges rather than small bombs and the barrels were mounted in series, set off-centre from each other to spread the fall of the projectiles. Each round weighed 390lb (177kg) with an explosive charge of 207lb (94kg) of minol. Trials were carried out from HMS *Ambuscade* in May 1943 and the first ship fitted with Squid was the Castle-class corvette *Hadleigh Castle*. Some seventy ships carried it by May 1945. A critical part of the weapon system was the advanced Type147B asdic, which determined the aim and moment of firing as well as the detonation time.[49] The first successful use was by HMS *Loch Killin* in July 1944. Each Loch-class carried two Squid mortars to fire a pattern of six charges designed to explode three on either side of the target, crushing the submarine's hull with the pressure of their explosives. In addition to Squids, a rail and two throwers for standard depth charges were fitted and the Lochs' gun armament included a single 4-inch weapon, a quadruple 2-pounder and either two twin 20mm Oerlikons or two single 40mm Bofors guns, as well as up to eight single Oerlikons. The far from elegant Lochs, which displaced 1,435 tons, could travel at 20 knots and had excellent endurance, being capable of steaming 9,500 miles at 12 knots.

We have noted that the first ship on which Squid was fitted for operations was HMS *Hadleigh Castle*, a Castle-class corvette. Although the Admiralty had decided to cease building Flowers in favour of frigates, there were many smaller shipyards that could not build Rivers and so the Castle-class was ordered. An improved version of the Flowers, modified for oceanic work, these included the revised longer forecastle of the improved Flowers, but were some 200 tons heavier and about forty feet longer. A single Squid was fitted, together with a depth-charge rail, a 4-inch main gun, a brace of twin Oerlikons and six single Oerlikons. Although more than 100 Castles were ordered, about half were cancelled and thirty-nine served with the Royal Navy, twelve with the Royal Canadian Navy and one with the Royal Norwegian Navy.

On Trafalgar Day, 21 October, Admiral Sir Dudley Pound died. He had resigned through ill-health four weeks earlier, having suffered a stroke during the Quadrant conference in August.

> Since 1939 he had borne a tremendous burden with unshakable resolution and calm confidence in the face of many setbacks and disasters. ... He shunned the limelight, and this combined with his natural modesty kept his accomplishments veiled from the public eye, and perhaps also resulted in their being insufficiently recognized in naval circles; for he was not the type of leader whose personality made an impact on the service as a whole. ... his contribution to the final victory at sea was immense, and we may be glad that he at any rate lived long enough to see the tide turn. His finest epitaph is, perhaps, Mr Churchill's remark that 'he was a true comrade to me'.[50]

Horton's tribute summarized the late First Sea Lord's contribution to victory in the Atlantic.

> *There* was, in truth, a fine man. He died from strain and overwork at the moment when, owing to his efforts and planning, the tide of war at sea against Germany had definitely turned in our favour. ... From *him*, I was always certain of a sympathetic reception, and wholehearted backing, whatever happened – and how that helps one in time of strain and stress![51]

Some believed that Pound had suggested that Horton be his successor, but Horton told a friend that he would have refused the post had it been offered:

he had 'Dönitz where I want him, and I intend to keep him there till the war is won!'[52] Sir Andrew Cunningham became First Sea Lord after Sir Bruce Fraser declined, pointing out that while he (Fraser) had the confidence of his own fleet, Cunningham had that of the whole Navy.[53]

Dönitz's transfer of his boats to the waters off Gibraltar did not have the hoped-for results even though he had achieved greater co-operation from the Luftwaffe which deployed long-range aircraft to home U-boats on to convoys between Gibraltar and the United Kingdom. In response the Admiralty re-routed the convoys, sending them farther west, within range of Allied aircraft from the Azores. Although Luftwaffe aircraft claimed some ships, losses from U-boats were negligible, even though convoys passed through concentrations of boats. Attacks were often half-hearted and not followed through. By November boats were remaining submerged by day and surfacing at night to recharge batteries or try to pursue convoys. No ships were lost on transatlantic routes and, by the end of the month, it appeared that the only U-boats in those latitudes were en route from Norway. Some passed through the Straits of Gibraltar into the Mediterranean to join their comrades there, bringing the Mediterranean force up to fifteen, but any effort to pass larger numbers through 'was severely punished by the combined efforts of aircraft based on Gibraltar and surface ships, which resulted in four submarines being sunk in the narrows'.[54]

In December only thirteen ships were lost to U-boats in all areas. GNATs continued to be used and, off North Africa, HM Ships *Cuckmere*, *Tynedale* and *Holcombe* became victims on the 11th and 12th. *Cuckmere* was able to reach Algiers but the others were sunk. *U-223* torpedoed *Cuckmere* while *U-593* sank both *Tynedale* and *Holcombe*. *U-593* paid heavily for her success as Allied ships and aircraft swamped the area to hunt her to exhaustion: in a thirty-two hour operation involving twenty-one sorties by Wellingtons *U-593* was eventually destroyed by the USS *Wainwright* and HMS *Calpe*, her crew becoming prisoners of war.[55]

The Admiralty's post-war publication comments on the inexhaustible nature of German ingenuity and the menace that the GNAT presented but notes that, towards the end of 1943, it was clear that, despite the numbers of U-boats at sea, 'their new captains lacked the fiery vigour of their predecessors'. Targets were there in plenty but sinkings dwindled as Allied countermeasures became more effective. Twenty Allied merchantmen (119,000 tons) were sunk by U-boats during September; twenty (97,000 tons) in October; fourteen (67,000 tons) in November; and thirteen (87,000 tons) in December. Although large figures, these paled in comparison with the heavy losses of June and November 1942 while U-boats destroyed between 1 September and 31 December 1943 were, respectively, eleven, twenty-six, nineteen, and eight – sixty-four in 122 days. Between September 1939 and December 1943, no fewer than 473 German and Italian submarines had been sunk.[56] (Uboat.net shows 397 U-boat losses between the outbreak of war and the end of 1943, with 243 lost in 1943.)

Those 243 U-boats were not the Kriegsmarine's only losses of 1943. The battle-cruiser *Scharnhorst*, sheltering in a Norwegian fjord with *Tirpitz* and the heavy cruiser *Lützow*, had remained a threat to the Russian convoys which resumed in November with the Home Fleet responsible for their protection. By then *Lützow* had moved to the Baltic but the heavier ships remained; *Tirpitz*, *Scharnhorst* and ten destroyers had sallied out of Altenfjord in September to bombard Spitzbergen. Plans were made to attack *Tirpitz* with X-craft, midget submarines, but the damage was less than hoped, although she was left incapable of putting to sea, a factor influencing the decision to resume Arctic convoys.[57]

On Christmas Day 1943 *Scharnhorst*, with five destroyers, sailed to intercept JW55B. Eight U-boats also deployed and Luftwaffe aircraft were to provide reconnaissance but were grounded by poor weather, leaving a U-boat to shadow the convoy; this was *U-601* which was first to spot it. Heavy seas also meant that the destroyers could not keep pace with *Scharnhorst* and Dönitz authorized Admiral Bey to carry on alone. Admiralty intelligence was soon aware that the battle-cruiser was at sea and Admiral Fraser knew that he might have to deal with the German ship. The escort force and *Scharnhorst* clashed on the 26th. On two occasions during the morning Fraser's cruisers drove off the battle-cruiser which was then lured into range of the guns of HMS *Duke of York*, Fraser's flagship. *Scharnhorst* was pummelled by the British battleship's heavy guns before being subjected to torpedo attacks by cruisers and destroyers. In the Arctic darkness the German ship slid below the waves, leaving only *Tirpitz* to threaten convoys.[58] Having been damaged badly in attacks by FAA and RAF aircraft, she was finally destroyed in November 1944 by Bomber Command with Lancasters of Nos.9 and 617 Squadrons, using 'Tallboy' 12,000lb bombs.[59]

Thus 1944 began with U-boats being the only real threat to convoys. Dönitz remained confident that he could still overcome the convoy defences and stated at a conference at Stettin on 20 January 1944 that, although the Allies had obtained the advantage at that point:

> The day will come when I shall offer Churchill a first-rate submarine war. The submarine weapon has not been broken by the setbacks of 1943. On the contrary it has become stronger. In 1944, which will be a successful but a hard year, we shall smash Britain's supply with a new submarine weapon.[60]

This section of Dönitz's speech was edited out of versions broadcast outside Germany. Apparently he still reposed great faith in the engineers and of the arrival of new and more effective boats.

Meanwhile some boats were back in the North Atlantic, working within some 350 miles of the Irish coast rather than their earlier operating areas some 700 miles out. During January they enjoyed some immunity from sustained air attacks due to the prevailing extreme weather conditions, but had little success against convoys. Elsewhere, two U-boats were sunk by aircraft in the Bay of Biscay in the first and final weeks of the month, *U-426* by an Australian Sunderland of No.10 Squadron on the 8th, and *U-364* by a Halifax of No.502 Squadron on the 29th. In between, weather conditions had restricted flying but, off the Azores and Cape Verde, US Navy CVEs and escorts had several successes, while the USS *Block Island* rescued forty-three of the fifty-man crew of *U-231*, sunk by a Wellington of No.172 Squadron, a detachment of which was based in the Azores. Two boats were destroyed off Ireland, one by a US Liberator of VB-103 operating from Dunkeswell in Devon, the other probably by its own torpedo. That month only thirteen merchantmen were sunk by U-boats in all waters, three in a prolonged attack on an Arctic convoy. Fifteen U-boats were lost, including six to aircraft and five to warships; two were possibly sunk by GNATs.[61]

On the day of Dönitz's speech at Stettin, Sir John Slessor handed over the reins of Coastal Command to Air Chief Marshal Sir William Sholto Douglas who had been AOC-in-C Fighter Command earlier in the war. Douglas continued Slessor's policy of interdiction in the Bay as well as using Beaufighter and Mosquito strike aircraft against U-boats and German surface vessels.

North Atlantic U-boat operations in February conformed to the same pattern as January with a concentration off Ireland to attack outbound Gibraltar and North American convoys. However, twenty boats were lost that month, including six to Walker's 2nd Support Group. The U-boat gathering off Ireland was an open invitation to support groups and Walker duly wrought havoc. His group was an excellent team with long experience in anti-submarine operations and Walker 'possessed an almost uncanny knowledge of where each submarine was likely to be found'[62] (he was not privy to Ultra intelligence). Three boats threatening two convoys were sunk in under seventeen hours. Once detected, a boat was hunted to exhaustion, a process dubbed 'Salmon'. Each boat was forced to dive deep and stalked until the killing attack was made. One hunt lasted from 10.00am to 5.00pm at the end of which *U-264* surfaced and scuttled herself, the entire crew being taken prisoner. In four cases, the U-boat was detected first by HMS *Wild Goose*. No merchant ship in the area fell prey to U-boats but *Woodpecker* was struck by a GNAT and lost her stern. Although taken in tow, she and her towing ship were caught in a gale and *Woodpecker* sank off the Isles of Scilly. The remaining ships steamed triumphantly into Liverpool to a rousing welcome.[63]

Another two boats, *U-406* and *U-386*, were sunk in the same area by HMS *Spey*, the senior officer's ship of B10. Commander Gerald Ormsby brought each to the surface with 'a single well-placed pattern of depth charges, to be sunk by gunfire'. On surfacing, *U-386*'s captain decided to fight back while trying to make a run for safety, but his boat was sunk by gunfire.[64] Among other boats destroyed was one north-west of the Lofoten Islands, sunk by a Catalina of No.210 Squadron. On the 25th Squadron Leader Frank French flew some 750 miles from his base, Sullom Voe in the Shetland Islands, a distance that limited the Catalina to only two depth charges. Two were enough: French dropped them with such accuracy that they straddled and destroyed *U-601*.[65] Aircraft also plagued the boats operating west and south-west of Ireland; machines from bases in Northern Ireland were joined by their comrades from south-west England and US Navy units, including VB-103 with its PB4Y-1 Liberators from RAF Dunkeswell in Devon. The American Liberators often flew out from Dunkeswell and into RAF Ballykelly at the end of their patrols.[66]

Into March the U-boats' anguish continued, with twenty-five lost; ships accounted for eight, aircraft for seven and joint action between aircraft and escorts a further five; yet another was lost to an air raid in port. Dönitz was trying to stretch Allied defences by dispersing his boats widely. Some U-boats in the Indian Ocean continued taking a toll, eleven of the twenty-three merchantmen sunk during March being in that ocean. Only one was sunk in convoy in the North Atlantic where boats continued to operate 'with great caution'. Harassed by aircraft, support groups and close escorts, they found it difficult to close on a convoy. Those who did knew that life expectancy was short. That must have been the case with Rolf Manke of *U-358*. His boat was detected on 29 February by 1st Support Group, under Commander Clive Gwinner DSO, who had commanded *Woodcock* in Walker's group, and forced down. Then began the longest U-boat hunt of the war. For thirty-eight hours, *Affleck*, *Gould*, *Gore* and *Garlies* – all Captains – stalked *U-358*, although *Gore* and *Garlies* ran low on fuel and had to make for Gibraltar to top up their tanks during the afternoon of 1 March. That left *Affleck* and *Gould* to continue the hunt. Eventually, Manke, with air and battery power running out after two days and a night submerged, surfaced, still prepared to fight. *U-358* unleashed a GNAT that hit and sank *Gould* before *Affleck* finished the U-boat with gunfire. Most of *Gould*'s crew were lost although Gwinner mounted a rescue operation after destroying *U-358* and picked up fourteen survivors in high winds and heavy sea. *U-358* was the second boat 1st Support Group had sunk in under a week. Little more than a week later, on 10 March, British and Canadian escorts carried out a hunt of thirty hours resulting in the destruction of *U-845*.[67]

One boat sunk in the Bay fell victim to two Mosquito Mark XVIIIs of Coastal Command's No.248 Squadron. On 25 March *U-976* was crossing the Bay with an escort of four destroyers and eight Ju88s when it was spotted by the Mosquitoes, which were accompanied by three Mosquito Mark VIs from No.248 Squadron. The Mosquito XVIII was a specialized version of the twin-engined fighter-bomber armed with a 6-pounder Molins gun, an anti-tank gun modified for use against U-boats. Nicknamed the 'Tsetse fly', this was the first occasion on which Mosquito XVIIIs sank a U-boat. While the Mark VIs battled with the Ju88s, shooting down four, the XVIIIs made five attacks on *U-976*, holing her hull in at least six places.[68]

By now convoys were assured of air cover in all but the worst weather conditions since machines from eleven escort carriers and seventeen MAC-ships deployed for their protection, either with convoys or support groups. Operating with Walker's 2nd Support Group on 15 March, one of HMS *Vindex*'s Swordfish detected and depth-charged *U-653*; depth charges from *Starling* and *Wild Goose* finished off the boat, the group's thirteenth kill. Swordfish from *Chaser*, protecting a convoy to the USSR, sank three boats in as many days using rockets.[69]

The *U-bootwaffe* was under intense pressure, so much so that April 1944 saw the lowest toll of merchant shipping for four years with only nine ships (62,000 tons) lost. Caution was the watchword among the U-boats whose operations in the North Atlantic were few, while many of the larger boats were en route to or from the Indian Ocean where they claimed no victims that month. With the loss of most of the *Milchkühe* the operational range of the smaller boats was much reduced. Of the Type XIV *Milchkühe* only two remained but *U-488* was sunk by US Navy escorts on 26 April and US carrier-borne aircraft and ships would destroy *U-490* on 12 June. Elsewhere aircraft from US Navy CVEs sank boats south of Nova Scotia and in the Cape Verde and Madeira areas. On Hitler's orders a strong U-boat force was maintained off Norway, not only to interdict convoys to the Soviets but as a precaution against a feared Allied landing.[70]

Dönitz was by now being very careful with his boats. The profligate use of radio signals had been stopped, because it was believed that Allied land-based HF/DF stations were using them to locate boats – the Germans did not appreciate that ships were also HF/DF-equipped; but there were still some transmissions. A number of boats were sending back weather reports which could be used to track down those boats and attack them, thus also depriving German commanders of vital meteorological information. Allied landings on the mainland were anticipated and the U-boats were one weapon with which to counter such landings. Germany's scientists and technicians had produced new 'secret' weapons, including the V-1 flying bomb – the first cruise missile – and the V-2 rocket, in addition to the glider bombs and GNATs already mentioned. The first of the new U–boats had been launched in April, two Type XXIII coastal boats in Hamburg. In May the first Type XXI slid into the water at the Blohm und Voss yard, also in Hamburg. Having convinced Hitler in May 1943 that the U-boat war had to be continued, Dönitz was placing his faith in these boats, and in the fitting of schnorkel equipment to existing boats; the latter measure would make older boats more effective and provide greater 'protection' against radar-equipped ships and aircraft. He hoped that two more Type XXIs would be launched in June, followed by another pair in July; production was to rise to six per month later in the year. But the *U-bootwaffe* had taken heavy punishment. Since Dönitz gained Hitler's agreement for continuing the campaign, 239 boats had been lost. The figures were even more frightening for the seventeen months from 1 January 1943 to 31 May 1944: 341 boats lost with 20,000 men either dead or taken prisoner. Production of new boats had outpaced losses so that 448 boats were in commission in June 1944. However, it had been easier to replace boats than men. Those lost or made prisoner had been replaced

> by scouring the surface fleet. Both the age and the level of experience of crews had fallen alarmingly. Herbert Werner, attending a course for prospective commanding officers in Gotenhafen earlier that year, had found only one beside himself from the U-boat arm. None of the others had even been on a submarine war patrol. Entirely lacking the seasoning that only action could provide, the instinctive feeling for when to make an alarm dive, when to fight it out on the surface, when and how to manoeuvre under depth-charge attack, when to play possum, he thought they 'stood almost no chance of survival, and neither did their crews'.[71]

The *U-bootwaffe* fought the final year of war with a large proportion of undertrained officers and crews, many of whom had little or no experience of submarine warfare. However, they would have a new 'search receiver' since a successor to Metox had been developed that could detect centimetric radar transmissions. (It will be remembered that an interim measure called Hagenuk had been unsuccessful.) This was Naxos which, operating between 2,500 and 3,750Mhz in the 8- to 12-centimetre wavelengths, could pick up ASV transmissions from about five miles (eight kilometres). In some respects Naxos was too sensitive and caused many boats to make unnecessary dives. However, Naxos I gave poor results since it had a vertically-polarized antenna whereas RAF radars were horizontally polarized. This problem was resolved with a new triple antenna with elements crossing at 45 degrees, in which guise the equipment became Naxos Ia; the maritime version was Naxos-U. In September 1943 the first equipment had been fitted to U-boats but its existence soon became known to the Allies since contacts were being lost as attackers closed on their targets. Since this had to be due to the boat detecting the ASV signal, a new radar, ASV Mark VI, was introduced, fitted with an attenuator allowing the operator to limit the power radiated, thus giving the false impression that the aircraft was not closing.[72]

However, there were other measures, including *Hohentwiel*, introduced in December 1943. A radar used by the Luftwaffe as ASV which was fitted to U-boats to detect aircraft, it was useful in limited conditions. Naxos's problems were overcome in its successor, *Fliege*, which gave good service but was rendered obsolete by 3-centimetre radar; the answer to this (ASV X in British service) was *Mücke*. (With *Mücke* the Germans had, for once, been ahead of the development of an Allied radar system.) U-boats also used a radar decoy called *Thetis* and a decoy called *Aphrodite*; the latter was a 3-foot-diameter balloon, attached to a float, flying 13-foot-long strips of aluminium foil from its cable and thus acting as did Window, the strips of foil dropped by RAF aircraft to confuse radars.[73]

Allied research had not been reined in. As we have seen 3-centimetre radar was developed and in use before the war ended. This came from the work of American laboratories to which the original British research leading to the cavity magnetron and 10-centimetre radar had been given. Kennedy quotes the Pulitzer Prize-winning American historian James Phinney Baxter III who, in his book *Scientists Against Time*, describes the cavity magnetron as 'the most valuable cargo ever brought to our shores' and 'the single most important item in reverse lease-lend'.[74] He also notes that by the end of the war, US industry had produced over a million cavity magnetrons and that 'As a small though nice bonus, the ships using it could pick out life rafts and lifeboats in the darkest night and foggiest day. Many Allied and Axis sailors were to be rescued this way'.[75] Terraine comments that 3-centimetre radar was but one of several American inventions of the second half of the war. 'Once roused, American warlike inventiveness quickly hit a fertile streak, and American production methods soon translated this into weaponry in lavish quantities.'[76]

Even the finest ASV radar would not allow an aircraft to detect a submerged submarine. In certain weather conditions, and in clear calm waters, the crew of an aircraft *might* be able to see the outline of a submerged submarine almost directly below them, but that was the limit. There was no airborne equivalent of asdic. This was something that scientists sought to develop and thus increase further the ability of airmen to detect and destroy U-boats. United States scientists enlisted the knowledge and experience of Victor Vacquier, a refugee from Russia, who had worked for Gulf Oil and developed the fluxgate magnetometer to find ore deposits. Working at the Airborne Instruments Laboratory at Columbia University, Vacquier applied his invention to the detection of submarines. This could be achieved by a magnetic anomaly detector (MAD) fitted to an aircraft. However, since the detector worked by finding magnetic anomalies, or distortions in the earth's magnetic field, in the sea, it had to be free from interference from metal in the fuselage of the aircraft, or electrical equipment aboard the machine, and so it was carried at the end of a boom on the tail or towed behind the plane.[77] (MAD equipment was carried first in US Navy blimps, or airships.) It was limited in ways similar to asdic since it could only find a submarine close to the aircraft's position and close to the surface.[78] By January 1943 the war diary of Western Approaches Command was noting that 'MAD trials from Catalina flying boat were postponed owing to breakdown of equipment'.[79] However, US Navy aircraft fitted with MAD equipment were soon deployed.

Since the Straits of Gibraltar had always produced difficult asdic conditions and not enough aircraft were available to provide a patrolling level sufficient to prevent submerged U-boats slipping through by night into the Mediterranean, a half dozen boats made the run successfully in January and February 1944.

Then an American Catalina squadron fitted with a device called the Magnetic Anomaly Detector (MAD) arrived at Port Lyautey and started to work over the Straits. This instrument, which enabled a submerged U-boat to be tracked from a low-flying aircraft, was well suited to conditions in those waters; but the presence of surface ships to co-operate with the aircraft was soon shown to be essential. On 24 February *U-761* was destroyed by British and American air and sea patrols with the help of MAD.[80]

The Catalina squadron was VP-63, dubbed the 'Madcats', which also claimed three U-boats sunk between February and May; the straits proved ideal for MAD equipment. Introducing MAD to service presented another problem: how to bombard a target directly below the aircraft. This was solved by developing a charge that could be fired rearwards before falling vertically, the retro-bomb, although Terraine writes that only one boat, *U-1055*, destroyed off Ushant on 30 April 1945, was ever sunk by this method.[81] The combination of MAD and retro-bomb was not best suited to conditions off the British Isles, but another proved more effective: 3-centimetre radar with another American invention, the sonobuoy, which was already in use. Sonobuoys

> could be dropped by aircraft and then kept an automatic hydrophone watch, transmitting the propeller noises from a submerged U-boat to the patrolling aircraft by wireless. ... used with the small acoustic torpedo [the Mark 24 mine] which could be dropped to 'home' on the U-boat, they had established themselves firmly in favour as an increasingly important weapon in the armoury of the anti-submarine aircraft.[82]

The first successful use of sonobuoys had been in July 1942; the first destruction of a U-boat through use of sonobuoys had been that of *U-658*, sunk by Hudson 'Y' of No.145 Squadron RCAF off Newfoundland on 30 October 1942.[83] Sonobuoys were also used in combination with MAD, producing an effective combination.

The MAD allowed an aircraft to localize a contact made with sonobuoys and the sonobuoys provided confirmation that the contact was, indeed, a submarine. In this combination MAD became the secondary system to the sonobuoy and would later become a mainstay feature of postwar NATO ASW techniques in the Atlantic.[84]

Thus the battle between the scientists continued unabated to the very end. As the conflict entered its final year the operations of both hunters and hunted would look very different from those of the earlier years of war.

Chapter Thirteen

The U-boats were quiescent during May 1944, claiming only four merchantmen (24,000 tons), the lowest monthly toll to date. Most smaller boats were being held at readiness in the Biscay or Norwegian ports to operate against the expected Allied landings in mainland Europe. Such operations would involve boats remaining submerged for long periods in the relatively shallow waters of the English Channel, a tactic possible only for U-boats fitted with a schnorkel. The larger Type IX boats, unsuited to littoral operations, continued operating farther afield. One, *U-852*, attacked by two Wellingtons of No.621 Squadron, was forced aground on the Somali coast where the survivors were taken prisoner by a landing party from HMS *Falmouth*.[1]

As well as the boat's war diary, *Falmouth*'s party also discovered a Focke Achgelis Fa330 Bachstelze glider-kite which had been developed to provide better observation for U-boats. Only Type IX boats could travel fast enough, 18 knots (20.7mph), to tow the kites, which worked by autorotation of their rotor blades, at heights of up to 700 feet, from where, in good conditions, a pilot could see over thirty miles. The simple machine was stowed on deck where four men could assemble and launch it in three minutes. A telephone connected the boat's captain to the pilot who, in emergency, could drop the connecting cable.[2] This was the first Bachstelze captured. (Germany led the world in the development of rotary flight in 1939 and introduced the first operational helicopters.)

U-852 has another distinction: her captain, Hans-Wilhelm Eck, and two of his crew were tried and executed for the murder of the crew of the Greek ship *Peleus* on 13 March. Eck was the only U-boat commander indicted for war crimes.[3]

Some U-boat activity continued in other areas during May, especially against the Russian convoys. The escort carriers *Activity* and *Fencer* provided cover in spite of adverse weather conditions, including six inches of snow on their flight decks, heavy seas and blizzards. *Fencer*'s Swordfish sank three U-boats in two days on RA59 while *Activity*'s Wildcats shot down one of two German aircraft that stalked the convoy, driving the other off severely damaged.[4]

By the end of May another twenty-three U-boats had been lost, the largest proportion, ten, to aircraft. Coastal Command had also initiated a major offensive in northern waters since it was realized that Dönitz might try to reinforce his Biscay flotillas from Norway. This operation began on the 16th when the first sighting and attack was made by a Sunderland of No.330 Squadron. Against intense fire the pilot pressed home his attack, even when his aircraft was hit and crew members injured. One engine was knocked out and another was 'vibrating violently'. Although it was believed that the boat had been sunk, this was not so.[5] The Sunderland was manned by Norwegians, No.330 Squadron being one of the RAF units formed for personnel from occupied countries; the squadron badge was a Viking ship in full sail 'in front of a sun in splendour' and its motto was 'Trygg Haver' (Guarding the Seas).[6] East of the Faeroes, where U-boats had hitherto not been much disturbed by aircraft, twenty-two sightings were made between the 16th and 31st. Thirteen attacks followed in which six U-boats were claimed sunk. In fact, five were sunk by aircraft and a sixth by HMS *Milne*.[7]

Dönitz had considered the problems of using U-boats to counter the Allied fleets when the landings in France began. Would it be possible to send boats into the Channel's shallow waters where escort ships would abound and aircraft patrol the skies? Could the boats remain in those waters? Could they achieve success sufficient to justify the risks? Certainly, only schnorkel-equipped boats could be deployed, and would have to remain submerged 'possibly for weeks at a time'. Operating submerged would mean no radio contact and hence no reports until the boats returned to base. Dönitz considered that the risks had to be taken as the outcome of the Allied landings would decide the subsequent course of the war; he believed that the U-boat was the only weapon that could make a 'wholly disproportionate contribution to success'.[8]

He felt that a single boat could achieve success by destroying just one ship loaded with tanks or other war *matériel* even if it were itself lost. Between 6 June, the day the landings began, and 31 August he noted thirty schnorkel-equipped boats deployed in forty-five operations in which twenty were destroyed for the loss of five Allied escort vessels, twelve merchantmen (56,845 tons) and four landing craft (8,404 tons), as well as an escort ship, five merchantmen (36,800 tons) and a landing ship damaged. Dönitz believed that this marked success. In reality it was a pinprick. His inflated claims suggest that he was trying to convince himself of success.[9]

In the Bay and Channel between 6 and 10 June Allied aircraft sighted three dozen boats by day and night, attacked twenty-three and sank seven. Remarkably, two, *U-373* and *U-441*, fell victims to one aircraft within thirty minutes: Liberator 'G' of No.224 Squadron, piloted by Flying Officer K. Moore, detected both with ASV off Ushant and attacked in bright moonlight. That forced a change of tactics, as U-boats then tried to creep through using schnorkel. However, by the end of the month, another twenty-three had suffered air attack; two were sunk by joint air/sea action and another three by escort ships alone. Losses continued elsewhere, especially in northern latitudes, so that by the end of the month another twenty-five U-boats had gone. One had been captured by US ships and aircraft, its crew made prisoner and the boat, Type IX *U-505*, taken to the United States where it is today on display in Chicago.[10]

Anti-U-boat operations in defence of the Operation NEPTUNE fleet had included Coastal aircraft patrolling a first line of defence to prevent the Biscay boats reaching the routes of the landing forces. This they had done exceptionally well as the boats had found to their cost. At the same time, many ocean escort vessels were allocated to defend the Normandy-bound armada, the escorts for convoys being reduced accordingly. In theory Dönitz's boats, more than seventy in number, could have penetrated the armada, endangering the entire operation.[11] That they were unable to do so is an indicator of the professionalism and teamwork of anti-submarine forces, both surface and air.

One attack in the northern transit areas resulted in another posthumous Victoria Cross. No.162 Squadron RCAF, equipped with Cansos, was on loan to Coastal Command and, between 3 and 30 June, sank five boats, but lost three aircraft, such was the ferocity of defensive fire. On 13 June Flight Lieutenant David Hornell in Canso 'T' spotted *U-715* and attacked. The boat put up a determined defence, badly damaging the Canso's wings.

Hornell's starboard engine was also damaged but he pressed on and sank the boat. Vibration in the damaged engine became so bad that the engine shook itself from its mounting and fire broke out in the wing. The flames could not be extinguished and the Canso was ditched, thanks to a 'superhuman effort' by Hornell. However, there were so many holes in the fuselage that it sank within twenty minutes. Then one rubber dinghy burst and the other capsized. It was twenty-one hours before a rescue launch arrived, by which time 'two men were dead, Hornell had lost his sight and, with two others, was in a state of exhaustion'. David Hornell died shortly afterwards. His valour and leadership were recognized by the posthumous award of the Victoria Cross.[12]

Recent events had precipitated a major change in U-boat operations. Trained primarily for oceanic operations, they made increasing use of schnorkels to crawl submerged along the coast to their patrol positions. If the water was deep enough, they rested on the bottom. Outlying rocks made radar detection very difficult, while eddies and tide-rips in the Channel's comparatively shallow water militated against successful asdic use. Even so, twenty-five U-boats were sunk in June. In all areas they sank eleven Allied merchant ships (58,000 tons). Off Normandy and in British coastal waters submarines sank only five merchant ships while another five were mined, 'an infinitesimal proportion of the great mass of shipping engaged in the operations and far less than we had a right to expect'.[13]

It was believed that U-boats in the northern bases had yet to be fitted with schnorkel equipment which led Coastal Command to launch an offensive in Arctic waters to catch boats on the surface charging their batteries while waiting for Russian convoys. This began in mid-July and proved 'most successful'. Over a week, long-range aircraft, sometimes 800 miles from base, attacked fifteen boats, sinking four and damaging three. One boat destroyed was *U-361* which was spotted on the surface well within the Arctic Circle by a Catalina of No.210 Squadron from Sullom Voe. The pilot, Flying Officer John Cruickshank, attacked immediately. The U-boat fought back with an intense barrage but Cruickshank pressed on. His first attack failed when his depth charges hung up. Making a second attack, even though his aircraft had been hit, his navigator killed, and he and three other crew members wounded, his charges dropped. Cruickshank's attack proved fatal for *U-361*, but he then had to get the damaged Catalina home. His wounds caused him to pass out several times during the five-and-a-half-hour flight but he refused morphia so as to remain conscious and able to assist his injured second pilot to land the flying boat. Before he could be removed from the aircraft, John Cruickshank had to be given a blood transfusion by the station medical officer. He was subsequently awarded the Victoria Cross, the only living recipient of the award in Coastal Command. His second pilot, Flight Sergeant Jack Garnett, received the Distinguished Flying Medal.[14]

Coastal Command's offensive, stretching from Arctic waters around the Lofoten Islands to Biscay, resulted in the destruction of over thirty U-boats and damage to some three dozen others. But success came at a price. Enemy action brought down thirty-one aircraft with another seventeen lost as a result of the hazards of operational flying, such as crashing when attacking, or adverse weather. Over 400 crew members died between May and 31 August and many more were wounded or injured, some of whom would never return to operational duties.[15] John Cruickshank VC was among the latter.

By the end of July another twenty-two U-boats had been lost. Nine had been destroyed by warships, including *U-333* on the 31st, the first victim of a Squid, mounted on HMS *Loch Killin*.[16] However, the month also saw the sudden death of Johnny Walker, who succumbed to a massive stroke on the 9th at the age of forty-eight. As with Sir Dudley Pound, Walker had overworked himself. He was on leave when he died, a day after receiving confirmation that his son Timothy had been lost in HM Submarine *Parthian* which had failed to return from a patrol in the Adriatic in August 1943; Timothy Walker had left his studies for the priesthood at the English College in Rome to join the Royal Navy as a rating.[17] Captain Walker was buried at sea from HMS *Starling* following a service in Liverpool Cathedral at which Sir Max Horton said of him:

In our hour of need he was the doughty protector of them that sailed the seas on our behalf. His heart and his mind extended and expanded to the utmost tiring of the body even unto death, that he might discover and operate means of saving our ships from the treacherous foes.[18]

Thus far in 1944 the *U-bootwaffe* had lost 155 boats. 'Badly mauled, though not yet defeated, they were now risking nothing more than was absolutely necessary.'[19] Truly mauled badly they were about to lose their French bases. As the Allies advanced out of Normandy, it became clear that the northern Biscay bases were untenable. Boats at Brest, Lorient and Saint Nazaire, all under immediate threat from Allied forces, were moved to la Pallice and Bordeaux, or southern Norway. The migration thus forced brought another opportunity to hunt boats down. Since the Luftwaffe could no longer operate over the Bay the boats were even more vulnerable and many attacks were made: ten boats were sunk. Three RCN destroyers, *Ottawa*, *Kootenay* and *Chaudière* accounted for *U-621* on the 18th and *U-984* two days later.[20] Australian aircraft of Coastal Command also claimed boats sunk. Three Allied merchant ships were sunk in the Channel over a three-week period and three U-boats in the same area by surface forces.

By the latter part of August the U-boats were abandoning the Biscay ports completely; some activity in the Channel was considered an attempt to divert attention from boats moving to Norway or Germany. Their departure from la Pallice and Bordeaux was hastened by bombing the fuel storage at both ports. Other boats operated off north Cornwall and between Scotland and Northern Ireland. Although not appreciated immediately such operations were a precursor to Dönitz's last offensive. No North Atlantic convoys were attacked during August, a month that witnessed the passage of the largest-ever convoy. HX300 consisted of 167 ships, including nine destined for Russia, and was escorted by ships of the Royal Canadian Navy. The ocean escort, C5, was led by the River-class HMCS *Dunver* (originally named after Verdun, Quebec, but the name was altered to avoid confusion) with five corvettes, and the convoy included MAC-ships and several oilers, which also carried spare depth charges. An official report notes: 'The feat reflects much credit upon the merchant ships and escorts, since the conduct of so large an assembly of ships presents many difficult problems.' That large assembly covered over thirty square miles of ocean in close order and the problems it met included much fog and bad weather. The ships bound for the USSR carried locomotives, explosives, tanks, cars, trucks, steel, food and machinery while those for the UK carried 1,019,820 tons of cargo including 307,874 tons of petroleum products, 216,676 tons of foodstuffs and over 10,000 vehicles.[21]

The departure of the U-boats from Biscay for Norway suggested a possible renewal of attacks on North Atlantic convoys. To counter this possibility, it was planned to move surface and air forces to northern waters, at the same time regrouping and strengthening escort and support groups. Although some larger boats still patrolled the Indian Ocean, operating from Japanese naval bases at Penang or in Batavia, and a few were in the eastern Atlantic, the majority were much closer to home, but their deployment demonstrated considerable prudence. The last two boats in the Mediterranean were destroyed during September, a month in which only seven Allied merchantmen (43,000 tons) were lost against the destruction or loss of twenty-three U-boats. The quiet time in the Atlantic continued into October, when a single merchantman of 7,000 tons was lost against fourteen boats, and November which saw another seven merchantmen (30,000 tons) lost against eight U-boats. November also saw the destruction of *Tirpitz* in her haven in Altenfjord, bombed by Lancasters of Bomber Command, thus removing the last major element of Hitler's surface fleet.[22]

Nine Allied merchantmen totalling 59,000 tons were sunk in December when fourteen U-boats met their ends, eleven to action by ships, aircraft, including bombers striking their bases, or mines; one Type IXD was lost off Java, probably due to a diving accident. *U-877* was lost on the 27th to the Castle-class corvette HMCS *St Thomas*, of C3, using a Squid mortar, the first RCN success with the new weapon.[23] The most unusual loss, however, was an indicator of how the submarine war was changing. On the morning of 18 December the lighthouse keeper on Wolf Rock, south of Land's End, reported that a U-boat had been washed up on the rocks but had then slipped off and was on the surface moving westward with men in the conning tower. *U-1209*, a VIIC fitted with schnorkel equipment, left Norway on 24 November, making most of her journey submerged. Following three days patrolling off Land's End, a merchantman was spotted through the periscope early on 18 December. As the boat prepared to attack, the navigating chief petty officer told the captain that he was making directly for the Wolf Rock. However, the captain disagreed and, in the ensuing heated argument, *U-1209* struck heavily on the bottom and scraped along. Thrown off and on rocks by a heavy swell, the boat was holed badly aft. With water rising rapidly in the diesel and motor rooms, she surfaced. Her stern was well down and the conning-tower hatch could not be opened. The boat submerged again and oil fuel was pumped out before she re-surfaced, whereupon the crew abandoned ship just before she sank. Most of the crew were picked up; the captain died of a heart attack on board HMCS *Montreal*.[24]

It was an ignominious end for *U-1209* and its young captain, Oberleutnant Ewald Hülsenbeck. That such a young man died of a heart attack seems unusual, but the trauma he had endured and the knowledge that he was responsible for the loss of the boat he had commanded since April may have combined with fatal effect.

The presence of *U-1209* not far from the Isles of Scilly is indicative of the resurgence of U-boat activity in the English Channel and neighbouring waters. Indeed, between Hülsenbeck's shipwreck and 29 December, five merchant ships and a frigate were torpedoed and sunk and another two merchantmen and another frigate damaged in those waters. Most counter-attacks had proved unsuccessful, although, on the 29th, HMCS *Calgary* sank *U-322* south of Weymouth. A Coastal Wellington was credited with sinking *U-772* off Cherbourg next day but the target was actually *U-486* which survived unscathed; *U-772* had already perished.[25]

With many boats fitted with schnorkels since spring 1944, there was already considerable experience in using these devices, which were not always popular with crews, although the degree of immunity from air or surface attack conferred was appreciated. Operating in littoral waters added another benefit: asdic performance was compromised considerably in such shallow waters while radar could be confused by rocks and debris, especially the detritus of war, floating in the waves. Many escorts were concentrated in the Channel and its approaches but with little success because of those difficulties. Such problems also faced Coastal Command as, while the enemy had been kept under, thus limiting greatly his opportunities to attack, use of the schnorkel and radar warning devices allowed him to elude detection. As a result, during the autumn when between fifty and seventy boats were known to have been at sea, sightings and attacks reduced significantly: September: 21 sightings, 10 attacks; October: 10, 3; November: 12, 10. 'It was a situation, moreover, that called for new countermeasures, for although the enemy was doing little damage to us … we were getting no better success against him and a stalemate was in view.'[26]

There was one noteworthy encounter with a U-boat south of Ireland on 17 December. The boat was *U-772* and the loss of her target would have been a tremendous morale blow for the United Kingdom. That target was the SS *Rimutaka*, a P&O ship operated by a subsidiary, the New Zealand Shipping Company, which had sailed from Liverpool on the 16th. On board were HRH Prince Henry, Duke of Gloucester and HRH Princess Alice, bound for Australia where the duke was to become governor general. *Rimutaka* had a significant escort, including the cruiser HMS *Euryalus*, two destroyers and the five frigates of B18. At 11.15pm on the 17th, HMS *Nyasaland** picked up a long-range asdic contact showing a submerged contact on *Rimutaka*'s port bow. Since the ships were about to alter course to port by 18 degrees, this would put the U-boat in an excellent attacking position. *Nyasaland* promptly made the alarm signal. The ships turned the other way and *Nyasaland* remained to hunt. At 11.38pm she made her first attack, followed twenty minutes later by a second. The explosions of her depth charges were followed by violent underwater detonations that lifted the frigate, while large quantities of diesel oil rising to the surface confirmed the kill.[27]

For this action *Nyasaland*'s captain, Lieutenant Commander John Scott, was awarded the Distinguished Service Cross, to which he received a Bar for his part in the sinking of *U-1014* off Malin Head in February 1945.[28]

During 1944 the *U-bootwaffe* had lost 249 boats from all causes, making this the worst year of the war for the force. Nonetheless, between fifty and sixty boats were operating in January 1945 with their main effort concentrated in the Irish Sea where they claimed five merchantmen sunk and two damaged.

---

* *Nyasaland* was a Colony-class frigate, one of a class of twenty-one ships built in the United States for transfer under Lend-Lease to the Royal Navy. The Colony-class was the equivalent of the US Navy's Tacoma-class patrol frigate, an adaptation of the British River-class.

Two U-boats were sunk by escorts in the area: *U-1051* was destroyed by ramming and depth-charging by HM Ships *Aylmer*, *Calder*, *Bentinck* and *Manners*; *U-1172* was accounted for by HM Ships *Tyler*, *Keats* and *Bligh*. The first of these was sunk south of the Isle of Man on 26 January and the second farther south next day. *Manners*, of B2, had been torpedoed by *U-1051* and her stern section was blown off. Her asdic operators kept contact with the boat, which *Manners* had not detected until the torpedo struck. B4 was carrying out an anti-submarine sweep east of Cork and its ships were despatched to the scene, to be joined by *Aylmer* of B5. Having provided medical care for *Manners*, which was taken in tow for Liverpool, the other ships began a sweep for the U-boat, which was lying on the bottom. After a patient search *Calder* pinpointed the target and fired her Hedgehog, which scored a direct hit. *U-1051* surfaced quickly whereupon *Calder* prepared to engage with gunfire but was pre-empted when *Aylmer*, which had just arrived, rammed and sank the boat. Thus ships from three groups were credited with destroying the U-boat.[29]

Of ten U-boats lost in January three were of the new Type XXI class, but none was lost in action: *U-2515* and *U-2523* were damaged beyond repair by bombing while *U-3520* was sunk by mines in the Baltic on the 31st; her crew of eighty-five perished.[30] Most boats lost at sea were sunk by warships; only those destroyed in dock were attributable to aircraft. Nonetheless, Coastal's patrols were effective in keeping the U-boats down. They were supplemented by US Navy patrol aircraft; the 'Madcats' of VP-63 were operating in UK and Irish waters, as were PB4Y-1 Liberators of Fleet Air Wing 7 (FAW-7) whose squadrons had been making regular runs out of Dunkeswell in Devon and Ballykelly in County Londonderry since 1944; their use of Ballykelly had been especially intensive in September.[31]

The use of schnorkel meant that Coastal's shore-based aircraft had no kills, but their constant presence over coastal waters restricted considerably the enemy's activity. Meanwhile Bomber Command attacked U-boat pens at Bergen and Blohm und Voss's building yard at Hamburg, in 'very successful' raids.[32]

The official history of the bomber offensive notes attacks on yards in which Type XXI and XXIII boats were being assembled:

bombing of the assembly yards began in a small way in November and December and in 1945 was much increased until in March and April devastating raids were made on Hamburg and Bremen.

Thus, the final result of all the planning and effort extending over two years was that only eighty type XXI U-boats were delivered to the German navy in 1944 and no more than thirty-nine in 1945. Only one of these became operational and that did no damage. The less ambitious programme for the type XXIII U-boats fared rather better. Sixty-three were delivered to the Navy and six became operational, doing some damage in the closing stage of the war.[33]

Dönitz's new wonder weapons were never truly to enter service, leaving the *U-bootwaffe* to persevere with schnorkel-fitted older boats. To counter them, minefields were laid around the British Isles with some success. On 12 March *U-260*'s crew landed at Galley Head in County Cork, claiming that their boat had been damaged by bombs. No bombing had occurred in the area, but minefields were thereabout.[34] Off the coast of Inishowen in County Donegal, *U-296* went missing the same day, presumably to minefields. (The destruction of this boat was claimed by a Liberator of No.120 Squadron on 22 March but the boat had been lost before then; the Liberator's attack was probably on a non–U-boat target.)[35]

Although the U-boats appeared to be fighting a losing battle, the Admiralty did not believe in complacency. The First Lord, Mr A. V. Alexander, introducing the Navy Estimates in the House of Commons in February, emphasized the importance of not assuming that the war had been won. In spite of many successes since mid-1943, and continuing success, he referred to the new types of German naval equipment, the innovative U-boats coming off the slipways, the resurgence of activity in British waters and the fact that the Germans 'were making great efforts to renew the U-boat war on a big scale'. Furthermore, he commented that the major German efforts and investment of resources to renew the submarine war indicated that Hitler still regarded it as 'his best hope of averting defeat against a nation which lives by seaborne supplies'. Alexander added that he considered this a 'highly significant fact' that he hoped would never be forgotten by his successors, the Admiralty or future governments.[36] Even while Alexander was issuing such advice to the House, his department was cancelling over fifty Loch-class frigates: it considered that the war would be over before these could be completed.

Morison comments that the Allied high command 'was seriously concerned over enemy submarine capability', a topic discussed by the Combined Chiefs of Staff at Malta in late-January and at Yalta in early-February. The 'most immediate problem' was presented by the schnorkel submarines, at least twenty-five of which were in, or moving into, British coastal waters, a 'most disturbing fact' as this was the first time U-boats had troubled shipping in these waters since 1941. These boats also had a radar detector device 'that offset the ASV radar in Allied aircraft and enabled them to dive before a plane could attack'.[37]

Dönitz found cause for optimism in January's operations and even in the losses sustained which, he noted, had declined very sharply, amounting to 10.4 per cent of boats at sea, lower than in 1940 and 1941 and only marginally higher than in 1942. He attributed this to the schnorkel's effectiveness and the 'indomitable enterprise of our U-boat captains and crews' which had transformed 'what started as a purely defensive delaying action ... into an offensive campaign in the enemy's coastal waters'. There the boats had even found some advantage from operating in shallow waters since the differing coastal configurations and tidal currents impeded anti-submarine operations by surface vessels. The success achieved in January provided encouragement for the deployment in British waters of boats due to be commissioned during February, despite the inherent risks, including the inevitable strengthening of Allied anti-submarine forces and the need for constant radio silence. It was felt that the opportunities justified the risks: 'every ship, laden with war material and bound for France or for the Scheldt estuary, which we could sink under the English coast, lightened the burden of our struggle ashore'.[38]

Although Dönitz saw operating without regular use of radio as a risk, it actually gave U-boats an operational advantage since silencing their radios deprived the Allies of intelligence garnered from Ultra intercepts and of HF/DF. The boats were spending so much time underwater that Allied shipboard and airborne radar systems had become almost impotent. Relying on schnorkel-mounted detectors and sky-search periscopes, the U-boats seemed to have found a 'silver bullet' that allowed detection of enemy aircraft and evasion of attack by them.

Allied anti-submarine forces around the British Isles were reinforced considerably. US Navy escort divisions deployed under Royal Navy command to combat the inshore U-boats. The RAF's airfield at Limavady, which was not ideal due to the nearby Binevenagh mountain, had become home to Nos.172 and 612 Squadrons' Leigh-Light Wellingtons in September 1944, thus increasing the muscle of No.15 Group, although 612 moved to Norfolk in December. While at Limavady both squadrons conducted comprehensive anti-schnorkel training, but the aircrews considered that their existing ASV would be unable to detect the devices. However, the new 3-centimetre ASV, APS-15, developed in the United States began to enter service with Coastal Command as ASV Mark X, although yet again Bomber Command had priority for the technology. 'With its improved definition the new radar had a definite edge over the earlier sets for Schnorkel detection, though if the sea was rough the old problems remained.'[39] Although it was said that the new 3-centimetre ASV could detect nails in planks floating in the water 'at a mile or two' this was an optimistic assessment.[40] It was, however, possible in calm sea conditions.[41] In April a Coastal Command Anti-U-boat Devices School was opened at RAF Limavady and continued in being until after VJ Day.[42]

The final campaign was hard fought and brutal, demanding much from personnel on both sides. Although U-boats had gained an operational advantage, this disappeared when an attack was made. Once Allied ships and aircraft knew the approximate location of a boat, it would be hunted to exhaustion. Moreover, some of that operational advantage was nullified by the basic navigational problems of being continually submerged. No navigational equipment was available to crews; accurate navigation depended on taking sightings of identifiable coastal features and thus using the periscope for long enough to spot those. Taking nocturnal star sightings was out of the question since the Kriegsmarine had no suitable device; the usefulness of any such instrument would have depended on clear skies, not something that could be guaranteed around the British Isles, especially during the winter months.

Paterson notes also that the presence of Allied vessels precluded using gyro-compasses and echo-sounders which created noise that surface ships could detect; thus navigational problems were increased.

> In general officers aboard the U-boats that were engaged in the war in British waters – including navigation NCOs – were young, often with little experience of navigation in the difficult tidal areas such as those found in the combat zone. Older, more experienced seamen had, by 1944, been promoted ashore to training establishments, or were preparing new crews for rejoining the war aboard the large Type XXIs.[43]

Twenty-nine new boats sailed for British waters from Norway during February, the largest monthly operational commitment.[44] Boats continued deploying during March, mostly into British waters but with some off Newfoundland and Nova Scotia, and others off Iceland and in the eastern Atlantic. Bomber Command was dropping mines to impede the passage of U-boats from Norway while also attacking, in concert with the USAAF, bases and building yards in Germany, The Netherlands and Norway.

February saw an intensification of the effort against the Russian convoys with the Luftwaffe using torpedo-carrying Ju88s in over 100 sorties; one merchant ship was sunk but four Ju88s were shot down, another two 'probably' shot down and three damaged by FAA fighters from the escort carriers *Nairana* and *Campania*. Fifteen merchant ships (65,000 tons) were sunk during February, but twenty-two U-boats were lost, including thirteen sunk by warships and one by an aircraft. Allied escort crews were becoming more familiar with using asdic in coastal waters and were finding schnorkel-equipped boats close inshore. Commander Phillip Burnett's B10 group, on loan to Portsmouth from Londonderry, sank three boats in two weeks off Norway and in the transit area between the Orkneys and the Faeroes.[45] The single boat lost to an aircraft was *U-927*, sunk off Falmouth by a Vickers Warwick V of No.179 Squadron. Some twenty escort groups, about 120 ships, were now hunting U-boats.[46]

The hunting groups were taking their toll of the U-boats which often lay on the bottom and could be mistaken for wrecks, or even rocks, but asdic operators were sharpening their skills as the cat-and-mouse game continued. Twenty-six boats were lost in March, although the Admiralty believed that thirty-four had been destroyed, including eight to warships. That figure included three destroyed by Commander Raymond Hart's B21 group between the 27th and 30th. Including the Captain-class frigates *Conn*, *Deane*, *Fitzroy*, *Redmill* and *Rupert*, B21 had been formed at Belfast in October; Hart already had an enviable reputation, having shared in the destruction of eleven U-boats. Despite many contacts, the group had not sunk any U-boats, but that changed on 27 March when *Conn*, *Deane* and *Rupert* ran down and sank *U-905* in the Minch, midway between the Butt of Lewis and Cape Wrath. Hart had split B21 into two divisions and, later that day, the other division, *Fitzroy*, *Redmill* and *Byron*, detected *U-722* between Skye and Eriskay, sinking her with depth charges.

> After this double victory … it seemed to be nothing less than wishful thinking that any more U-boats could be lurking in the Minches. However, Lieutenant Commander Hart kept the Group resolutely on the hunt, minutely investigating every nook and cranny in this 100-mile-long channel. Keyed up by success, and with renewed confidence in their prowess, the asdic crews were determined that if there were any more U-boats then they would certainly find them. Nothing succeeds like success and their double victory had put a very keen edge on 21 EG's deadly blade.[47]

Three days later, *Rupert*'s asdic operators picked up another definite contact in an inshore location about ten miles north-west of Enard Bay, in the waterway between the Hebrides and mainland Scotland. *Conn* and *Deane* were called in and *Rupert* steered them to a kill. *U-965* was the victim, although at the time it was believed to be *U-1021*.[48]

The group returned to Belfast and a heroes' welcome. A national press communique about the success was not released until mid-April, being delayed to include a fourth B21 victory, this time the sinking on 8 April of *U-1001* south of Ireland by *Fitzroy* and *Byron*. Four kills in twelve days was a remarkable achievement in the inshore campaign. Only one further patrol was carried out by Hart's group. Working around the north-west coast of Ireland, the group had no more kills but suffered the torpedoing of *Redmill* off Sligo Bay on 27 April.[49] The torpedo, probably a GNAT, was fired by *U-1105*, and twenty-four of *Redmill*'s crew died, some of whom are buried in Londonderry City Cemetery. *U-1105* was one of about ten boats given a rubber coating to foil asdic, turning them into 'stealth boats'. The coating seemed to work well on this boat, which gained the soubriquet 'Black Panther', but proved troublesome generally, tending to peel off under operational conditions.[50] It probably prevented B21's ships detecting *U-1105* and thus led directly to the torpedoing of *Redmill*, which, although towed to Londonderry, was declared a total loss.

U-boats claimed twelve merchantmen (58,000 tons) during March, nine in British waters; another three were sunk in the English Channel by midget submarines. Had the U-boats been manned by more experienced crews they might have achieved more. Their level of experience is indicated by *U-681* which was off the Isles of Scilly on her first war cruise on 11 March when her captain, Oberleutnant Werner Gebauer, took bearings from the Bishop Rock Light and the old lighthouse on St Agnes so that he could enter St Mary's Road. However, at 11.00am, while submerged at eighty feet, *U-681* hit a rock and, in trying to get off, suffered damage to hull and propellers. Gebauer was forced to surface where he decided that, since he could not dive, he would make for Ireland to abandon ship. He had not gone far on his 130-mile journey when he was spotted by a Liberator of VB-103 which attacked and dropped a stick of depth charges that sent the boat to the bottom; the Liberator summoned other aircraft and an escort group to rescue survivors.

The commander of *U-1003*, Oberleutnant Werner Strübing, had brought his boat all the way from Bergen on her second war cruise to a position north of Inistrahull Island off Malin Head in Ireland. On 23 March the boat was schnorkelling when, at 11.17pm, a look-out on HMCS *New Glasgow* heard a loud noise and reported, 'Low-flying aircraft approaching!' Almost immediately, the same look-out reported, 'Object in the water very close!' In the moonlight, the object was identified as a periscope and schnorkel some fifty to a hundred yards away on 'a perfect collision course'. Although obscured by a thick yellow pall of smoke mushrooming out around it, about three feet of the schnorkel was seen. Seconds later, periscope and schnorkel struck *New Glasgow*'s port side immediately below the bridge.[51]

Strübing had managed to hit a Canadian ship. With his boat damaged badly, he went to the bottom, staying there all night while depth charges detonated some distance away. He came up to sixty feet next day, 21 March, cruised submerged until dusk and surfaced to recharge his batteries but, before this was complete, was forced to dive again by approaching Allied ships. He struggled through the next day but his pumps, which had been running since he hit *New Glasgow*, finally failed not long after midnight on 22/23 March. He then surfaced and ordered his crew to abandon ship.[52]

Allied losses to U-boats rose to 73,000 tons, thirteen ships, in April, including four in the North Atlantic and seven in coastal waters. However, fifty-four U-boats were lost, the war's highest monthly total. Fourteen were destroyed in air raids on ports, nineteen by ships, eight by aircraft and two by mines. Another was sunk by Red Army artillery fire while being used to generate electricity.[53]

US Navy CVEs were still sinking U-boats while a Sunderland and B14 shared a kill in the Irish Sea and HMS *Viceroy* sank a boat off the Northumbrian coast, the wreckage from which included six dozen bottles 'of good brandy, fortunately none of them broken'.[54] Allied land advances were forcing U-boats out of the Baltic and into Norwegian ports as the Soviets pushed deeper into Germany from the east while the western Allies, who crossed the Rhine in late-March, did likewise from the west. In northern Italy, the Allied army group opened an offensive on 9 April that, by the end of the month, had broken the German armies, which surrendered on 2 May.

As the Red Army approached Berlin, Hitler committed suicide, having appointed Dönitz as his successor. Meanwhile, Allied bombers continued destroying U-boats in their bases or in shipyards while Coastal's strike aircraft, Beaufighters and Mosquitoes, plagued surface vessels and submarines with rockets and cannon. Operating from Scotland, they enjoyed considerable success in the Kattegat and Skagerrak. One attack by Mosquitoes, diving out of the sun, took three U-boats completely by surprise; the boats were overwhelmed by the firepower of the aircraft and one blew up, taking a Mosquito with it, while the others sank. Three Mosquitoes were damaged so badly that they had to land in Sweden. Ten days later the same Mosquito unit attacked another three U-boats with a minesweeper escort and sank one while damaging the others.[55]

On 4 May Dönitz signalled all U-boats at sea, ordering them to cease hostilities and return to base. However, he also told them:

My U-boat men!

Six years of U-boat war lie behind us. You have fought like lions. A crushing material superiority has forced us into a narrow area. A continuation of our fight from the remaining bases is no longer possible.

U-boat men! Undefeated and spotless you lay down your arms after a heroic battle without equal. We remember in deep respect our fallen comrades, who have sealed with death their loyalty to Führer and Fatherland.

Comrades! Preserve your U-boat spirit, with which you have fought courageously, stubbornly and imperturbably through the years for the good of the Fatherland.

Long live Germany![56]

Submerged boats could not receive the signal and some continued operations. Before the formal surrender of Germany was marked on 8 May, three Allied merchantmen totalling 10,000 tons were sunk, including *Sneland I* and *Avondale Park*, torpedoed in the Firth of Forth on the 7th, less than an hour before midnight, by *U-2336*, a Type XXIII, which carried only two torpedoes. *Sneland I* was hit at 11.03pm and *Avondale Park* three minutes later. *Avondale Park*, a Canadian vessel, was thus the last merchantman sunk by a U-boat in the Battle of the Atlantic. *U-2336* surrendered at Kiel on 15 May.[57]

In spite of Dönitz's surrender order, many captains continued as usual, some believing that, since he had issued so many fight-to-the-death signals, the order could not have come from him. As a result, at least fourteen boats were destroyed in action in that single week of May, eight by aircraft and six by warships. Coastal Command aircraft, both maritime patrol and strike, were kept busy, together with Second Tactical Air Force, attacking boats, mostly in Danish waters as they tried to flee to Norway. A Type XXIII, *U-2359*, was destroyed in the Kattegat on the 2nd by rockets from Mosquitoes of five squadrons, two RAF, one RCAF and one Norwegian. The last U-boat sunk by an aircraft was *U-320*, despatched off Bergen by a Catalina of No.210 Squadron which had sighted her schnorkel. FAA aircraft were also involved:

machines from the escort carriers *Searcher*, *Queen* and *Trumpeter* sank the U-boat depot ship *Black Watch* with a boat tied up alongside her in Harstad.[58]

The Battle of the Atlantic was over. Its sixty-eight months made it one of the hardest-fought struggles in history. Germany's attempts to strangle the United Kingdom's lifelines to North America and the rest of the world had been thwarted but at horrendous cost. Estimates of the numbers of dead and of vessels lost vary but over 100,000 lives were lost, including merchant seamen, naval personnel, passengers on ships, airmen and submariners. The *U-bootwaffe* had the highest loss rate of any combatant service during the war; as many as 32,000 were killed or missing, some 82 per cent of its personnel, with another 5,000 captured. Of 830 boats committed to operations, the Allies destroyed 696, a loss of 83.9 per cent.[59] Some 43,526 ships sailed in convoys, of which 2,452 were lost in the Atlantic (where 1,480 convoys sailed,[60] including the Arctic convoys, more than 1,000 were sunk in 1942 alone. The Merchant Navy lost 30,248 men[61] through enemy action, and nearly 11.5 million tons of shipping; the Merchant Navy Memorial in London bears the names of 23,837 seamen who have no graves but the deep; 8,000 others are buried in cemeteries worldwide. The Royal Navy lost 51,578 dead, 'a large proportion of which must be attributable to the U-boats' and almost half of the 341 British warships lost during the war were victims of the battle. To those grim figures may be added the many others who died in the Atlantic, including American, Canadian, Norwegian, Dutch and French naval personnel, and merchant seamen from all corners of the earth.

Dönitz's assertion that his men had been undefeated was countered by Admiral Sir Max Horton who ordered a formal surrender of the U-boat fleet at the Royal Navy's most important escort base, Londonderry in Northern Ireland. On Monday 14 May a small flotilla of eight U-boats, flying White Ensigns, with skeleton crews under Royal Navy guard, escorted by HMS *Hesperus*, HMCS *Thetford Mines* and USS *Paine* sailed up Lough Foyle into the river Foyle and the jetty at Lisahally where their commanding officers stepped ashore to surrender to Horton. The Germans were then taken to the nearby railway halt at Lisahally to board a train that would take them to a prisoner of war camp.

Chapter Fourteen

The longest campaign of history's most horrendous war was over. Although convoys and Coastal Command patrols continued for several weeks after VE Day, the danger was past. It had been one of the worst dangers Britain had ever faced with Churchill describing the U-boat menace as his greatest fear. He summarized the campaign:

> The Battle of the Atlantic was the dominating factor all through the war. Never for one moment could we forget that everything happening elsewhere, on land, on sea, or in the air, depended ultimately on its outcome, and amid all other cares we viewed its changing fortunes day by day with hope or apprehension.[1]

In contrast to Churchill's assessment, American historian Blair asserts that 'Contrary to the accepted wisdom or mythology, U-boats never even came close at any time to cutting the vital North Atlantic lifeline to the British Isles'.[2] Such an assessment can be made only in the light of hindsight and ignores the many factors that faced Churchill and those at the highest levels of command. There can be no doubt that Churchill's analysis that 'the Battle of the Atlantic was the dominating factor' is correct. The U-boat threat was very real and the toll in blood, steel and treasure was high. However, Blair's comment that the U-boatmen were sent out on suicidal missions is accurate, especially after May 1943.

Could the Germans have won the Battle of the Atlantic? The answer has to be 'yes' but with conditions. Those conditions include the element of luck, which no commander can ignore, as well as the vision of those involved. Had Hitler possessed a strategic maritime vision to match that of Dönitz, then Germany would have had a greater chance of victory. Even so, Germany's greatest chance of victory could only come from Allied, and especially British, errors or failures. In reviewing the conduct of the campaign, it may be seen that major errors were made by the Allies. While Churchill could claim that the U–boat menace worried him more than anything else, it seemed to take time to do so, as evidenced by his comment that 'Nothing of major importance occurred in the first year of the U–boat warfare'.[3] Perhaps this explains why it was February 1941 before he established the Battle of the Atlantic Committee (p.67). His failure to see immediately the importance of VLR aircraft for Coastal Command, as shown by his procrastination in what Pound called the 'Battle of the Air', is further evidence of an opportunity for Germany. Only Churchill could have ensured that sufficient VLR aircraft were available for Coastal Command and the fact that he delayed making a decision until the new year is not to his credit. Remember that Roskill comments that had Britain lost the campaign, 'history would have judged that the main cause had been the lack of two more squadrons of very long range aircraft for convoy escort duties'.[4]

Other factors ensuring Allied victory included the industrial muscle of the United States, muscle that had been honed by British money from 1938 onwards. A critical element of American industry was the ability of shipyards to produce speedily great numbers of both warships and merchantmen. The classic example is the Liberty ship, built to a British design on a prefabricated basis for final assembly in shipyards: 2,710 were produced, of which over 200 were lost, some due to failures in the original design.[5] The capacity of American yards to produce ships in such numbers – they also produced 694 tankers, and almost another 1,000 general cargo ships, in addition to warships and landing craft – meant that, once they were in top gear, Dönitz could never sink enough merchantmen to win the war. At one stage three Liberty ships per day were being launched; the record assembly time was that of the *Robert E. Peary*, which took only 111 hours to complete from the laying down of her keel.[6]

It is possible that the U-boat campaign might have damaged morale in the Merchant Navy so badly as to help the Germans to victory. Worse, in some ways, than the sinking of ships were the owners' practices of stopping seamen's pay when a ship went down, and of not paying merchant seamen between voyages. The latter practice, known as 'paying off', was not peculiar to wartime but owners chose to interpret the loss of a ship for whatever reason, including enemy action, as meaning the crew had been 'paid off'. This affected families since seamen could allot part of their pay to their next-of-kin at home to be paid on a monthly basis. On occasion the first a family knew that a father, husband or son's ship had been lost was the cessation of the allotment.

Since 15 September 1939 merchant seamen had been awarded a 'war risk payment' of £10 per month to those over eighteen and £5 to those under that age. This was intended to compensate for the risks the men took and encourage them to stay at sea. However, in May 1941, the government introduced the Essential Work Order for the Merchant Navy (EWOMN) making it illegal for a merchant seaman to leave the sea but guaranteeing that he would not be paid off between voyages and nor would his pay stop should his ship be sunk.[7] While this book has concentrated on the fighting services, it should not be forgotten that the Merchant Navy was pivotal to victory and that the men, women and boys of the service bore a heavy burden; of 185,000 merchant sailors who served during the war, almost 32,000 died.[8]

More than anything else, it was the recognition by the British government of the importance of the Merchant Navy and the convoys that ensured that sufficient resources were allocated to the Battle of the Atlantic. Those resources took the form, as we have seen, of more escort ships, of specialized small aircraft carriers, whether escort carriers or MAC-ships, and new and improved weapons systems for them, as well as detection systems, such as centimetric radar and HF/DF. In the air, more and better aircraft, ASV, air-dropped depth charges, acoustic torpedoes, and improved communications between ships and air support all played their part. In the background were the scientists and the intelligence experts, working on new weapons or communications or breaking the enemy's codes and reading his messages. Also behind the scenes were the men who trained the crews manning the escort ships, who developed tactics to beat the U-boats and who controlled the Submarine Tracking Room and the Trade Plot. In May 1943 all their efforts coalesced to force Dönitz to realize that his campaign had failed. Although Dönitz never accepted defeat, he was never to regain any advantage before the war ended. None of his innovations, whether new U-boats, schnorkels, new weapons, or detection systems, would turn the war to his advantage. The Type XXI boat was not going to change anything. Those who argue that it could have been a 'game changer' ignore the development of 3-centimetre ASV that could detect a schnorkel or a periscope and the advent of new Allied weaponry.

From 1943 on it became impossible for U-boats to operate in packs or on the surface at night. To claim that they could still wage war effectively is akin to saying that individual soldiers, albeit skilled marksmen, constitute an effective army. The Battle of the Atlantic had spurred research and development in many ways and the equipment and weaponry that would be familiar to NATO personnel involved in shadowing the Soviet submarine fleet can be seen to have originated in what was developed for the Battle of the Atlantic; MAD, sonobuoys, homing torpedoes all had their operational birth in the Atlantic.

A clear indicator of how the battle had turned may be seen in the request by the Ministry of Food in May 1943 to send a whaling expedition to the South Atlantic. A previous expedition, in January 1941, had been captured by a German raider and it had been decided that no more expeditions should take place until 'the end of the war'. However, it was considered that the situation had changed so much that 'escort through U-boat waters en route to the whaling grounds can be provided' as well as anti–raider cover.[9] That thoughts could turn to such mundane matters was surely proof that the Allies knew they had regained control of the seas.

Perhaps the greatest tragedy of the Battle of the Atlantic is that Dönitz continued to believe that he could wrest victory from the arms of defeat and persisted with a campaign that doomed many thousands, mainly young men, on both sides. While he is seen as an honourable leader and opponent, there can be no doubt that his fanaticism blinded him to reality and that he must bear the burden of guilt for the deaths of so many.

More than any other aspect of the war, the Battle of the Atlantic showed the lack of vision of political leaders in the inter-war years. The threat of Hitler's Germany was obvious and yet it took so long for the UK government to provide the Royal Navy with ships and weapons to protect trade convoys. While A. V. Alexander may have warned that the maritime travails of the war years should be a lesson to governments in the future and to service chiefs, it seems that nothing has changed. The UK has a small Navy, a merchant fleet that is a shadow of what it once was and a prime minister who can tell the House of Commons that the Royal Air Force can take a 'capability holiday' from the anti-submarine warfare role.

Sic transit gloria mundi.

Notes

Chapter 1
Much of this chapter is based on information from Terraine's *Business in Great Waters: The U-boat Wars 1916–1945*, especially from Part I: The First Round 1916–1918.

1. Elphick, *Life Line*, p.219.
2. Terraine, *Business in Great Waters*, pp.149 & 669.
3. Ibid, p.669; Elphick, op. cit., p.12.
4. Owen, *Anti-Submarine Warfare*, pp.11–17 for a summary of submarine development.
5. Hackmann, *Seek and Strike*, p.xxv.
6. Kemp, *Convoy Protection*, p.12.
7. Mahan, *The Influence of Sea Power on the French Revolution and Empire*, p.217.
8. Macintyre, *The Battle of the Atlantic*, p.19.
9. Ibid.
10. Ibid., p.18.
11. Kemp, op. cit., p.46.

Chapter 2
This chapter also owes much to Terraine's *Business in Great Waters*, especially from Part I: The First Round 1916–1918.

1. Terraine, op. cit., p.155.
2. Ibid.
3. Terraine, op. cit., p.157.
4. Wragg, *Plan Z*, pp.67–70; Terraine, op. cit., pp.203–6.
5. Terraine, op. cit., p.204.
6. Padfield, *Dönitz*, p.169.
7. Terraine, op. cit., p.169; see also Padfield, *Dönitz*, and Wragg, *Plan Z*, op. cit.
8. Padfield, op. cit., p.125.
9. Terraine, op. cit., p.171.
10. Padfield, op. cit., p.231.
11. Hansard, 5 Nov 1937.
12. Roskill, *Naval Policy*, p.451.
13. Conway's, *All The world's Fighting Ships*, pp.46–7.
14. Terraine, op. cit., p.179.
15. Nuremberg Trials Doc. L79, quoted in Wilmot, *The Struggle for Europe*, p.21.

37. Ibid.; Terraine, op. cit., pp.314–15.
38. Roskill, op. cit., p.365.
39. Adm, op. cit., pp.26–7.
40. Ibid., p.27.
41. Barnett, *Engage the Enemy More Closely*, p.262.
42. Macintyre, *BoA*, p.88.
43. Suhren, *Ace of Aces*, p.123.

Chapter 6
1. www.Uboat.net 24 Nov 2014
2. Ibid.
3. Hügel, interview with author, May 1995.
4. Padfield, *War Beneath the Sea*, pp.120–30; Adm, op. cit., p.31.
5. Terraine, op. cit., p.326.
6. Hinsley, *British Intelligence in the Second World War*, Vol. II, p.163.
7. Rohwer, paper, 'The Operational Use of Ultra in the Battle of the Atlantic', p.19; quoted in Terraine, p.400.
8. Terraine, op. cit., p.319.
9. Hinsley, op. cit., Vol. I, p.339.
10. Terraine, op. cit., p.327.
11. Roskill, op. cit., p.25.
12. Ibid.
13. Baker, *The Terror of Tobermory*, p.12.
14. Ibid., p.112.
15. Roskill, op. cit., p.359.
16. Baker, op. cit., p.120.
17. Ibid.
18. Ibid., p.136.
19. Ibid., p.135.
20. Ibid., p.136.
21. Williams, *Captain Gilbert Roberts RN*, p.85.
22. Ibid, pp.85–6.
23. NA Kew, ADM34/370, p.15.
24. Williams, op. cit., p.87.
25. Wragg, *The Escort Carrier (TEC)*, pp.27–9.
26. Terraine, op. cit., pp.396–9.
27. Ibid.
28. Ibid., Macintyre, *BoA*, pp.119–130; Kemp, *The Admiralty Regrets*, p.164; www.uboat.net 24 Nov 2014.
29. NA Kew, ADM234/370, p.19.
30. Williams, op. cit., p.91.
31. Ibid., p.88.
32. Ibid., p.92.

Chapter 7
1. Adm, op. cit., pp.30–1.
2. Ibid.
3. Ibid., p.31; Milner, op. cit., 93.
4. Milner, op. cit., p.92.
5. Adm, op. cit., p.34.
6. Ibid., p.30.
7. Price, op. cit., pp.54–8; Terraine, op. cit., pp.431–2; Macintyre, *BoA*, p.94.
8. Price, op. cit., p.59.
9. www.uboat.net 24 Nov 2014.
10. McGiffin, interview with author, Jan 1989.
11. Adm, op. cit., p.30.
12. Farndale, *The Years of Defeat*, p.111; Routledge, *Anti-Aircraft Artillery*, p.392; Doherty, *Ubique*, pp.253–9.
13. Macintyre, *BoA*, pp.92–3; NA Kew, ADM1/11312: Air protection for Atlantic convoys.
14. Roskill, op. cit., pp.476–7; www.uboat.net 30 Nov 2014.
15. www.navyhistory.org.au Naval Historical Society of Australia, Payne, 'The Catapult Fighters'.
16. www.cwgc.org
17. Payne, op. cit.
18. Wragg, *TEC*, pp.12–13.
19. Ibid., p.13.
20. Ibid.
21. Simons, *Consolidated B-24 Liberator*, pp.17–20 & 27–30.
22. Halley, op. cit., p.154.
23. Spooner, *Coastal Ace*, pp.27–8.
24. Ibid., p.125.
25. Ibid.
26. Ibid., pp.125–6.
27. Simons, op. cit., pp.37–42.
28. Morison, *The Battle of the Atlantic*, Vol. I, p.61. See also Chapter III.
29. Ibid., p.37 & 81.
30. Ibid., pp.36–7.
31. Barnett, *The Lords of War*, p.281.
32. Morison, op. cit., pp.36–7.
33. *New York Times*, 30 Dec 1940.
34. Ibid., 9 Feb 1941.
35. Ibid.
36. Ibid., 9 Mar 1941.
37. Weeks, *Russia's Life-Saver*, p.107.
38. Barnett, *Lords*, op. cit., p.282.
39. Ibid.

40. Quoted in NA Kew, CAB65; Morison, op. cit., p.33.
41. NA Kew, AIR41/47.
42. Morison, op. cit., pp.79–80.
43. Quoted in Morison, p.80.
44. Morison, op. cit., pp.84–5.
45. Lash, *Roosevelt and Churchill*, p.416.
46. Morison, op. cit., p.85; NA Kew, AIR41/47.
47. NA Kew, AIR41/47.
48. Morison, op. cit., pp.92–3; Parkin, *Blood on the Sea*, p.3; Macintyre, *BoA*, p.135.
49. Morison, op. cit., p.94; Parkin, op. cit., pp.3–6; Macintyre, BoA, p.136; www.uboat.net 2 Jan 2015.
50. Morison, op. cit., p.94; Rohwer & Hummelchen, *Chronology of the War at Sea*, p.94; www.uboat.net 2 Jan 2015.
51. Morison, op. cit., p.94.
52. Adm, op. cit., p.32.
53. Terraine, op. cit., pp.372–82.
54. Ibid.; Rohwer & Hummelchen, op. cit., p.82; www.uboat.net 2 Jan 2015.
55. Adm, op. cit., pp.34–5.
56. Macintyre, *BoA*, p.95.
57. Milner, op. cit., p.70.
58. Ibid., pp.70–1; Rohwer & Hummelchen, op. cit., p.82; Terraine, op. cit., pp.372–82; www.uboat.net 2 Jan 2015.
59. Adm, op. cit., p.33.
60. Ibid.
61. Ibid., pp.35–6.
62. Ibid., p.38; www.uboat.net 2 Jan 2015.
63. Dönitz, op. cit., p.229.

Chapter 8
1. Morison, op. cit., p.39.
2. Ibid., pp.39–40.
3. Ibid., p.40.
4. Ibid.
5. Ibid., pp.43–4.
6. Ibid., p.53.
7. Ibid.
8. Ibid., p.54.
9. Ibid., p.55.
10. Doherty, *Key*, p.21.
11. NA Kew, ADM116/4598: Projected United States' Bases in British Isles. Outstanding Financial and Technical Matters, 2 May 41.
12. NA Kew, ADM116/4598.

13. Milner, *Canada's Navy (CN)*, pp.89–90.
14. Macintyre, *BoA*, p.95.
15. Milner, *CN*, p.90.
16. Ibid., pp.90–1.
17. Ibid., p.93; www.uboat.net 4 Jan 2015.
18. Milner, *CN*, p.94.
19. Ibid, pp.94–5.
20. Ibid., p.97.
21. Dönitz, op. cit., p.197.
22. Ibid., p.161.
23. Ibid., p.162.
24. Ibid., p.195.
25. Ibid., pp.195–6.
26. Ibid., p.205.
27. Suhren, op. cit., p.118.
28. Ibid., pp.118–19.
29. Macintyre, *BoA*, p.133.
30. Suhren, op. cit., p.203.
31. Ibid., p.202.
32. Morison, op. cit., pp.129–30.
33. Dönitz, op. cit., p.202.
34. Ibid.
35. Ibid., p.219.
36. Ibid., p.221.
37. www.uboat.net 4 Jan 2015.
38. Macintyre, *BoA*, p.173.
39. Adm, op. cit., p.43.
40. Ibid.
41. www.uboat.net 4 Jan 2015.
42. Macintyre, *BoA*, p.137.
43. Adm, op. cit., p.39.
44. Macintyre, *BoA*, p.136.
45. Morison, op. cit., p.254.
46. Macintyre, op. cit., p.140.
47. Morison, op. cit., p.131.
48. Ibid., p.135.
49. Adm, op. cit., p.39.
50. Ibid., p.43.
51. www.uboat.net 12 Jan 2015
52. Adm, op. cit., p.44.
53. www.uboat.net 12 Jan 2015.
54. Morison, op. cit., p.139.

55. Suhren, op. cit., p.111.
56. Dönitz, op. cit., p.239.
57. Ibid.
58. Morison, op. cit, p.381; Roskill, *WaS*, Vol. II, p.203.
59. Roskill, *WaS*, Vol. II, p.203.
60. Adm, op. cit., p.42.
61. Rohwer & Hummelchen, op. cit., p.132; www.uboat.net 12 Jan 2015.
62. Chavasse, *Business in Great Waters*, p.8.
63. Ibid.
64. Macintyre, *BoA*, p.200; Owen, *Anti-Submarine Warfare*, pp.143–6.
65. Owen, op. cit., pp.143–6.
66. www.uboat.net quoting *U-427*'s war diary, 12 Jan 2015.
67. Terraine, op. cit., p.284; Kennedy, op. cit., pp.59–61; www.uboat.net 12 Jan 2015.
68. www.uboat.net, 12 Jan 2015.
69. Terraine, op. cit., pp.283–4.
70. Morison, op. cit., p.120.
71. Ibid., p.119.
72. Ibid., pp.119–20.
73. Ibid., pp.121–2.
74. Macintyre, *BoA*, p.149.
75. Adm, op. cit., p.45.
76. Morison, op. cit., p.121n.
77. Hughes & O'Loughlin, *Fermanagh in the Second World War*, p.5.
78. Roskill, II, op. cit., p.77.
79. Hendrie, op. cit., p.28.
80. Roskill, II, op. cit, p.77, but figure of 838 from Hendrie.
81. Hendrie, op. cit., p.28.
82. Roskill, II, op. cit., 77.
83. Hendrie, op. cit., p.29.
84. Roskill, II, op. cit., p.78.
85. Halley, op. cit., p.233.
86. Roskill, II, op. cit., p.78.
87. Ibid., pp.81–2.
88. Ibid., p.82.
89. Dönitz, op. cit., pp.227–8.
90. Quoted in ibid., pp.228–9.
91. Suhren, op. cit., p.123.
92. Nesbit, *Ultra versus U-boats*, pp.92–3.

Chapter 9
1. Spooner, *Coastal Ace*, p.31; information from Bulloch's logbook from Ernie Cromie, Ulster Aviation Society.

2. Spooner, op. cit., p.36.
3. www.uboat.net 15 Jan 2015; Spooner believed the boat to have been *U-254*.
4. Spooner, op. cit., p.40.
5. Ibid., pp.40–7.
6. www.uboat.net 15 Jan 2015.
7. Terraine, op. cit., pp.433–4.
8. Kirby, *Operational Research in War and Peace*, p.117.
9. Ibid., pp.91–4.
10. Pile, *Ack-Ack*, p.114.
11. Quoted in Terraine, op. cit., p.368.
12. NA Kew, AIR/II//117/3 (C) p.43.
13. www.hrmtech.com/SIG articles/coastal_command camouflage 15 Jan 2015.
14. Terraine, op. cit., p.197.
15. NA Kew AIR/II/117/3 (B), pp.305–6.
16. Blackett, *Studies in War*, pp.216–17.
17. Ibid., pp.214–15 & 235.
18. Terraine, op. cit., p.370.
19. Dönitz, op. cit., p.409.
20. Ibid.
21. Middlebrook & Everitt, *Bomber Command War Diaries*, p.338.
22. ACAS (Ops) to Harris, 14 Jan 1943, quoted in Webster & Frankland, Vol. IV, pp.152–3.
23. Dönitz, op. cit., pp.409–10.
24. Middlebrook & Everitt, op. cit., pp.343–4; 348–9; 352; 354–5 & 359.
25. Dönitz, op. cit., p.410.
26. Price, op. cit., p.72.
27. Ibid., pp.72–3.
28. Ibid., p.71.
29. Terraine, op. cit., pp.371–2.
30. AHB/II/117/3 (c) p.50, quoted in Terraine, p.371.
31. Dönitz, op. cit., p.408–9.
32. Halley, op. cit., p.190.
33. Price, op. cit., p.81.
34. Halley, op. cit., p.190.
35. Price, op. cit., pp.83–5.
36. Ibid.; www.combinedfleet.com/I-504; www.uboat.net 16 Jan 2015.
37. Rohwer & Hummelchen, op. cit., p.144.
38. Price, op. cit., p.86.
39. Ibid.
40. Ibid.; www.ussbennington.org 16 Jan 2015.
41. Price, op. cit., p.38; www.uboat.net claims only three D/Cs, 16 Jan 2015.
42. Dönitz, op. cit., p.232.
43. Ibid., pp.234–5.

44. Ibid., p.234.
45. Price, op. cit., p.88; www.uboat.net 16 Jan 2015.
46. www.uboat.net 16 Jan 2015.
47. Price, op. cit., p.88.
48. Ibid., pp.162–3.
49. Hendrie, op. cit., p.102.
50. Dönitz, p.235.
51. Patent GB106330A, Scotts Shipbuilding and Engine; RICHARDSON JAMES; 19 May 1916.
52. Jones, 'Give Credit Where Credit Is Due', *JMH*, Vol. 69, No.4, Oct 2005, pp.993–6.
53. Dönitz, op. cit., pp.353–4.
54. Jones, op. cit., pp.993–5 & 1007.
55. Owen, op. cit., p.156.
56. Dönitz, op. cit., p.265.
57. Milner, *CN*, op. cit., p.210.
58. Roskill, II, op. cit., p.199.
59. Terraine, op. cit., pp.471–5; Dönitz, op. cit., 255–64; www.uboat.net 16 Jan 2015.
60. Adm, op. cit., p.51.
62. Terraine, op. cit., p.346.
63. Quoted in Macintyre, *BoA*, p.25.
64. Roskill, II, op. cit., p.217.

Chapter 10
1. Roskill, II, op. cit., pp.291–8; Dönitz, op. cit., p.299.
2. Dönitz, op. cit., p.299.
3. Ibid., pp.321.2.
4. Ibid., p.315.
5. NA Kew, ADM199/631.
6. Adm, op. cit., p.56.
7. NA Kew, ADM116/4745.
8. Dönitz, op. cit., p.296.
9. Roskill, II, op. cit., p.218.
10. Dönitz, op. cit., p.320.
11. Quoted in Macintyre, *BoA*, p.168.
12. Padfield, op. cit., pp.313 & 318.
13. Roskill, II, op. cit., pp.356–7.
14. Ibid.
15. Roskill, op. cit., p.357. Rohwer & Hummelchen, op. cit., p.193
16. Milner, *BoA*, op. cit., pp.150–2.
17. www.uboat.net 16 Jan 2015

18. NA Kew, ADM230, A/S reports, Jan 1943, p.3.
19. Milner, *BoA*, op. cit., p.156; www.uboat.net 16 Jan 2015.
20. Macintyre, *BoA*, pp.176–7; www.convoyweb.org.uk; www.uboat.net 16 Jan 2015.
21. Macintyre, *U-boat Killer*, p.128.
22. Roskill, II, op. cit., pp.365–6 & 401.
23. Ibid; www.uboat-net 16 Jan 2015; www.convoyweb.org 16 Jan 2015; Padfield, op. cit., pp.322–8; Dönitz, op. cit., p.329.
24. Padfield, op. cit., p.327.
25. Roskill, II, op. cit., p.366.
26. Padfield, op. cit., pp.324–5.
27. Dönitz, op. cit., p.94.
28. Roskill, II, pp.367–8, quoted in Dönitz, op. cit., pp.329–30.
29. Roskill, II, op. cit., p.368.
30. Quoted in Chalmers, *Max Horton & the Western Approaches*, p.188.
31. Morison, *The Atlantic Battle Won*, p.16;. Roskill, II, op. cit., p.351.
32. Ibid., p.358; Milner, *CN*, pp.121–3; Blair, *The Hunted*, p.241.
33. Blair, op. cit., p.241.
34. Ibid., p.242; Milner, *BoA*, op. cit., p.154; Morison, op. cit., p.20.
35. Milner, *CN*, p.122.
36. Roskill, II, op. cit., pp.358–9.
37. Ibid., p.359; Milner, *CN*, pp.123–4; Conway's, op. cit., pp.38–9. The oldest was *Decoy/Kootenay*, launched in 1932; *Express/Gatineau*, *Fortune/Saskatchewan* and *Foxhound/Qu'Appelle* followed in 1934; *Griffin/Ottawa* in 1935 and *Hero/Chaudière* in 1936.
38. Roskill, II, op. cit., p.359.
39. Milner, *CN*, p.123.
40. http://archive.IWM.org.uk/The Battle of the Atlantic/Royal Canadian Navy 1943–1945.
41. Chavasse, op. cit., p.36.
42. Milner, *CN*, p.123.
43. Ibid., p.124.
44. Padfield, op. cit., p.319.
45. Ibid., pp.319–20.
46. Ibid., p.320.
47. Roskill, II, op. cit., pp.362 & 364.
48. Ibid., p.364.
49. Hendrie, op. cit., pp.214–19, Apps 11 & 12 Orbats.
50. Blair, op. cit., p.245.
51. Ibid., p.247.
52. Ibid., p.799.
53. Ibid., p.247; Hendrie, pp.214–19, Apps 11 & 12 Orbats.

54. Spooner, op. cit., p.137.
55. Simons, op. cit., p.92.
56. Spooner, op. cit., p.133n.
57. Roskill, II, op. cit., p.364.
58. Ibid., p.365.
59. Beesly, *Very Special Intelligence*, p.177.
60. Blair, op. cit., p.241.
61. Beesly, op. cit., pp.177–8.
62. Ibid., p.177n.
63. Roskill, II, op. cit., p.366.
64. www.uboat.net 17 Jan 2015.
65. Roskill, II, op. cit., p.366.
66. Ibid., p.367; NA Kew, ADM205/27 Washington Convoy Conference, March 1943.
67. Quoted in ibid., p.366.
68. MacIntyre, *BoA*, p.170.
69. Morison, p.23.
70. Ibid., pp.24–5.
71. Padfield, op. cit., p.319.
72. Hendrie, op. cit., p.62.
73. Roskill, op. cit., p.370.
74. Ibid.
75. Ibid., p.371.
76. U–boat Comd war diary, quoted in Padfield, p.329.
77. Gretton, *Crisis Convoy*, p.9.
78. Ibid., p.5.
79. Ibid., p.9.
80. Macintyre, *BoA*, p.184.
81. www.uboat.net 17 Jan 2015.
82. www.convoy.org 17 Jan 2015.
83. Rohwer & Hummelchen, op. cit., pp.206–7; www.uboat.net 17 Jan 2015; www.convoy.org 17 Jan 2015.

Chapter 11
1. Blackett, op. cit., pp.229–30.
2. Ibid., .p.230.
3. Ibid., p.231.
4. Ibid., p.232.
5. Ibid., p.233.
6. Spooner, op. cit., p.155.
7. Messenger, *ONS5*, p.28; www.wings–aviation.ch 17 Jan 2015.
8. Gretton, op. cit., p.149.
9. Ibid., p.150.
10. Ibid.

11. Rohwer & Hummelchen, op. cit., pp.208–9.
12. Ibid.; Roskill, II, op. cit., pp.373–5.
13. Messenger, op. cit., pp.48–9; Gretton, op. cit., p.151; Rohwer & Hummelchen, op. cit., pp.208–9.
14. Messenger, op. cit., p.49.
15. Rohwer & Hummelchen, op. cit., pp.208–9; Roskill, II, op. cit., pp.373–5.
16. Roskill, II, op. cit., p.374.
17. www.uboat.net 17 Jan 2015.
18. Roskill, II, op. cit., p.374.
19. Messenger, op. cit., pp.53–4.
20. Ibid., pp.54–5; www.uboat.net 17 Jan 2015.
21. Messenger, op. cit., pp.59–60; www.uboat.net 17 Jan 2015.
22. Roskill, II, op. cit., p.374; Messenger, op. cit., p.60; NA Kew, AIR27/911/42, ORB 120 Sqn
23. Dönitz, op. cit., p.338.
24. Ibid., p.339.
25. Messenger, op. cit., pp.62–7; Rohwer & Hummelchen, op. cit., pp.208–9; www.uboat.net 17 Jan 2015; Gretton, op. cit., p.153.
26. Messenger, op. cit., pp.60–1.
27. Chavasse, op. cit., pp.91–2; www.unithistories.com/officers/RN 17 Jan 2015.
28. Chavasse, op. cit., pp.92–3.
29. Ibid.
30. Ibid.
31. Ibid.
32. Ibid., p.93.
33. Ibid., p.97.
34. Ibid., pp.97–8.
35. Ibid.
36. Ibid.; www.uboat.net 17 Jan 2015.
37. Chavasse, op. cit., p.98.
38. NA Kew, ADM1/14453.
39. Ibid.
40. Macintyre, *U-boat Killer*, p.122.
41. Ibid., pp.122–3.
42. Ibid., p.125–30; www.uboat.net 17 Jan 2015.
43. Gretton, op. cit., p.154.
44. Adm, op. cit., pp.61–2.
45. Roskill, II, op. cit., p.376.
46. Gretton, *Convoy Escort Commander (CEC)*, pp.149–62; www.uboat.net 17 Jan 2015; Rohwer & Hummelchen, op. cit., p.212; NA Kew, AIR27/911/42, ORB 120 Sqn.
47. Gretton, *CEC*, pp.158–60.
48. Gretton, *Crisis Convoy*, p.154.

49. Gretton, *CEC*, p.161.
50. Dönitz, op. cit., p.341.
51. Adm, op. cit., p.62.
52. Macintyre, *NWAH*, p.82; Terraine, op. cit., p368.
53. Adm, op. cit., p.62.
54. Barnett, *Engage the Enemy*, op. cit., pp.582–3; www.uboat.net. 17 Jan 2015.
55. Terraine, op. cit., pp.618–19.
56. Smith, op. cit., pp.98 & 149.
57. NA Kew, ADM1/13523.
58. Smith, op. cit., p.149.
59. Herz, *Operation Alacrity*, pp.193–4.
60. Adm, op. cit., p.79.
61. Including Macintyre whose book *The Battle of the Atlantic* ends at this point.
62. Morison, *The Atlantic Battle Won*, pp.108–9.
63. Ibid., p.109.
64. Ibid., p.111.
65. Ibid., p.117.
66. Ibid., p.110.
67. Ibid., pp.109–10.
68. Price, op. cit., pp.147–64; Adm, op. cit., pp.68–70; Morison, op. cit., pp.99–105.
69. Hendrie, op. cit., pp.77 & 108.
70. www.uboat.net 19 Jan 2015.
71. Ibid.
72. Ibid.; Price, op. cit., pp.112–13.
73. Price, op. cit., pp.151–3.
74. Roskill, III, pt 1, pp.25–6.
75. Ibid., p.30.
76. Ibid., p.26; www.uboat.net 19 Jan 2015.
77. www.cwgc.org 19 Jan 2015.
78. Roskill, op. cit., p.27.
79. Colvin, *Flight 777*, pp.174–83.
80. Adm, op. cit., p.69.
81. Ibid., p.70; Morison, op. cit., p.125; www.uboat.com 19 Jan 2015.
82. Wood & Gunston, *Hitler's Luftwaffe*, p.188.
83. Roskill, op. cit., p.30.
84. Ibid.; www.uboat.net 19 Jan 2015.
85. Roskill, op. cit., p.30.

Chapter 12
1. Adm, op. cit., p.71.
2. Roskill, op. cit., pp.30–1.
3. Adm, op. cit., pp.71–2; Roskill, III, I, p.32; Bowyer, *Air VCs*, pp.332–3; *London Gazette*, 2 Nov 1943.

4. Terraine, op. cit., p.626.
5. Adm, op. cit., p.73.
6. Terraine, op. cit., pp.639–40.
7. Roskill, op. cit., p.41.
8. Schull, *The Far Distant Ships*, p.181.
9. Terraine, op. cit., p.641.
10. Ibid., pp.636–7.
11. Ibid., p.637; Roskill, op. cit., p.38; Adm, op. cit., p.73..
12. Terraine, op. cit., p.637.
13. Ibid.; Roskill, op. cit., p.38.
14. Adm, op. cit., p.73.
15. Terraine, op. cit., pp.637–8; Roskill, op. cit., pp.38–9; Padfield, op. cit., pp.365–7.
16. Terraine, op. cit., p.639.
17. Ibid., pp.640–2; Adm, op. cit., pp.78–9; Morison, op. cit., pp.160–1; Rohwer & Hummelchen, op. cit., pp.237–9; www.uboat.net 18 Jan 2015.
18. Roskill, op. cit., pp.41–2; Rohwer & Hummelchen, op. cit., p.239.
19. Rohwer & Hummelchen, op. cit., p.240; Roskill, op. cit., p.44.
20. Gretton, *CEC*, pp.163–6.
21. Ibid., pp.170–1.
22. Roskill, op. cit., p.44.
23. Gretton, *CEC*, pp.171–5.
24. Ibid., p.175.
25. Roskill, op. cit., p.45.
26. Ibid., p.46.
27. Ibid.
28. Ibid., p.47.
29. Herz, op. cit., p.200.
30. Roskill, op. cit., p.47.
31. Roskill, (p.47) gives 25, www.uboat.net gives 39, 19 Jan 2015.
32. www.uboat.net states: 1 interned; 2 in accidents; 1 lost without explanation and 1 'stricken from naval records', 19 Jan 2015.
33. Roskill, op. cit., p.48.
34. Burn, *Fighting Captain*, p.110.
35. Ibid., p.113.
36. Roskill, op. cit., p.48.
37. Ibid., p.49.
38. Ibid.; Burn, op. cit., p.118.
39. Roskill, op. cit., pp.49–50.
40. Ibid., p.50.
41. Dönitz, op. cit., pp.354–5.
42. Ibid., pp.355–6.
43. Ibid., p.357.

44. Franklin, *The Buckley-Class Destroyer Escorts*, p.7.
45. Collingwood, *The Captain Class Frigates*, p.7.
46. Ibid., p.33.
47. Ibid., pp.30–1.
48. Ibid., p.32.
49. Rawling, 'The Challenge of Modernization: The Royal Canadian Navy and Antisubmarine Weapons, 1944–1945', *SMH Journal*, Vol. 63, No.2, April 1999, p.363.
50. Roskill, op. cit., pp.60–1.
51. Chalmers, op. cit., pp.209–10.
52. Ibid., pp.210–11.
53. Roskill, op. cit., p.61.
54. Adm, op. cit., p.79.
55. Ibid., pp.79–80; www.uboat.net 20 Jan 2015.
56. Adm, op. cit., p.80.
57. Roskill, op. cit., pp.63–9.
58. Ibid., pp.80–9.
59. Adm, op. cit., p.97.
60. Ibid., p.81.
61. Ibid.
62. Ibid., p.82.
63. Burn, op. cit., p.140.
64. Adm, op. cit., p.82; www.uboat.net 20 Jan 2015.
65. Smith, op. cit., p.192; Blair, op. cit., p.515.
66. www.vpnavy.org/vp103_1940 20 Jan 2015.
67. Adm, op. cit., p.83; www.uboat.net 20 Jan 2015.
68. Adm, op. cit., pp.83–4; www.uboat.net 20 Jan 2015.
69. Poolman, *Escort Carrier*, pp.56–7; Adm, op. cit., p.84.
70. Adm, op. cit., p.84; Morison, op. cit., pp.283–4.
71. Padfield, op. cit., p.423.
72. www.uboat.net 20 Jan 2015.
73. Terraine, op. cit., pp.624–5.
74. Kennedy, op. cit., p.61.
75. Ibid.
76. Terraine, op. cit., p.661.
77. Dunmore, *Lost Subs*, p.120.
78. Terraine, op. cit., p.661.
79. NA Kew, ADM199/631.
80. Roskill, III, ii, op. cit., p.246.
81. Terraine, op. cit., p.661.
82. Roskill, op. cit., p.289.

83. Paterson, *Dönitz's Last Gamble,* p.116, in which the boat is identified as *U-568*; www.uboat.net 20 Jan 2015.
84. Paterson, op. cit., p.117.

Chapter 13
1. Adm, op. cit., p.87.
2. Smithsonian National Air and Space Museum: http://www.nasm.si.edu/research/aero/aircraft/focke_achgelis 21 Jan 2015.
3. Padfield, op. cit., pp.379–383.
4. Adm, op. cit., p.87; www.royalnavyresearcharchive.org.uk 21 Jan 2015.
5. Adm, op. cit., p.87.
6. Halley, op. cit., p.291.
7. Adm, op. cit., p.90; www.uboat.net 21 Jan 2015.
8. Dönitz, p.421.
9. Ibid., p.423.
10. Adm, op. cit., p.91; www.uboat.net 21 Jan 2015.
11. Adm, op. cit., p.90.
12. Ibid.; Bowyer, *Air VCs,* pp.373–6; Roskill, op. cit., p.59; *London Gazette,* 28 Jul 1944.
13. Adm, op. cit., pp.91–2.
14. Ibid., pp.92–3; Bowyer, *Air VCs,* pp.384–6; Roskill, op. cit., p.157; *London Gazette,* 1 Sep 1944.
15. Adm, op. cit., p.94.
16. NA Kew, ADM217/88, HMS *Loch Killin*; Blair, op. cit., p.605.
17. Burn, op. cit., pp.6, 12, 171–2.
18. Ibid., pp.171–2.
19. Adm, op. cit., p.93.
20. Ibid., pp.93–4; Milner, *The U-boat Hunters,* pp.168–9 7 281; www.uboat.net 21 Jan 2015.
21. Adm, op. cit., p.94; Blair, op. cit., p.606; www.convoy.org 21 Jan 2015.
22. Adm, op. cit., pp.95–7.
23. Rawling, *SMH Journal,* 63:2, op. cit., p.355.
24. Adm, op. cit., pp.96–7.
25. www.uboat.net 21 Jan 2015.
26. Adm, op. cit., p.96.
27. Ibid., p.27; Scott, interview with author, May 2000.
28. www.unithistories.com/officers/RN 21 Jan 2015.
29. Collingwood, op. cit., pp.53–4. He identifies the boat as *U-1172.*
30. www.uboat.net 21 Jan 2015.
31. www.vpnavy.org/vp103_1940 21 Jan 2015; Cromie, UAS.
32. Adm, op. cit., pp.97–8.
33. Webster & Franklin, III, p.274.

34. Adm, op. cit., p.98; www.uboat.net, which does not list *U-260* among the losses of March but in the index to all boats indicates that she was lost in this way.
35. www.uboat.net 21 Jan 2015.
36. Adm, op. cit., p.98.
37. Morison, op. cit., p.338; Paterson, op. cit., p.117.
38. Dönitz, pp.425–6.
39. Price, op. cit., p.217; Smith, op. cit., pp.137–8.
40. Elliott, *Allied Escort Ships*, p.524.
41. I am grateful to Sqn/Ldr Allan Thomas, a former Nimrod captain for this information. George Jackson also provided valuable information on MAD equipment.
42. Smith, op. cit., p.138.
43. Paterson, op. cit., p.117.
44. Ibid.
45. Adm, op. cit., p.98.
46. Ibid., pp.98–100.
47. Collingwood, op. cit., p.174.
48. Ibid.; www.uboat.net 22 Jan 2015.
49. Collingwood, op. cit., pp.174–5.
50. www.uboat.net 22 Jan 2015.
51. Adm, op. cit., p.100; Milner, *U-boat Hunters*, op. cit., pp.241–2; Morison, op. cit., p.340.
52. Adm, op. cit., p.100; Milner, op. cit., pp.241–2; Morison, op. cit., p.340.
53. www.uboat.net 22 Jan 2015.
54. Adm, op. cit., p.101.
55. Ibid., p.102.
56. Quoted in Padfield, *Dönitz: The Last Führer*, p.419.
57. Adm, op. cit., p.102; www.uboat.net 22 Jan 2015.
58. Adm, op. cit., pp.102–3; www.uboat.net 22 Jan 2015.
59. Ellis, *The World War II Databook*, pp.252 & 266; www.uboat.net, 22 Jan 2015.
60. Burn, *Fighting Commodores*, p.7.
61. Ellis, op. cit., p.269.

Chapter 14

1. Churchill, *Closing the Ring*, p.6.
2. Blair, op. cit., p.707.
3. Churchill, *The Gathering Storm*, p.371.
4. Roskill, II, op. cit., p.371.
5. Ellis, *Databook of World War II*, p.301.
6. Elphick, op. cit., p.22.
7. Ibid., pp.15–16.
8. Ibid., p.12.
9. NA Kew, ADM 1/15546.

Bibliography

Anon, *The Battle of the Atlantic. The Official Account of the Fight against the U-boats 1939–1945* (HMSO, London, 1946)

Baker, Richard, *The Terror of Tobermory: Vice Admiral Sir Gilbert Stephenson* (W. H. Allen, London, 1972)

Bailey, Chris Howard, *The Battle of the Atlantic: The Corvettes and their Crews: An Oral History* (Sutton Publishing, Stroud, 1994)

Barnett, Correlli, *Engage The Enemy More Closely: The Royal Navy in the Second World War* (Hodder & Stoughton, London, 1991)

——, *The Lords of War: Supreme Leadership from Lincoln to Churchill* (Praetorian Press, Barnsley, 2012)

Beesly, Patrick, *Very Special Intelligence: The Story of the Admiralty's Operational Intelligence Centre 1939–1945* (Hamish Hamilton, London, 1977)

Bennett, Geoffrey, *Naval Battles of World War Two* (Bt. T. Batsford Ltd, London, 1975)

Blackett, P. M. S., *Studies of War: Nuclear and Conventional* (Oliver and Boyd, Edinburgh, 1962)

Blair, Clay, *Hitler's U-boat War. The Hunters 1939–1942* (Weidenfeld & Nicolson, London, 1997)

——, *Hitler's U-boat War. The Hunted 1942–1945* (Weidenfeld & Nicolson, London, 1998)

Blake, John W., *Northern Ireland in the Second World War* (HMSO, Belfast, 1956; Blackstaff Press, Belfast, 2000)

Bowman, Martin W., *Deep Sea Hunters: RAF Coastal Command and the war against the U-boats and the German Navy 1939–1945* (Pen & Sword Aviation, Barnsley, 2014)

Bowyer, Chaz, *Coastal Command at War* (Ian Allan, Shepperton, 1979)

——, *For Valour: The Air VCs* (Grub Street, London, 1992)

Brooke, Geoffrey, *Alarm Starboard: A Remarkable Story of the War at Sea* (Pen & Sword Maritime, Barnsley, 2004)

Brown, David K., *Atlantic Escorts: Ships, Weapons & Tactics in World War II* (Seaforth Publishing, Barnsley, 2007)

Brown, Malcolm and Meehan, Patricia, *Scapa Flow: The Reminiscences of Men and Women who served in Scapa Flow in the two World Wars* (Spellmount Publishing, Stroud, 2008)

Burn, Alan, *The Fighting Captain: The Story of Frederic Walker CB DSO*** RN and the Battle of the Atlantic* (Leo Cooper, London, 1993)

——, *The Fighting Commodores: Convoy Commanders in the Second World War* (Leo Cooper, Barnsley, 1999)

Busch, Fritz-Otto, *The Drama of the Scharnhorst: A Factual Account from the German Viewpoint* (Robert Hale, London, 1956)

Butler, Daniel Allen, *Warrior Queens: The Queen Mary and Queen Elizabeth in World War II* (Leo Cooper, Barnsley, 2002)

Chalmers, Rear Admiral W. S. CBE DSC, *Max Horton and the Western Approaches* (Hodder & Stoughton, London, 1954)

Chesneau, Roger (ed), *Conway's All the World's Fighting Ships 1922–1946* (Conway Maritime Press, London, 1980)

Churchill, Sir Winston, *The Second World War* (12 volumes) (Cassell, London, 1949)

Colledge, J. J., and Warlow, Ben, *Ships of the Royal Navy. The Complete Record of all Fighting Ships of the Royal Navy from the 15th Century to the Present* (Chatham Publishing, London, 2006)

Collingwood, Donald, *The Captain Class Frigates: An operational history of the American-built Destroyer Escorts serving under the White Ensign from 1943–46* (Leo Cooper, Barnsley, 1998)

Compton-Hall, Richard, *Submarines at War 1939–1945* (Periscope Publishing, Penzance, 2004)

Destroyer Escort Sailors Association (Ed): *Trim but Deadly, Vol I* (Turner Publishing Co., Paducah KY, 1987)

——, *Trim but Deadly, Vol II* (Turner Publishing Co., Paducah KY, 1989)

——, *Trim but Deadly, Vol III* (Turner Publishing Co., Paducah KY, 1993)

Doenecke, Justus D., *Storm on the Horizon: The Challenge to American Intervention, 1939–1941* (Rowman & Littlefield, New York NY, 2003)

Doherty, Richard, *Key to Victory: The Maiden City in the Second World War* (Greystone Press, Antrim, 1995)

——, *The Battle of the Atlantic and the River Foyle* (NI War Memorial, Belfast, 2010)

——, and Truesdale, David, *Irish Winners of the Victoria Cross* (Four Courts Press, Dublin, 2000)

Ubique: The Royal Artillery in the Second World War (The History Press, Stroud, 2008)

Dönitz, Grand Admiral Karl, *Memoirs: Ten Years and Twenty Days* (Cassell, London, 2000)

Douglas, W. A. B., Sarty, Roger & Whitby, Michael, *A Blue Water Navy. The Official Operational History of the Royal Canadian Navy in the Second World War, 1943–1945*, Volume II Part 2 (Vanwell Publishing, St Catherine's, Ontario, 2007)

Dunmore, Spencer, *Lost Subs: From the Hunley to the Kursk* (Da Capo Press, Boston, 2002)

Duskin, Gerald L., and Segman, Ralph, *If the Gods are Good: The Epic Sacrifice of HMS Jervis Bay* (Naval Institute Press, Annapolis MD, 2004)

Edgerton, David, *Britain's War Machine* (Allen Lane, London, 2011)

Edwards, Bernard, *The Wolf Packs Gather: Mayhem in the Western Approaches 1940* (Pen & Sword Maritime, Barnsley, 2011)

Elliott, Peter *Allied Escort Ships of World War II. A Complete Survey* (Macdonald & Jane, London, 1977)

Ellis, John, *The Word War II Databook* (Aurum Press, London, 1993)

Elphick, Peter, *Life Line: The Merchant Navy at War 1939–1945* (Chatham Publishing, London, 1999)

Farndale, Gen Sir Martin KBE, *History of the Royal Regiment of Artillery: The Years of Defeat, 1939–41* (Brassey's, London, 1996)

Forester, C. S., *Hunting the Bismarck* (Michael Joseph, London, 1959)

Franklin, Bruce Hampton, *The Buckley-Class Destroyer-Escorts* (Chatham Publishing, London, 2003)

Freedman, Maurice, *Unravelling Enigma: Winning the Code War at Station X* (Leo Cooper, Barnsley, 2000)

Gretton, Vice Admiral Sir Peter KB DSO CBE DSC, *Convoy Escort Commander* (Cassell, London, 1964)

——, *Crisis Convoy. The Story of HX231* (Peter Davies Ltd, London, 1974)

Hackmann, Willem, *Seek & Strike: Sonar, anti-submarine warfare and the Royal Navy 1914–54* (HMSO, London, 1984)

Halley, James J., *The Squadrons of the Royal Air Force* (Air-Britain (Historians), Tonbridge, 1980)

Heathcote, T. A., *The British Admirals of the Fleet 1734–1995. A Biographical Dictionary* (Leo Cooper, Barnsley, 2002)

Hendrie, Andrew, *The Cinderella Service: RAF Coastal Command 1939–1945* (Pen & Sword Aviation, Barnsley, 2006 & 2010)

Herz, Norman, *Operation Alacrity: The Azores and the War in the Atlantic* (Naval Institute Press, Annapolis MD, 2004)

Hill, J. R. (ed), *The Oxford Illustrated History of the Royal Navy* (Oxford University Press, Oxford, 1995)

Hinsley, *British Intelligence in the Second World War* (HMSO, London, 1979–1990; the final volume was written by Sir Michael Howard)

Howard Bailey, Chris, *The Battle of the Atlantic: The Corvettes and their Crews: An Oral History* (Sutton Publishing, Stroud, 1994)

Isby, David (ed), *The Luftwaffe and the War at Sea 1939–1945* (Chatham Publishing, London, 2005)

Jane, Fred T., *Jane's Fighting Aircraft of World War II* (Random House, London, 2001)

Jordan, David, *Wolfpack: The U-boat War and the Allied Counter-attack 1939–1945* (Spellmount Publishing, Staplehurst, 2002)

Kahn, David, *Seizing the Enigma: The race to break the German U-boat codes, 1939–1943* (Frontline Books, Barnsley, 2012)

Keegan, John, *Battle at Sea: From Man-of-War to Submarine* (Pimlico, London, 1988)

Kemp, Paul, *Convoy Protection: The Defence of Seaborne Trade* (Arms & Armour Press, London, 1993)

——, *The Admiralty Regrets. British Warship Losses of the 20th Century* (Sutton Publishing, Stroud, 1999)

Kennedy, Paul, *Engineers of Victory. The Problem Solvers Who Turned the Tide in the Second World War* (Allan Lane, London, 2013)

Kirby, M. W., *Operational Research in War and Peace: The British Experience from the 1930s to the 1970* (Imperial College Press, London, 2003)

Lamont, A. G. W., *Guns Above, Steam Below, in Canada's Navy of WWII* (Melrose Books, Ely, 2006)

Nicolson, London, 1956)

Lash, Joseph P., *Roosevelt and Churchill 1939–1941. The Partnership that saved the West* (Andre Deutsch, London, 1977)

Lavery, Brian, *Churchill's Navy: The Ships, Men and Organisation 1939–1945* (Conway Maritime, London, 2006)

Macintyre, Captain Donald, *U-Boat Killer: Fighting the U-boats in the Battle of the Atlantic* (Weidenfeld & , *The Battle of the Atlantic* (B. T. Batsford, London, 1961) , *The Naval War Against Hitler* (B. T. Batsford, London, 1971)

Mahan, A. T., *The Influence of Sea Power on the French Revolution and Empire, 1793–1812* (Boston, 1894)

Mallmann Showell, Jak P., *Dönitz, U-boats, Convoys. The British Version of His Memoirs from the Admiralty's Secret Anti-Submarine Reports* (Frontline Books, Barnsley, 2013)

McAughtry, Sam, *The Sinking of the Kenbane Head* (Blackstaff Press, Belfast, 1997)

MacLean, *The Lonely Sea* (HarperCollins, London, 2010)

McQueen, Robert, *Hitler's Early Raiders* (Whittles Publishing, Dunbeath, 2011)

McShane, Mark, *Neutral Shores. Ireland and the Battle of the Atlantic* (Mercier Press, Cork, 2012)

Metzler, Jost, *The Laughing Cow: A U-boat Captain's Story* (William Kimber, London, 1955)

Middlebrook, Martin, and Everitt, Chris, *The Bomber Command War Diaries. An Operational Reference Book, 1939–1945* (Viking, London, 1985)

Miller, James, *Scapa. Britain's Famous Wartime Naval Base* (Birlinn Ltd, Edinburgh, 2001)

Milner, Marc, *The U-boat Hunters: The Royal Canadian Navy and the Offensive against Germany's Submarines* (Naval Institute Press, Annapolis MD, 1994)

——, *Canada's Navy: The First Century* (University of Toronto Press, Toronto, 1999)

——, *Battle of the Atlantic* (Tempus Publishing, Stroud, 2003, 2005)

Moore, Robert J., and Rodgaard, John A., *A Hard Fought Ship: The Story of HMS Venomous* (Holywell House Publishing, St Albans, 2010)

Morison, Samuel Eliot, *History of United States Naval Operations in World War II: Volume One: The Battle of the Atlantic, September 1939–May 1943* (Little, Brown and Company, Boston MA, 1960)

——, *History of United States Naval Operations in World War II: Volume Ten: The Atlantic Battle Won, May 1943–May 1945* (Castle Books, Edison NJ, 2001)

Nesbit, Roy Conyers, *Coastal Command in Action 1939–1945* (Sutton Publishing, Stroud, 1997)

——, *Ultra versus U-boats* (Pen & Sword, Barnsley, 2008)

Niestlé, Axel, *German U-boat Losses during World War II. Details of Destruction* (Frontline Books, Barnsley, 2014)

O'Kelly, Michael, *The Battle of the Atlantic 1939–1943* (privately published, 2014)

O'Loughlin, Joe & Hughes, John, *Fermanagh in the Second World War* (Northern Ireland War Memorial, Belfast, 2013)

Owen, David, *Anti-Submarine Warfare: An Illustrated History* (Seaforth Publishing, Barnsley, 2007)

Padfield, Peter, *Dönitz – The Last Führer* (HarperCollins, London, 1987)

——, *War Beneath the Sea: Submarine Conflict 1939–1945* (John Murray Ltd, London, 1995)

Parkin, Robert Sinclair, *Blood on the Sea: American Destroyers Lost in World War II* (Sarpedon, New York NY, 1996)

Paterson, Lawrence, *U-boats in the Mediterranean 1941–1944* (Chatham Publishing, London, 2007)

——, *Dönitz's Last Gamble. The Inshore U-Boat Campaign, 1944–45* (Seaforth Publishing, Barnsley, 2008)

Pile, Gen Sir Frederick, *Ack-Ack. Britain's Defence Against Air Attack during the Second World War* (George G. Harrap & Co., London, 1949)

Poolman, Kenneth, *Escort Carrier: HMS Vindex at War* (Secker & Warburg, London, 1983)

Potter, John, *Pim and Churchill's Map Room* (Northern Ireland War Memorial, Belfast, 2014)

Price, Dr Alfred, *Aircraft Versus Submarine in Two World Wars* (Pen & Sword Aviation, Barnsley, 2004)

Quinn, John, and Reilly, Alan, *Covering the Approaches. The War Against the U-boats: Limavady and Ballykelly's Role in the Battle of the Atlantic* (Impact Printing, Coleraine, 1996)

Ranalow, Eric, *A Cork Man at Sea* (n.p., n.d.)

Rohwer, Jürgen, & Hummelchen, Gerhard, *Chronology of the War at Sea, 1939–1945* (Greenhill Books, London, 1992)

Roskill, Captain Stephen W., DSC RN, *The War at Sea 1939–1945. Volume I: The Defensive* (HMSO, London, 1954)

——, *The War at Sea 1939–1945. Volume II: The Period of Balance* (HMSO, London, 1956)

——, *The War at Sea 1939–1945. Volume III: The Offensive: Part I: 1st June 1943–31st May 1944* (HMSO, London, 1960)

——, *The War at Sea 1939–1945. Volume III: The Offensive: Part II: 1st June 1944–14th August 1945* (HMSO, London, 1961)

——, *The Navy at War 1939–1945* (Collins, London, 1960)

——, *Naval Policy between the Wars* (Collins, London, 1968)

Routledge, Brig N. W. OBE TD, *The History of the Royal Regiment of Artillery: Anti-Aircraft Artillery, 1914–55* (Brassey's, London, 1994)

Sainsbury, Captain A. B., and Phillips, Lieutenant Commander F. L., *The Royal Navy Day by Day* (Sutton Publishing, Stroud, 2005)

Schull, Joseph, *The Far Distant Ships: An official account of Canadian naval operations in the Second World War* (Ottawa, 1961)

Simons, Graham M., *Consolidated B-24 Liberator* (Pen & Sword Books, Barnsley, 2012)

Smith, David J., *Action Stations 7: Military Airfields of Scotland, the North-East and Northern Ireland* (Patrick Stephens, Cambridge, 1983)

Spooner, Tony, DSO DFC, *Coastal Ace: The Biography of Squadron Leader Terence Malcolm Bulloch DSO and Bar DFC and Bar* (William Kimber, London, 1986)

Stearns, Patrick, *Q Ships, Commerce Raiders and Convoys* (Spellmount Publishers, Staplehurst, 2004)

Stern, Robert C., *Type VII U-boats* (Brockhampton Press, London, 1998)

Sturtivant, R., *The Squadrons of the Fleet Air Arm* (Tonbridge, 1984)

Suhren, Teddy and Brustat-Naval, Fritz, *Teddy Suhren Ace of Aces: Memoirs of a U-boat Rebel* (Chatham Publishing, London, 2006)

Terraine, John, *Business in Great Waters. The U-boat Wars 1916–1945* (Leo Cooper, London, 1989)

Thomas, David A., and Holmes, Patrick, *Queen Mary and the Cruiser: The Curacoa Disaster* (Leo Cooper, London, 1997)

Twiston Davies, David, *The Daily Telegraph Book of Naval Obituaries* (Grub Street, London, 2004)

Webster, Sir Charles, and Frankland, Noble, *The Strategic Air Offensive against Germany 1939–1945: Vol I – Preparation* (HMSO, London, 1961)

——, *The Strategic Air Offensive against Germany 1939–1945: Vol II – Endeavour* (HMSO, London, 1961)

——, *The Strategic Air Offensive against Germany 1939–1945: Vol III – Victory* (HMSO, London, 1961)

——, *The Strategic Air Offensive against Germany 1939–1945: Vol IV – Annexes & Appendices* (HMSO, London, 1961)

Weeks, Albert L., *Russia's Life-Saver: Lend-Lease Aid to the USSR in World War II* (Lexington Books, Lanham MD, 2004)

Whinney, Bob, *The U-boat Peril. A Fight for Survival* (Blandford Press, 1986)

Williams, Andrew, *The Battle of the Atlantic* (BBC Worldwide, London, 2002)

Williams, G. J., *HMS Wellington: One Ship's War* (Self-Publishing Assn, Hanley Swan, 1992)

Williams, Mark, *Captain Gilbert Roberts RN and the Anti-U-Boat School* (Cassell, London, 1979)

Wilmot, Chester, *The Struggle for Europe* (Collins, London, 1952)

Winterbotham, F. W., *The Ultra Secret* (London, 1974)

Winton, John, *Death of the Scharnhorst* (Cassell, London, 1983)

Wood, Tony, and Gunston, Bill, *Hitler's Luftwaffe. A pictorial and technical encyclopedia of Hitler's air power in World War II* (Salamander Books Ltd, London, 1977)

Woodman, Richard, *The Arctic Convoys 1941–1945* (John Murray Ltd, London, 1994)

Wragg, David, *The Escort Carrier in World War II: Combustible, Vulnerable, Expendable* (Pen & Sword Maritime, Barnsley, 2005)

——, *Plan Z: The Nazi Bid for Naval Dominance* (Pen & Sword Maritime, Barnsley, 2008)

——, *Fighting Admirals of World War II* (Pen & Sword Maritime, Barnsley, 2009)

Unpublished

Chavasse, Commander Evelyn H., DSO DSC RN, 'Business in Great Waters – war memories of a semi-sailor'.

Chavasse, Captain Paul M. B., DSC & Bar RN, 'A Sailor's War Memoirs'.

Cromie, Ernie, 'Notes on the Consolidated B-24 Liberator in Coastal Command service'.

Jeffery, Prof Keith, 'Canadian Sailors in Londonderry: A Study in Civil-Military Relations'.

Messenger, Charles, 'Atlantic Turning Point: Convoy ONS5 22 April–12 May 1943'.

Articles & Journals

Jones, Mark C., 'Give Credit Where Credit Is Due: The Dutch Role in the Development and Deployment of the Submarine Schnorkel', *The Journal of Military History,* Vol. 69, No. 4, October 2005, pp.987–1012.

Rawling, William, 'The Challenge of Modernization: The Royal Canadian Navy and Antisubmarine Weapons, 1944–1945', *The Journal of Military History*, Vol. 63, No.2, April 1999, pp.355–378.

National Archives, Kew, Richmond, Surrey

Space does not permit a complete listing of all the files examined at the National Archives. All the war diaries of Western Approaches Command have been consulted, with particular reference to the fortnightly reports from the Flag Officers-in-charge at Liverpool, Greenock and Northern Ireland throughout the war. These are in the series ADM199 as also are the convoy reports. Other Admiralty files studied include the convoy and anti-submarine warfare reports; ADM1/13523 on the subject of MAC-ships; ADM199/140 on the sinking of *Athenia*; ADM1/17599, the provisional Admiralty convoy instructions on the sighting of schnorkels or their smoke; ADM217/707 on the review of anti-submarine operations in Western Approaches in October/November 1944; ADM219/43, DNO studies; files from ADM205, the First Sea Lord's records; and ADM234/578, 'Naval Staff History: Defeat of the Enemy Attack on Shipping, 1939–1945: A study of policy and operations', Vol.Ia.

From Air Ministry files, those relating specifically to Coastal Command were consulted, including AIR2/3150 on convoy protection policy; AIR41covering the RAF's part in the maritime war and such subjects as the development of the Leigh Light (AIR41/47: 'RAF in the Maritime War – Vol. III, Atlantic and Home Waters', the official staff history, is held in this series) and AIR20/3095 which deals with air protection of Atlantic convoys, possible VLR bases in Greenland as well as other topics. The Battle of the Atlantic Committee records are held in the CAB series as are War Cabinet reports while the staff histories of the naval and air aspects of the campaign, as well as the German naval history of the U-boat war in the Atlantic, are to be found in the relevant ADM and AIR series. Churchill's interest in the campaign is shown by the daily reports of convoy escorts to be found in the PREM series while Ultra decrypts are in the DEFE and HW series.

Websites

www.wings-aviation.ch: An independent aviation website.

www.uboat.net: A comprehensive site with vast detail on U-boats, their service, weaponry etc., as well as on Allied ships.

www.unithistories.com/officers/RN: Biographical details of RN/RNR & RNVR officers.

www.cwgc.org: Details of all Commonwealth war dead.

www.vpnavy.org/vp103_1940: A history of US Navy patrol squadron VP-103.

www.nasm.si.edu/research/aero/aircraft/focke_achgelis: Smithsonian Institute National Air & Space Museum.

www.royalnavyresearcharchive.org.uk: A virtual museum on Royal Navy historical topics.

www.navyhistory.org.au: Naval Historical Society of Australia website.

www.hrmtech.com/SIG articles/coastal_command camouflage: Coastal Command camouflage and markings, based on official documents and published articles.

www.combinedfleet.com/I-504: Imperial Japanese Navy website.

www.ussbennington.org: USS *Bennington* history website.

www.convoyweb.org.uk: Website for Second World War merchant ships.

http://archive.IWM.org.uk/The Battle of the Atlantic/Royal Canadian Navy 1943–1945: Imperial War Museum online articles on the RCN in the Battle of the Atlantic.

Index